Google Analytics™

Third Edition

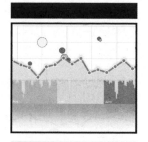

Google Analytics™

Third Edition

Jerri Ledford
Joe Teixeira
and Mary E. Tyler

Wiley Publishing, Inc.

Google Analytics™ Third Edition

Published by
Wiley Publishing, Inc.
10475 Crosspoint Boulevard
Indianapolis, IN 46256
www.wiley.com

Copyright © 2010 by Wiley Publishing, Inc., Indianapolis, Indiana

Published simultaneously in Canada

ISBN: 978-0-470-53128-0

Manufactured in the United States of America

10 9 8 7 6 5 4 3 2 1

For general information on our other products and services please contact our Customer Care Department within the United States at (877) 762-2974, outside the United States at (317) 572-3993 or fax (317) 572-4002.

Wiley also publishes its books in a variety of electronic formats. Some content that appears in print may not be available in electronic books.

Library of Congress Control Number: 2009934560

For Chip, because your interest is genuine,
and you help more than you know.
Thanks so much, Chipper!

About the Authors

Jerri Ledford has been a freelance business-technology writer for more than 10 years, with more than 1,000 articles, profiles, news stories, and reports online and in print. Her publishing credits include: *Intelligent Enterprise, Network World, Information Security Magazine, DCM Magazine, CRM Magazine,* and *IT Manager's Journal.* She has also written a number of books. When not writing, she divides her time between Alabama, Mississippi, and Tennessee, hiking, gardening, playing with electronic gadgets, and playing "tech support" for friends and family.

Joe Teixeira is currently the manager of web Intelligence at MoreVisibility, an online advertising agency. Joe has earned Google Analytics Authorized Consultant (GAAC) status for his company, which is an elite group of companies worldwide that provides support with the Google Analytics product. Joe also has a Google Analytics Individual Qualification (GAIQ), and is a Top Contributor on the Google Analytics Help Forum. He is also the sole contributor for his company's "Analytics and Site Intelligence" blog, and has appeared as a guest author this year on the official Google Analytics blog.

Mary Tyler is a professional technology journalist and a former software and web developer. She specializes in open source, enterprise software, intellectual property, motorcycles, and anything Macintosh.

About the Tech Editor

Todd Meister has been developing and using Microsoft technologies for more than 10 years. He's been a technical editor on more than 50 titles ranging from SQL Server to the .NET Framework. Besides editing technical titles, he is an assistant director for computing services at Ball State University in Muncie, Indiana.

Credits

Acquisitions Editor
Scott Meyers

Project Editor
William Bridges

Technical Editor
Todd Meister

Senior Production Editor
Debra Banninger

Copy Editor
Sadie Kleinman

Editorial Director
Robyn B. Siesky

Editorial Manager
Mary Beth Wakefield

Production Manager
Tim Tate

**Vice President and Executive
Group Publisher**
Richard Swadley

**Vice President and Executive
Publisher**
Barry Pruett

Associate Publisher
Jim Minatel

Project Coordinator, Cover
Lynsey Stanford

Compositor
Maureen Forys,
Happenstance Type-O-Rama

Proofreader
Nancy Carrasco

Indexer
Robert Swanson

Cover Illustration
Michael E. Trent

Acknowledgments

My new co-author, Joe Teixeira, deserves a great deal of praise. He jumped into this project and worked quickly to help ensure that you get the best possible book. Joe, thanks so much for all you've done. It's been great working with you, and I hope we'll have the opportunity to work together again soon.

We couldn't have created the book without the help of some very dedicated Googlites. To David Salinas, Brett Crosby, Christina Powell, Michael Mayzel, and Brandon McCormick, thanks for all your help and for pointing us in the right direction. And thanks to my very own Google Guy, Alex Ortiz. Your passion for and belief in Google Analytics comes through, my friend. I am more appreciative than you'll ever know for your answers and your efforts in ensuring that there are great screenshots for our readers to see.

There's also an entire team of people at Wiley who helped make the book possible. My thanks go to Todd Meister, our amazing (and super-patient) tech editor, Scott Meyers, and Mary Beth Wakefield (wonderful, helpful people), and Bill Bridges, who deals with my writerly eccentricities as if they were normal! It's because of his patience and attention to detail that my thoughts seem to flow well. Thanks to all of you (and to anyone I may have overlooked).

—Jerri Ledford

Thank you, Jerri, for this wonderful opportunity to co-author this book with you.

—Joe Teixeira

Contents at a Glance

Contents

Introduction

In late 2005, Internet behemoth Google purchased a leading web analytics firm, Urchin, and began offering the service free of charge to certain well-placed technology publications' web sites. Not long after that, Google launched the Google Analytics service based on the Urchin software, offering it to the general public as a completely free service. Response was incredible—overwhelming—and a quarter of a million new accounts were created overnight, with an estimated half to three-quarters of a million web sites tracked.

All of this caught Google unprepared, and people had to be turned away because there weren't enough resources to support everyone who wanted an account. Google began taking e-mail addresses for interested webmasters who couldn't be accommodated at launch.

How did this happen? How did Google so grossly underestimate the demand for Google Analytics? After all, at $200/month, Urchin did okay—it had good software and a relatively low price point for the industry, but it wasn't exactly inundated with clamoring customers.

Apparently, assessments based on Urchin's sales weren't exactly accurate. The demand for real analytics is huge, and the price tag of free is exactly the price tag that draws in the masses.

But what are analytics? Most webmasters know enough to realize that they need analytics. But do they know how to read them? How to use them? Are analytics just site stats on steroids, or can they be used by the average webmaster, who is a layman and not a professional, to improve the performance of a web site?

The answer is that, with Google Analytics, the average webmaster can use analytics to improve the performance of a site. And well over a half-million users have figured this out, using Google Analytics.

So many users have turned to Google Analytics and begun to make suggestions about the program that the design team at Google decided it was time to implement some new features and make the application easier to use. And that's how the Google Analytics 2.0 application was born. Then, continuing in that vein, Google Analytics has consistently been changed and updated as features have been added, changed, and removed.

The purpose of this book, *Google Analytics, Third Edition*, is to explain the concepts behind analytics and to show how to set up Google Analytics, choose goals and filters, read Google Analytics reports and graphs, and use that information to improve your web-site performance. Advanced information about topics such as filtering, goal setting, and e-commerce tracking, and more in-depth explanations of some of the theories of analytics, are among the new features added.

We provide numerous examples of the ways companies use these reports to do business better, and we illustrate how some of the functions of Google Analytics work. We have even included examples of web sites and usage patterns to help you understand the value of the reports and capabilities available through Google Analytics.

Overview of the Book and Technology

Google Analytics is a powerful tool for measuring the success of your web site, your marketing efforts, and your products and services. With that in mind, we strive to give you all the tools you'll need to begin using the program immediately if you've never used it before. That includes explanations of how to get started using Google Analytics, as well as chapters on how to find and use reports.

We've also tried to explain some of the concepts of analytics and what each of the Google Analytics reports means, in the grand scope of your business. Where it's appropriate, we tell you how these reports apply to our personal web sites; and where it's not, you'll find both fictional examples and examples of real companies that use Google Analytics.

What's new in this book is the advanced material that you'll see as well as fairly extensive updates to all the material that was included in previous versions. We include information that takes you beyond just getting into Google Analytics. Of course, you'll learn all about what's new with the program, but more important, you'll learn how to use the application for more in-depth analysis of your web-site statistics.

Using the advanced techniques and tips provided throughout the book, you'll be able to drill down deeper, find more specific information, and use information in ways that you never have before when using Google Analytics. There's even an entire chapter of advanced material to help you hack Google Analytics to gain still more value from the application.

How This Book Is Organized

The book is divided into several parts. Each part is arranged to help you understand Google Analytics better. In later parts, the chapters correspond with the Google Analytics user interface. Here's a quick map of what each part contains:

- **Part One: Getting Started with Google Analytics**—This part contains five chapters. After an opening Chapter 1, Chapter 2 introduces you to the concept of analytics and the reasons why you should use Google Analytics. And then, in Chapter 3, we help you get started using Google Analytics by walking you through setting up your Google Analytics account. Chapters 4 and 5 help you understand how to navigate through Google Analytics and make the best use of the dashboard features that the program has.

- **Part Two: Analytics and Site Statistics: Concepts and Methods**—Any web-site Analytics can be a little intimidating if you don't understand the metrics that are used. To help end confusion, this part of the book is designed to give you an overview of the concepts and measurement methods that are used in Google Analytics. Chapter 6 gives you the basic concepts of e-commerce. Chapter 7 walks you through the basic analytics concepts and metrics that you might find confusing. And Chapter 8 will help you get e-commerce reporting set up so that you'll have access to all that Google Analytics has to offer.

- **Part Three: Advanced Implementation**—There's much more to making use of Google Analytics than just setting it up and reading reports. Google Analytics offers a variety of features that let you really dig into information about your web-site visitors so you can reach more visitors and reach them better. In Chapter 9 you'll learn all about the advanced dashboard features that Google Analytics has and how you can use those features to your advantage. Chapter 10 helps you to understand and begin using filters to learn more about your site visitors. And in Chapter 11 you'll find everything you need to know about setting goals. Then in Chapter 12 we extend your knowledge of goals by introducing you to goal funnels and showing you how to set them up. AdWords integration is covered in Chapter 13, and Chapter 14 offers a wealth of hacking information that will allow you to extend the capabilities of Google Analytics.

- **Part Four: The Reports**—You'll find most of the information on reports in Google Analytics in the Reports section of the book. Each of these chapters follows the structure of the reports. Chapter 15 covers the visitor reports. Chapter 16 walks you through the traffic reports. Chapter 17 teaches you how to use the content reports. In Chapter 18 you'll learn all you need to know about the site search reports, and in Chapter 19 the event tracking reports are explained. Finally, in Chapter 20 you'll learn about the e-commerce reports. Through all of these chapters, we'll explain the reports in addition to giving you insight on how to best use them to improve your web-site traffic.

We suggest that whether you're interested in Google Analytics for marketing, content optimization, or e-commerce, you should skim through the whole book first. Even if you don't want to know which of the pages on your site sells the most gadgets, there is value to be found in these reports, and we show you where to find it.

Once you've read through the book, keep it near your computer and use it to refresh your memory on how to use a report or where to find it.

As noted earlier, each report is included in a chapter that corresponds with a report section in Google Analytics. We've tried to maintain a structure similar to that of Google Analytics to make it easier for you to find everything. If you don't know where something is located in the program, look at the illustrations in the book. They'll show you exactly where we found it.

One more note about the illustrations you'll find here. You may notice that some of them have no data. We've done this on purpose. Chances are that there will be areas of Google Analytics where data is not yet being collected. This is because you have to set up your web site and some of the reports and then give them time to collect data.

We're leaving these blank figures just so you can see what they might look like before you have data in them. In the majority of illustrations, however, you'll find varying amounts of data. In some cases, examples of micro-businesses are used, and in others we've included examples of larger businesses. Again, this is to help you understand the varying levels at which Google Analytics can be used to improve the effectiveness of your site.

Who Should Read this Book

Do you have a web site or blog that you'd like to track? Can you edit the HTML on that site? Are you web savvy but not an analytics expert? If that's you, you've got the right book. We tried to explain everything in the following pages in the context of how small-business owners and micro-business owners might need to use it. These concepts apply to home-business owners as well. There is a wide audience for Google Analytics. Our aim is to help the beginning and intermediate users become experts, so you'll find information in these pages that runs the gamut from very basic to quite advanced.

Depending on where you are with your Google Analytics account, you might be able to skim over certain sections of the book. For example, if you've already set up a Google account and your Analytics account, you can glance at Chapter 3 without paying too much attention to detail. If you haven't completed one or both of those actions, however, you probably shouldn't skip that chapter.

If you want, you can even skim through the whole book first and then come back and focus on only the sections that apply directly to your needs at this time. The great thing about *Google Analytics* is that it's designed to be a lasting resource. You can always pick the book up later if your needs change.

Tools You Will Need

As with any report that you create, there are a few supplies that you'll need along the way. With Google Analytics, it's fairly simple. First, you need a web site to track. It can be your own web site, your company web site, or even a blog site, so long as you have access to the HTML code for that site. You have to have access to the code because you need to alter the code so that Google can track your site.

In addition to your site, you'll also need access to the Google Analytics program. Signing up for Google Analytics is easy; you'll learn all about it in Chapter 3.

You may also want a Google AdWords account. It's not essential to have, but part of the true power in Google Analytics lies in its integration with Google AdWords. If you don't have an account and haven't even considered using one, read through Chapter 13 and then go ahead and sign up for the account if you think it will be useful. It takes only a minute, and you can deactivate your AdWords campaigns at any time.

Finally, throughout the book you'll find references to books on certain topics. These are not requirements, just suggestions that you may find useful if you want to know more about that specific topic. The books recommended here can be found through Amazon.com or any local bookstore. We've tried not to include anything obscure or hard to find.

Moving On

Enough. We've covered everything you're likely to want to know about using the book, so it's time to get on with it.

Have fun, and thanks for reading!

Part

I

Getting Started with Google Analytics

As analytics applications go, Google Analytics is probably the easiest (or at least one of the easiest) available in the market today. But don't let the simplicity of Google Analytics fool you. There's a lot of power to harness using Google Analytics, if you know how.

Before you can harness anything, though, you need to have a solid place to stand. That's what we're going to provide for you in this part of the book, from an application standpoint. In the chapters that follow, you'll learn why you want to use Google Analytics, and how to set up an account and install the tracking code. We'll also include some basics about navigating Google Analytics to help you move around as we dig deeper and deeper into the capabilities of Google Analytics in coming chapters.

If you're an advanced Google Analytics user, this part of the book will probably all be review for you. Feel free to skip ahead (or even just to skip around and skim through what's in these chapters for a refresher). Those who are new to Google Analytics probably need this information and should keep reading.

What's New in Google Analytics

Google, like every other software company on the planet, spends a lot of time and money on R&D (Research and Development). So it should come as no surprise that Google's programs, like Google Analytics, are in a constant state of flux. Even parts of the program that you might think are there to stay can change, literally overnight.

Google has gotten better about giving a little warning about elements of programs that disappear, but the company will still roll out a feature overnight and not let anyone even know it's in the works until it hits the page. Google Analytics is no exception to that rule, and in the year and a half since the last update of this book, lots of things have changed. Some reports have disappeared, others have turned up, and features have changed considerably.

Fortunately, the changes all seem to be good. There are still features that would be nice to have that don't exist in Google Analytics, but given time they'll probably turn up, and if they don't, then it's not likely that you'll miss them too much.

Two Years Equals Lots of Changes

So what's changed since the last edition of this book was released in August 2007? Here's the quick and dirty view of some of the most important changes:

- **Google Analytics Data Export API**: Google Analytics made the Data Export API available to all users. This API (which stands for Application

Programming Interface) allows programmers to deeply customize Google Analytics to work with other applications, or even as a customized stand-alone. The Data Export API isn't covered in this book, because it's most useful to developers and very advanced users.

- **AdSense and Analytics Integration**: Google Analytics and Google AdSense are now linked together so that you can view the success of your AdSense campaigns.

- **Cost Data Settings**: You can now change your cost data settings in Google Analytics. That's covered in Chapter 13, "AdWords Integration."

- **Motion Charts**: Google Analytics now has a feature called Motion Charts that gives you a new way to view the data that's available in your Analytics account. Motion Charts are covered in a little more depth later in this chapter.

- **TV Ad Metrics**: Now you can track your television ads using Google Analytics. You'll learn more about this new capability in Chapter 16, "Traffic Sources."

- **Advanced Segmentation**: The segmentation capabilities of Google Analytics have improved dramatically over the last couple of years. Advanced segmentation improves segmentation capabilities that previously existed and provides new features that allow for the creation of customized segmentation. These new features are covered in Chapter 5, "Account Dashboard Basics."

- **Custom Reporting**: Ever wish you could have access to reports that are more tailored to your specific needs? Now you can. Google Analytics has added a custom reporting feature that allows you to create reports that are truly meaningful to you specifically. You'll learn more about custom reporting in Chapter 9, "Advanced Dashboard Features."

- **Event Tracking**: Event Tracking is now a section of reports that are available to help you track events that take place on your site. You'll learn the basics of event tracking in Chapter 19.

- **Improved Training and Help Files**: Previously, the Google Analytics help files were frustrating at best. Trying to find something was like being caught in a House of Mirrors. Everywhere you turned, everything looked the same and there was no way to find the "real" answer to your question. Thankfully, that's changing. And in Appendix A, you'll find additional information about using these files and other resources that are available to you.

Lots of other, smaller changes have also been implemented. For example, the Site Overlay report has changed in appearance and the Reverse Goal Path report is going away soon (possibly even before you read this text).

Betas Galore

One thing Google is known for is its beta program. Google has often released a program or feature to the general population "in beta" to get feedback before releasing the final project. In fact, some programs have remained in beta for years.

Google Analytics isn't one of those programs, of course, but it does have features that are still in beta. These features are new additions since the last edition of this book, and it's not clear how long they'll remain in beta.

What that means to you is that these features are subject to change over time. They could even go away—completely go away. It will depend on how well users adopt the features, and what changes are suggested for improvements.

Custom Reporting

One of the beta features available in Google Analytics is custom reporting. This feature allows you to create reports that are customized to your specific needs. For example, if you want to know how your keywords are performing in specific countries, you can set up a custom report for that.

You can create a custom report using a metric of your choice, or you can use metrics and dimensions (which are segments of your site visitors) to further define analytics that are meaningful to your specific business or even to a goal that you've developed to move your business forward.

Creating custom reports is covered in Chapter 9. There you'll learn how to create a custom report that tells you exactly what you want to know about your site visitors.

Advanced Segmenting

A segment of your site visitors is basically a division or group. For example, you can segment visitors by visits that come from iPhones or even by returning visitors only. This gives you the control to look only at specific groups of visitors to see how they affect your web-site traffic or interact with your web site.

Google Analytics has always had segmenting capabilities, but the advanced segments that are offered now are a different type of grouping, brought on in part by the changing definitions surrounding analytics.

What used to be segments (campaign, keyword, language, browser, etc.) are now called dimensions. That's because a dimension can be a general source of data (a broad category), but it's not really going to mean much to you until you can dice it down and apply it to a specific group of visitors (or a segment).

The most useful data that you'll be able to pull from Google Analytics will be data that can be applied specifically to give you a clear picture of your average site visitor. So using segments along with dimensions is the key to teasing the value out of analytics.

One of the coolest features of the advanced segments available through Google Analytics is that you can create customized advance segments to help you break your web-site traffic down into groups that are meaningful to your business objectives.

Chapter 5 features more information about advanced segmentation and how to create advanced segments.

Motion Charts

The last new feature that should be pointed out right from the beginning is the addition of motion charts to some reports in Google Analytics. These charts are not well-suited to all the reports; however, for reports like New vs. Returning, you can use a motion chart to get a clear picture of the trends that multiple dimensions might indicate.

For example, using the motion chart, you can see how your keywords perform by conversion rate. This helps you to see which keywords are responsible for the most visits and which are responsible for the most conversions.

Motion Charts are automatically enabled on the reports for which they are available, as shown in Figure 1-1. Just click the **Visualize** button at the top of the report to switch to the Motion Chart. (You can always switch back by clicking on the name of the report again.)

As the name suggests, Motion Charts are actually moving charts. The movement helps you to see how your chosen metrics change over time. This allows you to see patterns where you might otherwise miss them. To activate the movement in the Motion Chart, click the Start arrow, shown in Figure 1-2.

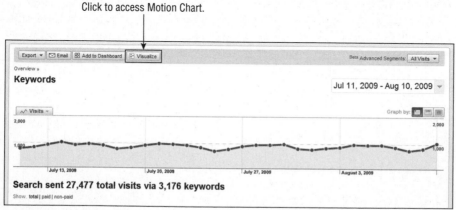

Figure 1-1: Motion Charts are another way to visualize your data segments and dimensions to spot trends you might not otherwise see.

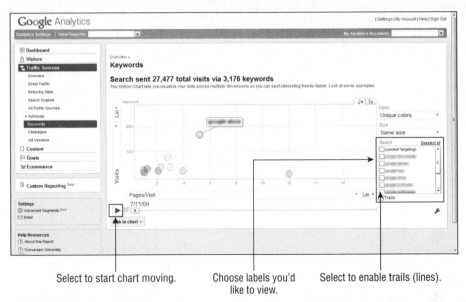

Select to start chart moving.   Choose labels you'd   Select to enable trails (lines).
                              like to view.

Figure 1-2: Controls allow you to start and stop the motion chart and change other visual elements.

You can also add labels to the bubbles on the chart by placing a checkmark next to the label that you would like to view in the scrolling list on the right side of the chart. Checking the Trails box will also add lines to the chart, making the paths of the bubbles clearer and easier to read, but note that the trails only show up for the bubbles for which you've enabled active labels.

You can also switch from the bubble visual to a bar graph, if that works better for you. You'll find the tab that switches between the two types of graphs in the upper-right corner above the graph.

In true Google fashion, too, there's more information hidden behind the labels of the bubbles in the Motion Chart. If you place your cursor over a label, you'll see the exact number (for whatever measurement you've chosen) appear on the X and Y axis.

The Motion Chart is just another way for you to visualize metrics that you're already tracking. And looking at something from a different aspect often helps you to see more clearly a picture that you might otherwise miss.

In all, Google Analytics has lots of new features to offer—features that are designed to help you get more from the metrics that you're monitoring. And learning how to use these metrics won't take you long. Like every other aspect of Google Analytics, there's more than meets the eye, but once you start using any of the new features, you'll find that they're worth the time it takes to get used to them.

CHAPTER 2

Why Analytics?

If you've picked up this book, you probably have at least a general idea of what Google Analytics is and does. You know it's a free application that Google makes available for web-site owners to measure their web-site traffic with. What you might not know is exactly why you want or need to measure this traffic. *They* have said that if you want to succeed, you should measure.

Yes, *they* have said this. And *they* advise you to know who visits your site. And obviously if *they* tell you to do it, then you should. But do *they* tell you why? (And for that matter, who are *they* and why do they think they know so much?)

We'll explain a little about why you should use Google Analytics as you go through this chapter. And try to give you some examples along the way. As for who *they* are …

Let's just say that they're the people who have "been there, done that," and they might even know a little about what they're telling you to do. So let's assume for now that *they* are correct and that you need Google Analytics, and then let's figure out why.

What Are Analytics?

According to the most basic definition, analytics are software programs that generate metrics. Metrics are measurements. And measurements can help you benchmark desired results. Now that may seem as clear as mud, but if you'll hang in for just a bit, maybe we can strain some of the mud out together and make the picture a little clearer.

Clarity starts with understanding a bit about what measurements are available for your web site and how those measurements are arrived at. Essentially, what most analytics applications measure is how many people come to your site, how they get there, and what they do while they're there. Of course that's not nearly as simple as it sounds, but it's a good basic description.

What's most important in that description may be the part about figuring out how those measurements are arrived at. And this is where things start to get a little complicated. First, there are a couple of ways to collect data:

- **Client-side data collection:** Uses data that's installed on the user's computer to collect data about that user's movements on the Web.

- **Server-side data collection:** Uses software that's stored on a web server to collect data about a visitor's movements on the Web.

And then there are also a couple of different measurement techniques:

- **Server logs:** Files of data, collected by a web server, about the visitors to a specific web site. Server logs are usually pretty unintelligible until they're processed by software such as *stats packages* or *log analyzers*.

- **Analytics applications:** Analytics applications, such as Google Analytics, take raw data (collected using a small snippet of JavaScript code) and create information out of that data that is understandable and can be used to improve a web site's performance.

NOTE Strictly speaking, stats packages and log analyzers could be used to analyze server logs to pull out information, in much the same way that analytics packages do. However, in the industry, the terms *stats packages* and *log analyzers* are usually used to refer to server logs, which are strictly data and not "information."

Collecting Raw Data

Let's start with the ways to measure. When we use the term "ways to measure" what we're actually referring to is the method by which *raw data* is collected. This raw data is nothing more than numbers—the number of people who visit the site, what pages they visit, where they enter your site, and where they leave your site. At this point, the information is not really usable unless you have a team of statistical experts that can translate it. But we'll get to that in the next section. Right now, all we care about is how that raw data is collected.

Raw data can be collected in one of two ways: through *client-side data collection* or through *server-side data collection*. The difference is not in what data is collected, but in how it's collected.

Client-Side Data Collection

Client-side data collection involves placing a bit of text in the client's—or site visitor's—web browser. This bit of text, called a *cookie*, contains anonymously identifying information that can then be collected by a piece of JavaScript code that's placed on a web page. This code is called a *tag* or *beacon*.

The tag or beacon is always on the lookout for the cookie, and when the cookie happens by (i.e., when you navigate onto a web site that has placed a cookie in your browser), the tag or beacon makes note of the visit. This is raw analytics data that has yet to be parsed into anything usable. At this point in the process, the data is sent to a *remote data collection server*, from which you (the analytics user) can view it, usually through the filter of an analytics application like Google Analytics, in nearly real time.

This method of data collection is called client-side data collection because the data collection actually takes place between the browser and the remote data collection server. You can envision the process as looking something like the diagram shown in Figure 2-1.

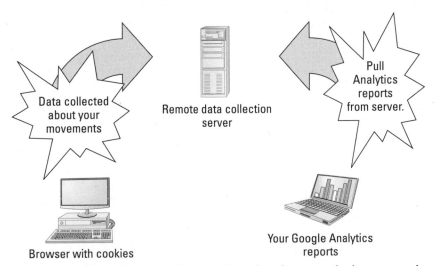

Figure 2-1: Client-side data collection takes place between the browser and the remote data collection server.

Server-Side Data Collection

The second method of data collection is server-side collection. This is a little different from client-side data collection, because it's actually a measurement of the number (and type) of files requested from the web server.

Each time a web browser requests a page (or file) from a web site, a notice to that effect is collected in a text file on the web server. Figure 2-2 provides an image that may be useful in understanding the difference between the two types of data collection.

> **NOTE** Although the information concerning a web page requested by a web browser is stored in a text file in some programs, it could also be stored as a binary file or even in a database. What determines how it's stored is the program that's collecting the data and how that program is designed to store the data once it's been collected. For our purposes (and to keep this simple) we're going to refer to data collected into a text file from this point forward.

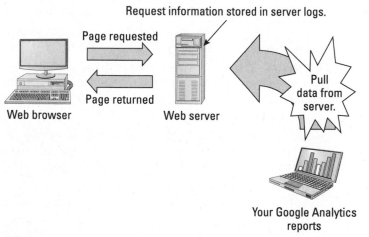

Figure 2-2: Server-side data collection takes place when a browser requests a page or file from a web server.

Server-side data collection is usually accomplished via server logs, which are tantamount to raw data. Nothing has been extrapolated from the data (e.g., there's no graphic showing exactly what percentage represents new visitors to your site and what percentage represents returning ones). However, that doesn't mean server-side data collection is without its merits. It's important, as you'll learn a little later in this chapter.

Right now what you need to understand is that server-side data collection results in a conglomeration of bits of data about web-site visitors collected into a text file. This data is also historical. The distinction between *historical data* and *real-time data* is important because it can mean the difference between being reactive and being proactive with your web-site management.

For example, let's say a page on your web site contains an article that's been picked up quickly by search engines and is drawing a lot of traffic to your site. You'll probably find out about this boost in traffic a lot faster if you're using client-side data collection than if you're just collecting data on the server side. That's because client-side collection gives you fast access to information collected, usually within two to four hours.

With server-side collection, the data is collected into a file throughout the day and then delivered to you at the end of the day. So you may actually not learn about your boost in traffic until you check in the next day. You've lost a day in taking advantage of the increased traffic, and your traffic-boosting article is now old news. Had you known a day earlier, you might have gotten some promotion out—an e-mail blast or some social-media action,

But don't forget—you will be learning some advantages to server-side data collection in the next section.

Measurement Techniques

Now, let's talk a little about the difference between raw data and information. That discussion starts with log files.

Log files were originally the only means by which you could collect web-site visitor data. A log file is a half million or so lines of data, collected into a file. Each time there's an event on your web site—whenever a visitor comes to the site, moves to a different page on the site, or clicks a link, another entry is made into that log file, adding to the bulk of it. This information is combined with other information about the visitor (what browser the visitor is using, whether this visitor is using broadband or not, and many other things).

Only people who bought really expensive software could figure out what the heck the half million lines of incomprehensible data really meant. Everyone else used little applications called *page counters*.

Using a page counter, anyone could see how many people had come to a page, because every time a person visited a web site the number on the page counter increased by one. As long as the counter didn't crash, corrupt its storage, or overflow and start again at zero, there would be a nifty little graphic of numbers that looked like roller skates (or pool balls or stadium scoreboard numbers or whatever you happened to prefer).

Around 1998, web-site statistics packages or *stats* came into common use among small to mid-sized businesses and home users. Stats packages—which are also called *server log analyzers*—basically collect data (in a log file) but leave you to analyze that data. So they tell you what happens; they just don't put what happens into any type of business context.

If you have Windows-based hosting, you may have a Windows-specific stats package, or your host may use the Windows version of one of the open-source stats packages. If you have hosting on a Linux web server running Apache (and about 60 percent of web servers fit this description), you'll most likely have Analog, Webalizer, or AWStats, and you may have all three. These software packages are open source under various versions of the *GNU Public License (GPL).* This neatly explains their ubiquity.

They're free as in freedom, but more important to this particular purpose, they're free as in beer. "Free as in beer" is very attractive to bottom-line-conscious ISPs and web hosts. While a good site-stats package will provide numerous important metrics to help you measure traffic and fine-tune your web site's performance, there are a few key things these stats just won't tell you. But we'll get into that later; we're not quite ready yet to address what stats *don't* say.

Where stats packages leave off is where analytics come in. Comparing what a good analytics package does to what a good site-stats package does is like having a major leaguer who's on steroids bat right before the Little League's MVP. One could be kind and say it's a Major League–to–Little League comparison, or like putting a man next to a boy, but the truth is that analytics are like site stats on steroids. Stats give you numbers—raw data. Analytics turn that raw data into usable information.

How Did Google Analytics Come to Be?

There are many analytics software packages that cost money, among them WebTrends, SiteCatalyst, and Manticore Technology's Professional Edition. The low-end price for web analytics is $200 per month. The high-end price? A couple grand a month is not unusual. To the microsite, the small site, the web merchant on a shoestring, the mom-and-pop site, the struggling e-zine, the blogger who aspires to be famous but isn't yet—that is, to most of the sites on the Web—even the low-end 200 bucks a month sounds like a lot of money!

Then, in mid-2005, Google rocked the boat, buying a small company called Urchin. Urchin was no Oliver Twist. It was, in fact, a runner-up for the 2004 ClickZ Marketing Excellence Award for Best Small Business Analytics Tool. Its product, Urchin Analytics, had a monthly cost on the low end—about $200 a month—and was designed for small businesses.

Six months later, Google did something completely unprecedented. It rebranded Urchin's service as Google Analytics with the intention of releasing it as a free application. Google pre-launched it to a number of large web publications, and shortly after that opened it to the public, apparently completely underestimating the rush of people who would sign up for a free, full-featured analytics service—a quarter of a million in two days.

Google quickly limited the number of sites that registrants could manage to three, although if you knew HTML at all, the limitation was pathetically easy to bypass. Google also initiated a signup list for people who were interested, which eventually morphed into an invitation system reminiscent of the controlled launch of Google's Gmail. Today, signing up is as easy as clicking the Sign Up Now link on the main page (which we'll get to in the next chapter). The moral of this story is, "Don't underestimate the attraction of *free*."

What Can Google Analytics Do for Me?

A better question might be: "What do you want your web site to do better?"

There are all sorts of possible *web-site metrics*—measurements you can take— about how many times files are accessed, how many unique IP addresses access the site, how many pages are served, and so on. Analytics can calculate the most popular pages, how long the typical person stays on the typical page, the percentage of people who bounce (or leave) the site from a particular page, and thus the percentage of people who explore the site more deeply.

You can look at a zillion different metrics until it makes you dizzy, sick, and hopeless. Fortunately, some metrics have more impact on your site than others. Which metrics matter? That depends on what your site is. If your site is content, there's one set of metrics that matters. If your site sells things, a whole different set of metrics matters.

We'll get to what matters to whom in future chapters, but the point we're making right now is that you have to figure out your web site's purpose. For content businesses (ones that normally supply free information on their sites), the most important things might be how much time the visitors spend, how deeply they dig, and how often they return. For a business concerned mainly with selling things, the most important things might be average time to sale, rate of shopping cart abandonment, and profit, profit, profit. Once you know what metrics are meaningful for your web site, you can use them to improve the site's performance. What do you do with analytics?

You improve your bottom line.

Here's a scenario for you. Mark owns a small rug store. It's nothing fancy, but the store does have the best prices in a three-state area, so it stays pretty busy.

Mark's wife, Anna, is his official webmaster. Anna doesn't have any formal training in web-site design, but through trial and error she has managed to put up an attractive site. The problem is, attractive doesn't necessarily translate into effective, and Mark and Anna want to know how effective the site is.

That's where Google Analytics comes in. When Anna first activates her Google Analytics account, she just watches it for a few weeks to see how much traffic the site gets, where it comes from, and what pages visitors spend the most time on.

After a few weeks, Google Analytics has given Anna enough information that she knows the planning pages of the web site are the ones that customers spend the most time on. She can also see that the majority of her visitors come from a link on their local Better Business Bureau site.

These facts help Anna and Mark make some decisions about their marketing budget. Marketing needs to be effective because there's less budget for it than a larger company might have.

Based on what they've learned from Google Analytics, Anna decides to create a monthly newsletter for the company, which includes decorating tips and tips for planning where and how to place a rug. She and Mark also decide to try AdWords for a few months to see how an AdWords campaign will improve the business.

To keep track of all of this new information, Anna sets up filters and goals in Google Analytics. Using the metrics returned by these filters and goals, she'll be able to see if her decision to build on the strengths of the web site actually turns into more sales.

Anna and Mark aren't real. They're (unpaid) performers in this little skit, but their story illustrates how you can use Google Analytics to improve your marketing, which in turn will improve your business. Your specifics might be different. But if you use Google Analytics as a tool to monitor and build marketing efforts, you'll find there are many benefits to knowing the who, what, when, why, and where of web-site traffic.

What Google Analytics Is Not

Google Analytics sounds like a miracle application to help you improve your business, right? It's a useful tool, for sure, but *Google Analytics is not magic*. It's not some mystical force that will automatically generate traffic to your web site. Nor is it the flashing neon sign that says, "Hey, you really should be doing this instead of that." And it's most certainly not the answer to all your web-site traffic problems. No, Google Analytics is none of those things.

It *is* a tool to help you understand how visitors behave when they visit your web site. What you do with that information is up to you. If you simply look at it and keep doing what you're doing, you're going to keep getting what you're getting.

You wouldn't place a screwdriver on the hood of a car and expect it to fix the engine. So don't enable Google Analytics on your site and expect the application to create miracles. Think of it as the tool that will help you figure out *how* to achieve your goals, and we'll help you understand how to use it better along the way.

CHAPTER 3

Creating Your Analytics Account

When Google purchased Urchin on Demand, industry analysts predicted that the merging of Google's technology with Urchin's capabilities would be a great relationship. Chalk one up for the analysts because it truly has turned out to be a marriage made in analytics heaven. Sure, there were some growing pains in the beginning, but combining a successful analytics program like Urchin with the power and simplicity of Google's technology has created an application that anyone can use.

It's not all roses and champagne, however. Even paradise has bugs, and Google Analytics isn't immune to them. Fortunately, the bugs have been pretty minor. You should have a minimum of frustration setting up Google Analytics. You could encounter a few issues, but we're going to walk you through those to make setup as painless as possible.

First, You Need a Google Account

With Google, the key to being part of the "in crowd" is having a Google account. Your Google account will open doors to all kinds of programs, including Google Analytics. And if you use any other Google applications, you probably already have an account.

Without a Google account you'd forever be an outsider, and you don't want that, do you? Signing up for one is easy. The amount of information required is minimal, just your e-mail address and physical location. In Figure 3-1 you can see the information required to create an account with Google.

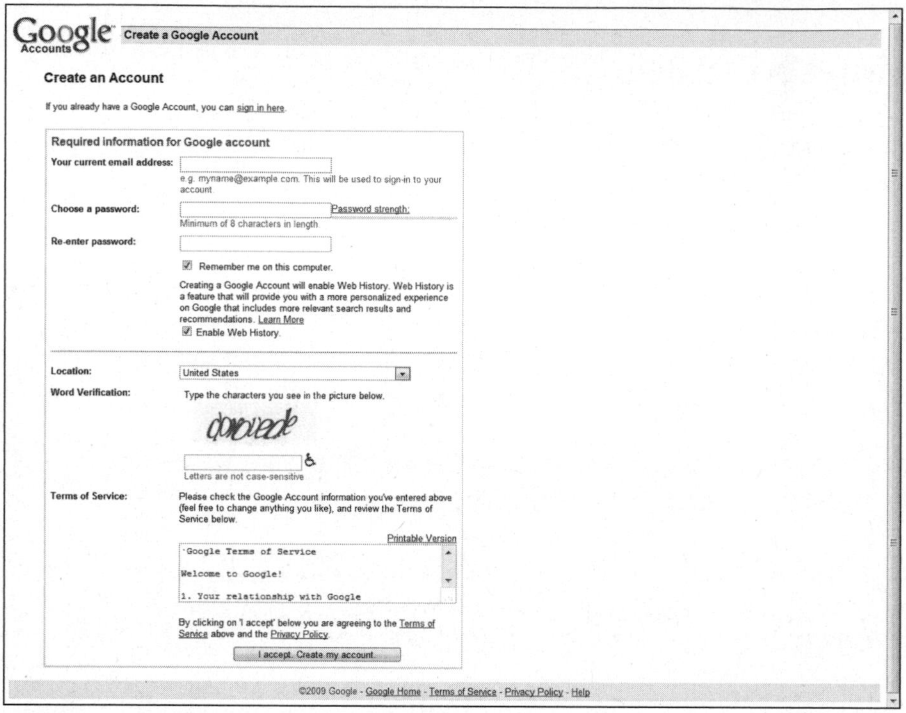

Figure 3-1: Google wants your e-mail address, your location, and a password to create an account.

You can sign up for a Google account through the main Google web page. Go to www.google.com and click the **Sign in** link in the top right-hand corner of the page.

On the page that appears you'll see a sign-in dialog box: this is where you would enter your username and password if you already had those. Since you're just now creating your Google account, you won't have that information yet. Instead, click the link below this box that says **Create an account now.**

On the Create an Account page, you'll enter your signup information. You'll be asked for your e-mail address, a password, and a location, and you'll have to fill in a *captcha* (or verification word). Once you've entered that information, read and accept the terms of service, and then click **I Accept. Create my Account.**

Google sends out confirmation e-mails for new accounts to prevent spam-bots from using bogus e-mail addresses. Within a few minutes you should receive a confirmation e-mail. When you do, click through the link in the e-mail to activate your account. Once that's done you'll have an active Google account.

Once created, your Google account becomes your unified sign-in for most of Google's applications, including iGoogle, Gmail, and Blogger (along with a couple dozen other applications).

Signing Up for Google Analytics

One Google application that your Google account won't grant you instant access to is Google Analytics. To begin using Google Analytics you do need to have a Google account, but you also need to go through the signup process specifically for Analytics.

To sign up for a Google Analytics account you need to start from the Google Analytics homepage, shown in Figure 3-2 (`www.google.com/analytics`).

From that main page, click the **Sign Up Now** link on the right side of the page.

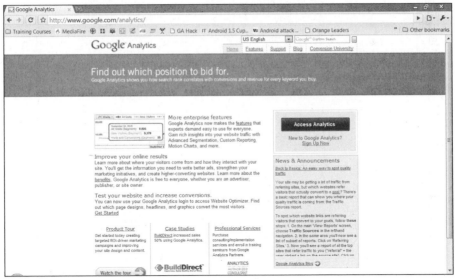

Figure 3-2: To sign up, click the Sign Up Now link.

Now, to the meat of the signup process. From the page shown in Figure 3-3, choose `http://` or `https://` from the menu, depending on whether your site is on a secure server or not. Then enter your site's URL.

Give the site a name, although Google Analytics will automatically enter the domain name for you. Choose the country where you're located. This sets the time zone menu to show only the correct time zones for your country, so don't choose France when you need Fiji. Next click **Continue**.

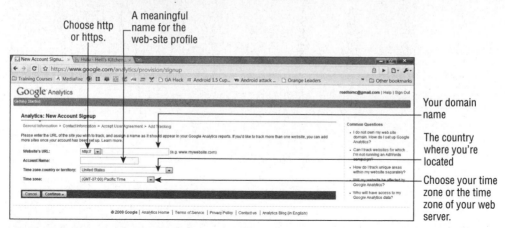

Figure 3-3: Enter your general information here.

PRIVACY, GOOGLE, AND YOUR DATA

Since the first edition of this book, we've fielded many questions about what Google may or may not do with your data. Buried deep in the Terms of Service (TOS) document is the following dense verbiage that explains this:

6. INFORMATION RIGHTS AND PUBLICITY. Google and its wholly owned subsidiaries may retain and use, subject to the terms of its Privacy Policy (located at http://www.google.com/privacy.html, *or such other URL as Google may provide from time to time), information collected in Your use of the Service. Google will not share information associated with You or your Site with any third parties unless Google (i) has Your consent; (ii) concludes that it is required by law or has a good faith belief that access, preservation or disclosure of such information is reasonably necessary to protect the rights, property or safety of Google, its users or the public; or (iii) provides such information in certain limited circumstances to third parties to carry out tasks on Google's behalf (e.g., billing or data storage) with strict restrictions that prevent the data from being used or shared except as directed by Google. When this is done, it is subject to agreements that oblige those parties to process such information only on Google's instructions and in compliance with this Agreement and appropriate confidentiality and security measures.*

Google's use of your data is governed by its privacy policy, located at http://www.google.com/privacy.html.

PRIVACY, GOOGLE, AND YOUR DATA *(continued)*

   Basically, this means that Google will share your information only when it's necessary to do so, and when your data is shared with a third-party company your best interests are protected. Google, being a rather large target, has already had to fight about what information it collects and uses, so you can be sure the company is careful with your data. But, as with all legalese, you should take the time to read through all the details of the TOS, understand them fully, and only then decide if you're in agreement.

Now, enter your contact information, as in Figure 3-4. In addition to filling in your name and phone number, you'll also need to select your country again. It's a little redundant, and it's not clear why selecting your country one time (as the time zone country on the first page of the signup process) isn't enough, but there must be a good reason, right?

Once you've entered your contact information, click **Continue** to move on to the next step in creating your Google account.

The next window contains the standard terms of service agreement (TOS), called Terms and Conditions. You should read the TOS. There's important information in it about how your site analytics may be used. Click **Yes, I agree to the above Terms and Conditions**, but only if you do agree with them. You should know, however, that if you don't agree to the TOS, you cannot create a Google Analytics account. When you've read through the TOS and agreed to it, click **Create New Account.**

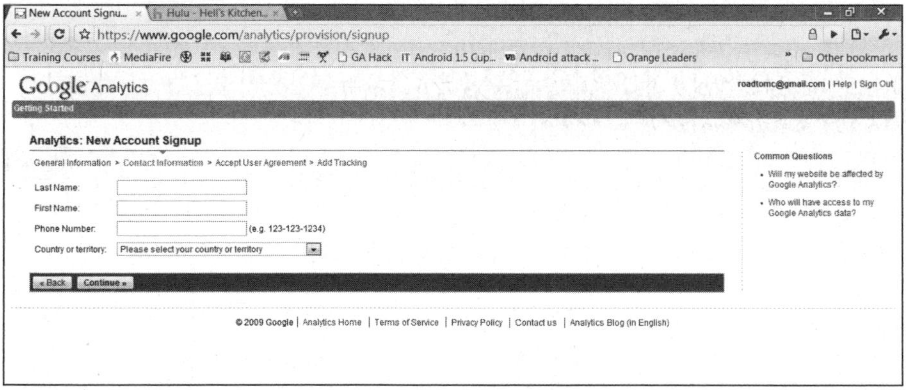

Figure 3-4: Enter your contact information here.

Adding Tracking Code to Your Pages

Just because you've created a new account, don't go getting a warm feeling yet of accomplishment. There's still work to be done. The next screen that appears, shown in Figure 3-5, is where the real work begins.

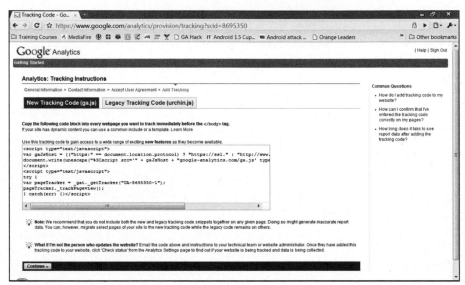

Figure 3-5: The Analytics tracking code must be added to every page of your web site that you want to track.

Analytics uses a snippet of JavaScript code to track the traffic on your web site. You have to place that code on your site before the Analytics tracking is activated. It's not hard to do, but finding the right spot to place the code could be a little difficult.

Technically, all you have to do, is copy the code that Google provides on this page and paste it into your web-site code before the </body> tag at the end of the page. But locating that closing body tag could take some time. As Figure 3-6 at the end of this section shows, the HTML code for a web page is the equivalent of a foreign language if you aren't familiar with HTML. And if you have a footer at the end of your page, the closing body tag (</body>) might not be right at the end of the page. Still, it should be in that vicinity, and a patient search should be all you need to find it.

NOTE If you use a template to create your web site, you can also use that template to insert the HTML tracking code you need to allow Google Analytics to track your site. All you have to do is insert an HTML element in the footer of the page. That should place the code properly so that Google Analytics can track your visitor data.

Now, let's talk a bit about that code and the placement of it. Placing the code immediately before the closing body tag is what Google recommends, because that prevents the JavaScript from interfering with other elements that load on a web page. It's a good solution, ensuring that Google Analytics collects information without affecting the performance of the page, but it does have its disadvantages.

Placing JavaScript code at the end of the page can result in your missing information about a small percentage of site visitors because:

- Returning visitors may navigate through pages quickly. If they're familiar with your site, your visitors might not wait for a page to load before clicking to another page. When they move on before the tracking code loads, they can't be counted.

- JavaScript near the top of the page could interfere with the Google Analytics Tracking Code. If there are other JavaScript elements further up the page that error out, that could cause other JavaScript on the page to be turned off, meaning you miss counting visitors.

- Tagging lots of pages can lead to missed or forgotten pages. This isn't strictly a tag-placement issue, but it is a tagging issue in general. Pages that aren't tagged can't be tracked.

In general these issues affect only a small percentage of the visitors to your site—less than 5 percent, according to analytics experts—but you need to know that Google Analytics isn't perfect. But even with these issues, it can still collect very useful analytics for you.

Getting back to installing the tracking code on your web page, once you've pasted the tracking code into the HTML on your site or created a module for the tracking code, you should save and republish the page. This may take a few hours or possibly even a day or two, but Google Analytics will automatically detect the correct placement of the code. Once you've copied the code from the Google Analytics web site onto the web pages you want to track, click **Continue** to move to the main Google Analytics account page, shown in Figure 3-6. We'll look at this page a little more closely in Chapter 4, "The Settings Dashboard," but before we get there, there's one more thing you need to know about the tracking code.

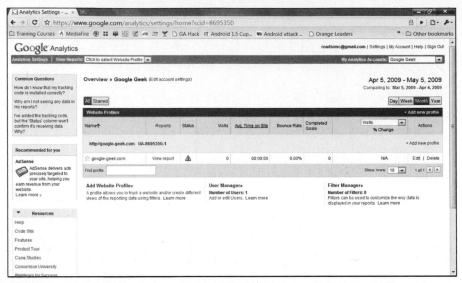

Figure 3-6: Analytics has many dashboards. This one controls your profile settings.

Google Analytics on Secure Pages (https)

A secure page has to use all secure resources. An unsecured resource could be a data-leak and compromise the secure nature of the page. Thus, using `http://www.google-analytics.com/urchin.js` to touch Google Analytics causes an error because it's not a secure resource. The protocol is `http://` rather than `https://`. If you have a shopping cart or you use a secure server for collecting customer information, you may well be tearing your hair out when the script that calls Google Analytics causes this error. There's an easy solution and a difficult solution.

The Easy Way

The easy way? Just use the secure source URL for all your pages. You'll have to modify the first portion of the tracker code, which looks like this:

```
<script src="http://www.google-
analytics.com/urchin.js"type="text/javascript">
</script>
```

It needs to look like this:

```
<script src="https://ssl.google-analytics.com/urchin.js"type="text/
javascript">
</script>
```

The second portion of your tracker code looks like this:

```
<script type="text/javascript">
_uacct = "UA-xxxxxx-1";
urchinTracker();
</script>
```

It will remain unchanged—except that your code will have your _uacct code filled in, of course.

The Hard Way

But that's the easy way! A real propeller-head doesn't do things the easy way, and in fact there *are* some reasons why you might not want to use the previous solution. For one thing, it would be considerate not to overuse Google's secure servers—and also considerate of the sites that are actually secure and would be slowed if the servers were hit unnecessarily. This would also discourage Google from purposely breaking the previous technique because said servers got abused. There is something to be said for doing something the right way, not just the convenient way.

The basic idea here is that you want to check if you're on a secure page or not, and then include the correct piece of code. This code replaces the first part of the script that you touched above in *The Easy Way*.

First, we'll do it in PHP:

```
if($_SERVER['HTTPS'])
{$GA_URL = "https://ssl.google-analytics.com/urchin.js"; }
else {$GA_url = "http://www.google-analytics.com/urchin.js"; }
print ("<script src='$GA_url' type='text/javascript'>\n</script>");
```

The "if" checks the global $_SERVER variable to see if it's using the https protocol (i.e., this is a secure page). If the page is secure, it sets the $GA_url variable to the URL for the secure version of urchin.js. If the page is not a secure page, the "else" clause sets the $GA_url to the non-secure URL. The print statement prints out the upper script tags. Your lower set of script tags (the one containing the $_uacct tag) remains unchanged.

Now, we'll give it a go in Javascript:

```
<script type="text/javascript">
document.write ('<script src="');
if (window.location.protocol == 'https:')
{document.write('https://ssl.google-analytics.com/urchin.js'); }
else {document.write('http://www.google-analytics.com/urchin.js'); }
document.write (' type="text/javascript"></sc'+'ript>');
</script>
```

The Javascript version is a tiny bit different. Rather than checking first and cobbling together the full script tag at the end, we first print the opening part of the script tag. Then we check the window's location property to see what protocol the page is using. If it's https—a secure page—we write the secure URL (remember, we've already written the opening part of the script). If it's not an https page, we write the non-secure URL. Then we write the last part of the script with a final `document.write`. Note that at the end of the `document.write` statement, the word `script` is broken up into two pieces as `sc'+'ript` so that the browser doesn't exit the script prematurely when it comes to a `</script>`!

The code for use of this technique ASP (CGI/Perl, Ruby, et al.) is left as an exercise for the reader. If you don't like typing the code, you can find it on our blog at `www.google-analytics-book.com` in the Code Samples directory.

Understanding the Tracking Code

The Google Analytics Tracking Code may look like just so much gibberish to you, but it all actually has a purpose. You don't need to understand all of it, however, so let's not dissect it completely.

There are two important elements to this code: your account number and the page tracking code. Both elements are labeled in Figure 3-7.

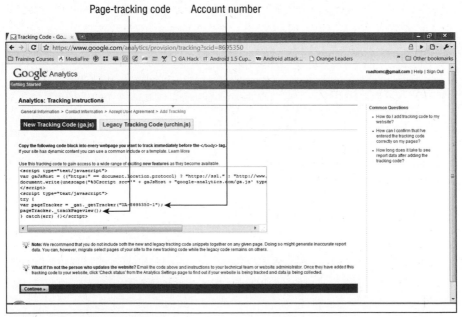

Figure 3-7: Your account number and the page tracking code are important elements to know.

The key piece of information in the tracking code is the line that begins uacct=UA and is followed by a seven-digit number. This number is unique to each web-site profile, and it tells Analytics which profile owns the ping your site sends when a page gets loaded.

The second piece of information in this code is the _trackPageview() tag. This little tag is the real workhorse within the code. It's the bit that pulls all the information you need from your web-site visitors. This information includes important stuff like what URLs the visitors see, what technology (browser, connection type, language settings) they possess, where they come to your site from, where they leave, and how long they stay.

In short, this single tag ensures that the data you need is collected by Google Analytics. You don't want to change this tag. There may come a time (especially as you read through Chapter 14, "Hacking Google Analytics") that you'll want to alter the tracking code in one way or another. You can do that (although Google recommends against it). But if you do, don't change this line.

Checking Tracking Status

Earlier (after you installed your tracking code in the first part of this section), you clicked through to your main Google Analytics account page. This is also called the Analytics Settings Dashboard, and it's the page that you'll see every time you sign in to Google Analytics. This is the central hub of your Google Analytics account, and it's from here that you can learn more about the status of your tracking code.

On your Analytics Settings Dashboard (which you'll learn more about in Chapter 4) you should see a grid for the web site on which you installed the tracking code. In that grid is a status column, indicated in Figure 3-8. This column is where you find the status of your tracking code, as indicated by an icon:

 Tracking not installed, unknown, or not verified. In other words, no information is being collected.

 Waiting for data. The tracking code is installed and recognized, but hasn't collected enough data to generate reports.

 Receiving data. The code is installed and detected, and data is being captured to populate your reports.

Tracking status

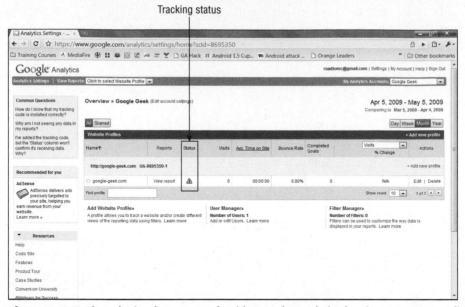

Figure 3-8: Each web site that you track with Google Analytics has its own account listing.

The detection of the code should be immediate, but it could take a couple of days for any analytics to appear. In the meantime, if you want a more detailed look at the status of your tracking code, follow these steps:

1. From the main Google Analytics account page, click **Edit** for the web site that you want to know more about.

2. You're taken to the Profile Settings page, shown in Figure 3-9.

3. Just above the upper right corner of the Main Website Profile Information box, you should see a tracking indicator (labeled in Figure 3-9). Click **Check Status** next to that indicator.

4. You are taken to the Tracking Code page, shown in Figure 3-10. Here detailed tracking status information is displayed at the top of the page, and tracking code at the bottom in case you need to reinstall it.

Analytics will say whether it detects your tracking code or not and whether it is waiting for data or receiving data. Depending on how busy your web site is, it can take several days to several weeks to get enough data into Analytics to make the graphs mean anything. Regardless, Analytics always shows a listing of your code on the Tracking Status page in case you misplace it somehow (for instance, during a site redesign). Click **Finish** when you're done with the page to go back to Analytics Settings.

Status indicator

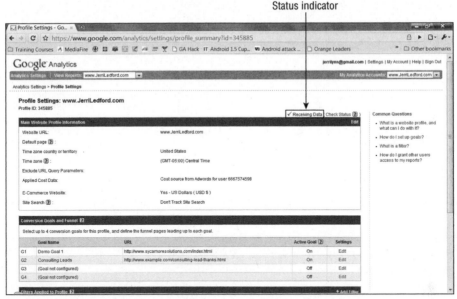

Figure 3-9: Tracking status is displayed on the Profile Settings page.

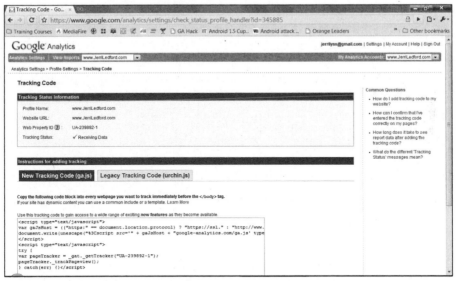

Figure 3-10: The Tracking Code page contains additional tracking information about your web site.

NOTE To track more than one page of your web site, you need to add the tracking code to every page you want to monitor. For example, if you have 15 pages in your web site and you want to track all of those pages, you need to place the code snippet on every one of those 15 pages. Any pages that do not contain the tracking code will not be monitored.

Once the tracking code is installed and collecting information, all the reports and graphics for your site metrics should appear in your Google Analytics account. Google Analytics is a historical analytics program, which means statistics are not tracked in real time. The statistical data that appears in your analytics reports will be one to two days behind. It's not a perfect solution, but despite the delay, the depth of information provided is both accurate and useful.

Navigating Analytics

By now you've had a taste of navigating through the Google Analytics site. You use an intuitive, point-and-click navigation method that lets you start at the most general of pages and takes you into more specific pages as you go on.

As you've already seen, when you sign in you're taken to the Analytics Settings Dashboard. If you click one of the **View Reports** links on that page, you're taken to the reports for the corresponding web site. The first page for each account (or web site) that you're monitoring is the Dashboard page. This page, shown in Figure 3-11, is an overview of the reports that are available to you through Google Analytics for that specific account or web site. It enables you to quickly see the most important measurements for your site.

From the Dashboard page you can navigate to every other report in Google Analytics. The navigation bar on the left side of the screen is where you'll find links to all the reports. Each section of reports is divided into a group that includes all the reports related to that aspect of analytics. If you click the title of the report section, the navigation bar expands to show links to each of the reports in that section.

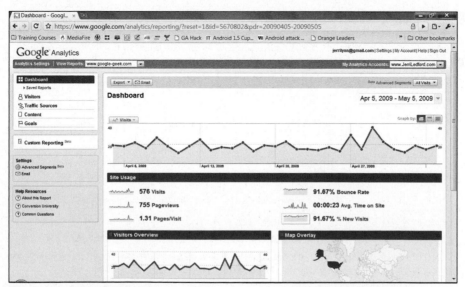

Figure 3-11: You'll find your most frequently used reports in the Dashboard.

Next to some reports within a section, you may notice there is a small arrow that points right. This arrow, shown in Figure 3-12, indicates there are additional reports under that category. For example, within the Visitor report section there's a category for Visitor Trending. When you click the Visitor Trending link, the navigation bar expands even further to show the reports available on that next level down. The important thing to remember, when navigating through Google Analytics, is that the more clicks you make, the deeper into the collected information you're drilling.

Indicates additional reports.

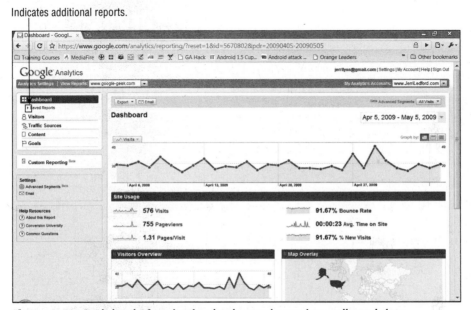

Figure 3-12: Each level of navigation leads you deeper into collected data.

One of the nice things about the Dashboard page is that it's completely customizable. You can quickly add the reports that you use most often to this front page by following these steps:

1. Navigate to the report that you want to include on the Dashboard. All the reports for each section of Google Analytics are located in the navigation bar on the left side of the screen.

2. Once you've reached the report that you want to add to the Dashboard, click **Add to Dashboard**, as shown in Figure 3-13.

3. The report is added to your Dashboard and a message (shown in Figure 3-14) is displayed on the current screen. The next time you view your Dashboard, you should see that report at the bottom of your screen.

Click to add report to Dashboard.

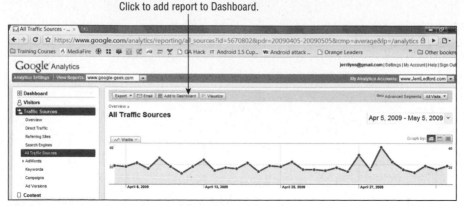

Figure 3-13: Customize the Dashboard by adding the reports you use most often.

Confirmation of addition to Dashboard

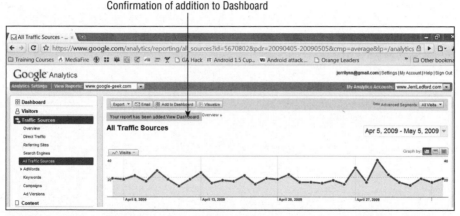

Figure 3-14: A confirmation message lets you know the report has been added.

You may find it irritating that this Dashboard system does not enable you to remove the Site Usage report that appears at the top of the page. You cannot remove it, and you can't move it to a different location on the page, which you *can* do with other reports that you place there.

To move a report from one place to another on your Dashboard, all you have to do is place your pointer over the gray bar at the top of the report. Your pointer will change to a four-pointed arrow. Click and hold that bar while you drag the report to the desired location. Using this method, you can arrange all your reports (except that Site Usage report) in any order that works best for you.

Finally, as you navigate through Google Analytics you may notice two buttons near the top of each report page. These buttons—**Export** and **Email**—indicate new functionality that users of Google Analytics have been waiting for. Use the **Export** button to export any report or Dashboard to a file. You have your choice of file types: PDF and XML are available for all reports, but CSV and TSV file formats are also available for some reports. If you want to export a report to one of these file types, all you have to do is navigate to the report, click **Export,** and then select a file type from the list that appears. After you click the link, a dialog box appears, prompting you to open or save the report. Use the dialog box to specify where you want to save the file and what the file name should be, and then click **OK**. The report will be saved.

When you click **Email**, you're taken to a page like the one shown in Figure 3-15. From this page you can send a report to an e-mail address as an attached file.

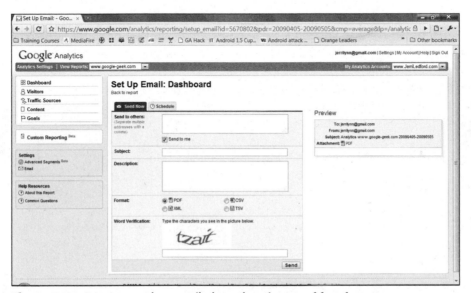

Figure 3-15: Reports can be e-mailed to others in one of four formats.

To send a report in e-mail, all you need do is add the e-mail address the report should be sent to, create a subject and description for the message, and then select a file format. On the right side of the page is a preview of the message that will be sent. When you've finished entering the information, enter the CAPTCHA (that's that funky word you have to type in for verification) and then click **Send**, and the message will be sent to the specified recipients.

The e-mail option also enables you to schedule a regular mailing of a report. If you click **Email** from within a report you'll be taken to the **Setup Email** page. From this page, click the **Schedule** tab. The page will reload and you'll notice that there is now a Date Range/Schedule drop-down menu, and that the **Send** button has changed to **Schedule**.

Set up your e-mail as you would if you were sending a single e-mail, and also set the schedule for the report you would like to send. You have some options there also for the type of the data you'd like sent. For example, if you choose

Weekly, the report that's sent will include all the data from the one-week period since the last report was sent.

Once you've set all the options, click **Schedule** and the message is scheduled to be sent, on the schedule you have chosen, to each of the recipients you specified. Once the message is sent you'll be returned to the report view, but a gold bar at the top of the report will display a confirmation that your report-sending schedule was set. In that bar there is also the link **Manage Scheduled Reports**. Click this link to view scheduled reports, stop sending them, or modify them.

If there is more than one report you would like sent on the same schedule, you can add a report to an existing schedule. Navigate to the report that you would like to include in the scheduled send, and click **Email** at the top of the page. When the page reloads and the e-mail form is showing, click the **Add to Existing** tab. This takes you to a page that displays the reports that you have scheduled to send at specific times. Select the schedule to which you would like to add the report and then click **Add Report**. The report is added to the existing schedule and you're returned to the report page.

In all, navigating through Google Analytics is pretty intuitive. And in coming chapters, you'll learn more about how to customize the interface to make it even more useful for your own needs. Now, however, you should be able to navigate through the basics of Google Analytics, and if you installed your tracking code properly, you should already begin to see some of the reports populating for your web site. They won't be truly useful yet, but you can navigate through them and become familiar with how everything works while Google gathers enough information to make them valuable to you.

The Settings Dashboard

It's one thing to collect data. Any web statistics program will do that. But to go beyond gathering data to producing usable information—that's something completely different. While most analytics programs produce almost any kind of data your heart could desire, they don't make it easy to use. And if you can't figure out what the data means, you can't use it to your benefit.

To produce meaningful data, even with the easiest of analytics programs, you have to set up the program correctly. Setup should be easy. The first dashboards, after all, were on horse-drawn buggies. Far from the technology of those horse-and-buggy days, most professional analytics programs require experienced professionals to configure them. Google Analytics is strictly do-it-yourself, with the simplest dashboards first. The more complex settings are no more than a few clicks deep.

Analytics Settings

When you log in to Google Analytics, the first page is the Analytics Settings dashboard shown in Figure 4-1. This dashboard is your gateway to creating and managing your profiles, controlling access to those profiles, and setting filters.

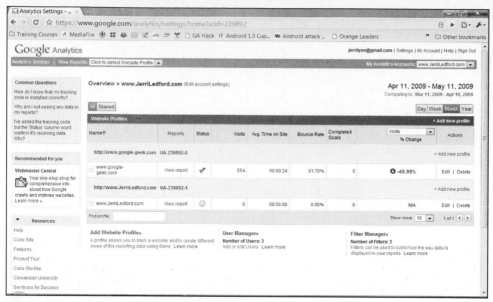

Figure 4-1: The main Google Analytics dashboard

The main (top) menu bar of the Analytics Settings dashboard has three basic choices: Analytics Settings, View Reports, and My Analytics Accounts. If you have more than one profile, you can select which one you'd like to view from the drop-down menu, as shown in Figure 4-2. Otherwise, the default profile (whichever one you added first) will load when you click **View Reports**. Jerri has two web-site profiles in her account: her freelancer's site, www.JerriLedford .com and the book-related web site at www.Google-Geek.com.

The My Analytics Accounts menu is where you access profiles from other analytics accounts that you may have or have access to. As Figure 4-3 shows, this menu contains the different accounts connected via your Google Analytics account. For example, the www.JerriLedford.com profile is the default in Jerri's account, whereas the SkateFic profile is the default in Mary's account. Using the Access Manager, Mary gave Jerri administrative privileges to the SkateFic profile. Jerri can see all the metrics and make changes to settings in the SkateFic profile.

WARNING One thing you should be aware of when adding someone else to your Google Analytics account is that once you grant that person access to your account, you're also granting him or her access to any other web sites that you're tracking. For example, Mary tracks multiple web sites within her Google Analytics account. Because Jerri has access to her account, she can also see all the metrics for each of those web sites. Use caution when adding other users to your account. However, you can add access to specific profiles, so make sure that when you add people, you add them where you want them, and restrict access to what you don't want them to see.

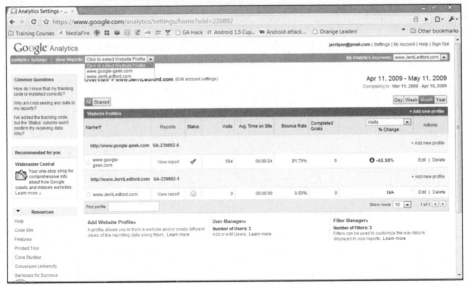

Figure 4-2: The Website Profiles menu contains up to five different profiles.

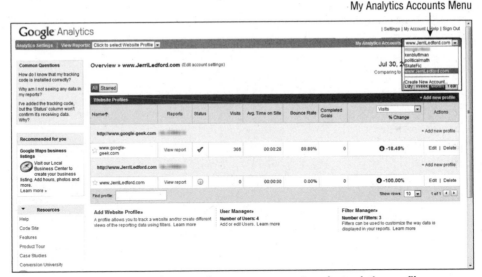

Figure 4-3: You can give other people access to your Google Analytics profiles.

Web-Site Profiles

How many web sites do you own? Do you have just one or do you collect them the way Monopoly players hoard hotels? Maybe you've got a web site and a separate blog or a personal site and an e-commerce one. If you have multiple sites to track, you know it can be a hassle to track each one separately. It takes time to keep up with each site, and it's always hard to come up with extra time.

Google Analytics makes it easy for you to track the analytics and metrics for multiple sites or even subdomains by creating profiles that you can manage from one location. Below the Analytics Settings ribbon is a Website Profiles table. This table contains all the links you need to administer your various profiles, to add a profile, or to change or delete a profile, along with some of the important metrics that you might want to see about your site, including the number of visits, average time visitors spend on the site, bounce rate, and goals completed for the site. We'll look much more closely at all these metrics in coming chapters, but for now just understand that they are probably the ones that you'll refer to most often.

In the Website Profiles table there's also a status category that gives you a quick look at the tracking status of each profile you've created. If for some reason your tracking code isn't working properly, you'll be able to see that very quickly in the Status column of this table.

Adding a Profile

When you sign in to Google Analytics for the first time, you'll be directed to a web site where you set up your first profile (you may remember doing this back in Chapter 3). Once you get that first profile set up you can add additional profiles through the Website Profiles dialog box.

Here's how to add a new profile to those you're tracking:

1. Below the Website Profiles table on the Analytics Settings dashboard, click the **Add Website Profile** link.

2. As Figure 4-4 shows, the information page for the new web-site profile appears. Select from the options to add a new domain or an existing domain to track. The new domain option is for a site that you are not currently tracking; the existing domain option is a portion, or page, of a site you're already tracking that you would like to track separately. (The way time zone information is presented may differ slightly among users.)

3. After you select the Profile Type, select whether your site is an HTTP site or an HTTPS site (HTTPS is usually used for secured pages, like checkouts or registration pages). Then enter the URL of the web site that you want to track in the "Add a Profile for a new domain" field.

4. If you're adding a page to an existing profile, click **Add a Profile for an existing domain**, select the domain name you want to add the profile to, and give the profile a name.

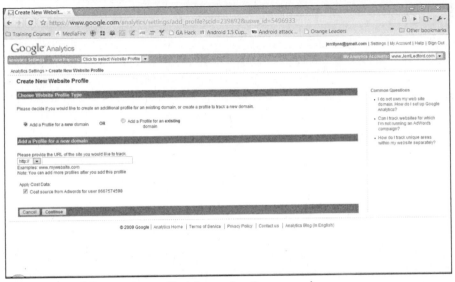

Figure 4-4: Adding a new profile takes only a few seconds.

5. Whether you're creating a profile for a new web site or an existing site, you'll have the option to connect your site to your AdWords account. If you prefer not to connect the two sites at this time, deselect the **Apply Cost Data** option checkmarked in Figure 4-4.

6. Click **Finish.**

7. You'll be taken to the Tracking Status screen, as shown in Figure 4-5. The code that makes it possible for Google to track your site is located below the heading "Instructions for adding tracking." Copy that code and paste it into your web page using the instructions that were covered back in Chapter 3. (It's OK if you need to flip back. We'll wait.)

NOTE As you're adding a web-site profile to your Analytics account, you may notice a few anomalies on your screen that don't appear to be present in the previous screenshots. For example, you may find that you have a section for "Time Zone," that you don't see here. If you're setting up your first Google Analytics web-site profile, you will be prompted for the time zone that you're in. After that first profile, however, you won't be prompted again. So the anomalies that you might encounter are related to first-time setup and should be pretty easy to decipher.

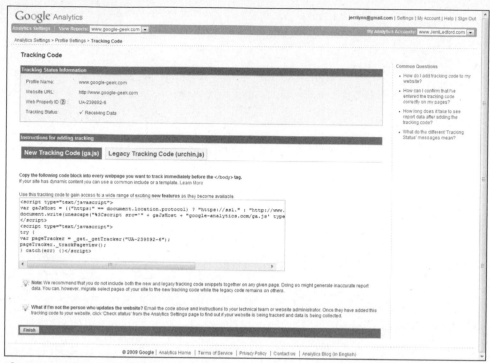

Figure 4-5: The Tracking Status screen shows status information and tracking code.

Checking Status

Once you've added the code to your web site, it will appear as pending in the Status category on your Analytics Settings dashboard. This means that Analytics is still gathering information. You should see the status of the tracking on your site, whether it is pending or receiving data. It could take a couple of days for Analytics to gather enough information to begin producing reports. When enough tracking information has been gathered, the tracking status icon will change to display a green checkmark. If you need a refresher on what the tracking status icons mean, you can find that information back in Chapter 3.

NOTE Even though Google Analytics may gather enough information within a couple of days to start showing you populated reports, many of the analytics measurements that you'll use won't be truly useful until data has been collected for two months or more. Because Google Analytics offers historical tracking, the true value of this data is how it varies over time. Try to be patient and not make too many decisions about how effective your marketing or SEO efforts are until there is really enough data to show you truly useful information.

Editing a Profile Name

Once you've created your Analytics profiles, you can edit or change the profile information by clicking the **Edit** link that's on the same row as the profile name in the Website Profiles table. The profile name is usually the URL of the web site you're tracking, though it might be something like "Web Store" if you're tracking the part of your web site where e-commerce takes place.

One of the new features in Google Analytics is the ability to change the default name for each web-site profile you have. To change a web-site profile name, use these steps:

1. Place your cursor over the default name for the web-site profile. You'll see a small pencil icon appear to the right of the name, as shown in Figure 4-6.

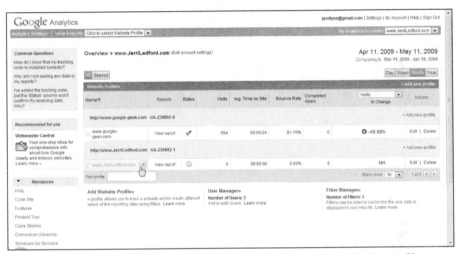

Figure 4-6: The pencil icon indicates that you can change the web-site profile name.

2. Click that icon and the Name textbox appears, as shown in Figure 4-7.

3. Delete the name in the box and type the new name for the web-site profile, then click **Save.** (Alternatively, you can click **Cancel** if you change your mind.)

4. You're returned to the normal Analytics Settings dashboard view, but the new web-site profile name is displayed in place of the old one.

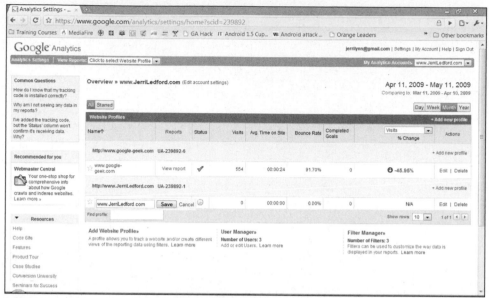

Figure 4-7: Delete the text in the textbox and replace it with the desired profile name.

Starring and Sorting Web-Site Profiles

Another new feature that you may have noticed in the Website Profiles grid is the faint star to the left of each profile name. If you've ever used Gmail or Google Docs, you're probably already familiar with this feature.

For those who are not, starring an item is a way Google provides for you to sort information. For example, maybe you're tracking analytics separately for 25 pages of the same web site (which is something that you *can* do). And let's assume that only five of those pages have AdWords ads associated with them, and you want to compare how well the ads are doing on each of the five pages. You can place a star next to each of those five pages so that you can quickly find only the sites that have AdWords ads and compare them.

Starring a profile is as simple as clicking the star to the left of the profile name (you can unstar it, too). When you click the star the first time, it turns yellow. When you click it again (or unstar the profile) the star goes back to being that faint outline.

Once you've starred a profile or group of profiles, you can sort them from the unstarred profiles using the buttons above the Website Profiles grid, as shown in Figure 4-8. Click the **All** option to list all web-site profiles you have created. It's also the default setting for the dashboard.

Click **Starred** to separate out only the starred profiles. The page reloads to display them without any profiles that you have not starred.

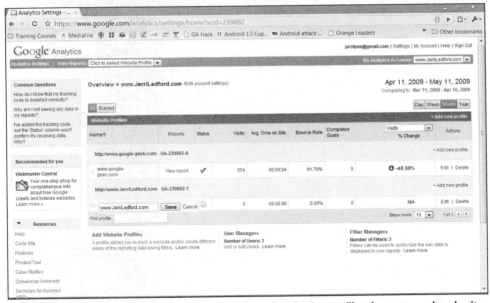

Figure 4-8: Use the sorting buttons to separate all web-site profiles from starred web-site profiles.

Editing Profile Settings

Back in Chapter 3 you caught a glimpse of the Profile Settings page when we were checking the status of the tracking code. There are many more capabilities on that page, however—all of which you'll find useful in managing your web-site profiles.

To reach the profile settings page for any web-site profile that you have set up, click the **Edit** link in the Actions column of the Website Profiles grid. The Profile Settings page, shown in Figure 4-9, enables you to manage four types of profile settings:

- **Main Website Profile Information:** Change the profile name or the URL of the site you're tracking, or set a default page—the index page for the site you're tracking. Add query parameters, set your time zone and currency settings, or specify whether you're tracking an e-commerce site or if you want site search capabilities tracked.

> **NOTE** Query parameters are variables that could possibly cause your web page to be counted more than one time. This duplication can skew your analytics, so it's important to add any query parameters that might make a page appear more than one time in your analytics. This includes session identifiers (such as `sid` and `session id`).

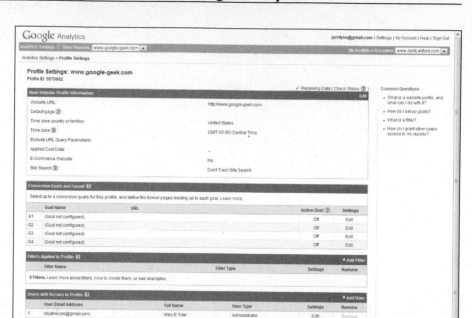

Figure 4-9: You can edit profile settings for several categories from this page.

- **Conversion Goals and Funnel:** A conversion goal is a target page you want users to reach. For example, if you want to drive traffic to sign up for your corporate newsletter, your conversion goal would be the thank-you page for the sign-up process. The number of people who actually reach the thank-you page is then counted toward the conversion goal. Funnels are pages that you expect your visitors to pass through to reach your conversion goal. You can specify up to four different goals, each with as many as 10 funnel pages. Those pages are then monitored to show traffic patterns and how users navigate through your site to your conversion goal—and where people drop out of the process that leads them to a goal. You'll learn more about creating and tracking goals and funnels in Chapters 11 and 12.

- **Filters Applied to Profile:** Filters help you achieve more accurate measurements of the traffic on your site. For example, you can choose to filter visitors who enter your site from a specific domain as a way to ensure more accurate reports. The most common use of this feature is to filter out traffic from your IP address. Say that your browser loads your web site's homepage when you open a new window. You don't want to skew data about real visitors by counting hundreds—if not thousands—of your own visits and page loads. A filter can tell Google Analytics to ignore anything that comes from your IP address, resulting in more accurate metrics. Filters can be quite complicated, especially when you begin to create advanced filters with Regular Expressions, so you'll find more information on this topic in Chapter 10.

▪ **Users with Access to Profile:** In many organizations, more than one person will want or need to have access to the information that Analytics collects and the reports that it returns. There are two levels of access: View Reports and Account Administrator. View Reports enables the user to look at any reports in that profile. Administrator privileges enable the user to make changes to View Reports and settings. This is where you add users for individual profiles, rather than the whole account. You'll learn a little more about access management in the "User Management" section of this chapter.

All these settings can be changed at any time. If you try something and it doesn't work, you can change it again until it does. Each web site you're tracking has its own profile settings, so you can manage each profile in a way that works best for that profile.

Deleting a Profile

Change happens, and it's a good bet that your needs will change over time. You may change the name of your web site, add profiles you want to track, or delete profiles. To delete a profile, navigate to the Analytics Settings page; then find the name of the profile that you want to delete. Click the **Delete** link in the Actions column of the same row as the name of the profile. As Figure 4-10 shows, you'll be prompted to confirm that you want to delete the profile. Click **OK** and the profile will be deleted.

Make sure you really want to delete the profile from Analytics before you click **OK**. Once you confirm, there's no way to get the profile back. If you change your mind, you'll have to recreate the profile from the beginning and you'll lose all your historical data.

NOTE Deleting a profile from your account will work only if you are tracking more than one profile. If you have only one, you cannot delete it. You can, however, create another profile and then delete the first one.

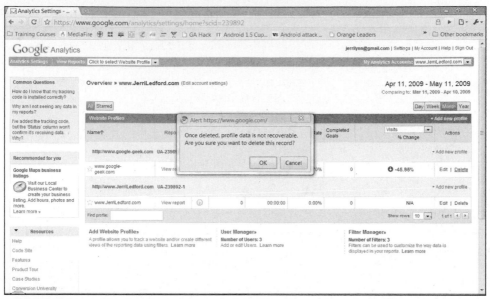

Figure 4-10: Confirm deletion of a profile before the process is complete.

User Management

One very helpful feature of Google Analytics is the ability to give other people—your IT manager or administrator, other executives, or your partner—access to your Analytics accounts. You can give them control over your Analytics accounts, enabling them to manipulate the accounts in much the same way you do, or you can limit the access to only viewing the reports.

If you've ever worked with someone else and had him or her inadvertently change something that you didn't want changed, you may be nervous about which privileges you grant to other users. The User Manager lets you control who can see what and who can do what with your whole account. You can control who has access to individual profiles from the settings page for each profile.

You can reach the User Manager from one of two places. You can access it either by clicking the Edit link in the Action column for the web-site profile you want to share, or by clicking the **User Manager** link located near the bottom of the Analytics Settings page. Using either method, you'll be taken to the User Manager dashboard, shown in Figure 4-11. From this dashboard you can add or remove users and manage those users' privileges.

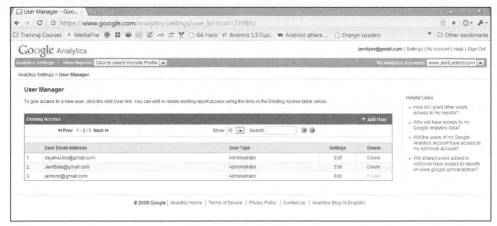

Figure 4-11: The User Manager lets you control who can access your account.

Adding a User

Recently there have been several studies about how executives want to be involved in the collection and reporting of business intelligence, such as the information gathered by Google Analytics. According to these reports, executives want to be right in the middle of the action. They want access to the reports and to receive information about what data is being gathered, how often, and from where.

Google Analytics is built for multiple users. If you have an executive screaming over your shoulder every day that he wants information about the ROI (return on investment) of your web site, Analytics makes it easy to overload him with all the information he could ever desire. All you need to do is add your executive as a user on one or more profiles.

To add a user to your profile, go to Analytics Settings ➪ **User Manager**. In the User Manager window is an Existing Access box that shows who your current users are and what levels of use each one is. Click **+ Add User** in the upper-right corner of the box to give another person privileges.

You'll be taken to the Create New User For Access page, where you should enter the user's e-mail address and name and set the access type, as shown in Figure 4-12. If you are allowing the user viewing privileges only, you can choose to permit access to individual profiles. If you select Account Administrator, the user, by default, will have access to all profiles and the profile lists will disappear. When you've entered the relevant information, click **Save Changes** and the user account will be created.

> **NOTE** When you're creating a new user profile, the user you are adding must have a Google account, and that's the e-mail address you should use to register the user for account access. If you use an e-mail address that isn't attached to an active Google account, the user won't be able to access the site. However, that person can use that address to set up a Google account that will then be able to access Analytics.

If you're not sure you want executives (or anyone else) to have complete control over your Analytics account, you can always add them to a report mailing list, which is covered in Chapter 6. This is an easy way to give your executives the information they demand without having them poking around in areas where they could create havoc.

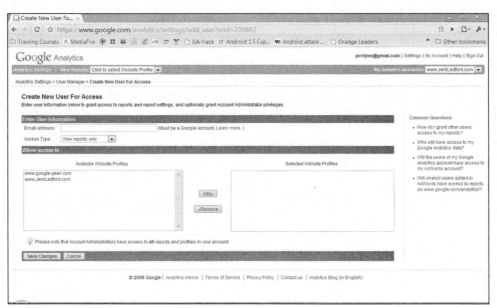

Figure 4-12: To add a new user, enter some simple information and click Finish.

Setting User Permissions

When selecting the Access type, you can set permissions so that your users have administrator access or authorization to "View reports only," as shown in Figure 4-13.

Administrator access to a profile gives the user the ability to do anything you (the owner) could do. That user can make changes to settings, add other users, and even delete the profile. That user can even hand out administrator privileges like beads at Mardi Gras. An inexperienced administrator can neatly sabotage a web-analytics strategy. "View reports only" allows the user to view reports but not to make any changes to the profile.

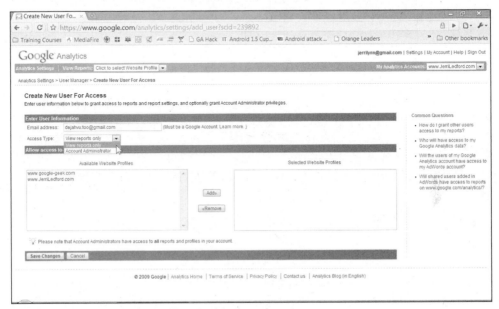

Figure 4-13: Set user permissions in this drop-down menu.

You can select and also restrict which web-site profiles the user can access. If you have multiple profiles for multiple sites, you can give users access to some and keep them out of others. For example, if you work in a big company, you can set up several profiles for your company's web site. You might have a profile of your site's web store for the e-commerce division, and another profile of the content pages for the editorial division.

Deleting a User

People leave. They find better jobs, get downsized, move to Tahiti, or transfer to different departments. In the business world, it's inevitable. Even in small family businesses, sometimes Mom and Pop choose to go separate ways. You need to have the ability to delete a user from your Analytics account. Google knows this and makes deleting users easy, even for non-propeller-heads.

To delete a user, go to Analytics Settings ⇨ User Manager and find the user you want to delete. Select the **Delete** option in the same row as the user's name.

You're once again prompted to confirm that you want to delete the user, as shown in Figure 4-14. Click OK and the user is immediately removed and no longer has access to that—or any other—profile.

Just be sure that you really want to delete the user, because once it's done, you can't undo it. You'll have to re-create the user's access.

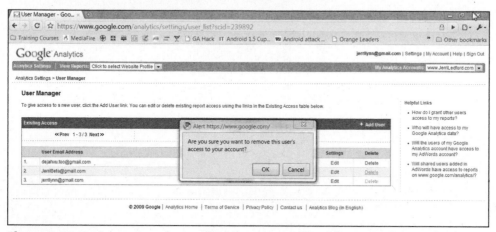

Figure 4-14: You're prompted to confirm that you want to delete users from your program.

Google Analytics makes everything point-and-click easy. It might take you a few minutes the first time you access the program to get it set up and become familiar with navigating through the controls, but once you're comfortable, adding and changing profiles and users is just a matter of clicking a few links.

Account Dashboard Basics

One feature of Google Analytics not only sets it apart from other analytics programs (such as AWStats) but also makes it much more valuable to the user. This feature is the graphic nature of the reports pages. Each report enables you to quickly see what the report is designed to tell you. At a glance you can see a metric that's meaningful and that you can use to determine the next action that you should take with your web site.

That graphic nature extends to the dashboard that you see when you first sign into a web-site profile. As you saw in Chapter 4, the Analytics Settings dashboard is pretty simple. Nothing like the dashboard that you'll encounter once you step one level deeper into Google Analytics.

Navigating from the Dashboard

When you first log in to a web-site profile, the default dashboard for that profile is displayed. On this default dashboard, shown in Figure 5-1, several reports are already added, but the one report on this page that cannot be removed is the top one, Site Usage. It's anchored at the top and cannot be replaced or moved. The controls for date ranges are also at the top of the page and cannot be moved. We'll cover date ranges near the end of this chapter.

Finally, you'll find advanced segmentation options anchored to the top of the page as well. This feature is still in beta testing at the time of this writing, but that doesn't mean it's without value. In fact, you should look closely at the segmentation capabilities in Google Analytics because they can give you a real edge when it comes to reaching your customers. But we'll cover that more in the "Sorting Data with Segmentation" section of this chapter.

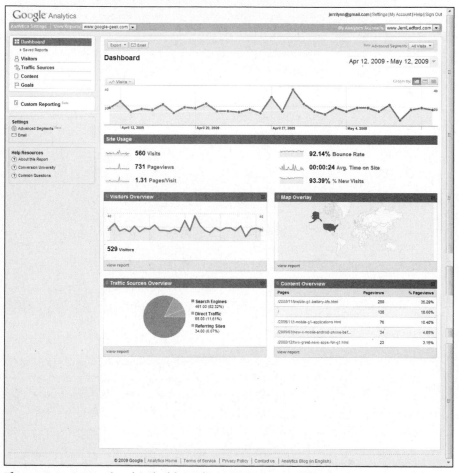

Figure 5-1: Customize the dashboard to meet your specific needs.

Standard Dashboard Modules

Before you begin customizing the reports that are displayed on your web-site profile, there is a set of standard (or default) reports—called Standard Traffic Reports—already in place. Google has determined that these reports are among the most frequently accessed by Google Analytics users. And they are, indeed, useful reports. They include:

- **Site Usage:** This report, shown in Figure 5-2, is the one you cannot remove from your dashboard. You also can't move it around. It's a useful report because it gives you a quick overview of your traffic statistics, but if it's not the most import report in your daily workflow you might find it frustrating that you can't move or remove it. You do have some options for interacting with this report, however, and we'll cover those options in the next section, "Interacting with the Site Usage Report."

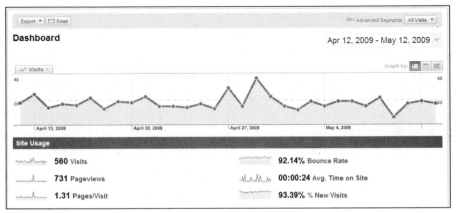

Figure 5-2: This report is an overview of how visitors interact with your site.

- **Visitor Overview:** This report, which is really just an unnumbered graph, lets you see at a glance how many visitors came to your site during the selected time period (shown in Figure 5-3). If you hover over a point in the graph, the exact numbers associated with the nearest inflection point (where the graph changes direction) are shown.

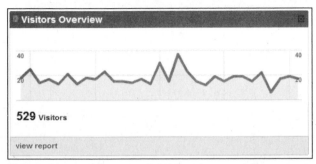

Figure 5-3: In this report, learn how many visitors came to your site during a given time.

■ **Map Overlay:** The Map Overlay gives you a quick graphic view of which continents your visitors are coming from. As shown in Figure 5-4, the continents are shaded, with white representing the location of the fewest visitors and bright green (the dark shading) the location of the most.

Figure 5-4: See where your visitors are coming from with the Map Overlay.

■ **Traffic Sources Overview:** The Traffic Sources Overview report shown in Figure 5-5 is a pie graph that illustrates the sources from which traffic was directed to your site. The graph is color-coded to quickly illustrate whether traffic came to your site directly or from search engines or other referring web sites.

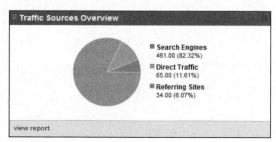

Figure 5-5: This report shows from where traffic came to your site.

■ **Content Overview:** This report, shown in Figure 5-6, lists the top five pages on your web site in terms of *page views*. Each of those five pages is linked to a Content Detail report, which provides additional information about it. In this module you'll also find the number of page views and the percentage of overall page views for each of the pages.

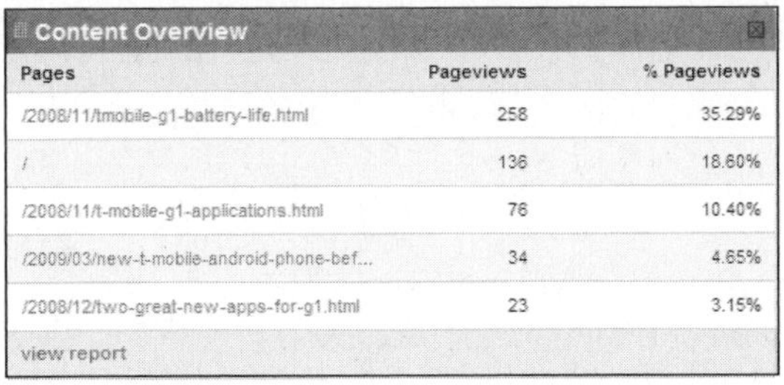

Content Overview

Pages	Pageviews	% Pageviews
/2008/11/tmobile-g1-battery-life.html	258	35.29%
/	136	18.60%
/2008/11/t-mobile-g1-applications.html	76	10.40%
/2009/03/new-t-mobile-android-phone-bef...	34	4.65%
/2008/12/two-great-new-apps-for-g1.html	23	3.15%

view report

Figure 5-6: Content Overview tells which pages on your site are most popular.

These mini-reports displayed on the main dashboard are called *report modules*. And they are all interactive. You can mouse over portions of the reports to see more details, or you can click selections within a report to dig deeper into the information contained there. For example, if you click the map in the Map Overlay module, you'll be taken to a detailed map for whatever country or territory you clicked on.

You can also remove all but one of these reports and replace them with your own selections. This makes the dashboard far more usable and more relevant to your specific needs. If you're part of a larger organization, you can also set up unique dashboards for different roles within your company. We'll talk more about adding and removing report modules a little later in the chapter.

Interacting with the Site Usage Report

Before we get into adding and removing report modules, the Site Usage report is screaming for attention. As previously mentioned, this report can't be removed from the dashboard, or even moved to a different area. However, it can be tweaked to meet your specific needs.

By default the Site Usage report displays the number of visitors (all visitors) to your web site—that would be new, returning, and repeat visitors. That information is represented by both a graph and additional drill-down options, as labeled in Figure 5-7. Don't think that you're stuck with this view, however. You're not.

You can change the information that's displayed in that report in a couple of different ways. First, you can click the tab above the graph that reads "Visits." When you click this tab the page expands to display additional options, as shown in Figure 5-8. Click the radio button next to any of the displayed options to change the information displayed in the graph.

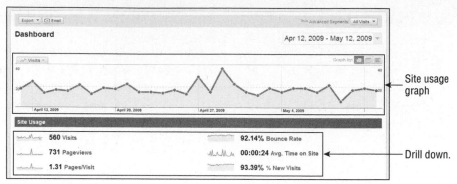

Figure 5-7: In the Site Usage report you can view top-level information
or drill down for more details.

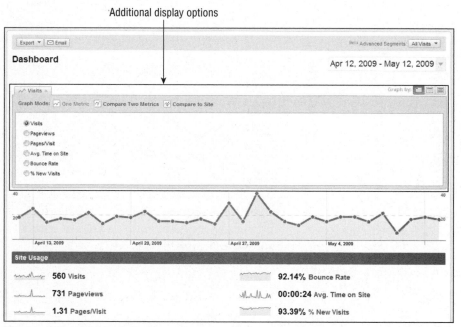

Figure 5-8: Additional display options for the graph are located on the tab above
the graph.

You can also achieve the same results by clicking the graph icon next to
each of the metrics listed *below* the Site Usage graph. Be aware, however, that
if you click the name of the metric (e.g., Visits, Pageviews, Bounce Rate) you'll
be taken to another page that displays more detailed information about that
specific metric.

We'll discuss all these reports in more detail in coming chapters. For now,
what's important is that you learn how to interact with the Site Usage report.

BARCODE: 0201700262714
LOCATION: bgen
TITLE: Strange gifts : eight stories of
DUE DATE: 05-12-2010

BARCODE: 0201801197116
LOCATION: bbkt
TITLE: The last cowgirl : a novel / Jana
DUE DATE: 05-12-2010

BARCODE: 0201801313374
LOCATION: bbkt
TITLE: Stormrage / Richard A. Knaak.
DUE DATE: 05-12-2010

BARCODE: 0201801295696
LOCATION: bbkt
TITLE: The graveyard book / Neil Gaiman
DUE DATE: 05-12-2010

And to that end, there are a couple more things you should know about this report.

The first detail you don't want to miss is that within the Site Usage report you have the option to compare some of the available metrics. As shown in Figure 5-9, you can choose to **Compare Two Metrics** or **Compare to Site.** When you select one of these options a new menu appears that enables you to choose the metrics that you would like to compare, or the graph changes to display the selected metric in comparison to the site average for that specific metric.

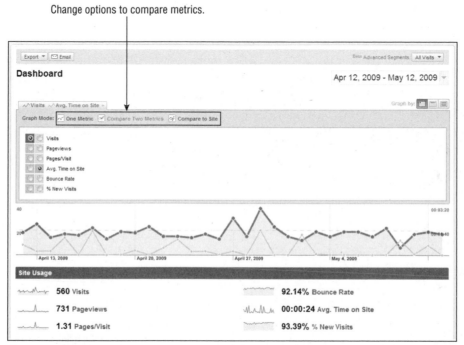

Figure 5-9: Compare metrics against metrics or against the site average for a clearer picture of site usage.

One more detail you might want to be aware of is the ability to change the time frame for the information displayed in the Site Usage report. Above the upper right corner of the Site Usage graph should be three small boxes that display figures that look like forms. These are actually date-range boxes that change the graph display to **Daily, Weekly,** or **Monthly.** Click any one of the boxes to change the display.

By default the display is set to Weekly. If you choose to view a different time-frame display and then later log out of your Google Analytics account, the next time you log back in to the account the displayed time frame will have reset to the default Weekly view.

You can access a lot more time-based capabilities through some of the controls in that upper right corner, but we're not going to cover those just yet. Keep reading, though, because you'll find more information about them in the "Working with Date Ranges" section of this chapter.

Adding Reports

Adding reports to your dashboard takes just a few clicks. First, you have to locate the report that you want to add. Using the navigation menu on the left side of the page, navigate to the report that you want to add to the dashboard. It can be any report that's not already there, and it can be as detailed a report as you would like. For example, if you go to the report **Content by Title** and then click one of the content titles to learn more about the number of visits to that specific page, you can then add to your dashboard the page that gives you that information. If your main focus is tracking your content, that might be a useful report to display.

Once you locate the report you would like to add to your dashboard, all you have to do is click the **Add to Dashboard** button, shown in Figure 5-10. If the add was successful you'll see an orangish bar that reads **Your report has been added. View Dashboard** appears below the **Add to Dashboard** button. This is a link back to your main dashboard.

NOTE You may also see the word "Overview" to the right of the addition-confirmation message. This is a link back to the main dashboard, just like the View Dashboard link.

When you navigate back to your dashboard, you should find the report you added at the bottom of the page. There are two things to remember here. The first is that the report shown on your dashboard is just a snippet of the information available in that report. To see the full report click the **View Report** link in the bottom left corner of the report preview. In some reports you can also click on information within the report preview to be taken to a deeper view of that information.

The other thing you want to remember is that with the exception of the Site Usage report that appears at the top of the dashboard, you can rearrange your report modules in whatever manner suits you. To rearrange report modules, place your cursor over the title bar of the report. As Figure 5-11 indicates, your pointer will change to a multidirectional arrow.

Click to add report to Dashboard.

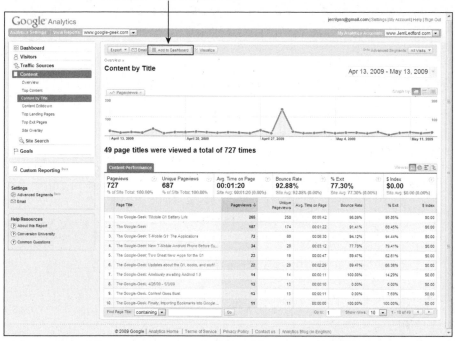

Figure 5-10: Adding reports to your dashboard is as easy as clicking a button.

Indicates the module can be moved.

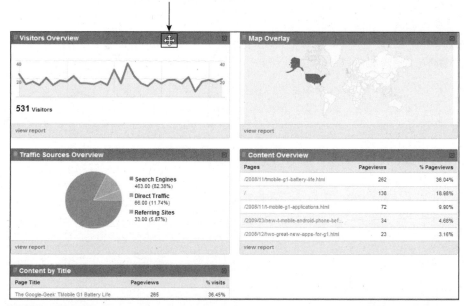

Figure 5-11: When the pointer changes you can grab and move the report module.

Next, click and hold that title bar. Drag the report, as shown in Figure 5-12, to its new location on the dashboard. You can move that report again at any time, to any location on the dashboard except for the top space, where the Site Usage report lives.

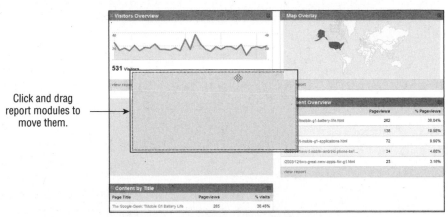

Click and drag report modules to move them.

Figure 5-12: Drag your report to its new location.

One thing you'll find about the ability to add and remove reports on the main dashboard is that you can arrange this dashboard in a manner that suits you. Creating special-purpose dashboards enables you to quickly see the information that's most important to you. But keep in mind that every web-site owner has different needs. To help you address those needs with special-purpose dashboards, we'll cover creating them in more detail in Chapter 9.

Deleting Reports

If you're adding report modules to your dashboard, then it's probably safe to assume that you'll also want to remove report modules from it. Removing the report modules is even easier than adding them. Each report module has a small black X in the upper right corner of the preview. To remove a report module from your dashboard, click this X. A dialog box appears that reads **Are you sure you want to remove this module from the dashboard?** Click **OK**. The report is removed from your dashboard, and if there were any reports beneath it, those are moved up to fill in the empty space.

If at some point you decide you want the deleted report back on your dashboard, then you have to go through the adding process again. Fortunately it's a simple process, so it won't be horrible if you accidentally delete a report.

Sorting Data with Segmentation

One more feature of the dashboards that you'll find handy is the Advanced Segments menu. At the time of writing, Advanced Segments is in beta testing, but it's just a new iteration of the *data segmentation* that's always been available in Google, so it's not likely to go away, though it could change a bit over time (and with Google Analytics, what doesn't?).

Data segmentation is a way of slicing and dicing the data you collect to give you additional insight into how your site visitors behave. For example, when you use segmentation, you might find that all the visitors to your site on the weekends are visiting from iPhones. That information can then be used to dictate the content you display on the weekends or the specials you run. Really, it's all about learning how your visitors interact with your site.

To that end there are many ways of dividing data into *subsets*, or *segments*. Google Analytics provides nearly a dozen different segments for you to use, as shown in Figure 5-13. You can access these segmenting options by clicking the **All Visits** tab on the upper right corner of the Site Usage graph. You also have the option of creating customized segments, which really makes your segmentation possibilities endless.

Click to open
segmenting options.

Figure 5-13: Segmenting your analytics data is one way to learn more about visitor behavior.

Enabling Segmentation

To enable a different segment from what is selected, just place a checkmark in the box to the right of the segment name. You can enable up to four segments at one time. Once you've chosen the segments that you want to view, click **Apply** and the Site Usage graph changes to illustrate the segments that you've selected. By default that graph shows the All Visits segmentation, but you have several other options to choose from:

- **New Visitors:** Shows new visitors
- **Returning Visitors:** Shows returning visitors
- **Paid Traffic:** Shows visitors that are the result of paid keyword ads (such as AdWords)
- **Non-Paid Traffic:** Shows all traffic that does not result from paid keyword ads
- **Search Traffic:** Shows all traffic that originates from a search engine result
- **Direct Traffic:** Shows traffic that is the result of visitors typing the direct address into the address bar of their browser
- **Referral Traffic:** Shows traffic that came from another site as a referral
- **Visits with Conversions:** Shows visits that result in conversions
- **Visits from iPhones:** Shows visits from iPhones
- **Non-Bounce Visits:** Shows visits that do not result in a bounce

When you're finished looking at the segmentation you can go back into the segment view and deselect the options you chose before, and then click **Apply** to return to the default view, or you can leave the view alone. The next time you log into that Google Analytics profile the graph will be reset to the All Visits segment.

Creating Custom Segments

Custom segments are where you will likely find your most valuable, most highly targeted information, because you can create customized segments that apply specifically to your business or web site. Use these steps to create a custom advanced segment:

1. From the Advanced Segments menu, click **Create a new advanced segment**. This takes you to a page where you can begin to create your advanced segment, as shown in Figure 5-14.

Choose a dimension   Drag it to the
or metric.   segment creator.

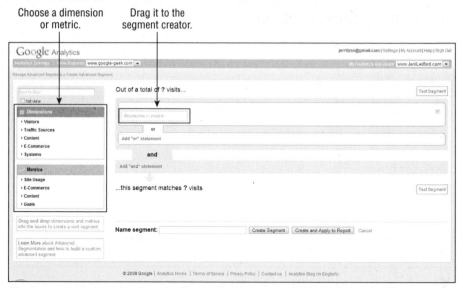

Figure 5-14: Create a custom advanced segment using the segment creator.

2. From the available dimensions and metrics on the left (shown selected in Figure 5-14) select the first comparison that you would like to use. Drag that metric to the **dimension or metric** box in the segment creator.

NOTE If you know exactly what dimension or metric you want to include in the custom segment you're creating, you can type the name into the search box above the available dimensions and metrics (where it says **type to filter**). Then select from the options that appear in the list below.

3. Once you drag a dimension or metric into the filter, the Condition and Value options appear, as shown in Figure 5-15. You must first select a Condition, then you can select a Value to pair with it.

4. You can add more than one dimension or metric to the segment that you're creating. Just remember that each one becomes an "or" statement. If you want to add an "and" statement, you should click the **Add "and" statement** link and then drag the dimension or metric that you want to use into the "and statement" area, highlighted in Figure 5-16.

5. Once you've added the dimensions and metrics that you want to use to segment your site visitors, give the new segment a name (the test won't run unless the segment has been named) and click **Test Segment**. This runs the segment equation to determine whether it will return results.

Choose Condition and Value.

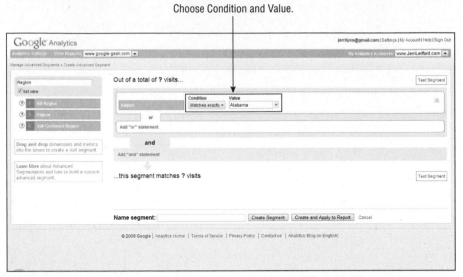

Figure 5-15: Choose a condition and value to further define the dimension or metric selected.

Add an additional requirement.

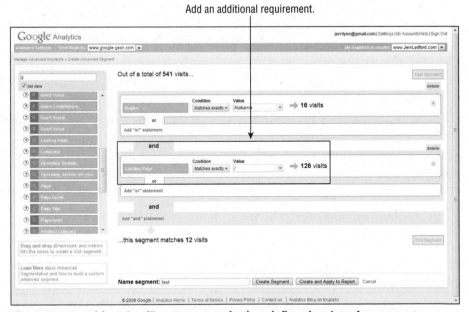

Figure 5-16: Add an "and" statement to further define the size of a segment.

6. If everything works properly in your segment test you can save the segment by clicking **Create Segment**.

It's important to note that with these custom segments you can also use Regular Expressions, which are a means in programming for writing a condition or filter. You'll learn more about Regular Expressions in Chapter 10, but once you do, you can apply them to your custom segments by using the **Matches Regular Expression** condition of a dimension or metric.

Once you've created a custom segment, you can apply that segment by selecting it from the **Custom Segments** section of the Advanced Segments menu. Once it's there, it behaves just like any other segment, and can be included in your data segmentation just like any other segment.

One last function that you might find useful with custom segments is the management function. From the Advanced Segments menu select **Manage your advanced segments**. That takes you to a page like the one shown in Figure 5-17.

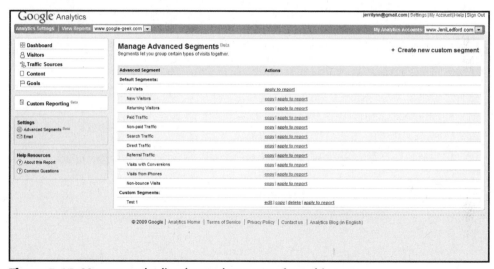

Figure 5-17: Manage and edit advanced segments from this page.

From this page, you can choose to edit, copy, or delete a segment, or apply one to the report. So if you create a custom advanced segment and then decide you need to change or delete it, this is the place to do it. And when you click **apply to report** you're taken back to the main dashboard, and the graph changes to reflect the segment that you selected.

Working with Date Ranges

Finally, we can look at date ranges. Date ranges are an important part of analytics, especially historical analytics, which are what Google Analytics provides. Although there isn't a huge lag—24 to 48 hours—the data that Google collects is not strictly *real-time*. That means the data isn't up to the minute. So when you're looking at your analytics reports, you're looking at activity that took place in the past.

Right there at the top of the page (actually inside the Site Usage report) you'll see a date range inside a drop-down menu. That's where the date-range capabilities are located, as Figure 5-18 shows.

Date range controls are located behind this menu.

Figure 5-18: The new location for date-range capabilities

Using the Calendar

The calendar in Google Analytics has a functionality that makes comparing date ranges much easier. Figure 5-19 shows that when you click the drop-down menu where the date range appears, the calendars expand for easy access.

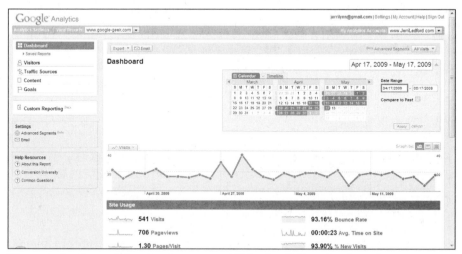

Figure 5-19: Expand the date-range capabilities by clicking the drop-down menu.

The default date range is set to one month, so you should see blue highlighting over the last 28 to 31 days. To change your date range, click the first day you would like to include in the range and then click the last day you would like to include. This should change the blue highlighting to reflect the range between those two dates.

> **NOTE** The default view for available dates is of three months—two in the past and the current month. However, you can go back to earlier months by clicking the small arrow to the left of the month names. It looks as if you can also advance to the future by clicking the arrow to the right of the month names. But that's just an illusion. Google doesn't provide predictive analytics, and if you try to move forward the program doesn't respond at all.

Once you've selected the range that you would like to view, click the **Apply** button and the reports on your dashboard will change to reflect the new date range.

There are other ways to change your dates, too. For example, if you want to quickly switch between weekly displays, you can click the small tab located to the left of a week to highlight it.

Another way to change the date ranges you're viewing is to highlight the date inside the textbox directly under the Date Range label. Type the new beginning date and then highlight the date inside the textbox to the right and type the new ending date. The blue highlighting will change to reflect the date range that you typed. Click **Apply** and the new date range will be applied to the reports on your dashboard.

NOTE When you change a date range, it applies to more than just the report previews on the dashboard. It is also applied to all the reports in Google Analytics.

Comparing Ranges

One other feature that you'll find on the Date Range module is the ability to "Compare to past." This feature enables you to compare two date ranges.

To use this feature, first select the current date range that you want to compare to the past. Then click the small box next to "Compare to Past." This will open a second set of date-range boxes, as shown in Figure 5-20.

Notice that the new date range is highlighted (in green on the actual screen) and that it is the same length as the previous date range. So if you're monitoring a month of data, your comparative range will also be a month in length.

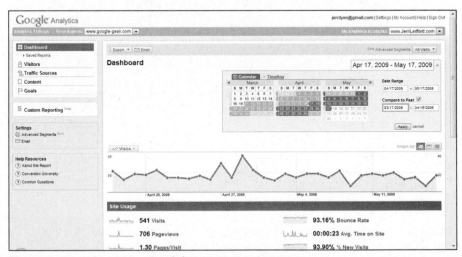

Figure 5-20: Select two sets of date ranges to compare.

You change the comparative date range the same way you changed the original date range. However, be aware that when you change the original date range, it will change the comparative range to match.

Once you have selected the current date range and the comparative date range, click **Apply** and both date ranges will be applied to your reports, as shown in Figure 5-21.

Figure 5-21: Comparative date ranges are shown as overlapped graphs.

When you finish comparing your date ranges, you can go back to a single date range view by deselecting the "Compare to past" option.

Using the Timeline

When you open the Date Range dialog box you will notice a second tab labeled Timeline. This view helps you visualize your date ranges by showing you a small bar graph, as shown in Figure 5-22.

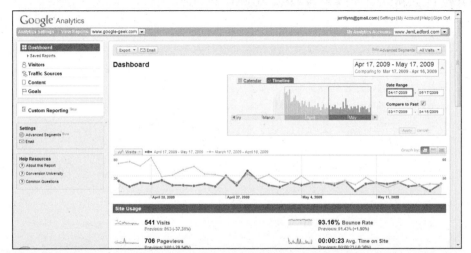

Figure 5-22: The Timeline feature gives you a different view of your date ranges.

The appearance of the date range view is the only change that you'll find on the Timeline tab. All the features of the date ranges and the comparative date ranges remain the same. To change the length of the timeline, grab one of the tabs at its right or left edge and drag it to the desired location. It's worthwhile to note that when comparing two timelines, you can overlap the time periods. This is easier to see in the timeline view than it is in the calendar view. One thing you should note, however, is that the Timeline feature does not change the graphics used in the various reports available to you.

There will be regular occasions when you need to change the date ranges that you're monitoring. Whether you're answering a question about the numbers from the last week or comparing this year with last, you'll find that date ranges are one feature you'll use all the time.

Analytics and Site Statistics: Concepts and Methods

Site analytics are useful for helping you to understand your web site's visitors and how they navigate through your site. The problem is that sometimes the analytics can be a little confusing. What exactly is the difference between a unique visitor and a new visitor, for example?

This part of the book is designed to help you understand just how site statistics are arrived at, and what they mean. With that information in mind you can move on to making your site statistics work for you.

E-commerce Concepts and Methods

One of the most common reasons people use Google Analytics is that they have a web site that sells products and they want to know how to improve sales, what brings people to the site, and what users do while on the site. But what if you're just getting started and someone has said to you that you need to have a product web site if you plan to have a presence on the Web? And what if those same people said you should also have Google Analytics, even though you're not quite sure what e-commerce is or what analytics are?

For all you know e-commerce and analytics could be some strange diseases that you really *don't* want, but that your competition would like for you to have.

It's not that dire, of course. E-commerce is all about selling products on the Web. And as you've probably figured out by now, analytics are about measuring the visitors to your web site and their behaviors. The trick, though, is making the two go hand in hand.

What Works in E-commerce

What works in e-commerce?

That's really a loaded question. And to be completely frank, it's a question to which there is no exact answer. In the past, some said you would never be able to sell anything more than books on the Web. Others said there was no way you could put a giant flea market on the Web and expect to make money. Amazon and eBay proved them wrong.

What works in e-commerce is whatever there is a demand for. That's an oversimplification, of course. You could expand that simple statement to be more accurate by saying that what works in e-commerce is whatever there is a demand for and whatever you can reach the right audience for. That's where Google Analytics becomes a natural partner to e-commerce, because what better way to learn if you're reaching the right audience than by understanding how those who come to your site use it?

Half of the fight when you're building an e-commerce business is reaching the right people with the right products. For example, a few years ago, everyone thought that you couldn't make a successful business out of selling electronic books (also called e-books). Yet even then a few companies were relatively successful with their endeavors, because they knew the market that they needed to target with these books. Of course, that was back before Google Analytics, so some of those successful companies used analytics applications that weren't free. Others used the free analytics programs that were available, but they were nowhere near as useful as what you'll find available today.

Today, too, the market for electronic books is much larger and growing every day. For example, Amazon probably recognized a growing number of electronic book downloads, which prompted the company to think about what it could do to capitalize on that market. That's where the idea for Kindle (the Amazon-branded e-book reader) came from, and why Amazon has had so much success in that particular market.

As you can see, successful e-commerce is starting with an idea—a way to meet a specific need that is either not being met at all, or is being met in a limited way—and then growing that idea by learning what your customers want. Just about any e-commerce business that you recognize as successful today can be categorized in that way.

A good example might be an e-commerce business like NewEgg (www.newegg.com) or TigerDirect (www.tigerdirect.com). Both of these are e-commerce businesses built around technology products. They both offer very specific types of technological gadgets at great prices. And they both target very specific audiences. NewEgg is a little more tech-oriented than TigerDirect.

What leads someone to start an e-commerce business is different from what helps that person to be successful. Maybe you start your little business because it's something that's dear to your heart. I've known people who started e-commerce businesses because the products they feature are ones for which they have a deep passion (think Christian jewelry or solar energy products). But having a passion about sharing a product is not enough to make an e-commerce business successful.

You must also have an audience—a group of people (other than your friends and family) who *want* or *need* to purchase the products that you are passionate about. And to be sure, it's easy enough to find a few people who will purchase just about anything. But a few purchases do not a successful e-commerce business make.

Which means there must be more, right?

Understanding Your Customers

Businesses in the real world—called brick-and-mortar businesses—become successful by knowing their customers. Those businesses spend millions of dollars each year studying how their customers interact with their storefronts.

Ever wonder why you can walk into any Wal-Mart in the world (and they are all over the world now) and see the image of every other store in the chain? That's because the marketing experts at Wal-Mart have studied their customers to learn what works and what doesn't.

Think about going down the pasta aisle of such a store. You'll find both pasta and pasta sauce on the shelves of that aisle. But you will probably also find fixtures attached to the shelves, sticking out slightly, that hold grated parmesan cheese. That's because someone took the time to analyze the shopping habits of Wal-Mart visitors and realized that most of the time, when visitors purchase pasta and pasta sauce, they also want to purchase parmesan cheese.

Now, if the parmesan cheese were located in another aisle, let's say in the dairy case with the other types of cheese, visitors might forget to pick up the cheese when they got to that part of the store. Having it available on the shelf, in the same vicinity as the pasta and the sauce, helps shoppers remember they need it.

Wal-Mart, being thorough, also has parmesan cheese available in the dairy case, along with the other cheeses. If you forget to pick it up while you're in the pasta aisle (and how many times have you stared directly at something and not seen it?), then seeing it in the dairy case *might* remind you to pick it up.

That tracking of customers' movements and buying habits is the real-world equivalent of Google Analytics. Various types of data (such as visitors' movements through the store, their purchasing habits, and even the time of day that they're shopping) are collected, and then later analyzed for patterns.

Google Analytics works the same way with your e-commerce web site. Installing Google Analytics is like putting up surveillance cameras, capturing transactions, and logging visits to your site, then pooling all that information together so you can see the patterns that are present in a very clear way.

Let's look at it like this. Say you've got an e-commerce site for books, and you notice that one particular title seems to be selling much better than the other titles on your site. By itself, that wouldn't mean much to you.

Then assume that you're seeing a lot of traffic coming from one particular web site. When you look at the web site from which that traffic is coming, you notice that there's a review of the book and a link back to your site because you have the best price on it.

Now you're starting to see a pattern emerge. People coming to your site from this review are buying the book that was reviewed. Leaving every other aspect of e-commerce and analytics out of this example, you can assume that *maybe* your site visitors would like to read reviews of the books that you offer.

You can test that theory, too, by putting a few reviews on your site and tracking visitors to those reviews who complete a purchase (either of the book reviewed or any other book). Then you'll know if it's just the review that's drawing people to purchase the book from your site, or if it's a combination of the book and something else or even some other facet of the linking page altogether.

This is a very simple example, but through it you can begin to see the power that analytics has when used to monitor an e-commerce web site. Using analytics you can catch short but revealing glimpses into the minds of the people who visit your web site.

What Measurements Matter

Once you understand that your e-commerce site first has to have an audience, and then that you should be monitoring that audience, you might wonder just what exactly you should be measuring with your analytics application.

Google Analytics does a pretty good job of laying out the basic needs. You should be monitoring visits, of course, but you also need to be monitoring visitor movements and behavior on your site.

Not only do you want to know where visitors come from, but you also want to know what visitors do while they're on your site. Do they come onto the site, surf through a dozen pages, and then leave? Why?

Analytics can give you the patterns that lead you to see why they are leaving. Analytics can also show you exactly the spot from which the visitor leaves. And though analytics won't tell you exactly why your visitors abandon your site, it might give you a glimpse into the possibilities.

Think about this. Suppose that you have an e-commerce site to which visitors come in large numbers. And looking at your analytics you see that the majority of your visitors surf through your site and put products in their shopping cart, but then leave your site during the checkout process, before they complete the purchase.

Using this information, you can assume there's something that's killing your sales. If you're tracking every step of the checkout process, you can even know exactly where in the process your visitors seem to slip away. Then you can examine that spot closely to learn more about what could possibly be wrong.

In our example, let's assume that visitors slip away once they hit the shipping information page of your checkout process. This could be because your shipping costs are prohibitively high. It could also be because users experience errors when they're trying to fill in their shipping information. But no matter what the reason is, if you know that you're losing most of your visitors on that shipping page, then you know where to look to find the exact problem.

Analytics works on the success side, too. If there's something that you're doing very well, you'll see that pattern also, because analytics doesn't just illustrate the bad things that happen with your site visitors. It also illustrates the good things.

For example, say you notice that one of your products is outselling every other product on your web site. Since you can see where your visitors are coming from and you find that the majority of them are not coming through your AdWords ads, then you might recognize a pattern that indicates your visitors are coming from an article on another web site.

Watching that traffic as it navigates through your web site, you may also see that most of your sales come from visitors led to your site by that outside link. You can then look at the page that's pushing visitors to your site to learn what's so compelling about it. Maybe there's something on that site that you should be emulating on your own site.

But you shouldn't limit your interest in e-commerce measurements just to your visitors' movements and the fact that they do or do not make a purchase. Monitoring your products, the average amount that visitors spend during a purchase, and even how long it takes a visitor to commit to finishing a purchase transaction can also tell you important things about your site visitors. If you're monitoring the time it takes visitors to commit to a purchase and you learn it takes them three visits (on average) before they complete the purchase, then you know that you've got to either keep their attention for three visits, or find a way to decrease the amount of time it takes them to make the decision to purchase.

The average amount of a purchase is an indicator of how well your product layout is working. The higher the average amount of the sale, the better you're doing (excluding high-ticket items, of course). That usually means your visitors are buying more than one item, which could be a reflection that your product selection is not only good, but also well targeted. But low sales might indicate that you could lay out your product selection better to help users find similar or complementary items that would catch their interest and help them make the decision to buy additional items.

With e-commerce measurements (as with all analytics), it's all about understanding what it is that your site visitor wants or needs. Analytics can give you a glimpse into the patterns of your web-site visitors. Then, using those patterns, you can make some educated guesses as to what you could be doing better, doing differently, or adding to your arsenal of possible efforts.

To some, e-commerce seems like a mystery. It is, in a way. But the best way to reduce the amount of mystery in e-commerce is to be prepared by understanding your consumers—your site visitors. Analyze your visitors in the same way that brick-and-mortar stores analyze their shoppers. Then you'll begin to gain an understanding of how to go from having just an e-commerce business to having a successful e-commerce business.

CHAPTER 7

Basic Metrics and Concepts

When you begin looking at your Google Analytics metrics, you might find some of them confusing. In fact, some metrics simply make you think, "How in the world did they come up with that number?" It's a problem that's plagued analytics users since the very first analytics applications hit the market.

Understanding just what exactly is being measured (and how) is easily half or more of the process of understanding your visitors' behavior. For example, if you don't know that there are differences among visits, new visits, and unique visits, then you're not going to be able to fully understand how those metrics affect you. What follows is a quick and dirty primer on just what some of the metrics that you'll find in Google Analytics mean.

This is not a comprehensive guide by any means. But it's my hope that when you're finished with this chapter you'll have a clearer understanding of how Google arrives at the metrics that it displays, and what those numbers mean to you as far as building and capitalizing on web site traffic are concerned.

Identifying People and Not-People

Generally, visits to your web site that are counted in Google Analytics are made by "people," meaning actual people (to the best that Google can determine) using web browsers to view your web site. In actuality, Google Analytics counts

IP addresses (from your web browser) as people. But there are many visits to your web site that don't actually come from people using a web browser. These "not-people" are applications—*spiders*, *crawlers*, and *robots*—that are assigned the task of reviewing your web site for some reason.

For example, search engines use these critters for the purpose of examining and classifying your web site for search engine results that are returned when someone searches for a topic or phrase through the search engine. However, how a visit from a person and a visit from a spider, crawler, or robot are executed is what determines how these two classes of visitors are quantified.

Visitors—actual people using web browsers—are classified by *IP address*. In the simplest explanation, your web browser requests a page to display for you from a web server, and in that request is a header that identifies where the request is coming from. It contains your web address, in the form of an IP address. (That's that funky-looking number that you sometimes see associated with web sites. It might look something like `196.255.86.86.0` (not a real link). That is the numerical equivalent of a web address like `www.example.com`.) This IP address represents your actual location on the Web.

Think of it like your house location, and for the moment let's assume the "web page" you want to see (the one you've requested) is actually a package that needs to be delivered to your house.

What happens when you request that package is that you provide a location for it to be delivered to—a house number, street, city, state, and if necessary a country. Without that information, the package could not be delivered to you.

When you think of the web page your browser has requested in these terms, the IP address can be thought of as an address (or route) that leads right down to the local web server that provides your Internet access. The IP address is specific to your location on the Web.

When a "not-people" visitor—a crawler, spider, or robot—wants to look at your web site, it also sends a request. What differs is the way the critter identifies itself. Rather than saying, "Hey, this is what I want and this is how you know me," the crawler says, "I need only this specific information and I'll take it with me." It's almost the cyber-world equivalent of going past a drive-through window. The crawler identifies itself in the same way your web browser does, and it also usually provides a name or some other credential (e.g., a Google web crawler identifies itself as Googlebot).

> **NOTE** I'm using "crawlers" from this point forward to refer to all crawlers, spiders, and robots. There really is no difference, so they're generally all lumped together.

To be slightly more technical about these crawlers, when they request a web site, they request a stripped-down version of the site. The crawler doesn't need all the aesthetics that you and I need or want to see on a web site. The crawler is interested in more serious elements such as keywords, links, and the location of elements (such as headers).

The next major difference is in how the crawler identifies what it wants. Rather than tell the web server it wants a page, it tells the web server that it wants information from the page. This is usually accomplished when the crawler identifies itself as a *user agent* (such as Googlebot) by sending an *HTTP request* that asks for a different version of the web site.

The really confusing part comes when you realize that sometimes Google Analytics doesn't recognize the difference between people and not-people.

Google Analytics is, after all, only an application, so there are limitations to what it can infer from appearances. And if the crawler *appears* to be a web browser, Google Analytics can't tell the difference.

Crawlers don't always identify themselves as crawlers. What does that mean for you? Simply put, it means that there is a margin of error in your Analytics visitor data. It's generally a small margin of error, and considered acceptable in analytics, but a margin of error nonetheless.

Visits and Visitor Metrics

A visitor is a visitor all the time, right? Well, not if you're an analytics program. Analytics programs look at visitors from several different angles to see just how exactly those visitors qualify as visitors on your site. Are they new? Have they been here before? How long has it been?

It's a confusing mess of nuances and detail. But once you understand all the little things that make the numbers work, you get a much better picture of your site visitors and how well you're doing at keeping them interested in your web site.

Hits vs. Pages

Rather than starting with visitors, let's start our journey into analytics basics with a topic that's caused confusion for a lot of years. Hang with me for a few moments; this will start to make more sense soon. Background first:

The first few years that web sites were a reality, webmasters drew a lot of pride from the number of *hits* their web pages garnered. Hits were such a big deal that any webmaster worth his salt placed a hit counter on his web site for all the world to see (this was, after all, bragging rights). And these hit counters could be pretty stylish, too. In fact, the cooler they were, the more attention they drew, meaning more people saw (and took note of) the number of hits showcased. High numbers of hits were to be envied.

There was one small problem with this method of counting, though. As it turned out, hits were a pretty worthless metric because to a web server, any access of any document—a page, a script, a multimedia file, an image, or any other element classified as a document—counted as a hit. And depending on how the web page was designed, a single page, loaded one time, could count multiple times, creating the illusion of multiple hits.

As analytics became better understood, this disparity between hits and page views became more apparent.

Naturally, a new metrics blossomed—*page views*. Now, if we're just going to get straight to the truth here, page views as a metric are a much better measurement than hits. Page views in analytics don't refer to what you might think of as a page, that being everything included on the page. Separate elements can still qualify as pages (in the same way that those elements previously counted toward hits).

Typically, certain technologies, such as Flash, AJAX, media files, downloads, documents, and other elements that can be included on a web page can be counted toward page views in analytics. This doesn't usually include requests for images or Cascading Style Sheets, which used to be included in the number of hits a page received.

Even with the misleading nature of hits and page views, the metric for page views can still be useful. Hits as a metric are pretty much useless these days, but the metric for page views can give you an understanding of which pages (or elements of pages) are working for you. You can also look at the number of page views per visit to determine the depth of the visit, and if you track this information over time you may find patterns that you can use to change and improve the content offerings on your web site.

Visits, Unique Visits, and New Visits

When you're discussing how metrics are derived, this is where the waters go from murky to downright muddy. Understanding what counts as a visit, a visitor, a unique visitor, a new visitor, a returning visitor, and a repeat visitor will have you ready to throw mud pies at the lunatic who came up with these metrics. (Also, Google uses the term Absolute Unique Visits to refer to Unique Visits in Google Analytics reports.) We're not going to throw mud pies, of course. Instead, let's see if we can figure out just how each of those metrics is derived, and how each affects your analytics measurements.

A good place to start clarifying how visitors are counted is with some definitions from the Web Analytics Association (WAA):

- **Visits:** A visit is an interaction, by an individual, with a web site, consisting of one or more requests for an analyst-definable (that's an element of the page that can be tracked) unit of content (i.e., page view).

- **Unique visitor:** The number of inferred individual people (filtered for spiders, crawlers, and robots), within a designated reporting time frame, with activity consisting of one or more visits to a site. Each individual is counted only once in the unique visitor measure for the reporting period.

- **New visitor:** The number of unique visitors with activity including a first-ever visit to a site during a reporting period.

- **Repeat visitor:** The number of unique visitors with activity consisting of two or more visits to a site during a reporting period.

- **Return visitor:** The number of unique visitors with activity consisting of a visit to a site during a reporting period, who also visited the site prior to the reporting period.

THE WEB ANALYTICS ASSOCIATION: AN ANALYTICS STANDARDS BODY

The Web Analytics Association is a standards body for web analytics. This group includes consultants, educators, and vendors, all working together to reach a standard set of guidelines for web analytics and the measurements associated with analytics.

Back in 2006, WAA formed a committee to develop some standard analytics definitions that would help users understand how certain metrics were derived. Those standards were released in 2007 and are the definitions that are used in this (and other) chapters.

To learn more about WAA, its mission, and how you can get involved, check out its web site at `http://www.webanalyticsassociation.org/`

Each of these metrics is a different measurement, but sometimes the difference is nothing more than a subtle (but important) nuance in the way the visitor is counted. Understanding these subtleties begins with understanding how visitors are counted.

New, Returning, and Repeat Visits

By now you know that Google Analytics uses cookies to count visitors. The very first time a visitor comes to your web site, a cookie containing a unique identifier is placed in the visitor's web browser. That's how visitors are recognized each time they begin a new *session* (or visit) on your site.

On that very first visit, the cookie is issued and the visitor is counted as a visit. However, because it's the first time this person has visited your site in this reporting period, he or she is also counted as a unique visitor, and because it's this person's first visit *ever* to your site (at least from the computer that person is using at the time), he or she is also counted as a new visitor.

It would seem that a unique visitor should be a person coming to your web site for the first time ever, but that's not really the way it works. A unique visitor can actually be someone who's been to your web site before, but not in the same time period that's being monitored. So let's say that you're monitoring your web statistics monthly, and during January, Suzie comes to your web site for the very first time ever. On that visit, she's counted as a visitor, a unique visitor, and a new visitor.

Then Suzie gets enthralled with some other web site, so she doesn't return to your site again for at least 30 days (the default reporting time period in Google Analytics). But in late February she remembers your site and stops by again.

This time Suzie is counted as a visit, a unique visitor (because this is the first time in this reporting period that she's stopped by), and a return visitor (because although she's a unique visitor, she *has* been to your site before, so she's not a new visitor).

If Suzie decides to come back to your site later that same day or the next day (assuming she's still in that 30-day reporting period), she's then counted as a visitor, a repeat visitor (because she's returning in the same reporting period), and a return visitor, but she won't be counted as a unique visitor, because she's already been counted as unique for the reporting period.

See, subtle differences. But these subtle differences can provide a wealth of information about a visitor or group of visitors. For example, what if your number of unique visitors is high, but your number of new visitors is low?

My first thought in that situation would be that your site has good *stickiness*— visitors who have been to the site before are returning at relatively regular intervals. But the low number of new visitors would indicate that you're not being found often enough. This could indicate that you need to step up your *search engine optimization (SEO)* or marketing efforts. And if you're already pushing heavily in those areas, then you might need to examine your efforts more closely to see what you could change or improve.

The way visits and visitors are counted can be a little confusing, but once you understand who qualifies to be included in what metric, what you're seeing in your Google Analytics account begins to make more sense—even though in Google Analytics the metrics that you have are labeled visits, absolute unique visits, and new visits.

SESSION TIMEOUTS

One factor in how visits are calculated is called session timeouts. This isn't represented by an actual metric of any type by Google Analytics, but it can affect the number of visits, return visits, and repeat visits that you might see.

A timeout happens when a visitor comes to your site and then goes idle for a period of time. In the case of Google Analytics, a visitor who's been idle for 30 minutes has the session terminated. Even if the visitor begins to surf your site again after that 30-minute period, this person is now counted as another visitor. This can cause single visitors interrupted by something (like screaming kids or a telephone call) while they were on your site to be counted as two visitors.

You can change the default session timeout for Google Analytics by altering your Google Analytics Tracking Code. All you have to do is change the highlighted line in the following code sample to reflect the number of seconds (yes, seconds, not minutes or hours) that you would prefer to use as a session timeout. Google's default of 1,800 seconds, for example, can be changed to 3,600 seconds, making the timeout take effect after one hour of idleness.

Change session timeout:

```
<script type="text/javascript">
var gaJsHost = (("https:" == document.location.protocol) ?
    "https://ssl." : "http://www.");
document.write(unescape("%3Cscript src='" + gaJsHost
    + "google-analytics.com/ga.js'
type='text/javascript'%3E%3C/script%3E"));
</script>
<script type="text/javascript">
try{
var pageTracker = _gat._getTracker("UA-xxxxxx-x");
pageTracker._setSessionTimeout("1800");
pageTracker._trackPageview();
} catch(err) {}
</script>
```

Visit Duration

Another metric that you might find helpful is the "duration of visit" metric. This is a measurement of how long visitors spend on your site and you'll find it in two separate reports in Google Analytics: the Time on Site and Length of Visit reports. I'll look at both of those reports in more depth in Chapter 15, so for now let's just examine what is meant by visit duration.

When visitors enter your web site, they are "clocked in," so to speak, much as you would punch a clock when going to work. Since Google Analytics is monitoring visitors by a unique identifier (in the form of a cookie), a time stamp is made in the server logs when that unique identifier shows as being present on your web site. That identifier is tracked as the user navigates through your site. Then, when the visitor leaves your site—either by closing the browser or by navigating to a different web site—another time stamp is created. It's as if the user "clocks out" of your site. The out-time stamp is then subtracted from the in-time stamp to determine the total time the visitor spent on the site.

Depending on the analytics program you're using, that information can be aggregated or segmented in different ways—as average time spent on site, average time spent per visitor, or even average time spent per page per visitor. In the case of Google Analytics it's given as the average time spent on the site and the percentage of visits in a given duration.

But why should you care how long a visitor spends on your site?

Simply put, you can equate the length of time a visitor spends on your site with the amount of interest your site generates for that visitor. For example, if a visitor navigates into your site and spends 10 minutes looking through your content, it's a safe bet that you've captured that person's interest. Additionally, the longer a user spends on the site, the more likely that user will be not only to return at a later time, but also to reach whatever goal conversion you may have set up for visitors.

On the other hand, if you have a visitor who comes to your web site and stays only a few seconds or even leaves immediately, you can infer that something is wrong—either the visitor found your site through an unrelated search, or found your site through a related search but didn't find what was being sought. The visitor also, apparently, found no indication that the desired information could be found by digging deeper into your site. Either way, a high number of these ultra-short-duration visits—called *bounces*—indicates there could be a problem that you need to address.

Bounces and Single-Page Visits

A bounce can be slightly more complicated than simply equaling someone who came to your web site and left immediately. Strictly speaking, a bounce is considered a single-page-view visit. What that means is that a person who comes to a page on your site and navigates to no other pages, but instead leaves from that same page, may not be considered a bounce. He or she could, instead, be considered a single-page visit.

A bounce is all about interaction. Remember how a single page can represent multiple page views? Well, that's what separates a bounce from a single page view. For example, if a visitor clicks into your site and immediately clicks the Back button, then this will probably be considered a bounce. But if the same user clicks into your site, allows it to fully load, and spends a few seconds glancing at the content (in other words, interacting with the page), then this could be considered a single-page visit instead of a bounce. This is especially true if there are elements on your page such as videos that the visitor allows to load before clicking away.

The distinction between the two metrics is important, because a bounce tells you there was nothing of interest to the visitor on the page. A single-page visit means your first page was marginally interesting, but not interesting enough to draw the visitor deeper into the site. Both numbers, however (when they are high), are indicators that you need to concentrate on improving your web-site targeting. If either number is high, you're drawing the wrong visitors or not providing what the right visitors need.

In Google Analytics, the bounce rate is the same as the rate of single-page visits. Google counts visitors who come to your site on one page and leave from that same page without navigating to other pages within the site as bounces. The number of visitors who "bounce" away from your site is then compared to the number of all site visitors and a percentage is arrived at that represents the bounce rate.

Traffic Metrics

As valuable as visitor and visits metrics are, they aren't the only metrics from which you can gain insight. Where visits and visitor metrics tell you about user behavior, traffic metrics tell you what brings visitors to your site. What draws (or pushes) users to your site? Do they come to it directly? Or do they navigate in from another web site or marketing campaign?

All these are important elements of how users find your site that you need to understand. Consider them measurements of how users find you and how well you're tapping into the relevant sources. They're also a good means of finding new avenues through which you could be driving (or pulling) traffic.

Direct Traffic, Referrers, and Referring URLs

Direct traffic is a measurement of the number of people who come directly onto your web site. That can mean visitors who type your web-site address directly into the address bar of their web browsers, but it can also mean visitors who click into your web site from a link they have saved to their favorites. Unfortunately, in Google Analytics there is no way to tell the difference. So for the purposes of this metric, it could be either.

When a visitor comes to your web site, he or she is visiting with a web browser, which communicates with the web server to tell it what site the user wants to see or where this user wants to go next. So when a user opens his or her web browser and types a URL into the address bar, the browser sends a request to the web server for the URL that the user typed into the browser.

The request is formatted with a header that contains information about where the request came from. In the case of the user who types a URL directly into the address bar, that header contains no information about where the request came from. This is read by the web server as "no referrer" or "direct navigation." That's where direct traffic comes from.

But suppose this user is on another web site and clicks through a link to your web site. In that case the web browser includes in the referrer field of the header the URL of the web site the user was on when he or she clicked the link leading to your site. That becomes the referring URL. It's the "page URL that originally generated the request for the current page view or object," according to the WAA.

As tidy as this all sounds, sometimes it's not all that clear-cut. For example, say a user clicks a link that leads to your web site from a page that's part of a *frame set*. Frame sets are web pages designed around a set of frames that separate page elements. This can make them appear to be several different pages, rather than a single cohesive page. So when the user clicks a link on the framed page, the web server has to determine the original page from which the request is coming. And sometimes that can be a little confusing.

It's also possible that the visitor clicks a link to your site from a subdomain within a web site. Again, the web server has to track that subdomain back to the original domain for the purposes of identification. So in some cases, rather than the subdomain showing as the referrer, the actual domain shows as the referrer. It can, at times, be misleading when you're looking at your metrics.

For the most part, however, the referrer or referring URL is the place from which the visitor came to your site. And this can be handy information to have.

For example, a few years ago I was tracking the referrers to my personal web site. What I found was that a web site with which I had partnered about five years earlier was still referring visitors to my site. A lot of visitors. I no longer had a relationship with that site, but after reviewing my metrics I saw the need to rekindle that relationship. It was an existing avenue of traffic for me, based on an old listing. Adding a new listing turned the traffic up a notch and brought better targeted results from that particular referrer.

Keywords and Phrases

One last measurement that you might want to understand a bit about before we move on to e-commerce metrics: *keywords* and *keyword phrases*. These are the terms visitors use to find you when they use search engines. Let's say you're looking for a recipe for chicken cacciatore. When you type that keyword phrase into a search engine, the first result that you're likely to see will be for a web site like the Food Network or AllRecipes.com. That's because these sites have been optimized for this particular keyword or keyword phrase.

Keywords are used to classify your site for search engines, but they can apply to your site in one of two ways. Paid keywords or keyword advertisements (such as those you can create with Google AdWords) are keywords and keyword phrases that you spend advertising dollars to target. These keywords are used in advertising campaigns that draw visitors to your site when they search for a specific keyword. If you're using a paid keyword advertising campaign, your site needs to be well optimized for the keywords that you're targeting, because when visitors find you through one of those advertisements they're searching for something pretty specific. It would be a shame to pay for those visits and then lose the visitors as bounces because you're not meeting their needs.

The other type of keyword is *organic*. Organic keywords are the keywords and keyword phrases visitors use to find your site but that you don't pay for. These you can consider bonuses. Search engine crawlers will automatically classify your web site based on content. Part of that content is the words that you use on your pages, and the ones that are repeated most frequently are keywords.

If you find that your site is being classified by organic keywords, you should consider trying to capitalize on these keywords, assuming they're reaching the right target market. Organic keywords are hard-won victories in drawing traffic.

In Google Analytics you'll find metrics for keywords, and metrics for AdWords (paid keywords). These will help you understand what words and phrases visitors are using to find your site.

These are the basics of how Google Analytics (and other analytics programs) arrives at the metrics it provides for you about your site visitors. You could probably spend a lifetime learning about the different metrics and how they're calculated, but it's not necessarily a requirement for understanding what Google Analytics is trying to tell you.

Once you understand the basics you'll understand how your visitors interact with your site, and isn't that the ultimate goal of using Google Analytics anyway?

CHAPTER 8

Setting Up E-commerce

Google Analytics has the ability to collect product revenue, item information, and transaction data from sales that happen on your online store in a very special e-commerce report section. This section appears below the Goals report section when enabled, and also appears throughout the Google Analytics interface in a tab or as an additional trending graph, custom report, and advanced segmentation options.

To be able to collect this highly valuable information, you will need to roll up your sleeves and put on your technical hard hat—because there is some custom programming and possibly an obstacle or two to negotiate along the way. Even if this isn't your gig—that is, even if you are not a technically savvy individual—you can still take in the information in this chapter, which will enable you to understand how e-commerce data looks in source code format. This will come in handy for diagnostic purposes if there are ever issues, bugs, or garbled data in your e-commerce reports.

> **NOTE** If you'd like to read about the metrics, reports, and insights that you'll be able to obtain from the E-commerce section, then before reading this chapter flip back to Chapter 6 and forward to Chapter 20. The present chapter deals mostly with the programming and implementation side of e-commerce with Google Analytics.

Enabling E-commerce within Your Profile(s)

The very first step in activating e-commerce reporting within your Google Analytics profile(s) is selecting **Yes, an E-Commerce Site** from within the Main Website Profile Information editing screen as shown in Figure 6-1. Click **Save Changes** at the bottom of this page, and you're done on the profile side of things! This is arguably the easiest thing that you'll ever do. Now let's mention a few other things before moving on to the coding/implementation part of e-commerce.

First, don't forget that you'll have to do this for every profile you want to track e-commerce data with. Second, don't forget that your profile is going to display the correct currency—select the currency of choice from the **Currency displayed as** drop-down menu shown in Figure 8-1. (There are more than 20 currencies from around the world to choose from, but keep in mind that Google Analytics will not perform currency conversions for you—you'll have to do that on your own.) Finally, a little-known fact: even if you forget to edit your profile, e-commerce data will still be collected and processed by Google, which stores it within its data centers. So if you have e-commerce coded correctly on your web site, and don't remember about turning it on until later, all collected data will still appear throughout your profile. This is one of the only situations with Google Analytics in which data can be "recovered," (even though the data has been there the whole time).

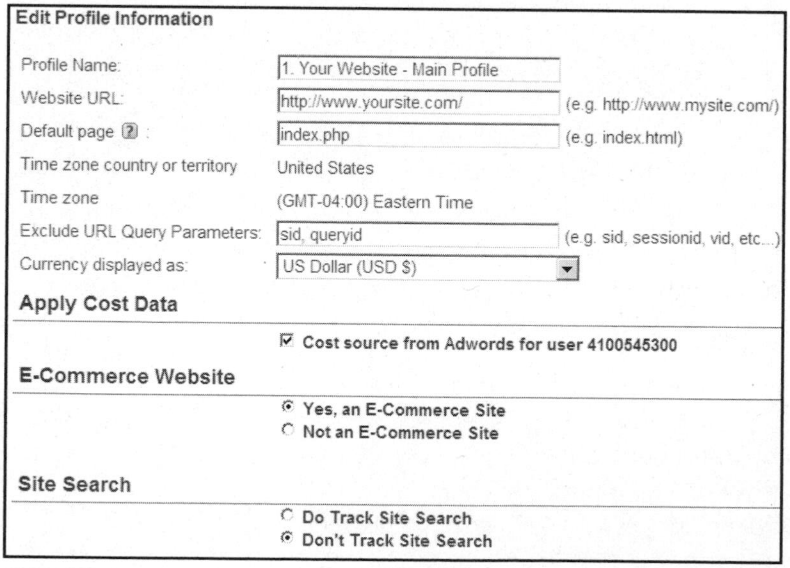

Edit Profile Information

Profile Name: 1. Your Website - Main Profile
Website URL: http://www.yoursite.com/ (e.g. http://www.mysite.com/)
Default page [?]: index.php (e.g. index.html)
Time zone country or territory: United States
Time zone: (GMT-04:00) Eastern Time
Exclude URL Query Parameters: sid, queryid (e.g. sid, sessionid, vid, etc...)
Currency displayed as: US Dollar (USD $)

Apply Cost Data

☑ Cost source from Adwords for user 4100545300

E-Commerce Website

⦿ Yes, an E-Commerce Site
○ Not an E-Commerce Site

Site Search

○ Do Track Site Search
⦿ Don't Track Site Search

Figure 8-1: E-commerce profile settings

The Google Analytics E-commerce Code

Now comes the fun part! Luckily, most template-driven e-commerce platforms can easily be edited to allow for e-commerce tracking. Even some popular platforms—Google Checkout, osCommerce, ZenCart, and several others—are beginning to adopt this very important piece of the Google Analytics pie with patches, version upgrades, and modules. However, even if you use a self-made platform or content-management system, it should be a task that you or your webmaster can accomplish without too much hassle.

The "basic" Google Analytics e-commerce code will look like this:

```
<script type="text/javascript">
var gaJsHost = (("https:" == document.location.protocol )
? "https://ssl
." : "http://www.");
document.write(unescape("%3Cscript src='"
+ gaJsHost + "
google-analytics.com/ga.js' type='text/javascript'
%3E%3C/script%3E"));
</script>
<script type="text/javascript">
try{
var pageTracker = _gat._getTracker("UA-XXXXXX-X");
pageTracker._trackPageview();
pageTracker._addTrans(
      "555667", // order ID - required
      "Clothing Store", // affiliation or store name
      "21.99", // total - required
      "1.09", // tax
      "", // shipping
      "Boca Raton", // city
      "Florida", // state or province
      "USA" // country
   );
   pageTracker._addItem(
      "55567", // order ID - required
      "123123456456", // SKU/code - required
      "T-Shirts", // product name
      "Green Shirt - Large", // category
      "21.99", // unit price - required
      "1" // quantity - required
   );
   pageTracker._trackTrans();
} catch(err) {}
</script>
```

There are three methods in this script that collect and send transaction data to Google Analytics. They are:

1. **The _addTrans method:** This method collects the primary order information, like the order ID, the total, and the location of the customer making the purchase. The order ID in the _addTrans method is what associates this transaction with the items in the _addItem method(s).

2. **The _addItem method:** This method collects all product information, like the name of the product, the SKU/code, the unit price, and the quantity ordered. For orders with multiple unique products, a unique _addItem method must be printed out for each separate item ordered. (Example: If someone orders two green T-shirts and one red sweater, there should be two _addItem methods printed out—one for the two green T-shirts, and one for the red sweater.)

3. **The _trackTrans method:** This method is called at the very end of the code and is the method that sends the data to Google for processing. The _trackTrans method sends a separate __utm.gif request, meaning that e-commerce data is sent separately from visitor data from the _trackPageview method in the Google Analytics Tracking Code.

This code should be placed on the very last page of your cart or processing system (the order confirmation, receipt, or thank-you page). If you have multiple purchase points using different order confirmation pages on your site, then each order confirmation page should be coded for Google Analytics e-commerce.

Obviously, the values in the _addTrans and _addItem methods in the aforementioned coding example are just samples to show you what you'll see if you view the source code of the receipt/confirmation page after an actual order has been completed. Check out the next section ("General E-commerce Coding Guidelines") for some important details that will save time and a few headaches along the way.

General E-commerce Coding Guidelines

There are so many different ways to print the actual transaction and item values into the Google Analytics e-commerce coding module that we could dedicate an entire chapter of this book to it. It can be done in PHP, ASP, .Net, ColdFusion, or JSP, and it can be programmed in any way you want with most types of e-commerce platforms—as long as when you view the source of the page you can see the transaction and item details within the e-commerce module, and as long as the second _utm.gif request gets sent to Google for processing.

However, we do have the space to show you one example of how this is done in PHP. The following is the analytics.php page from osCommerce, and it shows how the order ID, _addItem, and _addTrans data is collected and then printed into the final confirmation page of osCommerce's very popular e-commerce system, checkout_success.php.

NOTE Some comments and extra line breaks have been removed from the following example to save space.

This example is from the Google Analytics module for osCommerce by Clement Nicolaescu (osCoders.biz) on 11/15/2005, with beta modification on 01/15/2008 by Tomas Hesseling (boxershorts.nl) and Mathieu Burgerhout, released under the GNU General Public License.

```php
<?php

// ############## Google Analytics - start ##############

// Get order id
    $orders_query = tep_db_query("select orders_id from " . TABLE_ORDERS
. " where customers_id = '" . (int)$customer_id . "' order by date_
purchased desc limit 1");
    $orders = tep_db_fetch_array($orders_query);
        $order_id = $orders['orders_id'];

// Get order info for Analytics "Transaction line" (affiliation, city,
state, country, total, tax and shipping)

// Set value for  "affiliation"

        $analytics_affiliation = ''

// Get info for "city", "state", "country"
    $orders_query = tep_db_query("select customers_city, customers_state
, customers_country from " . TABLE_ORDERS . " where orders_id = '" .
$order_id . "' AND customers_id = '" . (int)$customer_id . "'");
    $orders = tep_db_fetch_array($orders_query);

    $totals_query = tep_db_query("select value, class from " .
TABLE_ORDERS_TOTAL . " where orders_id = '" . (int)$order_id . "'
order by sort_order");
// Set values for "total", "tax" and "shipping"
    $analytics_total = '';
    $analytics_tax = '';
    $analytics_shipping = '';

     while ($totals = tep_db_fetch_array($totals_query)) {

        if ($totals['class'] == 'ot_total') {
$analytics_total = number_format($totals['value'], 2, '.', '');
$total_flag = 'true';
} else if ($totals['class'] == 'ot_tax') {
```

```
$analytics_tax = number_format($totals['value'], 2, '.', '');
$tax_flag = 'true';
} else if ($totals['class'] == 'ot_shipping') {
$analytics_shipping = number_format($totals['value'], 2, '.', '');
$shipping_flag = 'true';
}


    }


// Prepare the Analytics "Transaction line" string

$transaction_string = '"' .
$order_id . '"," ' .
$analytics_affiliation . '","' .
$analytics_total . '","' .
$analytics_tax . '","' .
$analytics_shipping . '","' .
$orders['customers_city'] . '","' .
$orders['customers_state'] . '","' .
$orders['customers_country'] . '"';


// Get products info for Analytics "Item lines"

        $item_string = '';
    $items_query = tep_db_query("select products_id, products_model,
products_name, final_price, products_tax, products_quantity from " .
TABLE_ORDERS_PRODUCTS . " where
orders_id = '" . $order_id . "' order by products_name");
    while ($items = tep_db_fetch_array($items_query)) {
            $category_query = tep_db_query("select p2c.categories_id,
cd.categories_name from " . TABLE_PRODUCTS_TO_CATEGORIES . " p2c, " .
TABLE_CATEGORIES_DESCRIPTION . " cd where p2c.products_id = '" .
$items['products_id'] . "' AND cd.categories_id = p2c.categories_id
AND cd.language_id = '" . (int)$languages_id
. "'");
            $category = tep_db_fetch_array($category_query);


        $item_string .=  "pageTracker._addItem(\n\"" .
$order_id . "\",\"" .
$items['products_id'] . "\",\"" .
$items['products_name'] . "\",\"" .
$category['categories_name'] . "\",\"" .
number_format(tep_add_tax($items['final_price'],
$items['products_tax']), 2) . "\",\"" .
$items['products_quantity'] . "\");\n";
    }


// ############## Google Analytics - end ##############

?>


pageTracker._addTrans(
```

```
<?php echo $transaction_string; ?>

);

<?php echo $item_string; ?>

pageTracker._trackTrans();
```

There are two required fields in the _addTrans method that must be filled in. These are Order ID and Total. The other fields—Affiliation, Tax, Shipping, City, State, and Country—are all optional (but it's recommended that you make use of them).

There are four required fields in each _addItem method that must also be filled in for proper item data to be sent to Google Analytics. These four required fields are Order ID (which must be identical to the order ID in the _addTrans method), SKU/Code, Unit Price, and Quantity. In the _addItem method, Product Name and Category are the optional fields.

The SKU/Code field must be populated for every _addItem method you print. If you have an order with multiple _addItem methods, and the SKU/Code field is not used for every item, then only the last item with the SKU/Code field filled in will be recorded. This will cause big data discrepancies on the reporting side.

Avoid using any "special" characters in the names or values for every field. Characters like currency symbols ($ and €, for example), will cause missing or unrealistic data in your reports. Other characters that will cause problems are quotation marks (" and "), which can cause the entire transaction to not be reported, as well as trademark or copyright symbols, letters from non-English language sets (vowels with tildes, circumflexes, umlauts, and grave/acute signs), and several non-ASCII, non-UTF-8 symbols. It's best to steer clear of symbols altogether and stick to letters, especially in the names of products, where most errors seem to occur.

Stand-alone zeros in numerical fields (Total, Tax, Shipping, Unit Price, and Quantity) are to be avoided at all costs, as these can also cause problems. Instead of using zeros, simply leave the field blank—don't skip it entirely. Our first coding example in this chapter shows the Shipping field not being used in the _addTrans method:

```
pageTracker._addTrans(
"555667", // order ID - required
"Clothing Store", // affiliation or store name
"21.99", // total - required
"1.09", // tax
"", // shipping
"Boca Raton", // city
"Florida", // state or province
"USA" // country
);
```

The comma is another character that will break your e-commerce data and cause more headaches for you. Commas are very often used in fields, but these support only integers. Don't separate your thousands places with commas with Google Analytics E-commerce.

The Country field in the _addTrans method supports the two-letter country code (US), the three-letter country code (USA), or the full name of the country (United States). Feel free to use any one of these.

Keep in mind that the last two fields in the _addItem method—Unit Price and Quantity—should not be multiplied together. Google Analytics will do the math for you, so if, for example, you multiply a unit price of 1.25 by a quantity of 3, it will appear in the e-commerce source code as 3.75, which Google will then multiply again by 3 for a whopping 11.25, which will make your product revenue data highly inaccurate.

Currency conversions (dollar to euro, euro to yen, etc.) are not handled by Google Analytics, so they must happen on your end before the GIF request. Again, remember that Total, Tax, Shipping, and Unit Price are integer fields.

E-commerce Tracking on Subdomains and Separate (Third-Party) Domains

Oddly, tracking your shopping cart on a subdomain or on a separate/third-party domain has absolutely nothing to do with the actual e-commerce tracking code itself. However, it's vital that you implement the following steps if your cart resides on a separate subdomain or fully separate domain. By default, Google Analytics expects that all tracking for each UA number will happen on a single domain—if a visitor goes from your main domain to another subdomain or fully separate domain that has your same Google Analytics Tracking Code, you'll lose the original visitor session information, and a new set of cookies will be created for that visitor. This means that unique visitor counts and reports like the New vs. Returning report will be negatively affected, but more importantly, referral information will be lost, resulting in all e-commerce transactions being credited to "direct/(none)," or to your own web site as a referral.

> **NOTE** You can arrange to track two subdomains/full domains in the same profile with Google Analytics in the same way that I'm about to demonstrate, whether you have an e-commerce storefront or not. It bears repeating that this is a vital element of tracking visitors in the same profile between sub-domains and separate domains. I'll briefly review this part of this chapter, as well as covering some other neat workarounds (or "hacks") in Chapter 14.

If your shopping cart resides on a separate subdomain/full domain, there are some site-wide coding changes that you'll need to implement. These are covered in the following section.

Tracking E-commerce on Subdomains

If your site spans multiple subdomains, like `www.yoursite.com`, `blog.yoursite.com`, and `shopping.yoursite.com`, you will need to update your Google Analytics Tracking Code on all pages of all subdomains to include a call to _setDomainName, as the example here shows:

```
var pageTracker = _gat._getTracker("UA-XXXXXX-X");
pageTracker._setDomainName(".yourwebsite.com");
pageTracker._trackPageview();
```

Adding a call to _setDomainName and defining your domain as shown allows the hash value that is created by the Google Analytics Tracking Code to "accept" visitors from any subdomain of `.yourwebsite.com`. Notice the leading period in front of the domain name within the _setDomainName call; this leading period must be present on each subdomain's tracking code, or you will experience visitor tracking problems (you can also use _setDomainName without the leading period). Whatever you do on one subdomain (use the period or don't use it), you must replicate that exactly on any other subdomain.

Once you implement this _setDomainName call within the Google Analytics Tracking Code on all pages on all of the subdomains you wish to track, e-commerce transaction data will be properly credited to the right referring sources, saving campaign and keyword data as well.

Keep in mind that the only thing you have to add to the Google Analytics Tracking Code for tracking subdomains is the call to _setDomainName—you don't have to edit the tracking code beyond that.

Tracking E-commerce on Separate/Third-Party Domains

Tracking multiple domains, like `www.yoursite.com` and `www.website2.com`, is a bit more involved than simply tracking subdomains. Here we'll not only have to make changes to the Google Analytics Tracking Code on both web sites; we'll also have to pass cookie information via HTTP from the first site to the second site. Here's how that is accomplished:

1. Modify the Google Analytics Tracking Code on both web sites to include calls to _setAllowLinker and _setAllowHash, as this example shows:

```
var pageTracker = _gat._getTracker("UA-XXXXXX-X");
pageTracker._setAllowLinker(true);
pageTracker._setAllowHash(false);
```

```
pageTracker._trackPageview();
```

Here, the call to_setAllowLinker has a value of true, and immediately below that, the call to _setAllowHash has a value of false. _setAllowLinker activates linking capabilities between this web site and another web site (where this Google Analytics Tracking Code will also be placed), while _setAllowHash rewrites the way the domain is "hashed" in the cookies, allowing any domain with Google Analytics Tracking Code and the exact same UA account number to read visitor cookies from this site.

2. Add either _link or _linkByPost to all links and forms sending visitors to and from each web site—it must be added to links and forms on BOTH sites.

   For all hyperlinks (text or image), add the _link function within the anchor tag (<a>) as an onClick event, as shown here:

```
<a href="http://www.otherwebsite.com/"
onClick="pageTracker._link('http://www.otherwebsite.com/')
;return false;">Click here to go to our other web site!</a>
```

   For all form buttons (Submit, Add to Cart, Checkout, etc.), add the _linkByPost function within the corresponding form tag (<form>) as an onSubmit event, as shown here:

```
<form action="http://www.otherwebsite.com/processing.php" name="form"
method="post" onSubmit="pageTracker._linkByPost(this)">
```

Web-site owners using third-party sites for e-commerce or form processing may be able to arrange with their vendors to add the GA tracking code. But some vendors (PayPal is one) won't do this.

Once the Google Analytics Tracking Code is properly implemented on both your original (or first) site and the third-party (or second) site, and once all your links or forms have had _link or _linkByPost added to them, you should visit your own site and perform a quick test to see if your e-commerce cross-domain tracking is successfully working. To test, click a link that you know will take you to the third-party site, and that has had _link or _linkByPost added to it. Once the third-party site loads, you should see a URL in the address bar of your browser that contains a very long string of query parameters, like this example:

```
https://shopping.othersite.com/
store.php?StoreID=54321CartID=
123456789&ItemID=1a2b3c4d5e6f7
g8hLanguageID=001&__utma=1.185
```

```
8684020312326400.1250039919.12
50039919.1250039919.1&__utmb=1
.1.10.1250039919&__utmc=1&
utmx=&__utmz=1.1250039919.1.1.
utmcsr=(google)|utmccn=(Green
+Hats++National+Campaign)|utmc
md=(cpc)&__utmv=-&__utmk=2012
17070
```

Everything from the end of the fourth line (starting with &__utma=)of the URL onward is your cookie information, which in this example was successfully sent via HTTP (in the address bar, in layman's terms) to the second site. Now, when shoppers make purchases on your shopping cart, their correct referral information will receive the credit for the sale, instead of your getting those nasty self-referrals or extremely high volumes of "direct/(none)."

A Few Important Notes about Tracking E-commerce on Third-Party Domains

By far the number-one item not implemented by webmasters everywhere is the _link or _linkByPost function—especially on the second domain. If a user clicks a link from your original site to the second site, and _link is present, cookie information for that visitor's session gets sent via HTTP, just as our previous URL example showed. However, if a customer decides to keep shopping or clicks a link in your navigation header or footer, and if _link or _linkByPost is not present, the cookie information that was just appended to the end of the URL of the second site will get left behind, causing you to see referrals from the second web site being credited for transactions.

We understand that implementing _link or _linkByPost may mean a lot of manual work for the IT team, but the marketing/SEO departments will definitely appreciate these efforts.

It's crucial that the _setAllowLinker function on the second site be set to true, exactly like our coding example from earlier. This is why you will always see it recommended to update the Google Analytics Tracking Code on all pages of both web sites. This way you won't have to worry about which page is coded with what function. More importantly, it's basically a requirement to do so, because on most web sites the second domain can be accessed by means of the Checkout or View Cart links/buttons.

Keep in mind that all points covered in this chapter are the "standard" implementations of cross-domain tracking for your e-commerce storefront. You may have to install a workaround or two if you still aren't able to properly track your e-commerce platform, even after correctly implementing these instructions. For example, if there are redirects present on the second domain (which may strip off the cookie URL parameters), or if the second domain isn't accepting query parameters in the URL (sometimes on purpose to avoid spamming), you may have to tweak your implementation a bit to get it working. Queries on .NET postbacks, and several other workarounds have been successfully implemented to accommodate Google Analytics e-commerce tracking among multiple domains.

E-commerce Tracking with Google Checkout; Other E-commerce Platforms

One of the most widely used checkout processes on the Internet today is Google Checkout. Merchants that provide Google Checkout as a checkout option get to display the Google Checkout button on their web sites, as well as a Google Checkout badge on their Google AdWords ads. Naturally, Google Checkout also provides the ability to track orders in Google Analytics with just a few additions to your source code.

To begin tracking your Google Checkout e-commerce sales within your Google Analytics account, perform the following steps:

1. Ensure that e-commerce tracking is enabled in your desired profile(s) by selecting **Yes, an E-Commerce Site**, as outlined in the beginning of this chapter (Figure 8-1).

2. You are going to need to ensure that the Google Analytics Tracking Code is moved higher up in the source code, above the source code for the Google Checkout button. The safest way to ensure this happens is to move the Google Analytics Tracking Code immediately before the opening <body> tag. If the Google Analytics Tracking Code is not moved you will experience difficulties with tracking your Google Checkout sales in Google Analytics.

3. On every page that uses a Google Checkout button you will need to add the following few lines of JavaScript code. Ensure that this is placed immediately below the Google Analytics Tracking Code that you just moved:

```
<script src="http://checkout.google.com/files/digital/ga_post.js"
 type="text/javascript"></script>
```

4. Next, on every form that is displaying the Google Checkout button you will also need to add this line of code; it is a hidden field that must be present in order for e-commerce data to be collected:

```
<input type="hidden" name="analyticsdata" value="">
```

5. Additionally on every form displaying the Google Checkout button you must also add an onSubmit call within the actual <form> tag (the setUrchinInputCode function), exactly as shown in this example:

```
<form action="..." method="POST"
onsubmit="setUrchinInputCode(pageTracker);">
```

This is how all your Google Analytics/Google Checkout Tracking Code should look on one page, starting at the top with your Google Analytics Tracking Code and finishing at the bottom with the actual Google Checkout form and button:

```
<script type="text/javascript">
var gaJsHost = (("https:" == document.location.protocol)
? "https://ssl." : "http://www.");
document.write(unescape("%3Cscript src='" + gaJsHost +
"google-analytics.com/ga.js'
type='text/javascript'%3E%3C/script%3E"));
</script>
<script type="text/javascript">
try {
var pageTracker = _gat._getTracker("UA-XXXXXXX-X");
pageTracker._trackPageview();
} catch(err) {}</script>

<script src="http://checkout.google.com/files/digital/ga_post.js"
  type="text/javascript">
</script>

<form action="..." method="POST"
onsubmit="setUrchinInputCode(pageTracker);">
    <input type="hidden" name="cart" value="...">
    <input type="hidden" name="signature" value="...">
    <input type="hidden" name="analyticsdata" value="">
    <input type="image" name="Google Checkout" alt="Fast checkout
through Google" src="http://checkout.google.com/buttons/checkout.gif?
merchant_id=YOUR_MERCHANT_ID&w=180&h=46&style=white&variant=text&loc=
en_US" height="46" width="180"/>
</form>
```

NOTE The previous example of integrating Google Checkout transactions with your Google Analytics account assumes that you are using Digitally Signed Checkout XML API Requests. If you use Server-To-Server Checkout API Requests you will need to modify the form handler to extract the value of the analytics data field that is going to execute when someone clicks to purchase with Google Checkout. You will also need to add the <analytics-data> element to your API. Exact steps for Server-To-Server Checkout API can be found on code.google.com/apis/checkout.

Tracking Other E-commerce Platforms

To be honest, it's really a roll of the dice as to which third-party e-commerce platforms are going to provide integration with the Google Analytics e-commerce tracking module. This is *not* to say that any non-Google e-commerce system isn't a solid and a reputable one, only that for many reasons some vendors simply cannot support code customizations at this time. (However, several vendors are beginning to release patches and software updates to specifically accommodate Google Analytics.)

At present PayPal does not have a reliable, standard way to track Google Analytics e-commerce transactions. PayPal simply is not allowing JavaScript to be inserted into its checkout and processing pages, which reside on its servers, and so you may be out of luck. Yahoo! Store merchants may install the Google Analytics e-commerce tracking module on its confirmation/receipt page, but may experience challenges in properly tracking referrals from the original site to the Yahoo storefront. Some custom-designed e-commerce storefronts or content-management systems do not have simple ways to install custom code outside of a template or an include file, and this makes it time-consuming and difficult for web developers to get everything working correctly.

However, other popular carts offer more flexibility with Google Analytics, such as osCommerce (whose coding I showcased an example of earlier), ZenCart, Volusion, and several others. It would take several other chapters, and quite possibly a book, to display every single instructional guide for every cart out there. My best advice for you is to visit one of the following URLs, which come from official vendor forums and download pages. These are by far the best resources if your web site uses one of these popular solutions.

- **osCommerce:** Community Add-Ons: Google Analytics Module:
  `http://addons.oscommerce.com/info/3756`

- **Zen Cart:** Support forum thread: Google Analytics Add-Ons:
  `http://www.zen-cart.com/forum/showthread.php?t=43907`

- **Volusion:** Knowledge Base: Google Analytics in 2 Steps:
  `http://www.volusion.com/support/KB_Article.asp?ID=201`

- **Yahoo! Store:** Google Analytics Yahoo! Store Self Installation:
  `http://www.mystore-solutions.com/google-analytics.html`

- **Miva Merchant:** Community Forum: Gilligan's Google Analytics Module for 5/5.5:
  `http://extranet.mivamerchant.com/forums/showthread.php?t=18585`

- **Joomla!:** Google Analytics Tracking Module:
  ```
  http://extensions.joomla.org/extensions/site-management/
  site-analytics/1233
  ```

- **Drupal:** Google Analytics:
  ```
  http://drupal.org/project/google_analytics
  ```

- **DotNetNuke:** Marketplace: Google Analytics 2008 2.0:
  ```
  http://marketplace.dotnetnuke.com/p-320-google-analytics-
  200820.aspx
  ```

- **Magento:** Installing Google Analytics on Your Magento Stores:
  ```
  http://magentoexpert.co.uk/2009/04/21/installing-google-
  analytics-on-your-magento-stores/
  ```

If I didn't list your cart you can get in touch with your vendor and specifically ask what it can do for you in terms of e-commerce tracking. If your IT or webmaster designed the cart, work with this person to implement the Google Analytics e-commerce module. The primary key to tracking Google Analytics e-commerce is the answer to the question, "Can we install code on it?" If the answer is no, there may not be much you can do. If yes, the e-commerce tracking world—no matter the language or environment—is your oyster.

Advanced Implementation

Getting started with Google Analytics is easy enough. Just create an account and paste a bit of code into your web-site code. But there's so much more to Google Analytics than just the basics.

This part of the book walks you through some of the more advanced implementation of Google Analytics. For example, did you know that you can customize dashboards for specific needs? Or that you can set up goals, filters, and funnels for your web site to help you track how your visitors move through your site?

You can. You can also connect your AdWords account to your Google Analytics account, and there are numerous ways you can hack Google Analytics to further customize it to meet your needs. This is the part of the book where we show you how to do all of that.

Advanced Dashboard Features

You've already seen how useful the dashboard in Google Analytics can be. What you may not have considered is that it's also useful for creating a quick snapshot of your web-site analytics for special purposes. For example, if you're the marketing manager for the web site being tracked in Google Analytics, you'll need to know different information from the webmaster or an executive.

Of course, the reports that you need (or think you need) as a marketing manager (for example) might be different from the reports that some other marketing managers might think they need. What it all comes down to is that you have quick access to the reports that tell you *the most important metrics* that you want or need to track. Those metrics are usually determined by your specific organizational requirements, which is why the metrics you need are probably going to be very different from the metrics another person needs.

There are some pretty good guidelines about what you should include on any dashboard, however, no matter what the purpose of that dashboard might be. In fact, there are three principles you should follow, no matter whom you're creating a dashboard for:

- **Show metrics in context:** This is the most important principle for creating any dashboard for any reason. A metric that's just a number tells you nothing about your web site. However, a metric that's in context can open your eyes to a whole new world of information. For example, if you learn that your bounces are down 1 percent, it's hard to know if that's good or bad. However, if you have contextual information that shows that bounces are down 1 percent this month but had been up 5 percent last month, then you've got something you can work with. Now you see that there's been a 6 percent drop in bounces, meaning that whatever you changed in your site is working either to help attract the right visitors or to hold visitors on your site.

- **Select only meaningful metrics:** When you're creating a dashboard for any purpose, it's important that you know which metrics are actually meaningful and which are not. For example, if you're creating a marketing dashboard and you've just launched a marketing campaign in New York, one of the metrics you might want to include on your dashboard is a drilldown of the Map Overlay focused on the state of New York. You can even take that further and drill down to a specific city if that's the information you need to know. Just remember that needs for information change. Fortunately, changing the reports included on the dashboard is fairly easy.

- **Keep it simple:** You've heard this admonition before, but that's because it's really good advice. Even in creating your dashboards you need to keep it simple. If you have more than four to six reports (in addition to the Site Usage report) on your dashboard, then you've probably got too much going on and should consider creating a report instead of a dashboard (we'll take a look at how to create custom reports in the "Creating Custom Reports" section of this chapter). Ideally, you want to be able to print your dashboard on a single page, so that at a glance you have the most important information about your web site available to you.

Creating Special-Purpose Dashboards

With those few principles in mind you can begin to create a dashboard that's specific to your role, and that provides the information you need at a glance. And creating dashboards, or changing them, is as simple as navigating to the report you want to include in the dashboard.

As you learned back in Chapter 5, almost all the reports available to you in Google Analytics can be added to your dashboard. So for example, if you want to include metrics about a specific page of content that you're tracking (literally down to the page level), all you have to do is navigate to the page that displays that report and then click **Add to Dashboard**.

Once the report is on your dashboard, you can change the order in which reports are displayed by clicking and dragging them around the page.

NOTE Remember, the Site Usage report is one that doesn't move and can't be removed from the dashboard. All the other report modules that you place on your dashboard can be rearranged or removed at your pleasure.

User Access to Dashboards

One frustrating element of the dashboard is that you can create only one per sign-in address for your analytics account. If you happen to hold multiple roles in your computer (marketing manager and webmaster, for example) you'll have to have multiple sign-in e-mails in order to create different dashboards for each of your different roles. It's frustrating, but at this time it's not possible to create multiple dashboards and switch between them.

The same holds true if there are multiple people whom you've given access to Google Analytics. You can't create a single dashboard that is automatically pushed out to them. Those people can rearrange their dashboards to suit themselves, without any input from you at all. This isn't ordinarily a problem, unless there is a specific metric that you want to be certain your users can see. Then you'll need to tell your users what your expectations are.

Sharing Your Dashboard Information

One thing you can do when you create a dashboard that you want to share with multiple people is to send it to them via e-mail. This was covered back in Chapter 3. If you need to, flip back for a refresher.

Remember, too, that you can set reports up to send automatically. This enables you to "set it and forget it." Once you've created an automatic report delivery, it will continue until you change it.

Suggested Dashboards for Specific Roles

Analytics can be a lot of different things to different people. Fortunately, with the new dashboard capabilities you can have different dashboards for whatever roles you play in your organization.

Below you'll find examples of several different types of dashboards. These are just suggestions for how your dashboard might look under different circumstances. Your actual dashboard could vary considerably, depending upon your specific needs. Feel free to use these examples or not, whichever works best for you. And remember, too, that you can change your dashboard at any time; you might start with an example and find later that you need to add or remove modules.

Executive

Executives tend to need just a basic overview of everything. Most executives don't want (or need) to know the specifics about what pages get the most visitors and how long those visitors stay on the site. In general, what an executive needs to know is how many visitors came to the site, where they came from, how many of them were new, and what area of the world they reside in.

To meet those needs, an executive dashboard might have these reports on it:

- Site Usage (this is a default report)
- New vs. Returning
- Map Overlay
- All Traffic Sources
- Visitors Overview

That example dashboard might look like the one shown in Figure 9-1. Also notice that in this picture date-range comparisons are included. This helps to put the information in each of the report modules on the dashboard into perspective.

NOTE When you change the date range on any of the report modules that you include on a dashboard, this changes the date range for all the report modules on that dashboard. If you want to change back to the original report (without the date comparisons) you have to open the calendar controls (you learned about this in Chapter 5) and deselect the **Compare to Past** option and click **Apply**. Alternatively, you can log out of Google Analytics and then log back in; the calendar will be reset to the default view.

Of course, it's also possible that your executive dashboard won't look anything like this. What appears on that dashboard and how it's arranged are entirely dependent upon your specific needs.

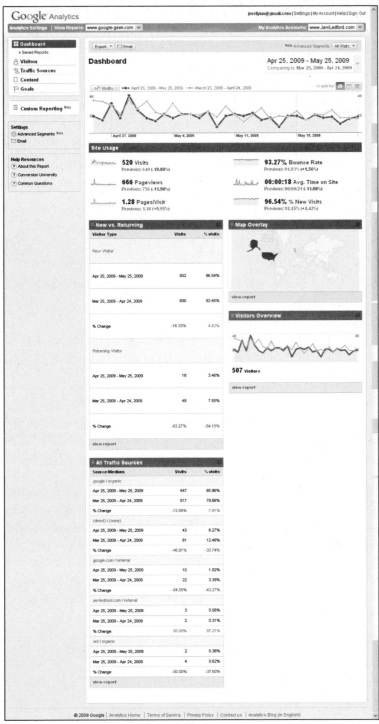

Figure 9-1: An example executive dashboard

Marketing

A marketing manager's job is vastly different from that of an executive. Marketing managers are looking for how well their marketing campaigns perform. It's all about return on investment for them. So when marketing managers create dashboards, it isn't unusual for them to include reports that allow them to see how pay-per-click advertising is performing, how keywords are performing, and how many goal conversions happen each day. Some of the reports that a marketing manager might include on a dashboard are (with the source of each in the "tree navigation" at the left of the Figure 9-2 screen):

- Site Usage (default)
- Keywords (Traffic Sources)
- AdWords Campaigns (Traffic Sources)
- Campaigns (Traffic Sources)
- Ad Versions (Traffic Sources)
- Goals Overview (Goals)
- Total Conversions (Goals)

Your marketing dashboard might resemble the one shown in Figure 9-2.

Webmaster

As a webmaster, you're constantly worried about the differing factors that affect how your web site is displayed. Everything from the browser your visitors use to find your site to the color capabilities of their screens can affect how your site works for them. And every webmaster knows that usability is a key factor in designing a site.

So as a webmaster, you might want to see reports that tell you what content was most viewed on your site, what types of browsers and operating systems most users have, even how visitors move through your site. All these things can be included on your dashboard. Unfortunately, because Google Analytics is cookie-based, not server log-based, there are no reports to show 401 errors (attempts to access pages that don't exist or attacks on the site) or 301 redirects.

As a webmaster, you might have a dashboard like the one in Figure 9-3. It could include the following reports:

- Site Usage (default)
- Keywords
- Browsers and OS
- Goals Overview
- All Traffic Sources
- Goal Abandoned Funnels
- Visitor Loyalty

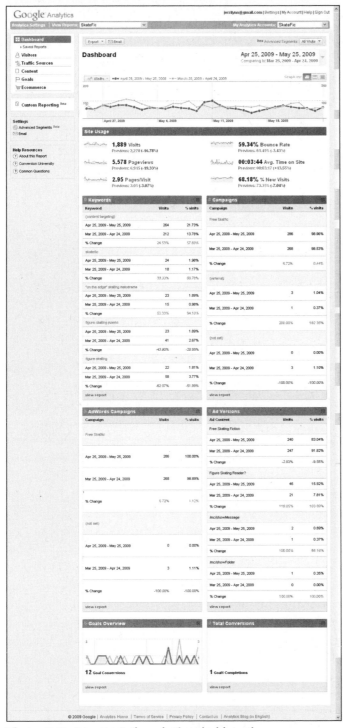

Figure 9-2: A suggested marketing dashboard

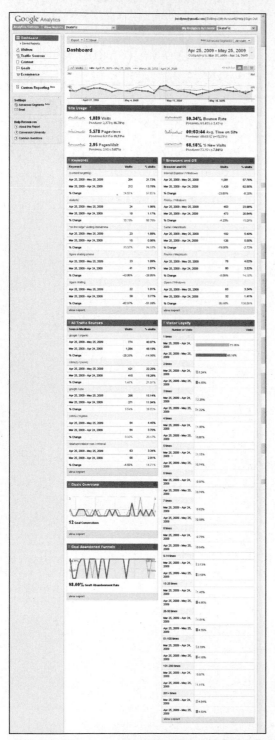

Figure 9-3: An example webmaster dashboard

Small Business

Small businesses vary so much that it's hard to decide what an Analytics user might need on a dashboard. It's going to be very different from one business to another. However, some basic reports are always a good place to start for small-business owners. You can see those reports in the example of a small-business dashboard in Figure 9-4. Remember, however, that those reports can be changed as needed—this just may be a good starting point. This small-business dashboard contains these reports:

- Site Usage (default)
- Traffic Sources Overview
- AdWords Campaigns
- Keywords
- Content Overview
- Goals Overview

Notice that all these reports are overview reports. If you are a small-business owner and start with this example, but find you really need reports that are more in-depth, you can always add or remove reports according to what suits your specific needs.

If your business is primarily local, you might want to add a drilled-down map view of your city or regional area. If you're heavily invested in AdWords campaigns, you might want more details than just the overview. And if you're concerned with stickiness, you'll want a bounce-rate report.

Content Site

SkateFic.com is a content site. People don't go there primarily to buy stuff; they go there to read stuff. The main focus is content. It can be articles, a newsletter, a blog, or whatever type of content (including audio and video) you choose. But there are certain reports that are key to the operation of a content site. If your main focus is that type of site, the dashboard shown in Figure 9-5 is a good place for you to start.

Here's what's included on that dashboard:

- Site Usage (default)
- Top Content
- New vs. Returning
- Bounce Rate
- Depth of Visit
- Map Overlay

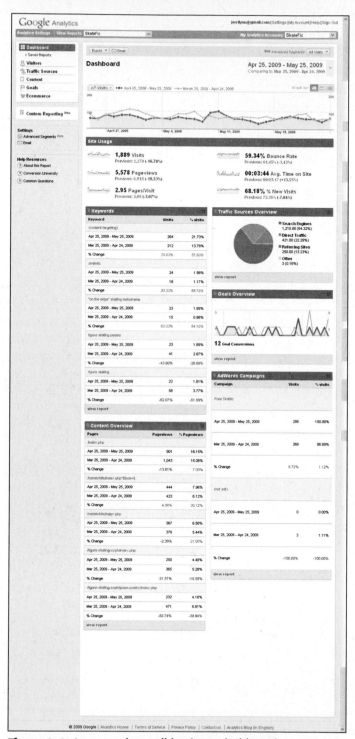

Figure 9-4: An example small-business dashboard

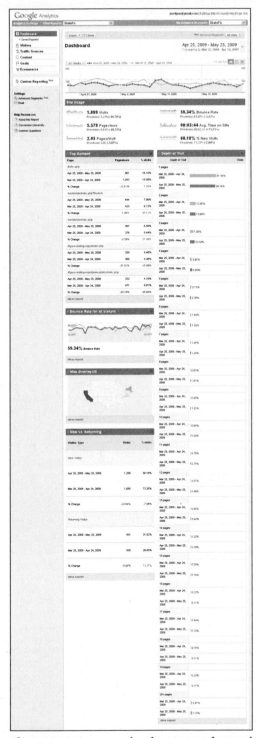

Figure 9-5: An example of a content-focused dashboard

In addition to the reports shown for this dashboard, if you sell a few things on your content site or if you use AdWords to draw new readership, you may also want to include some of the e-commerce or AdWords tracking reports. This is especially true if you offer content on your site for sale (e-books, special reports, teleseminars, and so on). However, even if you're selling nothing on your site, you can take advantage of some of the e-commerce capabilities by assigning value to your content. You'll learn more about how to do that in Chapter 11.

E-commerce Site

One reason Google Analytics is so wildly popular is that it has capabilities for everyone with a web site. E-commerce sites have always presented a special problem for tracking and analytics programs because they are designed a little differently from normal web sites. However, Google has taken the time to add more bulk to its e-commerce offering. If your main focus is an e-commerce dashboard, you might expect it to look something like the one shown in Figure 9-6. Here's what's included on that dashboard:

- Site Usage (default)
- E-commerce Overview
- Goal Conversion Rate
- Average Order Value
- Products
- Transactions

In some instances you may prefer to include more detailed reports than these. Or perhaps you want to add reports that show you the funnel navigation for a specific goal. All this can be done with the new dashboard capabilities in Google Analytics. You can add or remove reports at any time.

Local Business Only

Local businesses often need to know how many of their users come from their local community. This is especially true if the local business is a brick-and-mortar one that uses the web site as a draw for local sales. If you have one of those local businesses, there's good news. You can set up a dashboard that includes only location-based information (or you can add the suggested reports to your regular small-business dashboard). That dashboard might look like the one shown in Figure 9-7. Here are the main reports on geographics:

- Site Usage (default)
- Map Overlay
- Keywords

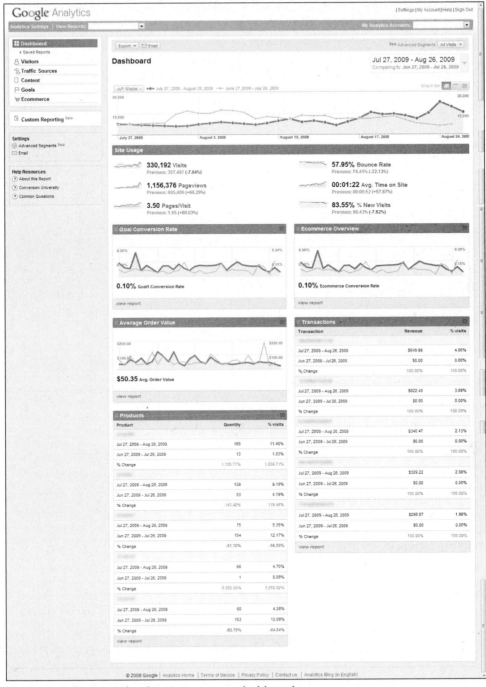

Figure 9-6: An example of an e-commerce dashboard

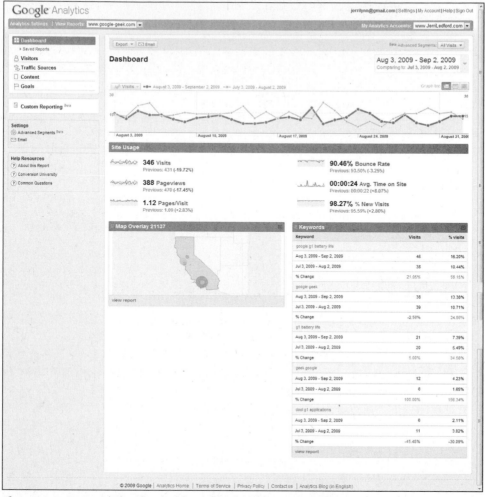

Figure 9-7: An example of a dashboard for local business only

The flexibility of the dashboard makes Google Analytics even more usable for you. All too often, users have wished they could have the information they needed at their fingertips. Now they can. And there are only a few limits to that information. For example, you can add only 12 reports to your dashboard at any given time, but in most cases your most frequently used information will be in four to six reports. And of course there's the annoyance of the Site Usage report that you simply can't do away with. And it doesn't look as if that's going to change in future iterations of Google Analytics, so you might as well get used to it.

Apart from those minor points, the dashboard provides useful capabilities in analytics and workflow. Everything you need is right there, and drilling deeper into the data is as simple as clicking a mouse.

Creating Custom Reports

One last capability that we should cover in this chapter is creating custom reports. Custom Reporting, which is in beta testing at the time of writing, is a capability that enables you to customize reports with the data that you want to see, displayed in the manner that's most useful to you.

Custom Reporting actually takes advantage of two different types of data to enable you to create reports that meet your specific needs:

- **Dimensions:** These are attributes for visitors or campaigns. They are usually text-based measurements (rather than numerical measurements), and they'll represent the rows in your custom report. For example, if you want to track the number of new visits to your web site by city, then "city" would be a dimension.

- **Metrics:** The complement to attributes is actual measurements, and that's what metrics are—numbers. So in the previous example about tracking the number of new visitors by city, the metric is going to be the *number* of visitors.

It's important that you understand what metrics and dimensions are, because not all metrics work together with all dimensions. As a matter of fact, there are enough metrics and dimensions that won't work together that Google has created a chart to help you understand what works with what. You can find that chart at `https://www.google.com/support/googleanalytics/bin/answer.py?answer=99174`.

How the Report Is Created

The actual process of creating a custom report (when you know what you want to illustrate) is point-and-click easy. It's a process that you can complete in a few simple steps:

1. From within any dashboard view in Google Analytics (for which you have administrative privileges) click **Custom Reporting** on the left side of the page. This takes you to the Custom Reporting Overview page.

2. To begin creating a custom report, click **Create new custom report**. You'll be taken to the report creation page shown in Figure 9-8.

3. Begin by giving your report a name. To do that, click the **Edit** link next to the custom title at the top of the page. This opens the title for editing, as shown in Figure 9-9. Once you've edited the title, click **Apply** to save the changes.

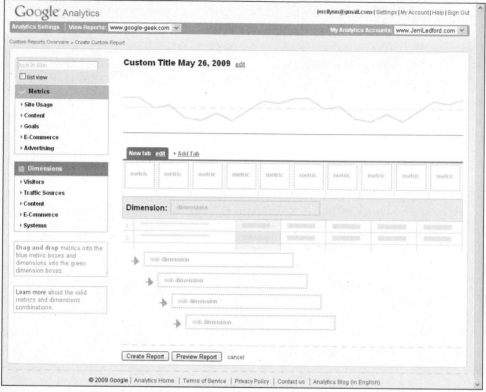

Figure 9-8: Use the report creation page to create a custom report for your specific data needs.

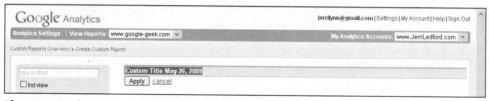

Figure 9-9: Give your custom report a title that's descriptive to you.

4. Next, choose a metric for which you want to create a report. Going back to our previous example, let's track the number of new visitors to your web site, by city. The metric you want to use in this report is the visitors metric: you can either navigate to it (using the blue buttons) or type "visitors" into the search bar and click the magnifying glass.

5. When you find the metric you want to use, all you have to do is click and drag that metric to the **metric** box on the report, as shown in Figure 9-10.

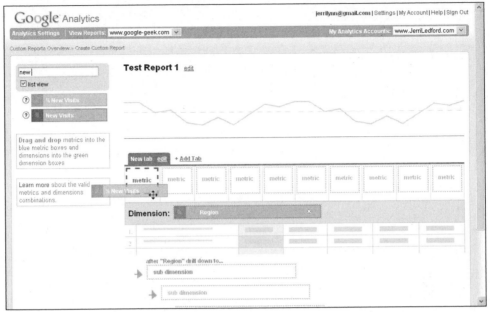

Figure 9-10: Click the desired metric and drag it to an available metrics column on the table.

You can add as many as 10 different metrics to your report. Each metric appears in its own column. Let's add another one to this report, just to make it a little more interesting. Let's say you also want to track the bounce rate for each state. Add the Bounce Rate metric the same way you added the New Visitors metric: search for it, then click and drag it to one of the **metric** columns.

6. Next we need to add the dimension. We want to know how many visitors and bounces there are for each state, so we'll choose **Region** for this dimension. Search for Region, and when you find it, click and drag it to the **Dimension** row, as shown in Figure 9-11.

7. Finally, you can add sub-dimensions down to four levels. For example, if you want to drill down to sub-regions (geographically), you should find the Sub Continent Region dimension and drag it to one of the sub-dimension boxes.

8. Once you've added the metrics, dimensions, and sub-dimensions that you want included in your report, you can test the effectiveness of your design by clicking **Preview Report**. A new window will open with a preview of the report that you've created, as shown in Figure 9-12. (I've renamed my report as Test Report 1.)

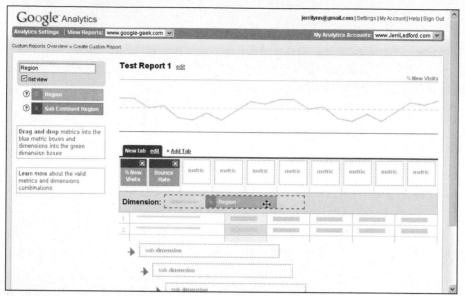

Figure 9-11: Next, add an attribute to the Dimension row.

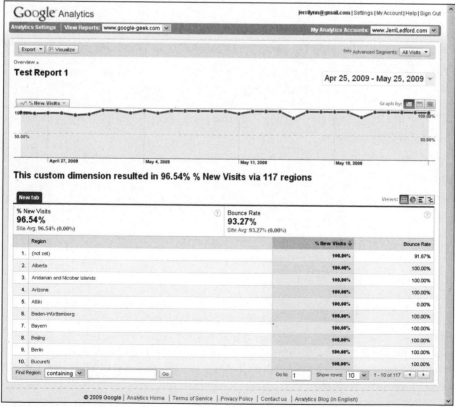

Figure 9-12: The report preview looks exactly as the finished report will look.

9. If you're satisfied with the report, close the preview window and select **Create Report**. The report is saved, and you'll automatically be taken to the report view. From here you can add the report to your dashboard or navigate to other reports, just as you would from any predefined report within Google Analytics.

Editing and Managing Custom Reports

Once you've navigated away from your report you might wonder where to find it again, if you didn't add it to your dashboard. The process is a little obscure, but you'll find the right port just behind the **Custom Reporting** button that you clicked to create the report. If you click it again you'll be taken to Custom Reporting Overview, shown in Figure 9-13. This is where you'll find the report you just created (along with any others you create in the future).

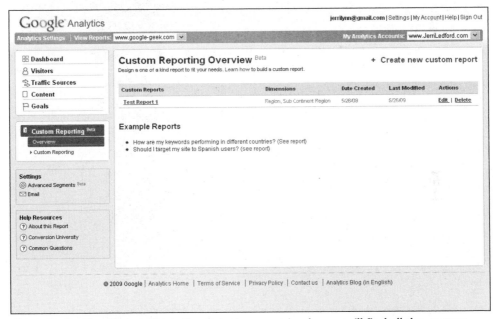

Figure 9-13: The Custom Reporting Overview page is where you'll find all the custom reports that you've created.

To access the report from this page, click the report title. That takes you to the report display page. You can also edit or delete the report, using the links to the right of the report name. If you click **Edit** the report creation page is opened: here you can add, remove, and change elements of the report. When you're finished, click **Save Report** again, and you'll be taken to the completed view of that report.

If you click the **Delete** option for a custom report you'll receive a confirmation message prompting you to confirm that you really do want to delete the report. If that's the case, click **OK**. Otherwise, click **Cancel** to return to the previous view of the Custom Reporting Overview. As always, use caution when deleting custom reports. Once you delete a report, there's no way to get it back.

CHAPTER 10

Filtering Analytics Data

Most people look at a bolt of fabric and see nothing more than cloth. A seamstress looks at it and sees a shirt. The data collected by Google Analytics is just about the same—it's meaningless until you view it from the right perspective. That's when it begins to look like something useful.

In Google Analytics a filter provides the right perspective. Filters help to separate data into two categories: the data used to create reports and the data that has no value to you. Google Analytics provides filtering capabilities that help you see through the myriad facts, numbers, and values it collects.

Using Filters to Further Segment Visitors

Suppose Google Analytics simply collected information about your web-site statistics and then dumped that data in your lap without any kind of organization. It would take you longer to make sense of the statistics than it takes for a toddler to clean his room.

To help you understand the meaning of the facts that Google Analytics collects, data goes through filters. These filters can exclude information collected about certain domains or IP addresses (an Internet site's numerical address), or they can simplify complex sets of numbers or facts, making them easier to understand.

Because understanding data can be a real chore, Google has created a standard set of filters that give you the ability to separate your collected metrics by plugging in key pieces of information or patterns expressed in a language called *Regular Expressions,* also known as RegEx. More about that later (although you'll see some RegEx wildcards in the following examples). The following standard filters are located in the Filter Type drop-down menu on the Create New Filter page:

- **Exclude all traffic from a domain:** This filter enables you to exclude visits to your site from a specific Internet site. This is especially helpful if your company web site gets a lot of visits from people on the corporate intranet looking for dirt to dish on their coworkers.

- **Exclude all traffic from an IP address:** Remember that girl who had a crush on you and now follows you everywhere, making untoward suggestions for weekend activities? She visits your web site 150 times a day from her always-on cable modem connection 68.68.68.68. You could filter out that IP. But say she also uses her dialup connection, which has the IP address 68.68.68.67. This filter will also exclude information about visits that match a particular kind of pattern. Filtering on `68\.68\.68\.6[78]` will match either 68.68.68.68 or 68.68.68.67 and will keep her obsession from screwing up your web-site metrics. Now, if you could only use a filter to keep her out of your favorite restaurant.

> **NOTE** Some unsavory characters have discovered ways to mess around with your stats and analytics. One way they skew the numbers is by copying your web site's source code (which they use to create their own site) and leaving your Google Analytics code embedded within it. Another is by copying your source code to the header on their web site. In either case, the result is screwy measurements for your site. To straighten out your measurements you need to use a filter that excludes the rogues' IP addresses from the data that Google Analytics collects.

- **Include only traffic from a specific subdirectory:** Your hot new product finally has a page on your web site, and now you want to know how much traffic that one part of the site gets. Disappointingly or not, this filter will show you how your baby is doing at the expense of all the other data on your site. "Include only" will include only the specific information that you tell it to.

In addition to the filters that have obvious purposes, you can create custom filters that separate out the information you don't want or that isolate the information you do want. Custom filters enable you to:

- **Exclude:** This filter will exclude from visits data that matches a certain pattern. Say you want to collect information only on your catalogue's regular products, not on the sale ones. All sale products have a special e-commerce item code that begins with SALE. You could filter the Item Code field to exclude any hits from those e-commerce items by filtering with SALE.* as the pattern.

- **Include:** Just as you can exclude, you can choose to include information that matches a certain pattern. Say you want to measure only the visitors who have really high screen resolution because you're going to launch a new game that requires it. You could include traffic for which the Visitor Screen Resolution matches \d\d\d\d x \d\d\d\d, which would match only those resolutions consisting of two four-digit numbers.

TIP The custom Exclude and Include filters are much more flexible than the predefined filters that Google has included. You can use pattern-matching with any of the data fields that Google monitors, not just the domain, sub-domain, or IP address. Use these custom filters to drill deeper into the vast field of data that's available to you.

- **Search and replace:** Much like the search-and-replace function in your word processor, this filter lets you search for specific types of information related to user visits and replace it with other information.

- **Uppercase/Lowercase:** Got something against capital or lowercase letters? Use this filter to change them. Why? Maybe your web developer is lazy and sometimes used title style for tokens and sometimes all caps. Google Analytics doesn't know that there's no difference between Sale and SALE. With the uppercase filter you could change Sale to SALE, or with the lowercase filter you could change Sale and SALE to sale, which would make for much more accurate metrics.

- **Advanced:** Do you wish you could exclude one pattern at the same time that you're including another? You can. Simply use an Advanced filter that looks at multiple pieces of information at one time. Advanced filters are trickier than avoiding anthills in Mississippi, though, and Google documentation is circular, but that's why you bought this book, right? We'll help you figure out how to create advanced filters that work for whatever filtering you might need to do. Before we get there, though, you're going to need to understand a little more about the language used to create advanced filters.

A Short Lesson in Regular Expressions

Creating many of the Google Analytics filters requires some knowledge of Regular Expressions. Don't get too excited. Regular Expressions aren't phrases like "Well, bless her heart"—the Southern disclaimer for every comment uttered under any circumstance. Life couldn't be that easy.

A Regular Expression is a string of text that uses characters, numbers, and wildcards to match patterns in a string of characters. RegEx, which is a simplified term for Regular Expressions, has been accused of being obtuse, and that is not wholly unjustified. While basic RegEx is pretty easy, patterns can be complex, and RegEx follows right along.

The characters and numbers used in a Regular Expression are the same ones you use in English every day: letters A–Z (and a–z), numbers 1–9, and certain symbols from your keyboard. The wildcards are specific symbols or combinations of symbols. Here are the wildcards used in Regular Expressions:

. A period by itself will match any single character: a letter, number, punctuation, or space, but not an end-of-line character such as a carriage return. To match a literal period, use \ . This uses the backslash to *escape* the wildcard and make it literal.

* An asterisk added to a character or wildcard will match zero or more of the previous items. So x* will match a string with nothing in it, and it will also match x, xx, xxx, or any number of x's in a row. More generally, . * matches nothing (an empty string) or any series of characters (including numbers and punctuation but not including end-of-line characters). But take great care with the * modifier; it's greedy, meaning that it seeks the largest match possible—not always the one you mean. Say you have a paragraph with several sentences ending in periods. You would think that . *\ . would match the first sentence, but it doesn't. It matches the whole paragraph!

+ A plus sign added to a character or wildcard will match one or more of the previous items. Use this modifier when you definitely know you don't want to match an empty string or when you want to require that a particular character be present. So x+ will match x, xx, xxx, and so on, but not a blank string or a string of characters with no x's in it.

? This will match zero or one of the previous items. So x? will match x and xx but not xxx. Adding ? to * produces something interesting. Remember that we talked about . * being greedy—that it produces the largest match possible, which is not always what you want? Well, . *? de-greedifies . * faster than jail time drains the avarice from a CEO. Still want to match the first sentence of that paragraph? Well . *?\ . will do it. You can also use ? with the + modifier to the same effect. The pattern .+? will match at least one character in a non-greedy way.

{ } Use curly braces to repeat an exact number of times. So [0-9]{4} will match any group of exactly four digits. You can also have several values inside curly braces. So {2,5} will match any two or five characters.

( ) Put parentheses around a part of a pattern when you want to store that tidbit for use later. To reference that stored bit of text you use escaped numbers: \1 for the first saved bit, \2 for the second, \3 for the third, and so on.

[ ] Put square brackets around a list of characters you want to match. So when we wanted to match both 67 and 68 in your crazy crush's IP address, we used the pattern 6[78], which matched both. Don't make the mistake of putting a word in square brackets and thinking you'll match the word. You won't. It's strictly character by character. Use alternation with the | to match words.

- This creates a range in a list. So if you want to match any digit, you can use [0-9] rather than [0123456789].

| The vertical bar or pipe character is used for alternation. Think of it as the word *or*. Say you wanted to match *this* or *that* . You'd use a pipe: this|that.

^ The carat has two possible matches depending on where it is. If it's inside square brackets, it means *not*. So [^0-9] means anything that is not a digit. But when you find ^ outside of square brackets, it means *at the beginning of the line*. So ^Help will match the word Help if it appears at the beginning of a line.

$ Just as the carat is the beginning of the line, the dollar sign is the end of the line or field. So help me$ will match only if that phrase appears at the end of a field (or if it's followed by an end-of-line marker like a carriage return or line feed).

\ Escape any wildcard. When you escape a wildcard, it becomes a literal. When you escape certain literals, they become wildcards (for example, \d represents any digit and comparable to [0-9] but quicker to type). Only certain literals can become wildcards when escaped. What happens if you escape something that doesn't have a special meaning? Nothing. You're safe. You can even escape an escape, like \\, which you'll need to do if you want to match a literal backslash. RegEx behaves like Amelia Bedelia, a beloved character from a series of children's books who takes every direction completely literally unless you tell her not to.

Here are some additional tips that you'll need for working with wildcards in Regular Expressions:

- The characters ^ and $ represent the beginning or end of an expression. They're called *anchors* and can speed up the processing of your request when used properly.

- Use | to group patterns together. For example, if you need to return graphics with the extensions .jpg, .gif, .bmp, and .png, you don't need to escape the period in front of each extension. Instead, you can use the expression \.(jpg|gif|bmp|png) to group the pattern (and preserve the exact text of what you've matched).

- The expression .* matches everything, so don't forget how greedy it is! Use .*? when you don't want to match everything and its dog and cat and bird and fish and—well, you get the idea. Also remember that .* and .*? will match the empty string (i.e., nothing) as well as strings containing characters. If you definitely want to make sure that you're not unintentionally matching empty strings, make sure to use .+ or .+? instead.

- Keep it simple. The more complex you make your Regular Expressions, the longer they will take to process. With a very complex Regular Expression you also introduce more opportunity for error. As my editors are fond of telling me, add only what you have to and leave everything else out.

You could spend months—even years—learning Regular Expressions and still not learn everything there is to know. What you need to know right now is that you will need some simple Regular Expressions, like the ones in the preceding examples, to create an advanced filter. Of course, more advanced expressions will result in more advanced filtering capabilities, so if you'd like to know more than what's here, check out the sidebar later in this chapter for some additional resources on Regular Expressions.

A Slightly Longer Lesson on Regular Expressions

As with most programs you run on your computer, Regular Expressions was developed rather than just springing like Athena from the mind of the creator. It's one thing to understand what the symbols mean and quite another to be able to read or write one. As one reviewer of the first edition properly pointed out, we didn't have enough examples. So in the coming section we're going to provide the RegEx for certain situations you might commonly encounter as a webmaster.

Matching an IP Address

In the last section we talked about wildcards that match various subsets of characters. The most flexible, powerful, and dangerous character is the period (aka dot). The period will match any character except the end-of-line marker (\n in RegEx-speak). It will match letters of either case, digits, punctuation, spaces, tabs—you name it. It will even match periods. So how do you match a literal period?

To make the wildcard period into a literal period in a Regular Expression, you escape it by putting a backslash in front of it like this:

```
\.
```

So say that you want to match the specific IP address 192.168.0.1. You could write the RegEx like this:

```
192.168.0.1
```

It would match `192x16830,1` as well as `192.168.0.1`. Instead, write the following:

```
192\.168\.0\.1
```

Now the RegEx parser knows that you mean "Match literal periods," not "Match any character."

What if you want to match a range of addresses? Say that you'd like to match the addresses `192.168.0.1` through `192.168.0.5`. It's still fairly easy:

```
192\.168\.0\.[1-5]
```

Don't forget that escaping works for a variety of wildcards. For example, the ampersand is a wildcard. You should always escape it with the expression `\&`. You can create some wildcards by escaping letters: \n means end of line, and \t means tab. To refer to a previous match that you have saved by putting it in parentheses, escape a number. The first match is \1, the second match is \2, and so on. Sometimes you even need to escape the escape. Use \\ when you want to match a literal blackslash.

What happens when you escape a character that has no special meaning when escaped? Nothing. If you escape a character that is not a wildcard when escaped, nothing happens.

Matching a Directory Name

The first thing you need to do when putting together a Regular Expression is think about what the pattern is. How does it begin and end? Are there markers that appear every so often? In programming-speak, these are called *delimiters*. If you've ever opened a CSV file (created by Excel) in a text editor, then you've seen that it's all comma-separated values. The comma is the delimiter.

So what kind of delimiter does the directory structure of your web site have? Let's look at a hypothetical URL:

```
http://www.example.com/serials/ote/index.php
```

See how the forward slashes separate the protocol `http:` from the domain name `www.example.com`? Then there are forward slashes between each two directory names. You can use RegEx to match the serials directory in order to filter information. First, the name of the directory we want to match:

```
serials
```

Next, the delimiters—the forward slashes come before and after the directory name:

```
/serials/
```

Now, let's say that `example.com` has an old, basically abandoned domain name, `anotherexample.com`, which still points to the active site, much as `egroups.com` still leads to `groups.yahoo.com`. So we can't just put the whole `http://www.example.com/` in the pattern, because sometimes it's `http://www.example.com/serials/` and sometimes it's `http://www.anotherexample.com/serials/`.

We don't know exactly what comes before the directory we want. We also have a variety of serials, and each of those serials has a lot of different documents. So we need to express this understanding that there's some stuff before and some stuff after the directory name `serials`.

Yes, "some stuff" is a technical term. In RegEx, `.+` means "some stuff." We're going to use `.+` instead of `.*` because `.*` might match the word *serials* by itself, and we want to make sure it has some stuff before and after. So, placing `.+` before and after our current expression, we get this:

```
.+/serials/.+
```

Wait a minute. Why are the slashes important? Couldn't we do just as well without them?

Nope. If we wrote the RegEx like this:

```
.+serials.+
```

then it would match things like this:

```
http://www.example.com/skating-serials-rule.html
```

It fits the pattern, after all, being some stuff before and after the word *serials*. Without the delimiting forward slashes, you can end up matching things you don't intend to match. Now, do we need to make those `.+` matches not-greedy? It probably wouldn't hurt. One web site's owner might be fairly careful about what she names things. For example, the owner might use the word *serials* only for that directory name. So there's no way for the RegEx to mess up even if it's greedy. But what if the original owner sells the site and the new owner does not follow that careful naming convention?

Better safe than sorry:

```
.+?/serials/.+?
```

Matching a Variable Name/Value Pair

Some URLs, like product catalogue pages, end like this one with a question mark and a series of variables:

```
http://www.example.com/catalogue/index.php?ItemID=4963
```

A variable is something that can change. In this case it can be one ID or another and identifies the catalogue item you want to display. But say you don't want to display that meaningless number in the Google Analytics results. Say you want to display something meaningful to the average human … like your boss.

First, just as an exercise, let's develop a generalized expression for a name/value pair. The name part of the pair can be letters and numbers, but must always start with a letter. The value, for this example, will always be a four-digit number. Names and values in URLs are always separated by an equals sign. Let's also say that we know there is never more than one variable in the example site's URLs. For this example, let's also try to use escape sequences when we can—it makes for more human-readable RegEx.

OK, we need the first character to be a letter. You can denote that letter as `[a-z]`. Because we want one or more letters at the beginning, we need a plus sign as well, like so:

```
[a-z]+
```

Now, the rest of the name can be letters or numbers. We could write it like `[a-z0-9]` or we could use the escape shorthand and write `\w`, which matches any word character. Now, since we want to allow a number to be included, but do not want to require it, we need an asterisk rather than a plus sign. Make sure not to put a space between the characters inside the square brackets. We don't want any spaces in our *name* tokens! Now we have the following:

```
[a-z]+\w*
```

That's our Name token. We know that the Name token is always followed by an equals sign. So that's next:

```
[a-z]+\w*=
```

Now, we know that the value is always going to be a four-digit number. We can express that in a couple of different ways. You could, if you wanted, repeat `[0123456789]` four times, but that would be long, long, long, long. You can also write `[0-9][0-9][0-9][0-9]`, which is still long. If you like escape sequences you can write four digits as `\d\d\d\d` (note that here we don't need the square brackets). Or, if you are a propeller-head, you can write `\d{4}`, which means "digit, exactly four times." And let's say that we want to capture that four-digit number for use later. We need to put our expression in parentheses for that. For clarity's sake, let's use the `\d\d\d\d` notation:

```
[a-z]+\w*=(\d\d\d\d)
```

Wow! We actually developed something that might be useful.
Not.
There's not much point in being able to match any name/value pair. For filtering, you want to be able to match particular ones. So let's replace that generalized Name pattern with the literal one used in our example URL:

```
ItemID=(\d\d\d\d)
```

But let's also add a bit more complexity. Let's say that the item number is not always going to be four digits. It could be from one to four digits. How would you write that? There are all kinds of complex ways, but you don't need to rack your brain for them because there's one simple way:

```
ItemID=(\d+)
```

Huh!?
The reason we can write it that way is that we know this RegEx will only match digits. A `\d` won't match the `&` that delimits variable pairs on the hind end. And we know that the filter will either reach the end of the URL or there will be an ampersand and the match will complete. And if someday you have more than 9,999 items in your catalogue, your filter isn't going to break when it sees `ItemID=10000` (five digits).

But what if we want to be able to use letters and numbers in our values? You may well want to do that if you need to capture a long, complicated session ID. It's not too difficult. Remember that we decided that `\w*` meant letters and numbers (word characters, really, but let's not be nitpicky). But in this case we don't have to have a letter first. So we need a + instead of a *:

```
ItemID=\w+
```

LEARN MORE ABOUT REGULAR EXPRESSIONS

If you're interested in learning more about Regular Expressions, these resources will give you something to chew on:

Beginning:
   Beginning Regular Expressions, by Andrew Watt. ISBN: 0764574892.

Intermediate:
   Regular Expressions: The Complete Tutorial, by Jan Goyvaerts. ISBN: 1411677609.

Advanced:
   Mastering Regular Expressions, by Jeffery Friedl, ISBN: 0596002890.

Articles on the Internet:
   "Regular Expressions" Wikipedia entry: `http://en.wikipedia.org/wiki/Regular_Expressions`
   "Common Applications of Regular Expressions," by Richard Lowe at 4GuysFromRolla.com:
   `http://www.4guysfromrolla.com/webtech/120400-1.shtml`
   "Understanding Basic Regular Expressions Patterns," by Tom Archer at Developer.com:
   `http://www.developer.com/net/cplus/article.php/3485636`

   Don't worry that these articles are a few years old. The information included in them is still relevant and useful. You can find more resources by Googling "How to +Regular+Expressions."

Again, we don't have to worry about the ampersand or the end-of-line. But what if your site has two different catalogues? Or if a combination of variables has a meaning? Like this:

```
http://www.example.com/index.php?CatID=1A&ItemID=4309
```

Say that Catalogue 1A is Ice Resurfacers, and ItemID 4309 is the Zamboni Deluxe 9000. If you want to capture these two variables separately you could use these two separate Regular Expressions, which we have already developed:

```
CatID=(\w*)
ItemID=(\d+)
```

What if you want to capture them together? You can just *concatenate* them—a fancy propeller-head term that means moosh together.:

```
CatID=([\w]*)\&ItemID=(\d+)
```

Notice that the ampersand (`&`) in this pattern is escaped. In RegEx the `&` is a wildcard meaning "the whole match," so if you intend to use it as a literal (an actual ampersand) you need to escape it.

In Analytics we wouldn't do a compound pattern like this. In the "Advanced Filters" section you'll see what we would do. But first let's take care of the administrivia of creating and assigning filters.

Managing Filters

Setting up filters begins with the Filter Manager, which is located near the bottom of the Analytics Settings dashboard. Click the **Filter Manager** link—not the **Learn More** link, which will take you into the Help system—and you'll be taken to the dashboard shown in Figure 10-1.

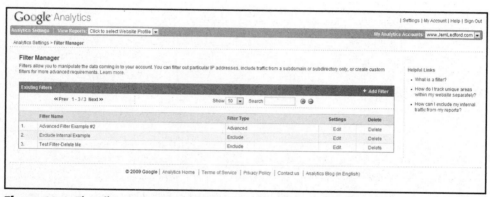

Figure 10-1: The Filter Manager dashboard is where you create, manage, and delete your Analytics filters.

Creating New Filters

To set up a new filter, click the **Add Filter** link in the upper right corner of the Existing Filters box. This opens the Create New Filter page shown in Figure 10-2.

Enter the filter name, filter type, and domain name, if necessary. Then select a web-site profile to apply the filter to and click **Save Changes**.

> **NOTE** If you have multiple domain profiles on your Google Analytics account, you can apply the same filter to all the domains (or any number of them) at one time. For each domain you want the filter applied to, highlight the domain name in the Available Website Profiles menu and click Add. The domain will be moved to the Selected Website Profiles menu. Complete the filter setup, and the filter will be applied to all selected domains.

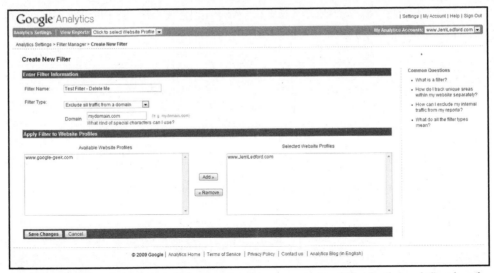

Figure 10-2: The Create New Filter page is where you start creating both predefined and custom filters.

You'll be returned to the Filter Manager Dashboard, and as Figure 10-3 shows, your new filter will appear in the Existing Filters box.

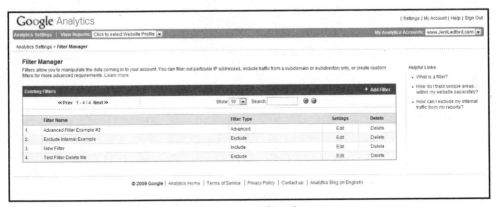

Figure 10-3: New filters appear in the Existing Filters box.

For example, if you want to create a filter to exclude the internal traffic from your network because your homepage is set to the front page of your web site, from the Filter Manager you would select **Add Filter**. Now, as shown in

Figure 10-4, enter a filter name; for the purpose of this example, we'll use the name Exclude Internal Example.

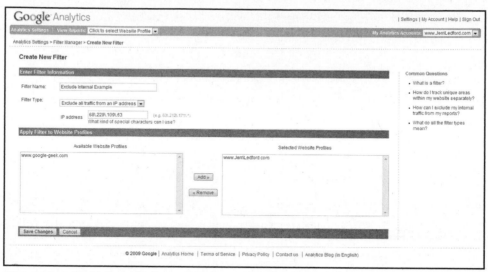

Figure 10-4: Exclude traffic from your own IP like this.

Next, go to **Filter Type** and select **Exclude all traffic from an IP address**. When you select this option the IP Address field will automatically show a default IP address. This is an example address and should be changed. Replace the address with your own IP address. Don't forget, this is RegEx: make sure to escape the periods in your IP address.

Finally, select the web-site profile to which you want to apply the filter and click **Add** and then **Save Changes**.

Now you have set up your first filter to exclude any internal traffic to the web site that you're measuring.

NOTE You can find your IP address by going to www.WhatIsMyIP.com. But remember that if you're on a dialup connection your IP can change every time you dial in. In that case you will probably want to contact your ISP and ask them what range of IP addresses your dialup number uses. Then create a Regular Expression that will match that range. You'll lose some visitors who might happen to use the same dialup that you do, but there's nothing that can be done about that. If you're on DSL or a cable modem, it will probably change every two to six months. So if you filter your own traffic out you should make a point of checking your IP address at least quarterly.

There's one more thing you need to understand about filters, and that's the order in which they are applied. Many people have trouble with Google Analytics's filters because they don't realize that the filters you apply to a website profile are applied in the order in which they are set.

If you happen to have an exclude filter set as the very first filter, only what remains after the filter action will be affected by the next filter in the list. Unfortunately, these sorts of effects are most often found by trial and error, as in "Why the heck isn't such-and-such data showing up?" Duh … it's excluded. This is where you conk yourself on the head and reorder the filters. This is easy enough. From your Analytics Settings page, click **Edit** in the same row as the web-site profile for which you want to change the ordering of the filters.

On the Profile Settings page, navigate down to the Filters Applied to Profile box and click the **Assign Filter Order** link, as shown in Figure 10-5.

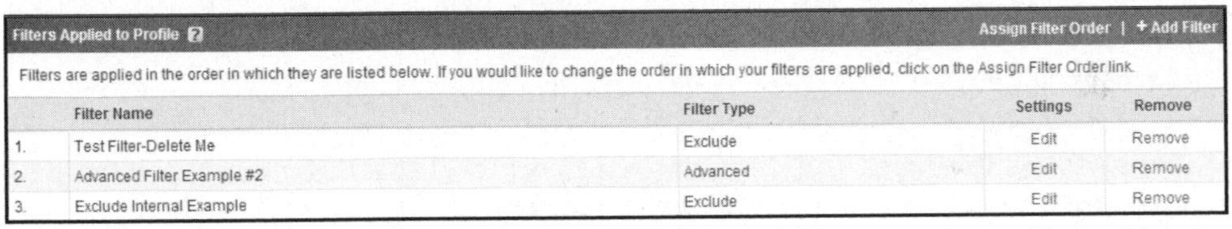

Figure 10-5: In the site profile you can see the order in which filters are applied to data.

You are taken to a page like the one in Figure 10-6. Highlight the filter you want to move and then click the **Move up** or **Move down** button to rearrange your filters into the order in which you want them to be accessed.

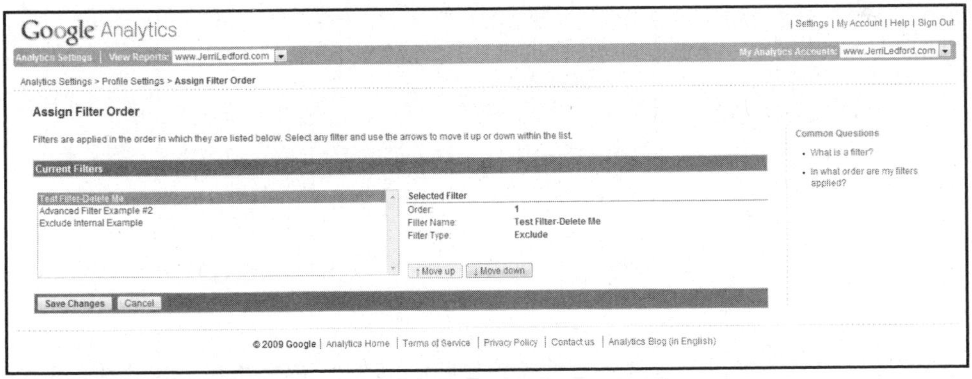

Figure 10-6: Rearrange the order in which filters are accessed.

FILTER VALUES IN PREDEFINED FILTERS

If you're using the filters that Google Analytics already has predefined, there are a few fields that you might want to know a little more about. Here's a quick list of the fields you might encounter and how you can use them:

Domain: This enables you to determine a complete domain or a portion of a domain that you want to filter. So if you want to keep your brother-in-law's traffic out of your stats (because you share a domain) you could set up your filter to exclude his subdomain (`sub.domain.com`) by using the expression `sub\.`

IP Address: You can filter an IP address or a range of IP addresses using Regular Expressions to tell Google what to look for.

To filter a single IP address, like your own, enter the IP address like this: `192\.125\.1\.1`.

To filter a range of addresses (as you would if you worked in an office with multiple computers, each with its own IP, such as `192.125.1.1` to `192.125.1.25`) you would use the expression `192\.125\.1\.[1-9]|1 [0-9]|2[0-5]`.

To filter two or more addresses, which you might need to do if you have two separate local area networks, use a | symbol between the addresses. This technique is called *alternation* and the vertical bar is read as "or." If you want to match `192.168.0.1` or `10.0.0.1`, the expression is `192\.125\.1\.1|10\.0\.0\.1` and is read `192.125.1.1` or `10.0.0.1`.

Subdirectory: Again, you can use Regular Expressions to include (or exclude) the subdirectory of a site. So if you wanted to include a specific subdirectory (and exclude everything else), the expression that you would use is `subdirectory/` (where you replace the word *subdirectory* with the name of the subdirectory you want to include).

Translating RegEx into English can be confusing, even for experienced users. This is not to say that it's too hard for us mortals. Rather, if you find RegEx tough going, don't feel dumb, because you're in good company. RegEx is a cryptic language—and maybe it's new to you. That makes it seem even harder than it really is. The more you use Regular Expressions, the more it will make sense. Until you're comfortable with the language, you may need to refer to the opening portions of this chapter to help you figure out how to write the Regular Expressions you'll use in your filters.

Custom Filters

When you're creating a new filter, one option you have is to create a custom filter. When you select the **Custom filter** option, as shown in Figure 10-7, the menu for custom filters expands to show you additional options for that filter.

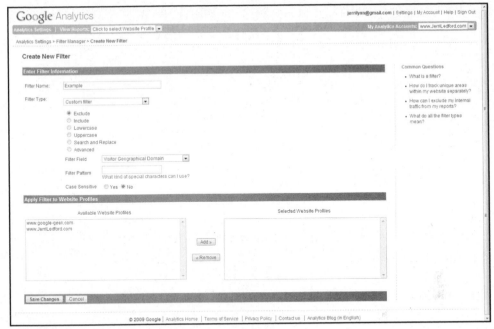

Figure 10-7: Additional options on the custom-filter menu

These custom filters can be used to dig deeper into the statistics that Google Analytics collects. Use them to filter for specific activities, such as by including only a subset of traffic or excluding a select type of visitor. You can also perform search-and-replace functions and rely on a table function to clarify the data returned. Let's look more closely at each of those types of filters.

Include and Exclude Filters

Include and exclude filters are just what they appear to be—filters that include or exclude specific data. But the custom include and exclude filters go beyond simply filtering web-site domains and IP addresses. With these filters you can choose to include or exclude specific fields or capabilities. If you don't want to know about any of the users hitting your site who have Java capabilities installed, you can choose to exclude them. Or maybe you want to include only the users who have Java capabilities. In that case all the visits from users who don't have Java capabilities will be discarded, and you'll see information only from those who do.

Here's what you need to remember:

- **Include filters** include only the data that matches the inclusion pattern and discard everything else.

- **Exclude filters** exclude only the data that matches the exclusion pattern and include everything else.

The reason it matters? Multiple include and exclude filters can result in no traffic at all. Say you want data only from users who use IE7 with Java turned off. So you include only the data from people with Java turned off. Then you exclude all the people running all browsers other than IE7. What if there are no users among your visitors running IE with Java turned off? Right. No data.

Think of it this way. When you decide to buy a car, you go to the lot and first choose a model that you like. That choice (which you could call an include filter because you want to include only cars of that specific model) cuts your options down by at least half and probably more.

Then you decide that you want this specific model only in blue. You've added another include filter that reduces your number of choices again.

Your last decision is that you don't want a standard transmission. Now you've added an exclude filter and the result is that there might not be any cars on the lot you can choose from. Include and exclude patterns work the same way to narrow your results.

Search-and-Replace Filters

Ever look at something and have no clue why you're looking at it? Chances are, if you were looking at it from a different perspective you'd understand it immediately. Let's say you're selling Jet Skis, snowboards, and surfboards through your web site. Each category of items appears on a single dynamic page. Which page you get is determined by the category ID tag on the end of the URL: 1000 for surfboards, 2000 for Jet Skis, and 3000 for snowboards. When you look at the metrics you'll need to remember what those numbers mean, because Analytics will show your results by the category number. If you have more than three categories—whoa, baby! Unless you have a photographic memory, learning all the category ID numbers could take forever.

On the other hand, if you can convert those numbers to readable, easy-to-understand text on your reports, your hair might not go gray for another month or so.

That's what a search-and-replace filter does. This nifty tool lets you replace a matched expression with a different string or group of numbers or text in order to turn mundane, hard-to-recognize results into something immediately understandable. You can use the search-and-replace filter to change those mundane category IDs to something that has meaning. Like this:

Go to Analytics Settings ➾ **Filter Manager** ➾ **Add Filter** and then enter a filter name. For this example we're using Search & Replace Example. From the drop-down menu select **Custom Filter** and then click the radio button beside **Search and Replace**.

A new information section that has to this point remained hidden (Google doesn't want to scare you with confusing stuff before it's necessary) appears. In the Filter field, select **Request URI**.

Now, for Search String, type **/docs/document.cgi?id=1000**. (This is just for the example, not for your actual site. For your site you would replace this information with the actual part of the URL that you want to find.) Then, for Replace String, type the information you want to replace the search string with. Let's use **surfboards**.

Now you can select whether you want to make this filter case-sensitive. In most cases you do not want case-sensitive searches. For now, leave it alone.

At this point your filter should look like the one pictured in Figure 10-8. All that's left is to select the web site you want the filter to apply to and click **Save Changes.**

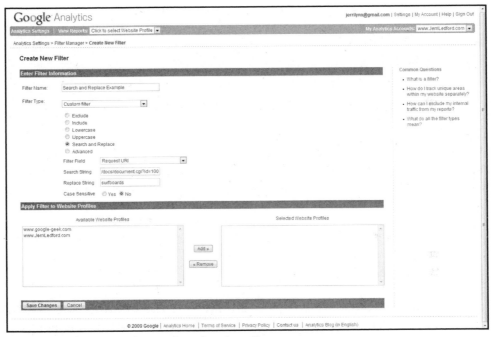

Figure 10-8: An example search-and-replace filter

Now you're seeing the meaningful label surfboards instead of ID=1000, which really means something only to your web server. You won't have to wonder if your customers are looking at surfboards. The answer will be right in front of you in an easy-to-read format.

Lookup Table Filters

NOTE At the time of this writing, Lookup Table functions are disabled in Google Analytics. You can use existing lookup tables, but Google is not installing new ones. We've included information on lookup tables in this chapter so that when they go live again, you can use them.

But what if you have more than three generic items in your catalogue? What if you have a hundred models of surfboards and 55 different Jet Skis and hundreds of snowboards? You're not going to want to enter a different filter for each model, but you might want to be able to break down your metrics by model as well as by general category.

Like search-and-replace filters, lookup table filters substitute something understandable for the incomprehensible numbers on the ends of your URLs. But there are some differences. Let's look at the surfboards again. Say your product IDs are set up like this: `http://www.supersurf1ng.com/catalog.php?id=1691` (where the number represents the specific product ID of a particular model of surfboard). The lookup table filter takes the product ID and compares it against a big list of possible values and their corresponding substitutes. When it finds the one that matches, the filter does the replacement with the value that corresponds to the value you looked up. This is like search-and-replace with a range of possible finds and replacements. And this requires Google's help.

To begin using a lookup table, the first thing you need to do is create a spreadsheet saved as a *tab-delimited plain text file* with the format discussed in the following paragraphs.

In cell A1, type **# Field**. In cell B1, type **request stem**. Now, in column 1, list all the possibilities for your product ID. In column B, list the corresponding replacement value for each product ID. For example, our surf shop's spreadsheet looks like Figure 10-9.

	A	B
1	# Field	request stem
2	1691	Super Surfer
3	2010	Jet Ski Max 2010
4	3055	Awesome Fun Snowboard D23

Figure 10-9: The basis of a lookup table filter

Once your spreadsheet is complete, save it as a tab-delimited plain-text file with the extension .lt for lookup table. If you're using Excel you'll probably receive a program prompt that tells you that you can save only the active sheet, not the whole workbook. This is exactly what you want to have happen, so click **OK.**

NOTE If you run into problems with your file being named something other than .lt (.lt.xls, for example) you may need to disable the "Hide Extensions of known file types" option. You'll find this in the Control Panel under the **Folders** option.

Now you have to send the sheet to the folks over at Google for processing. Attach the file to an e-mail to `analytics-support@google.com`. And because a human will be reading your message, make sure you specify which account and web-site profile you want the table applied to. Then wait. It could take a few days for the team at Google to get you fixed up, so be patient. When it does get you ready to roll, you need to create an advanced filter to put that file to use. You'll learn how to do that in the next section.

Advanced Filters

Advanced filters are where things get hinky because creating one isn't as easy as picking two options from a list and then clicking OK. You actually have to work a little to put an advanced filter into place. The payoff is that you can create filters that meet your specific needs, including customized tracking for advertising campaigns and specific measurements.

Creating Advanced Filters

Now that you understand just enough about the other types of filters to be dangerous, it's time to learn how to create advanced filters. Buckle up. It's going to be an interesting ride.

Step back just a bit and remember where we were with the lookup table filters. We're going to continue that example by using the surfboard information to create an advanced filter.

You start creating an advanced filter just as you would start creating any other type. Go to Analytics Settings ➪ **Filter Manager** ➪ **Add Filter**. The Create New Filter page appears. Enter a name for your filter (for this example I'm using Advanced Filter Example); then, from the **Filter Type** drop-down menu, select **Custom filter**, as shown in Figure 10-10.

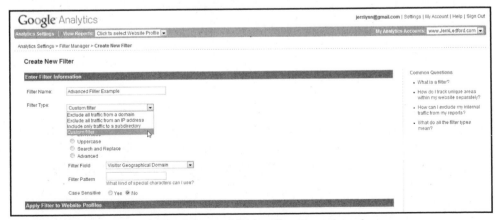

Figure 10-10: The custom filter is located in the Filter Type drop-down menu.

The custom filter menu expands to show several options. Select the radio button next to the **Advanced** option, as shown in Figure 10-11, and the advanced filter fields appear on the page.

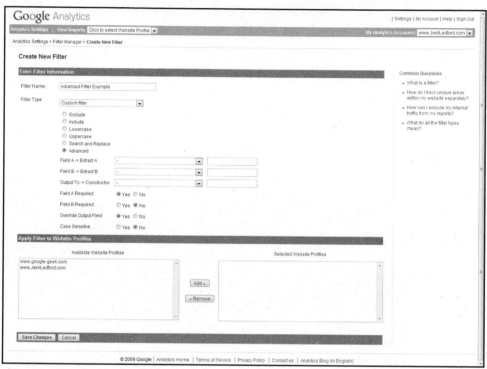

Figure 10-11: Advanced filters use a combination of input data and RegEx to produce the output.

What you'll see next looks scary. Don't panic. Advanced filters have three fields that you need to understand. Each field has two parts: a data source (Field A, Field B) or destination (Output To) and a Regular Expression (Extract A, Extract B, and Constructor). Field A and Field B and the associated Extract A and Extract B are inputs. You're going to capture information in those inputs. Output To is exactly what it says—the data you're going to change. The Constructor uses Regular Expressions to show what changes you want made to the Output To data, based on the inputs from Extract A and Extract B.

Sorted that out yet? Good. Let's do an example.

Say that all your surfboards have IDs in the 1000s. And miracle of miracles, you've sold and/or discontinued so many surfboards that you have more than a thousand surfboard IDs. Now you want to have the surfboard IDs be in the 10000s, with the first thousand reserved for the legacy boards. But you want only to count them that way; you don't want to have to change the numbers in your catalogue.

NOTE This may not be the most realistic of examples, but it's a good one for showing how advanced filters work. In the next section we give some real-life examples. Never fear.

In order to capture the fields you need to enter two pieces of information. The first is the source of the data you want to capture. You select this from the drop-down menu shown in Figure 10-12. Field A, Field B, and Output To all use the same menu.

Figure 10-12: You can cull your fields from many possible sources.

NOTE To see what all the filter fields represent, search Google Analytics Help for "filter fields represent."

For Field A select Request URI. This is the part of the URL of the incoming page after the hostname—the `www.your-domain-here.com`. For this example, that is `catalog.php?id=1691`. We'll also assume that we know all the IDs are going to be four-digit numbers. Now you need to enter a Regular Expression in the Extract A textbox to the right of the Request URI menu line. The one we developed earlier in the chapter for a four-digit number was as follows:

```
id=(\d\d\d\d)
```

But that captures all the digits in one clump, and it captures all possible four-digit IDs. You want only IDs that begin with the digit 1 and you want to capture only the last three digits. So you modify that RegEx to this:

```
id=1(\d\d\d)
```

Enter that in the Extract A field. Remember that the parentheses in the Regular Expression mean we're capturing the part of the source data that matches the pattern we've described. That's the connection between Extract A and the RegEx in the parentheses. Whatever part of the RegEx you put in parentheses will be what Extract A captures.

We are not going to use Field B for this example, so leave the data source as -.

Now for the output. First you have to choose what data you're modifying. Choose **Request URI** from the Output To menu. Next, let's develop the RegEx, which will describe the changes we want made. What are we changing? Right, the ID. So the first part of the RegEx is this:

```
id=
```

We want to go from a four-digit number beginning with 1 to a five-digit number beginning with 10 (from 1000s to 10000s). So you want to specify the first two digits as a literal 10:

```
id=10
```

Here's the meat of the change. We've captured the three digits after the 1 in the original ID. We need to refer to them in the Constructor. How? Easy. There's only one set of parentheses in the pattern for Field A, so the reference is $A1. (Most propeller-heads read $ as "string" as in "string A one."). So now we need the digits we saved from Extract A:

```
id=10$A1
```

You come out with the filter shown in Figure 10-13.

How should this work in practice? Let's say our ID is 1691. The pattern in Extract A matches 691 and saves it in $A1. Then the Constructor builds id=10691.

Let's do another. Say the ID is 2353. What happens?

You're right! Nothing happens. Why not? Because id=1(\d\d\d) won't match 2354 at all.

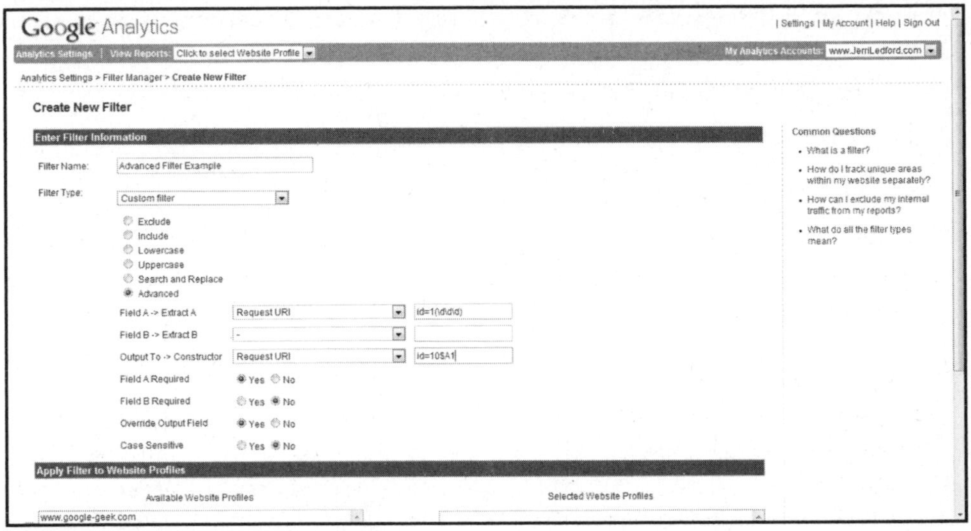

Figure 10-13: Your nearly finished filter.

Now that we have some confidence that our RegEx is right and we've set the filter up correctly, we can move on to the other options. If you're using only one field, of course you want to require that the data you're trying to access and match in that field be present. No data and the filter won't apply to that page view. So in this example we want to click **Yes** for Field A Required and **No** for Field B Required. In this example the ID output field already exists; we want to override what is already there with our new value, so we click **Yes** for Override Output Field. We want the filter to match ID, id, Id and iD, so we click **No** for Case Sensitive. At the bottom of the page you can select which profiles will use the filter and then click **Finish**.

Now let's extend this example a little bit. We have our same four-digit numbers, but let's say that in addition to the product ID (itemID) we also have a category ID (catID), like this: catalog.php?itemID=1691A&catID=2900. Note that the itemID is now four digits and a capital letter and the catID is just four digits. Now, you want to append the first two digits of the catID to the end of the itemID with a hyphen between them, and you want to take the letter on the end of the itemID and put it on the front. If there's no category ID in the URI, don't worry about it.

We need to make a couple of changes to the filter. First, choose Request URI for all three sources. Next, the RegEx for the itemID needs to change. It's itemID instead of just ID. And we want to capture the digits and the letter separately, so we need two sets of parentheses. With the modifications, it looks like the following:

```
itemID=(\d\d\d\d)([A-Z])
```

We'll also need to use Field B and Extract B in this example to capture the category information. We need to capture the first two digits; they'll need parentheses around them in the RegEx. The pattern for Extract B looks like this:

```
catID=(\d\d)\d\d
```

With those two things in place, we can work on the output. We want to modify the `itemID:` and add the letter to the front, and add the partial category ID, if it exists, to the back. Now, note that we have two captures from Extract A. The four-digit number is `$A1` and the letter is `$A2`.

> **NOTE** When you capture multiple parts of a Regular Expression (by using several sets of parentheses) the notation is $ followed by A for Field A or B for Field B, and then a number: 1 for the first set of parentheses, 2 for the second set, 3 for the third, and so on. The first match in Extract A is $A1. The second match in Extract A is $A2. The first match in Extract B is $B1. The second match in Extract B is $B2. And so on.

We'll have `itemID=` plus the second match from Extract A (the capital letter), plus the first match from Extract A (the four-digit number), plus a dash, plus the first match from Extract B (the first two digits of the `catID`). That looks like this:

```
itemID=$A2$A1-$B1
```

Just a little bit more and we'll be done. Field A is required, but Field B is not. So click **Yes** for Field A Required and **No** for Field B Required, **Yes** for Override Output Field and **No** for Case Sensitive. The filter will come out looking very much like Figure 10-14.

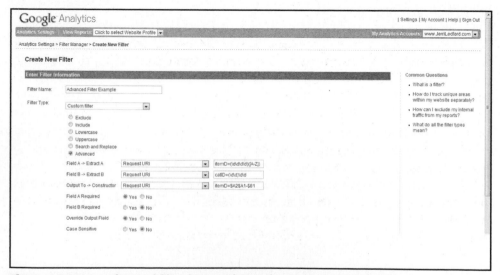

Figure 10-14: An advanced filter for an advanced user (congratulations)!

Let's look at some boundary conditions. These are situations in which the filter might fail—problem areas. For example, what will happen if there is no `catID`? It's not required, so the filter won't run screaming from the room. Here's an example:

```
catalog.php?itemID=1234B
```

There's no `catID`. So there also won't be any `$B1`. The Constructor will build `itemID=B1234-` and go no further. In the real world a situation like this may or may not be a bad thing. You might want to require that there be a Field B, or you might just cope with the fact that some `itemID`s might end up with a dash and no partial `catID`.

Another boundary condition: What if there is no `itemID`? Well, Field A is required. The filter is going to be bypassed because it will not apply. This is only a problem if you miss counting visits because of it.

Now that we've mastered the basics of advanced filters—is that ever a contradiction in terms!—let's look at some real-life uses for them with examples based on real filters used by real businesses.

Improve Your SEO/CPC Reporting with Filters

One thing drives many web-site owners wild when they look at their Analytics reports: the results of search engine optimization (SEO) efforts and AdWords sometimes muddy the waters so much that you can't see what each is doing alone. There's a way to deal with this. Simply create one profile that sees only organic search engine traffic from the biggies and another that only sees *cost per click* (CPC) traffic. To do this you of course need to filter the data coming in.

Organic Traffic Only

First, create a new profile for your web site, then go to **Analytics Settings** ⇨ **Profile Settings** ⇨ **Add Filter to Profile**. Name your new filter Organic SE Traffic Only. Choose "Custom filter" for the filter type and click the **Include** radio button. Now, for Filter Field choose Campaign Source and for Filter Pattern simply type **google|yahoo|msn|aol**, as shown in Figure 10-15.

This will include all your organic traffic from all search engines, but no direct traffic and no referrals from old domain names. Now that we have all the search engine traffic in, we want to get rid of the CPC traffic.

Create a new filter. Name it CPC Traffic Out. Set your filter type to "Custom filter" and click the **Exclude** radio button. Choose **Campaign Medium** from the **Filter Field** drop-down and enter **cpc** as your **Filter Pattern**, as shown in Figure 10-16. This filter will filter out Google AdWords traffic.

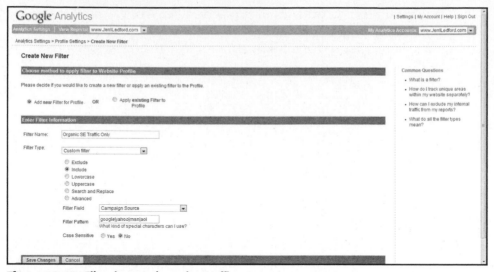

Figure 10-15: Filter in search engine traffic.

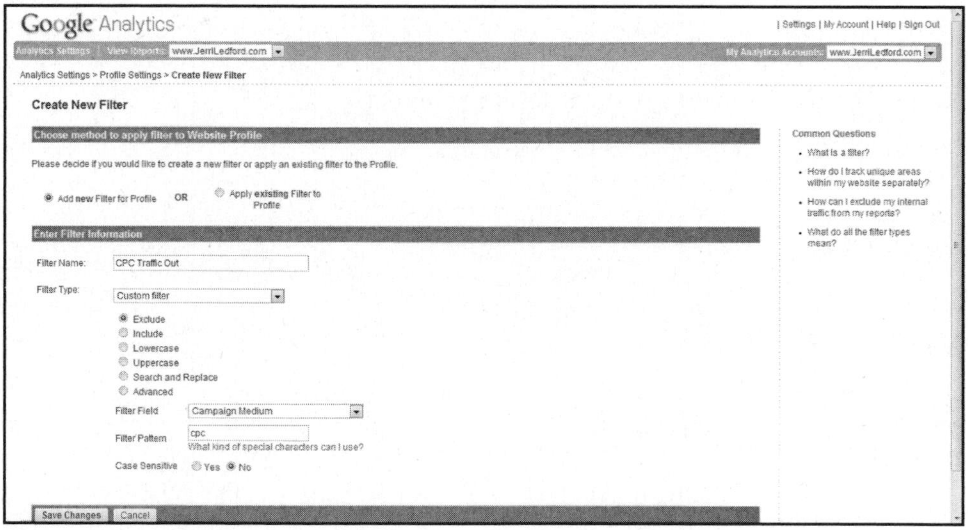

Figure 10-16: Filter out CPC traffic.

NOTE If you do CPC advertising with Yahoo!, MSN, or AOL, they may have different ways of denoting their CPC campaigns, which you will also have to filter out. You may do this in a separate filter or by using a vertical bar in your pattern, as we did earlier with the search engine names.

If you want only CPC traffic, your Include filter would have **Campaign Medium** as its Filter field, and the filter pattern would again be **cpc** alternated with whatever campaign markers your other CPC advertising providers use. Remember that you can't run these two filters in the same profile! You'll filter out all your traffic.

As you can see, filters have real-world uses for determining what traffic from your site comes from what source, how valuable it is, and numerous other facts that you might want to know. Creating a custom or advanced filter might not be the easiest thing you've ever done, though. Fortunately, lots of people who participate in Google Analytics community forums are happy to share the filters they've developed, so if you can't figure something out, you can ask questions in one of these forums (like the Google Analytics group on Google Groups). If you still can't figure it out, there are always authorized Google Analytics Consultants who can help you out.

Editing and Deleting Filters

Filters don't run off to Tahiti to hang out under palm trees and slurp umbrella drinks. But you may find now and then that they need a vacation—maybe a permanent one. So you need to know how to change or delete them. (And Tahiti could still be a problem if the boss spent a week there and came home with some grand ideas that require different analytics.)

Before the tropical high wears off, change your filters and then ask for a big raise. We can't help you with the raise, but we can tell you that you change or delete filters by clicking the **Edit** or **Delete** links in the Existing Filters box.

Editing will take you to the same page you saw when you set up the filter, and then you can change anything about the filter that you want (or need) to change. Just click the **Finish** button when you're done and the changes will automatically take effect.

> **NOTE** If you need to keep a filter around but don't want it to be applied anymore, edit the Apply Filter to Website Profiles list so that it's not applied to any profiles. Then you can keep the filter but not have it mucking with your data anywhere.

When you select the option to delete a filter, you are prompted to confirm that you truly do want to delete it, as shown in Figure 10-17. By now you should be familiar with this routine. The confirmation is there for your protection, so double-check everything and then click **OK**, and the record is deleted.

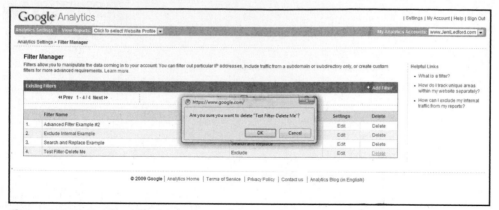

Figure 10-17: Confirm that you want to delete the selected filter.

The Power of Filters

What you can do with filters is limited only by your ability to create them. If you're not familiar with Regular Expressions, it is well worth your time to learn more. Like any new language RegEx can be confusing in the beginning, but as you become familiar with how the wildcards work it will get easier to create Regular Expressions for your advanced filters. Before you know it you'll be filtering with the best. Don't worry: those monkeys in the back room banging away at keyboards won't care that you're filtering them out as long as you keep them supplied with bananas.

CHAPTER 11

Setting Goals

What's the point of tracking web-site metrics if you don't have some reason for tracking them? It's like jumping on the interstate in your super-efficient car with no particular destination in mind. You've got the vehicle to get somewhere, and the road to follow—and you're not doing this for the joy of travel. But without a destination, how will you know if you're headed in the right direction?

That's where goals come in. They're the "where you're going" of collecting user data. Why do you want to know how many users dropped off your e-commerce web site during the checkout process or how many people signed up for your newsletter? Because knowing will help you decide if you've reached your goal of providing an easy, effective way for users to accomplish whatever goal it is they (and you) have in mind.

Google Analytics actually has a capability that enables you to decide where you want to go and then gather data to show how fast you're going, how far you've gone, and whether you're getting there at all. You can add goals to web-site profiles so you can track your progress toward those goals.

Before we get any further into the specifics of Google Analytics' goal capabilities, let's run through some of the management-speak you'll encounter in this chapter. The keywords are *objectives*, *goals*, and *specifics*.

- **Objectives:** An objective is your big picture, or what you want the big picture to look like when you're finished. An objective for a company that imports and sells Russian nesting dolls might be to sell more dolls and make piles of money. It's a long-term outlook.

- **Goals:** If objectives are long-term aims, goals are shorter-term aims. What has to happen for you to sell more nesting dolls? And specifically, what do you want to accomplish with Google Analytics? Your goal could be to increase sales by 20 percent and to do it using Google Analytics.

- **Specifics:** Now you're getting to the heart of what you want to accomplish, both in the short term and in the long term. Specifics are the how—the action steps—of goal-setting. A good set of specifics for the nesting-doll goal would be to use Google Analytics to find the most efficient way to funnel traffic to a sales confirmation page (the "Thank you for placing your order" page that appears after an order has been approved), to reach a sales goal within six months, and to generate proof of your efforts and successes in the form of reports to get the boss off your back.

Now, back to an important question: If you don't have goals is there still a reason to have analytics? The answer is yes—but be aware that without goals you'll get a lot less out of your analytics. They won't be as focused, which means they won't be as valuable. And (I think we've said this before) analytics is all about gaining as much value as you can from your web-site traffic, right?

Understanding Goal-Setting

Pop quiz: What's a frequent response to the question, "Why do we need this or that technology, application, or program?"

Give up? Try "Because it's the best." To which the typical reaction is to scratch your head and keep your mouth shut because you don't want to look like a complete idiot to the obvious genius trying to explain that having the best means the tech gods smile on you, revenues flow from the heavens, and the door on the corner office automatically opens.

Yeah, right.

Every technology, application, or program should have a purpose to fill: a goal to reach that leads to the big-picture objective. If you're putting a firewall in place, the purpose (or goal) of that firewall is to keep the wrong sort of people off your network. And if you want to track analytics, what you track will be determined by the business problem that you're trying to solve with your web site.

Of course, this whole theory assumes that you have taken the time to develop a web site for a purpose. Are you selling a product, collecting customer information for marketing purposes, or trying to recruit the next downline star for your network marketing group? You need a goal. Simply saying the business problem is the goal isn't enough. Yes, you want to sell more of your Russian nesting dolls. But that's your objective, and alone it isn't enough to drive business or increase sales. And trying to track that goal will have you pulling your hair out by the roots.

What you need is a goal or set of goals that specifically tracks the behavior that leads to the sale of the nesting dolls. So the goal we mentioned earlier—to increase sales by 20 percent and do it using Google Analytics—is more measurable than a goal of simply selling more nesting dolls.

That's an important point: to be effective you need a goal you can measure or track. With that goal in mind you can develop a set of *metrics*, or specifics, that shows how visitors navigate through the site to complete the sale. The information returned by these metrics will illustrate what works and what doesn't, making it easier for you to alter your marketing campaign or customer approach to achieve your goal.

For example, to the real-estate giant RE/MAX, driving traffic to the RE/MAX web site seemed like a good goal. A study conducted by the National Association of Realtors in 2004 found that nearly three-quarters of all home buyers begin their search for a new home online.

But simply driving traffic online isn't enough. It's like herding cattle in the direction they're already going. You sit in the saddle and let the horse follow the cows while you watch the scenery.

RE/MAX needed to do more than just drive traffic to its web site; it needed to turn online traffic into sales—that is, make conversions. Kristi Graning, senior vice president of IT and e-business for RE/MAX, said that instead of just pushing users to the Web and tracking how many visitors the site had, the company created a goal to help people find a house and select an agent, which follows the general objective of increasing sales.

To reach the goal, RE/MAX used Google Analytics to learn more about why people were visiting the RE/MAX web site, where they were coming from when they visited the site, and how they behaved while on the site.

Those analytics were then turned into a strategy—the specifics—to make it easier for people to find houses and select agents. Then RE/MAX redesigned its web site to better suit visitors' property-search behaviors, to capture lead information that was then passed to agents, and to track the lead-to-sale-conversion rate.

RE/MAX set a goal it could act on and then went to work using Google Analytics to create strategies to reach that goal.

Why Set Goals?

There's some consensus in the business world that those who set goals tend to get further than those who do not. Look around your organization, circle of friends, or family group. How many of the people there have solid goals and can voice those goals in a clear, understandable way?

Now consider where those people are in comparison to Cousin Danny, who really doesn't seem to have any goal in life, or colleague Jenny, who's very happy with her current position in your company. Contrast that with your manager, Amy, who always knows where she's going and what she wants to do, or your dad who retired at 55 after a lifetime of careful saving. Do the people with goals accomplish more than the people without goals? You bet they do!

Setting analytics goals works the same way. If you have a clear, reachable goal in line with your overall objective, there's a better chance you'll take action to achieve that goal. It's the difference between passive and active. If you're passive, the world happens to you. If you're active, you make the world happen.

Setting goals is the precursor to action. You set a goal with an overall objective in mind. Then you can choose specifics that will make things happen so you reach that goal.

Choosing Which Goals To Set

Here's where the waters start to muddy just a bit. How do you know what goals to set? No worries. It's easy. There's this glass jar with the word GOALS painted on the front. Someone in the office has it. Just reach in and pull one out.

Okay, maybe that won't work. But it still seems to be some people's approach. They grab at thin air and hope that something will magically appear for them to latch on to. Instead, try asking yourself this question: What business am I really in?

It's not fate, magic, or divine intervention that makes a goal great. It takes a solid understanding of your business—or your objective—and how your web presence fits in to that larger picture. If your business is management training, how will your web site improve that business? Maybe you want to expand training beyond your local area by offering online classes to management wannabes still living in their parents' basements. You could also use your web site to gather sales leads by enticing potential management trainees (or even corporations that might need your services) to sign up for a monthly newsletter.

What you need to accomplish with your web site is what should drive your goals in Google Analytics. A good goal for your management training business might be to increase sales by providing training services that are more accessible to individuals and companies in the region (or the US or the world).

That goal applies to the actions your management training company takes with your web site.

Ultimately, you determine your analytics goals by your specific situation and needs. A goal that puts you on a path toward fabulous results might put a similar company on a path toward certain doom. So examine your business. Determine what *your* needs are. And then create goals that help you fill those needs.

One company that truly understands the business it's in is the Warren Featherbone company. Back in the 1800s Warren Featherbone made corset stays—those horrid, rigid pieces of hard material that ensured a woman couldn't slouch or bend at the waist. Obviously, corset stays went out of style. So in the 1920s Warren Featherbone got into bias tape. That's a sewing notion that simplifies making secure hems on fabric that frays.

Over time, however, customers' needs changed again. No longer did customers have time to sew all the garments their families wore. There were even— gasp—women who couldn't sew!

Because the Warren Featherbone company knows what business it's in—the fabric and clothing business—it shifted gears yet again to meet the needs of the customer. Until recently Warren Featherbone sold kids' clothing under the Alexis label. These days the company focuses on other industries such as health care and education.

Warren Featherbone completely understood its business, which led to a clear understanding of its objectives and the survival of the business—something that's nearly unheard of today—all because it's a company that can create and achieve effective goals.

Now, let's see if we can help you do the same thing.

Monetizing Goals

It's one thing to set up your thank-you page as a goal, and quite another thing to know what reaching it is worth. For an e-commerce site, the value of a goal is fairly easy—it's the value of the transaction. For an e-commerce site, the value of a page of content can be figured using sales that result from that page. But for a content site, it's not so apparent what the value of a particular page of content is, or how much a new subscriber to the mailing list is worth.

OVERWHELMED? OR IS THIS ALL TOO SIMPLISTIC?

At this point some readers are going to be completely overwhelmed by the sheer volume of skills they're being expected to master. That's okay. Some of this stuff *is* rocket science. Don't feel dumb if you're not getting it. Meanwhile, other readers may be saying, "This stuff is too simple, I really need XYZ, why aren't those stupid authors giving it to me?! My company needs professional-level analytics help, not this dumb book."

Both kinds of readers need professional intervention, which you get from companies such as MoreVisibility (www.morevisibility.com). MoreVisibility offers high-end services to companies that need more than a how-to book can provide, and it also helps out mom-and-pop web sites that are up RegEx Creek without a paddle.

Content-Site Goals

The content-site issues aren't as intractable as they first seem, but getting a goal value does require some voodoo and wand-waving. Your content has to lead to some monetary gain. It may not be immediately apparent what the gain is.

For a site where the primary purpose is marketing, there's a sale down the line. That sale is worth something and you probably have some information about how many of your leads turn into sales. For a publication, where the content *is* the product, the monetary gain involved is usually revenue from advertising. You have information on returning visitors and on page views per visitor, and you probably know what your average (or even specific) ad revenue from a page is.

Goal Value of a Sales Lead

The easy case is when your content collects leads that end in an offline sale. Let's say, for example, that you sell consulting services. Your average sale is $2,300. And you know that you get one sale for every 23 leads. You've set up a goal that is similar to the one in Figure 11-1. (Don't worry that you don't know how to do this yet, we're going to show you later in this chapter. For now, this is just an example.)

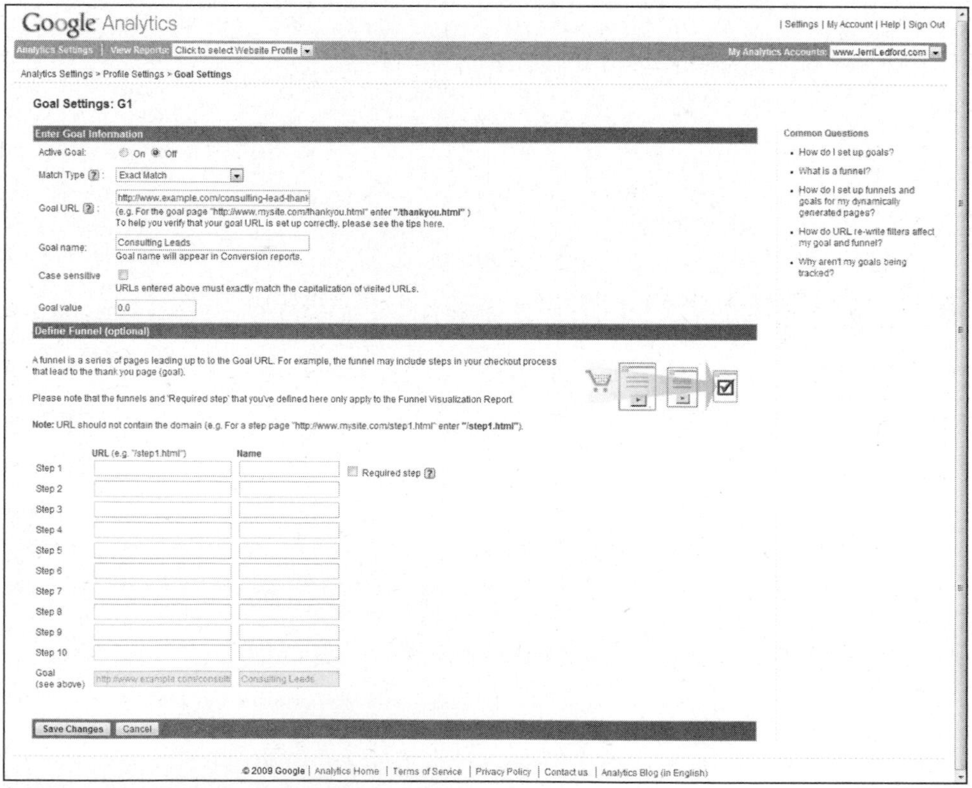

Figure 11-1: A simple lead-acquisition goal

There's no funnel to define, so you can leave that blank. You'll want to choose the right kind of match for the structure of your individual site's URL. The calculation for the goal value is fairly simple: Average Sale/No. of leads = $2,300/23 = $100.

NOTE Funnels are the paths that users take to reach whatever goal you have determined. You'll learn more about funnels in Chapter 12, "Funneling Visitors to Their Destination."

So each time you get a lead, it's worth $100. That's your goal value, as shown in Figure 11-2.

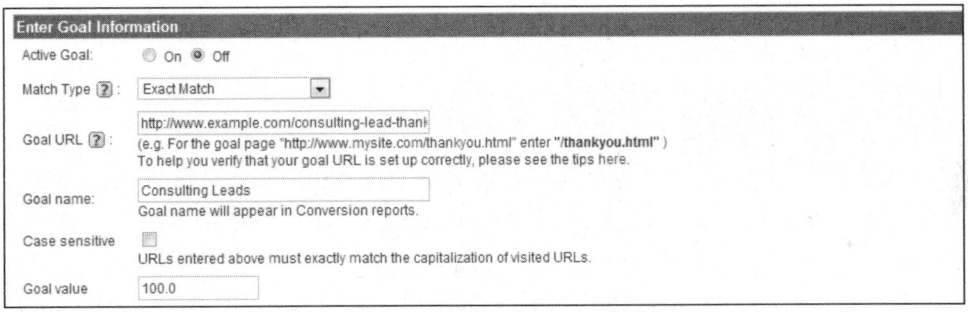

Figure 11-2: The goal value for each lead goes in the Goal Value field.

NOTE You can do a similar calculation even if your numbers are not as neat as the ones in the preceding example. For instance, if you're getting three sales for every 10 leads, that's one sale for every 3.33 leads. Just divide your $2,300 by 3.33 and you'll see that each lead is worth about $690.

Now, when you acquire a lead because the visitor made it to the goal page, the financial data will flow into your reports. If you have AdWords integrated or you track other advertising campaigns, those costs will go into reports and you will begin to see ROI (return on investment) calculated. (Chapter 13 is all about integrating your AdWords account with your Google Analytics account.)

Goal Value of a New Subscriber

What if you're not selling anything? Suppose you run an advertising-supported content site. This model applies both to sites that are small mom-and-pop operations and to large operations such as Salon and the *New York Times*. Like many content sites, yours probably has an announcement or headline e-mail that you send out when there is new content. A reader who signs up to receive content announcements obviously intends to return. This can be quantified.

Now you need some data. Click **View Report** for the appropriate Google Analytics profile, and go to the Visitors: New vs. Returning report. Click **Returning Visitor** (below the overview graph). Now, click the **Dimension** drop-down menu and choose **Source**, as shown in Figure 11-3.

Figure 11-3: If you're tracking sources, you can see where people are coming from.

Now, if you scroll down a bit, you'll see a list of whatever sources you are tracking. We're going to assume for the moment that you have set up all the URLs in your content announcements with tracking for the source (more about how to do that later in the chapter). For the sake of this example, say that the content announcement URLs are tagged as `DejahsPrivateIce.com`. Announcements account for 178 visits (12.7 percent), as shown in Figure 11-4.

Take note of one more number from this report—the number of pages per visit. In this case, it's 4.71.

NOTE These two numbers should be representative of the traffic your content announcement brings in every month. You'll have to look at several months or at a longer period of time to get an idea of what the correct numbers are.

Remember, this is an estimate; it's not going to be exact. The important thing is to get as close as you can so as not to overcount or undercount by too much. For example, when we change the date range to a full year instead of just a month, we get 2,010 visits (12.66 percent) and 4.61 pages per visit. Those numbers are very close to the monthly percentage (12.73 percent) and 4.71 pages per visit. This means we have a pretty good estimate. If possible, use a yearly figure—unless you had a wildly atypical year. But if you don't have a year of data to go on, use a monthly estimate and update it quarterly until you do.

We're going to use the monthly numbers, even though they are slightly less representative, because they are close enough. We have 178 visits at 4.71 pages per visit; that's 838 pages.

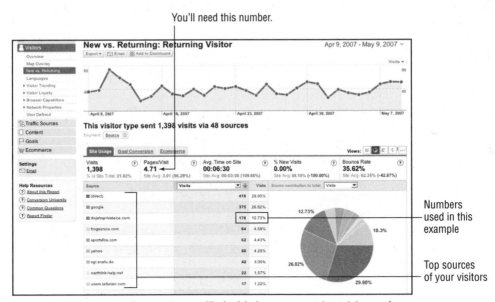

Figure 11-4: Source of returning traffic holds key to returning-visitor value.

Now on to the next key piece of information. This has to come from your advertising aggregator (like AdSense). If you use AdSense, log in and you'll see a report much like the one for `SkateFic.com` in Figure 11-5.

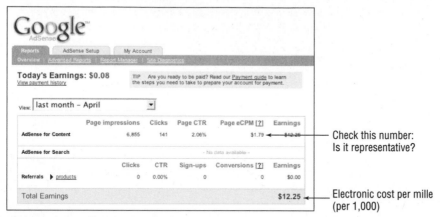

Figure 11-5: What's your CPM?

Locate the eCPM (that's electronic cost per mille, or thousand) for a representative time period. It may be last month, or this month, or today, depending on how much you make on advertising. You may choose a different time frame if you choose. This is your call. If you overestimate, your goals value will be inflated. If you underestimate, you'll undervalue your content-announcement subscribers. We chose "last month" as our time period, since the total payment of $12.25 for that month was fairly representative of what the site brings in—don't laugh, it pays half the hosting.

The eCPM for that time period is $1.79, which means that we made $1.79 for every thousand ad impressions. Let's assume that each of your pages holds a standard Google AdSense vertical banner showing four ads. That's four impressions per page, and 250 pages will make a thousand impressions. You have to show 250 pages to make $1.79, so each page in our example is worth $1.79/250 or $0.00716.

Putting that all together, we have 838 page views worth $0.00716 each, or $6 altogether. Okay, so it's not a huge amount, but it's for a single month for a low-traffic site.

Now we need one last piece of information: the number of absolute unique visitors—actual people who visited your site in a stated period, regardless of how many times they visited. (You can find more about these visitors in Chapter 15.) Go to **Visitors ⇨ Visitor Trending ⇨ Absolute Unique Visitors** and read off the number of absolute unique visitors for a typical month, one without any unusual circumstances to skew the numbers. In this example April 9 to May 9, 2007 is such a period. In that month there were 3,238 absolute unique visitors to `SkateFic.com`. (We haven't given you the screenshot for this, but if we had, you would see 3,238 in big type at the top.)

Now go to **Visitors ➪ Visitor Loyalty ➪ Loyalty** and look at the same time period. Read off the number of visitors who visited only once, as shown in Figure 11-6. Although there were a fair number of return visits, a lot of first-timers didn't come back, so this is a picture of at least moderate disloyalty. However, it's the ones who did come back that we're interested in.

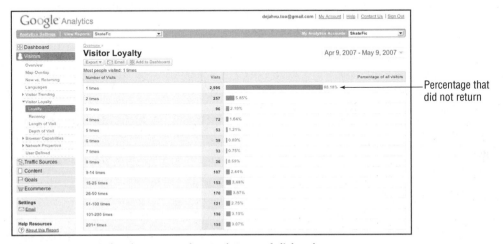

Figure 11-6: Results show a moderate degree of disloyalty.

The number of one-time visitors in Figure 11-6 is 2,995, which means that some of those 3,238 absolute unique visitors from the other chart (remember, we're counting actual individuals here) did not drop out after just one visit during the period. In fact, 243 of them apparently were interested enough in the site to come back one or more times. These folks have value and are responsible for those six dollars in AdSense revenue. Divide 6 by 243 and you find that each of these 243 returning visitors is worth just under two and a half cents a month.

How much is a visitor worth over a lifetime? It's hard to say. You have to make some sort of assumption or use some heavy-duty software to send out tailored e-mails to every subscriber. If you assume in the preceding example that a visitor will keep returning for three months, then each new subscriber is worth about seven and a half cents. If you think this person will be back for a year, then 30 cents might be closer to right. If you assume people will visit and revisit over the course of years, then you might make even more. This estimate is your call, based on whatever final total you think is likely.

Now, whatever that number is for you, put it in the "Goal value" box shown earlier in Figure 11-2.

Goal Value of a Content Page

What if the pages you want to get people to visit are just content pages? To work with these, you have to know what a content page is worth. This may require some extra tracking or custom reporting. We'll do this example with AdSense, but if you use a different ad aggregator, it may have similar tools. Ask tech support for information about your aggregator.

Log in to AdSense. Click the **AdSense Setup** tab right below the Google logo. Click **Channels** in the menu (just below Setup). Now click **URL channels** and then **+ Add new URL channels** and you'll come to the screen shown in Figure 11-7.

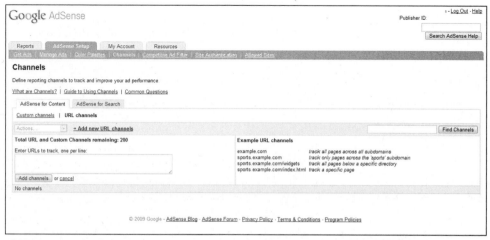

Figure 11-7: Track revenue on single pages (or groups of pages) using AdSense channels.

Now enter the URL you want to track. You can track a specific page, all the pages in a directory, all the pages in a subdomain, or all the pages in a domain. AdSense provides a neat little shorthand beside the entry box in case you forget how to enter the URL to track what you want to track. Click **Add channels**.

Tracking Dynamic Pages

One thing that Google doesn't say in the reminders is how to track dynamic pages. If you want to track dynamic pages—ones with name/value tags that control the output of the page—you should just use the bare URL before the question mark. For example, on `SkateFic.com`, Chapter 1 of the serial *On the Edge* is produced by the following URL:

```
http://skatefic.com/serials/ote/chapters/index.php?Chapter=1
```

To track that chapter alone you would enter the whole URL. But every chapter in the serial gets produced by the same script. The only thing that changes is the number after `Chapter=`. If you wanted to track the revenue from all the chapters you would enter the URL up to `index.php`, excluding the `?` and everything after it. After adding the channel you can turn it on or off, or remove it altogether, from the result screen shown in Figure 11-8.

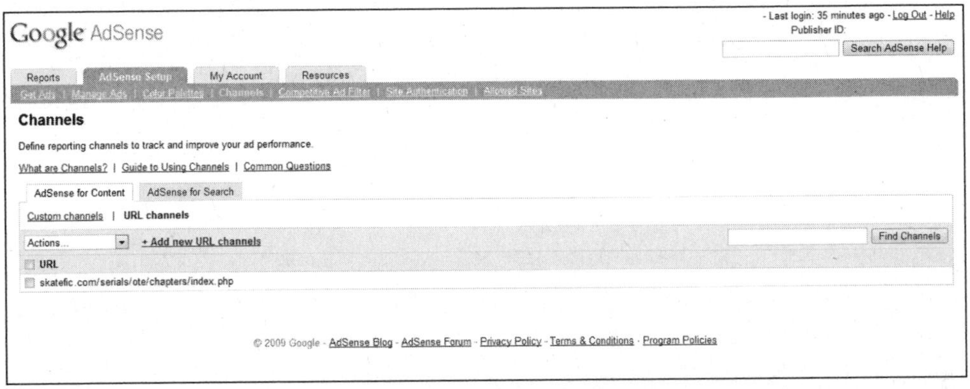

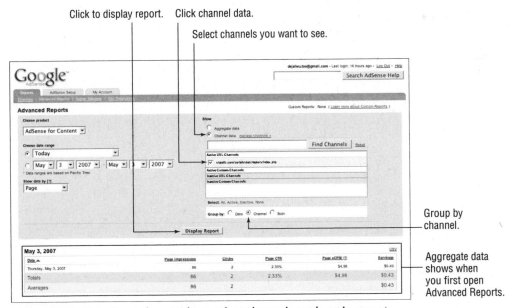

Figure 11-8: From this screen you can turn your new channel on and off or delete it.

Now, to see the data on your new channel, click **Reports**. Then click **Advanced Reports**. Then click the **Channel data** radio button. The channel controls will appear and you can select the channel (or channels) you want to see, and then click the **Group by Channel** radio button at the bottom, as shown in Figure 11-9.

Figure 11-9: Use channel controls to select channels to show in report.

Unfortunately, AdSense will not process historical data. So you'll have to wait a short time—anywhere from a couple of hours to a couple of weeks, depending on how busy your site is—to generate the data you need. You may want to wait a month or more, to generate typical data. If you don't want to wait *that* long, keep checking back so you can fine-tune your page value as time goes on.

So have you waited a bit?

Then click **Display Report**. You'll see something similar to Figure 11-10.

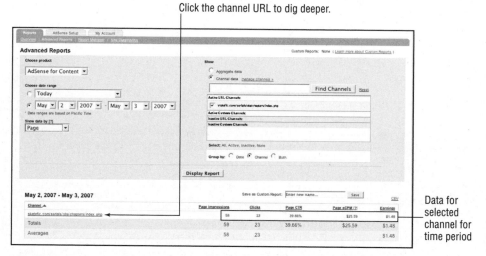

Figure 11-10: A two-day report for the *On the Edge* channel of advertising

If you click the URL for the channel of interest you can break performance for that particular channel down by day, as shown in Figure 11-11.

This is actually the same view you would get if you clicked the Group by Both radio button instead of Group by Channel before you displayed the report.

At any rate, the tidbit of interest is the total earnings. We're assuming this total is representative of how much revenue the page usually generates. But this may not be a good assumption.

The total is based on a very small sample size (only two days in this case). You want the total you use to be based on at least 30 days. That will give you some level of confidence that it's statistically accurate. And if your traffic is distinctly cyclical, you may want to be careful not to use your highest days' values, but rather to include the whole cycle in your total.

Finally, take the Total Earnings and divide it by the Total Page Impressions—not the Total Clicks. In this case it's $1.48 divided by 58, or $0.026. This is the goal value of any page in that channel (i.e., any chapter in the serial *On the Edge*). Once you have this monetary value you can use it to measure the performance of your pages.

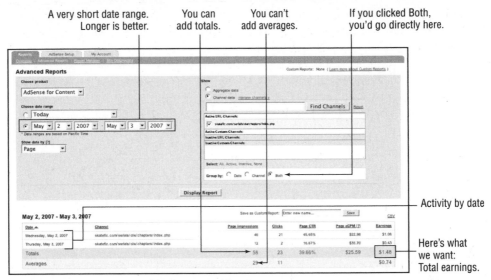

Figure 11-11: The *On the Edge* channel by day

Setting Up Goals

When you first set up a web site for tracking on Google Analytics, you're given the option to create goals for the site. Most people don't set those goals up at the very beginning because they're not sure what they're doing. That's OK. You can set the goals up anytime you're comfortable with the process.

It'll be easy. We'll lead you through the steps. All you have to provide is the goal.

To set up a goal after you've created your web-site profile, go to Analytics Settings. Under the Website Profiles menu, find the profile to which you want to add the goal. Click the **Edit** link in the same line as the web site's name, and you are taken to a page like the one in Figure 11-12.

The Conversion Goals and Funnel menu is the second box on the page. It lists the name of any goals you've created, the URL of those goals, and a status area that shows whether the goal is active or not. Click the **Edit** link in the line of the goal number you want to change or set up.

> **NOTE** Google allows only four goals for each web-site profile you set up. If you need to track more than four goals for your web site you should set up another web-site profile for a section of your site. This enables you to have four goals for that section and four goals for any other section of the web site that has its own profile.

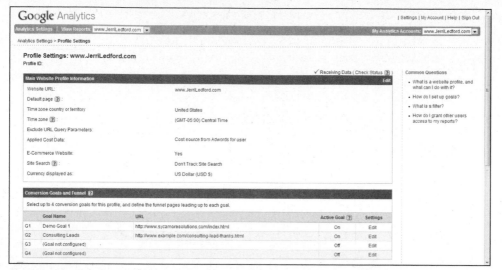

Figure 11-12: Create goals in the Conversion Goals and Funnel menu.

After you click the **Edit** link you are taken to the Goal Settings page shown in Figure 11-13.

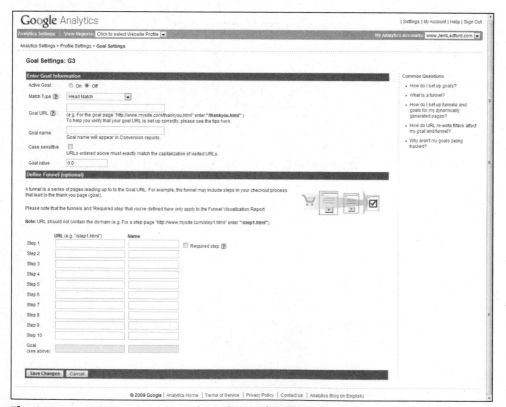

Figure 11-13: Create a goal to track on the Goal Settings page.

Choosing the Right Goal Information

As you're setting up your goals, there are a few things you should understand about the fields on the Goals setup pages. Some of these fields are required, others are optional. Here's the information you need to enter to create a new goal:

- **Active Goal:** Select the **On** or **Off** radio button to activate or deactivate your goal.

- **Match Type:** There are three options for Match Type. Exact Match requires the URL to be exactly what you've entered as the funnel or goal URL. Use Head Match when you always have the same URL but have user or session identifiers after the URL that are unique for each visitor. You can also specify a Regular Expression Match, which is useful when you're dealing with subdomains.

- **Goal URL:** This is the web page within your site that you want your customers to reach. If you have an e-commerce site, the Goal URL might be the purchase confirmation page after the transaction has been submitted. It could also be a confirmation page on a site where the goal is for users to sign up for a newsletter.

- **Goal Name:** Choose the name you want your goal to have. For the preceding example the name Purchase Complete would be a good choice.

- **Case Sensitive:** Select this option if URLs must exactly match the capitalization of goal URLs.

- **Goal Value:** You learned how to determine the value of a goal earlier in this chapter. This is where you enter that information.

- **Define Funnel:** For every goal URL there is a logical way that consumers reach that goal. In the case of the e-commerce site a funnel might include the index page, the products page, the shopping-cart page, the checkout page, and then the goal URL, which is the confirmation page.

A funnel is used to measure how often users take the logical path to your goal URL. If they deviate from that path frequently, you know that what you think is the logical path may not be logical for the consumer. This enables you to redefine the funnel and creates additional opportunities for you to reach your customers.

Enter the URLs for the funnel in this section.

NOTE In concept, funnels sound pretty easy to figure out. In practice, they're a bit harder than they sound. Don't worry that you don't understand funnels completely right now. We'll cover those in more depth in Chapter 12, Funneling Visitors to Their Destination.

When you finish entering all the information requested, click **Save Changes** and your new goal will be created. Then you'll be able to see it in your goals list, as shown in Figure 11-14.

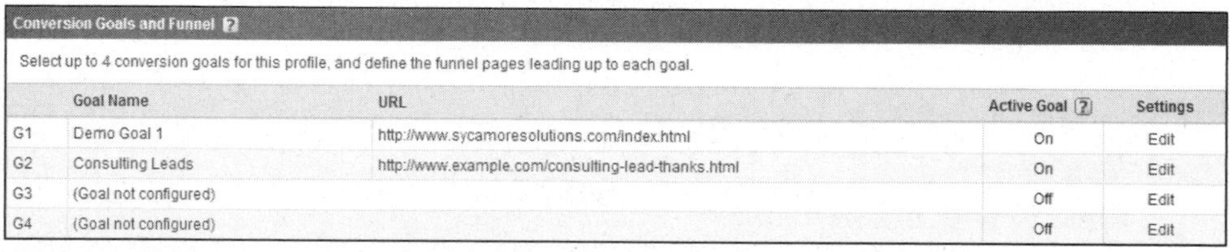

Conversion Goals and Funnel ⏻				
Select up to 4 conversion goals for this profile, and define the funnel pages leading up to each goal.				
	Goal Name	URL	Active Goal ⏻	Settings
G1	Demo Goal 1	http://www.sycamoresolutions.com/index.html	On	Edit
G2	Consulting Leads	http://www.example.com/consulting-lead-thanks.html	On	Edit
G3	(Goal not configured)		Off	Edit
G4	(Goal not configured)		Off	Edit

Figure 11-14: Once created, goals appear on your Profile Settings page.

TIP To quickly determine how many goals you have set for a particular web-site profile, all you need to do is look in the status column on the Analytics Settings page. The number of goals for each web-site profile is displayed there, but you can't see the actual goals.

Editing and Inactivating Goals

Like the other functions of Google Analytics, editing goals is easy to do. To edit your goals, enter the Goals Settings screen by going to **Analytics Settings ⇨ Profile Settings** and then click **Edit** in the same line as the goal number that you want to edit or delete.

If you're editing the goal, your pre-populated Goal Settings screen will appear, as shown in Figure 11-15. All you have to do is edit the information that you want to change and click **Save Changes**.

The one failing here is that you can't actually delete a goal once you set it up. You can change it or turn it off, but you can't remove it entirely. It's not a problem unless you happen to be the minimalist type who can't stand clutter. In that case, having an unused goal just floating around in your web-site profile might drive you a little crazy, but it won't hurt anything at all.

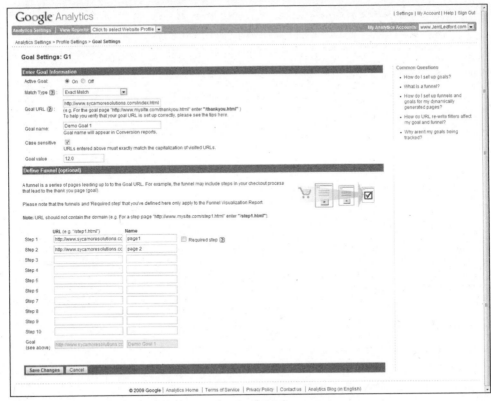

Figure 11-15: Make your changes on the Goal Settings screen.

Measuring Goals That Result in Conversions

Goals and goal-setting in Analytics can be confusing. All the information you've seen up to this point has been about goal conversions and how many are happening on your site, and about the process of setting up goals in Google Analytics.

Now it's time to put those goals to work—to actually achieve the goal conversions that you've only considered so far. Ultimately, all your web-site efforts are probably about goal conversions. And what follows will help you understand the conversions happening on your site and how to achieve more of them where possible.

That's where the goal-related reports in Google Analytics come into play. Using these reports you can quickly see which of your goals are effective and which might need to be restructured to ensure that, ultimately, the conversion you seek is achieved.

Goals Overview

The first of the goal reports is the Goals Overview report, shown in Figure 11-16. It gives you a quick glance at some of the most important metrics in goal tracking and conversions.

Figure 11-16: The Goals Overview report is a snapshot of the metrics available.

NOTE The Goals section of Google Analytics may prove elusive to you. If you don't see a Goals section in your report menu, it's because you have not yet set up your goals. Once you set up the first goal, the Goals section becomes visible and available.

On this overview page you'll find a graphical representation of the number of goal conversions completed by your visitors for each goal you have established for your site. You can have up to four goals for a profile (Google calls a web site a profile, and you can have more than one profile for each web site, so if you need more than four goals you can set up another profile for your site).

Each goal on the report is a link to a Goal Detail report, as shown in Figure 11-17. This report provides information on the total conversions, conversion rate, and abandonment rate for each goal. Each of these metrics links to another report (such as Total Conversions, Conversion Rate, and Goal Verification), each of which will be covered in more depth later in this chapter.

You'll also notice there are links on the right side of the page that lead to further data analysis. Again, each of these links leads to another report, including the following:

- Languages

- Network Locations
- User Defined
- Browsers
- Operating Systems
- Browser and Operating Systems
- Screen Colors
- Screen Resolutions
- Java Support
- Flash
- Map Overlay
- Goal Funnel

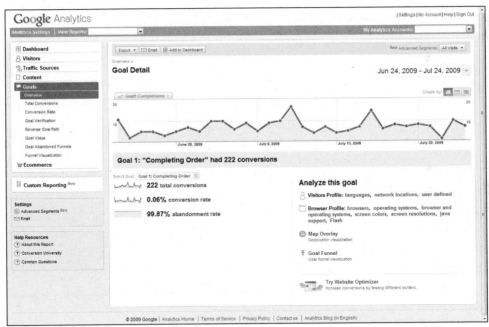

Figure 11-17: The Goal Detail report adds details on conversions and abandonment.

Most of these reports will be covered in future chapters, so we won't go into detail about them right now. Just realize that each of those terms, which you'll actually see in blue, will lead you to yet another level of reporting detail, which will help you more clearly understand your web site's visitors.

The Goals Overview also contains the Goal Conversion Rate module, which leads you to the Conversion Rate report. The Total Goal Value module leads to the Goal Value report.

The purpose of the Goals Overview is to give you a quick glance at some of the most accessed metrics associated with goals and conversion rates. That's not to say all of these metrics will necessarily be meaningful to you. Perhaps they are, but there are other metrics that are *more* meaningful. Unfortunately, like all the overview pages (except your main dashboard), this one cannot be altered to show the metrics you prefer to have shown.

Total Conversions

Conversions are the number of goals that have been reached by your site visitors. And those goals can be anything you want them to be, whether they have monetary values or not.

So what's the purpose of the Total Conversions report, shown in Figure 11-18?

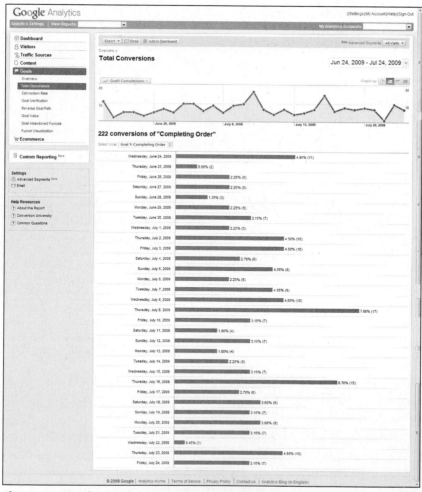

Figure 11-18: The Total Conversions report shows how many goal conversions occur each day.

It's nothing more than a quick glance at the number of conversions you had for each goal during a given period.

And why is it important?

If you're not getting goal conversions, there's a problem somewhere. Or if you're getting goal conversions but they're low, you can see this at a glance and then dig deeper into the information in later reports to find out why you aren't getting these conversions.

If you happen to be getting a very high number of goal conversions or an unbalanced number of goal conversions across all your goals, that's important information, too. Either of these cases should lead you to investigate what's working and, if necessary, what's not.

As you investigate, the question becomes, Are my conversion numbers good? And if they're not, how do you increase those numbers?

There may not be easy answers to those questions. How many conversions is enough? Obviously, you'd like every visitor who comes to your site to reach a conversion goal. But 100 percent conversion is probably unrealistic. So you have to decide what your target goal is. Then, if your numbers aren't showing the goal's being met, it's time to try something different. Maybe users aren't finding the link to sign up. Or maybe the newsletter/announcement list isn't portrayed in a way that interests users. This is where you need to decide what's enough and what needs to be done if what you have doesn't reach that criterion.

The problem with establishing goals (as you may remember from earlier goal discussions) is that it is not always easy to know what the right goal is. If you're looking at three different reports, you'll quickly see that not all goals are created equal. Some will naturally be more successful than others. However, if you find that you've created a goal that doesn't result in conversions, you know something is fundamentally wrong with that goal. Something needs to be changed. You're challenged with figuring out just what it is. Fortunately, some of the other reports in this section may help on that front.

Conversion Rate

In the Conversion Rate report, shown in Figure 11-19, each of your goal conversions for any given day—remember that you can have up to four goals per website profile—is shown as a percentage. You can quickly see what percentage of your visitors is reaching the page you've established for each goal.

You may notice that this report is very similar in appearance to the Total Conversions report. In fact, it contains much of the same information, but presented differently. Where the Total Conversions report showed you the number of conversions for each goal, this report shows you the percentage of change in goals over the designated time frame.

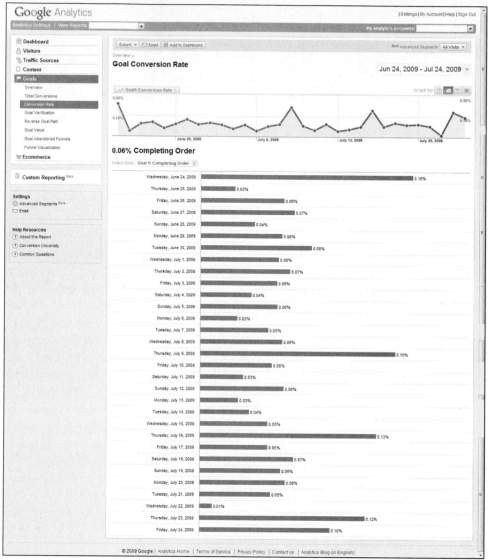

Figure 11-19: The Conversion Rate report shows conversion percentages by day.

The information is presented differently so you can see whether the number of goal conversions is increasing or decreasing without having to flip back and forth between different reports.

You even use the information in much the same way as the information from the Total Conversions report. However, here you can also use it to see whether conversion for one of your goals is increasing or decreasing. If you can correlate that information with any changes you've made during the specific time period shown, you can attribute those changes to the difference and either repair the damage you've done or use what you've learned to improve other goal conversions.

Goal Verification

When you set a goal for your site, it's possible to set a directory as the goal page. If you've ever done that, have you wondered how many goal conversions from that group of pages are actually attributable to each page? The Goal Verification report, shown in Figure 11-20, illustrates exactly which of those pages is responsible for goal conversions. It gives you a measurement for the goal pages viewed by users.

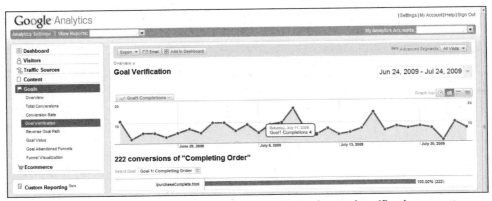

Figure 11-20: View the pages that led to a conversion in the Goal Verification report.

So how is this report useful? Well, in truth, it's not all that useful if your goal is on the front page of your web site. However, if you have a directory of pages as your goal (for example, you want people to reach a specific category of products, each with its own page), you will eventually want to know which of those pages within the directory led to the goal conversion. This is where you'll find that information.

Once you have the information, you can use it to determine which pages within a directory are the most useful or most valuable. That information can in turn be used to gain more conversions from those pages or to improve conversions on other pages.

Reverse Goal Path

We've already established that not every visitor is going to use the same path that you've designated as a funnel to reach a goal conversion. And the path those users take can hold valuable clues as to how they navigate through your site. This is especially helpful if all users, even those who don't navigate through your funnel, reach a goal conversion through a specific page.

The Reverse Goal Path report, shown in Figure 11-21, shows you exactly how users reach your goal-conversion pages.

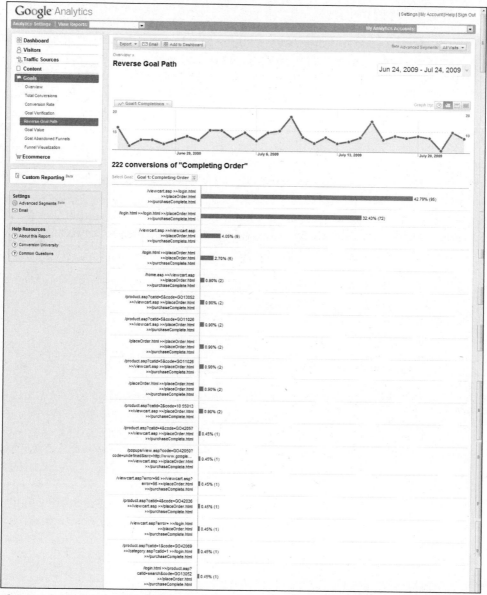

Figure 11-21: Reverse Goal Path shows how users reached goal-conversion pages.

You can also use this report to find out exactly what pages are required for a user to feel comfortable making a conversion.

NOTE Although the Reverse Goal Path report is a relatively useful one to have, much of its value can be found in other reports that are available on Google Analytics. For that reason (and because Google is always improving its products to make them more useful) this report will soon be removed from the Goals reports section. If you're currently using the report and haven't saved all the data that you need from it, you should do so immediately so that you don't lose that information when the report is removed from Google Analytics. When will that be? Well, Google hasn't said, so it could be anytime.

Goal Value

The Goal Value report, shown in Figure 11-22, illustrates the daily value of each of your goals. Now, if you run an e-commerce site, a goal value should be very easy to define. However, if you run a content site, defining a value for your goals might be a little harder. But we gave you some information on just how to go about defining that value earlier in this chapter—Monetizing Goal Values. If you missed it, you might want to flip back and read it. It's interesting stuff. Really.

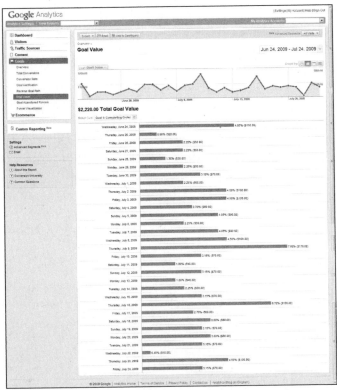

Figure 11-22: The Goal Value report shows the daily value of goal conversions.

The goal value helps you to see how valuable your goal conversions are. If you have a goal conversion that's less valuable than you projected it would be, you may need to consider redefining the goal, evaluating the navigation path, or changing the way the goal is marketed.

It's not an exact science if you have a content site, but at least it gives you a monetary value to work with.

And a Couple More...

There are a couple more reports included in the Goals section on Google Analytics, but we're not going to address them in this chapter. Those reports—Goal Abandoned Funnels and Funnel Visualization—will make far more sense to you if we show them in the context of the funnel information that we're presenting in Chapter 12, Funneling Visitors to Their Destination. So keep reading, there's still more to learn…lots more.

As we've established, goals are important. They're a guiding light that leads to conversions. But what good is a guiding light if it's far enough away that you don't know what path to follow to reach it? That's where funnels will help. Think of them as the pathways that you want to lead your visitors through to ensure that they reach the conversions you need. And with that in mind, turn the page.

CHAPTER 12

Funneling Visitors to Their Destination

One of the most useful—and yet most underused—features of Google Analytics is the ability to track visitors through your web site to the completion of a goal that you've set up. Remember from the last chapter (Chapter 11: Setting Goals) that goals are a pretty important part of monitoring the traffic on your web site.

But what good does it do to have a goal if you don't know how visitors reach that goal? Well, you can look at other reports (such as the Goal Verification report) to see if your goal was reached, but all that tells you is that visitors performed whatever action that goal represents—like signing up for a newsletter or reaching the confirmation page for an order.

How did users get to that point? If you left them to their own devices, some of them probably would get there accidentally. But much as with goal conversions in brick-and-mortar stores, few site visitors will reach those conversions without some help. That's why you go through specific steps when you enter a store: browse the products, make a selection, go through the checkout line, make a payment, receive a receipt. If you're lucky, you'll also receive a "Thank you, please visit us again," and a smile.

That process—from product selection through receiving a receipt—is considered a funnel. It's the most likely path that visitors to a store will take, and at each step the merchant leads you along to the next. In the case of product selection, advertisements and coupons are a helping hand. When it comes to checkout, many merchants keep multiple lines available to make it easier for you to get through them (because who wants to stand in line for 20 minutes for milk and bread, right?).

The checkout process is also guided. A cashier rings up your purchase, gives you a total, and then provides options (such as cash or credit) for your payment. That payment, of course, results in a receipt. You can walk away with your purchases without ever knowing that you've been funneled through a process that the merchant can monitor to learn if there are problems in one area or another that cause people to abandon their purchases.

What's a Funnel and Why Is It Important?

By definition, a funnel is the most likely path that users will take to reach a goal conversion. It's called a funnel because it can easily be visualized that way: at each step a percentage of visitors will drop off, leaving fewer visitors to ultimately reach the goal. A visualization of this process might look something like what you see in Figure 12-1.

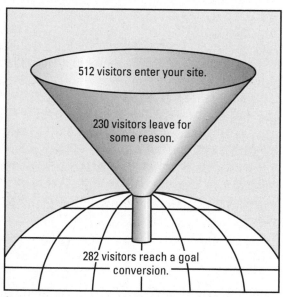

512 visitors enter your site.

230 visitors leave for some reason.

282 visitors reach a goal conversion.

Figure 12-1: The number of visitors who start the defined path to a goal conversion is rarely the same number who complete that goal.

Here's an example. Let's say that you have a product web site, and that one of your goals for that site is to have visitors purchase a particular product. You can create a funnel that walks visitors from that specific product's page through the four-step checkout process and ultimately to the goal page—the "Thanks for your order" page.

Each step in that process (there are six steps in this example) can be monitored to show you how many people enter the process, how many complete the process, and where they fall off. That tells you what pages in the process there could be problems with. For example, if one step in the checkout process is for users to enter payment information and you accept only PayPal, you might find that a lot of your visitors drop off at that point. You're losing sales because your payment methods are too restrictive. If you were to implement other payment types, you might see less *abandonment* during the payment process.

In another scenario, after monitoring your funnel you find that you're losing visitors at the shipping page. This could indicate that users are finding your shipping charges too high, or perhaps the page is too hard to enter information into, confusing the visitors who may then just abandon the process. What's important in using the funnel is that you can see there's a problem—and then can investigate to learn what might be causing it.

Now you understand why we skipped creating funnels in Chapter 11. It's not because they're unimportant. On the contrary, funnels are so important (and so underused) that they really deserve a chapter all to themselves. Using funnels, you can determine why some visitors behave the way they do on the way to reaching a goal. For those visitors who do reach the goal, you'll have a record of what works. But for those visitors who never make it to the final step, there's also a record of what's not working. And what's more, there are records of where those visitors went when they abandoned the funnel process, which could also be a clue to what's going on in their minds.

Here's an example. Let's say you've set up a funnel for one of your e-commerce goals that includes the shopping cart as the first stop in the funnel process. After monitoring this for a while, you notice that the drop-off rate during that first step is phenomenal. That should prompt you to examine what's happening.

The most likely cause for that drop-off is probably just that people are looking at their shopping cart many times as they shop through the available products on your web site. It's common behavior, but it can skew your numbers. It's also the main reason that you're advised not to use the shopping cart page on your site as a step in your funnel process.

So how do you know what steps to include? We'll get to that in the next section, "Establishing Funnels." Right now it's important to understand that funnels, when done properly, can give you great insight into the behavior of site visitors, but when done wrong can lead to misleading numbers that can skew your understanding of that behavior.

Oh, and one more thing. To this point, I've referred to funnels as being used by e-commerce sites. And truthfully, that's the most common use for a funnel in Google Analytics. It's very easy to track the sales process from one point through the completion of a sale. But that doesn't mean you can't use funnels for content-related goals as well. You can. And you can do it in much the same way.

Establishing Funnels

Having funnels in place makes sense, right? Good. Now let's figure out how to put them there. First I'm going to walk you through the actual process of creating a funnel, but along the way you'll learn more about how to define funnel pages and what makes one type of funnel setup more useful (and usually more accurate) than another.

We're even going to get into some of the quirks that Google Analytics funnels have. You knew it wasn't going to be entirely easy, didn't you? Nothing ever is. But once you understand that Google Analytics sometimes counts pages in a screwy manner, it will help you understand the numbers that you're looking at when you're creating the funnels that you'll use to determine visitor behavior.

Buckle up and let's get started. This should be an interesting ride.

Creating Standard Funnels

Creating a standard funnel is a relatively straightforward process. The first step is to determine what pages you'll include in the funnel. Then you can go about setting up that funnel. After that it's just a matter of waiting for Google Analytics to collect enough information about the funnel process to be useful to you.

It's the first step here that's going to be the most frightening. Determining what pages to include in your funnel can be a bit tricky. Remember the funnel example in the last section that included the shopping cart as one step in the funnel process? It screwed up the numbers for the process, and that's not something you want to have happen.

Determining Funnel Steps

The funnel process should include the most logical steps in the process that visitors will take to reach your goal. For example, one way to use funnels is to track the success of AdWords campaigns. Say you have a campaign that's designed to bring users into your site at a specific page and your ultimate goal with the campaign is to get users to sign up for your company newsletter.

You can use some clearly defined steps to create a funnel in this scenario:

1. The first stop is the campaign landing page. How many users are landing on that page?

2. Now visitors will probably fill out some kind of form to be included in your newsletter mailing list. That's a logical second step.

3. For the sake of this example, let's say the third step is verification that the visitor does indeed want to be included on the mailing list.

4. Then the final step (and what *should* be your goal step) is the confirmation page, where visitors receive a thank-you message for signing up to get the newsletter.

You would include those four steps in your funnel. Suppose you just wanted to know how many people came to your site through the campaign and how many people completed goals. Could you set the funnel up with only Steps 1 and 4?

You could. Google Analytics lets you define funnels with one page or as many as 10. However, creating a funnel that shows only the landing page and the confirmation page will give you some seriously strange numbers that you won't know what to do with.

To begin with, the funnel will probably show that 100 percent of the people who come in on the campaign landing page abandon the goal that you have set for them. But you'll likely also see a percentage of people who complete the goal and reach the confirmation page. How can that be?

Google tracks everyone who lands on the first page that you've set for that funnel. However, to reach the confirmation page, visitors have to click through two other pages. And when they reach Step 4, it's going to appear to your funnel as if the original visitors have all defected and other visitors (from some unknown location) have signed up for the newsletter. You won't have any information from the intervening steps.

This is not only very misleading, but it strips you of the ability to collect the information that really matters. You can get a sense of the number of people who complete the goal, but it's not going to be entirely accurate. And if you're not tracking Steps 2 and 3 in the funnel process, then you can't tell where you're losing visitors. So you may have a funnel, but it's basically useless to you.

Instead of creating a nightmare like this, you need to be sure that you're choosing well-defined steps in the process for leading your visitors to the confirmation page (or whatever goal it is that you have set up).

Remember way back when I suggested that, left to their own devices, most store visitors wouldn't follow through with a sale? That's where your funnel steps serve double duty. Not only do they enable you to view the movements that your visitors make, but within the pages of that funnel you can take site visitors by the hand and tell them, "OK, do this first, now this, then that, and one final step before we're finished." This enables you to lead your visitors right where you want them to go.

You're not always going to get the steps in your funnel exactly right the first time around. You may determine what you think is the best funnel by reviewing previous analytics for the pages that you want to include—but then you may find that visitors are actually taking a different path to reach the intended goal. You can learn about this by looking at the Top Content report and then drilling down to Entrance Sources and even Entrance Paths.

For example, if you were to look at the top entrance source (or the place where visitors come from) for the second page in our example funnel, the source *should* show that the top entrance page for that URL is the landing page defined in your AdWords campaign. If it isn't, you know there's something that needs adjusting—whether it's the AdWords campaign or the landing page is something you'll have to determine through research (and possibly even some consulting help).

It may take a little trial and error, but over time you should be able to hone your funnel steps to the point where they provide really useful information about visitor behavior.

Setting Up a Standard Funnel

Setting up a funnel isn't nearly as intimidating as defining the funnel. It's actually part of the process you'll go through when you're setting up a goal. Remember our old friend the Goal Settings page (shown in Figure 12-2)? You can get to it by logging in to your Google Analytics account, selecting **Edit** beside the web-site profile for which you want to create a goal or funnel, and then selecting **Edit** again by the name of the goal to which you want to add a funnel.

Since we covered creating goals in the last chapter, I'm not going to walk you through that again. Let's assume you already have a goal set up for which you want to create a funnel. You need to have a goal first, so if you don't have one you can use the information in Chapter 11 to create a goal, then add the funnel before you save the changes on the Goal Settings page.

To create a funnel all you need do is fill in the URL boxes and assign each step in the funnel a name in the Define Funnel section of the page, as shown in Figure 12-3. (Note that the information filled in on this form is there for example purposes and does not relate to the text that follows.) You may notice that the Goal URL is already filled in on this form before you start creating your funnel. That's because this URL is created automatically when you add a goal to your web site. Remember that, essentially, your goal is likely to be a conversion of some type.

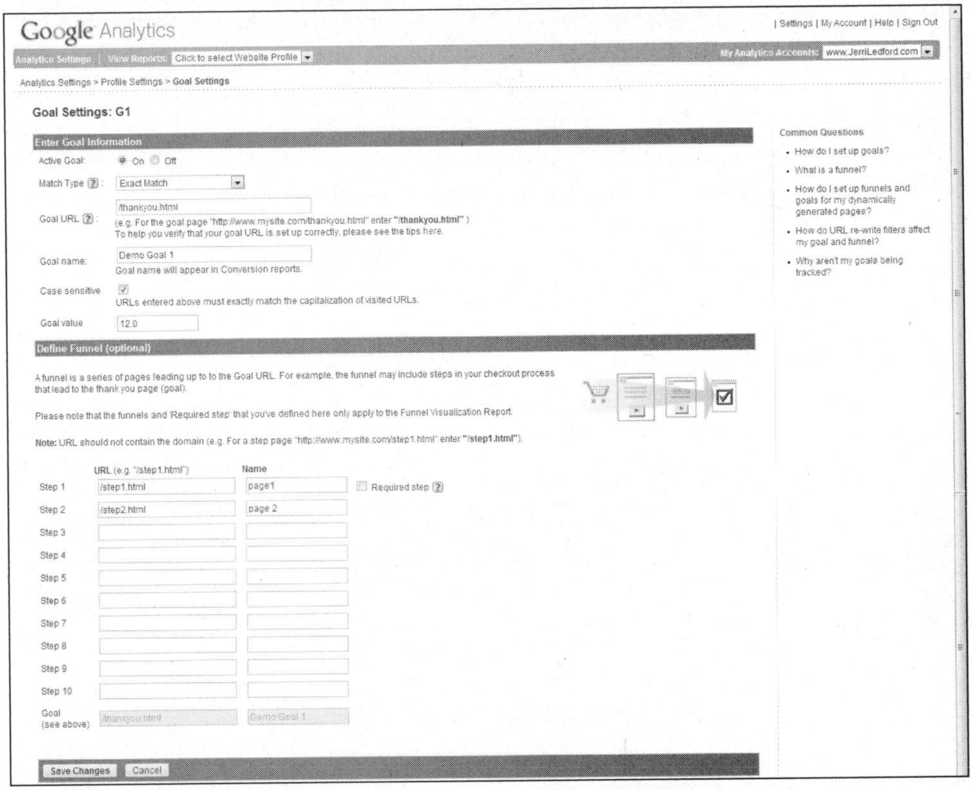

Figure 12-2: The Goal Settings page is where you'll find the form needed to create a funnel for your goal.

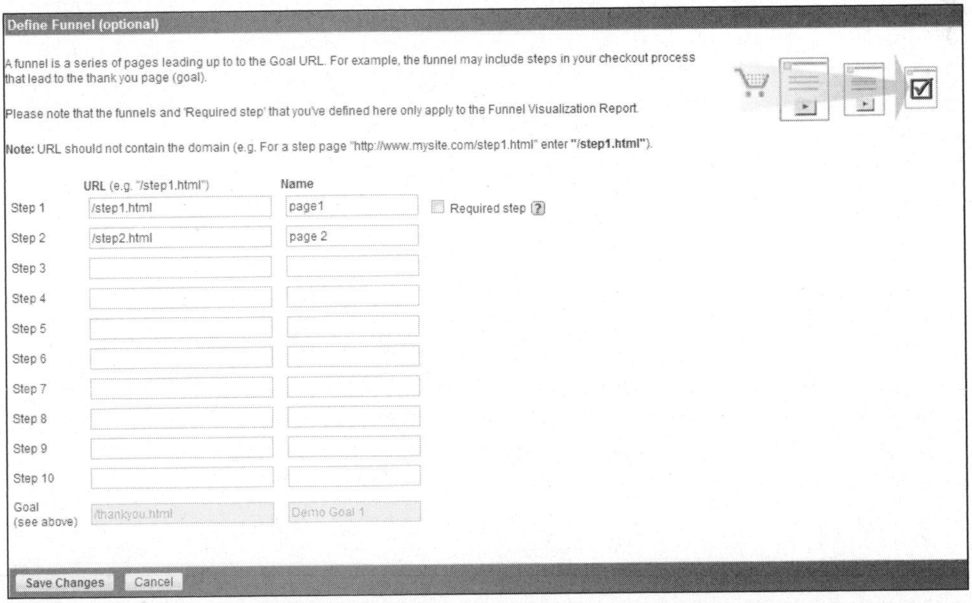

Figure 12-3: Fill in the fields of the Define Funnel form to create a funnel for the goal you have set (or are setting).

Going back to the beginning of creating a funnel, the URL you enter for each step of the funnel should be the URL for the page you're tracking. (This URL will be a partial one for each particular step. You'll see a note about this just above the form.) For example, if you're creating a funnel that tracks five steps in a sales process—landing page, billing, shipping, order review, confirmation—each page will be different, so each URL should be different. Table 12-1 illustrates how the URL relates to the steps in a funnel:

Table 12-1: Funnel URLS

STEP NUMBER	URL	NAME	ACTION TRACKED
1	`http://www.example.com/landing_page`	Landing Page	Visitor landing on a page associated with marketing campaign
2	`http://www.example.com/billing`	Billing	Visitor completes billing information
3	`http://www.example.com/shipping`	Shipping	Visitor completes shipping information
4	`http://www.example.com/order_review`	Order Review	Visitor reviews and submits order
5	`http://www.example.com/confirmation`	Confirmation	Visitor receives "Thank you for your order" message. This URL will already have been in place as the "Goal" URL once you set up a goal (or conversion goal) for your site.

NOTE When you're defining the steps in your funnel, make sure that your tracking code is installed on each page that's included in the funnel. This is an essential step in tracking these pages. Without the tracking code Google Analytics has no way of knowing whether visitors make it to that page or not. If you're not sure how to install the tracking code, flip back to Chapter 3 for instructions.

One thing you'll notice is that the final step of the funnel, the Goal URL (which in this case is the confirmation URL), is already in place when you begin to define the funnel. This is because you had to enter the goal URL when you created the goal at the top of the page. There's no need to include this goal URL a second time, and, in fact, if you do, it will cause your funnel to do strange and squirrelly things (like showing no actual goal conversions, because the previous URL will be the same as the goal URL).

NOTE One thing that you might not know is that you can use Regular Expressions when defining your funnel URLs. Regular Expressions can help you define a URL, or they can cause problems if you're not careful. For example, if you make the first step of your funnel `www.example.com/` (or you can skip the `www` part of the URL and just use `/`) then each page after that is going to be a problem, because every page on the site will have something that follows the `/` (e.g., `www.example.com/billing` or `www.example.com/confirmation`). You can overcome this problem by using the full URL and not leaving a `/` character as the final character in the first step.

One more thing you need to take note of as you're creating your funnel is the option next to the first step to make that step a requirement for a goal conversion. This is an option that you want to use carefully. If you require that the first step be completed before a goal conversion is counted, you're going to miss tracking people who might come into the funnel process in the second or subsequent steps. This is because what you're telling Google Analytics (in essence) is that anyone who completes the goal but does not complete the first step in the funnel doesn't matter. They may reach your goal, but they might as well be invisible if they didn't land on that first page in the funnel process.

Use caution when deciding to make that first step mandatory. There might be an occasion for which you need that option, but for most goals that's not the case. So, unless you're really certain, leave the "Required step" option unchecked.

Once you've finished defining your funnel, click **Save Changes** at the bottom of the page to save the goal and funnel. Now all you have to do is allow some time for Google Analytics to collect data about the funnel process you've set up. Then you can begin to analyze the data.

Creating Nonstandard Funnels

The process above is great if you have a standard funnel that's all contained within your own web site. But what if you have a funnel that includes a step that's on a subdomain or a different domain altogether?

You can do that. too. It just means that you'll have to first be sure the Google Analytics code is included on the page you want to track (even if it's on a different domain), and then you'll need to be sure that you use the exact URL for the page that's included in the funnel. So if you're using a shopping cart that's hosted on another service, you need to be sure that the shopping cart's domain is included in your tracking, and that when you're tracking actions that take place on the shopping cart's domain, you use the exact URL for that other domain.

You'll learn more about tracking different types of shopping carts in Chapter 6.

Funnel Quirks

Although the funnel function in Google Analytics is one of the most useful features of the program, it does have some strange quirks. For example, if you're tracking a funnel that *does not* have a required first step and a visitor enters the funnel process at a later step—like the last step—and completes the goal conversion, Google Analytics will *backfill* the previous steps.

What that means is that on your Funnel Visualization report, even if the user only hit one of the steps in the funnel, Google Analytics will provide information in the previous steps as if the user actually went through them, provided that user reaches a goal conversion.

This is misleading because, even if you have a funnel set up so that a user can reach the goal conversion without going through the funnel, it's still going to look as if this user followed the funnel steps. At this time there's no way to stop Google Analytics from backfilling that information. But it is something we would like to see changed in future versions of Google Analytics.

Another little quirk that's related to the backfilling issue is that Google doesn't particularly care in what order your visitors accomplish the funnel's steps. So, for example, if a visitor comes into your site and completes a goal conversion using the funnel steps, but takes Step 2, then 3, then 1, then 4, and then the conversion, Google Analytics won't show you that complicated path. It simply shows that the funnel steps were completed, and that the goal conversion was reached.

Why is this important? If your funnel steps are out of order (meaning they're not particularly user-friendly for site visitors), you won't be able to tell that. What you'll see is that you have a large number of abandonments during the funnel process, but determining why will be very difficult. It won't be impossible, but you'll have to dig through other reports to get the clear picture.

This is another aspect of Google Analytics funnels that we'd like to see improved in the future. But even with these quirks, I'm holding on to the opinion that the funnel capabilities and reports are some of the most valuable information you can pull from Google Analytics. In fact, let's take a closer look at the two reports available to you so you can get a full picture of how this all comes together to provide insight into your site visitors' behavior.

Tracking Funnel Results

Having funnels is all great and wonderful, but what about tracking the results of those funnels? Google Analytics has two reports, both found in the Goals section of the analytics reports, that let you see very clearly what works and what doesn't in your funnel pages.

Goal Abandoned Funnels

You already know that funnel navigation is the process by which you gently nudge, or funnel, your site visitors to a conversion page. You might think of it as taking site visitors by the hand and leading them through the site, one page at a time. On each page you give them a reason to want to go to the next, and then the next, until they've reached the conversion page. At that point the objective is to have built enough desire in the visitors that the process becomes a goal conversion.

Unfortunately users often abandon the process, resulting in what's called an *abandoned funnel*. The Goal Abandoned Funnels report shows you exactly what percentage of people who start a funnel navigation process abandon it. The report, shown in Figure 12-4, gives you a clear picture of how often your funnel process is ineffective.

When you view this report, one thing you need to remember is that a funnel is simply an indicator of how *you* think your visitors will navigate through your site to reach a specific goal. You can require that users hit certain pages, but even then not everyone thinks the same, so you could be missing out on conversions because you think differently from your users.

And in Figure 12-4, nearly all the data shown indicates that users abandoned a funnel before they reached the goal of "completing order." Obviously something is set up wrong in this funnel, because otherwise the abandonment rate would not be nearly 100 percent. However, for example purposes, this shows you how the Goal Abandonment Funnel report might look.

In short, this is a tool, nothing more. Use it to figure out where you're losing users along their journey to goal conversions. If you think your users should hit a specific page as they make their way through purchasing a specific item, but they don't hit that page, view the pages they do hit and learn why their behavior is different from what you expect. That information will help you better understand your site users, and then you can create pages and content that specifically meet their needs.

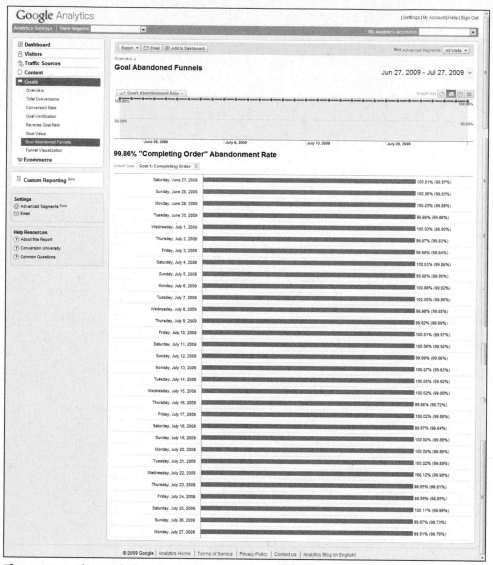

Figure 12-4: The Goal Abandoned Funnels report shows how often visitors abandon a funnel before conversion.

Funnel Visualization

Here's where things start to get a little bit interesting. This is one of my favorite reports in Google Analytics. Throughout these pages you've seen information about defining a navigation funnel to lead users to a goal page. If you've been scratching your head and thinking, "How do I do this?" you're about to have your question answered.

First there's a bit of philosophy to remember here. Water poured into a funnel has no choice about where to go. But visitors in your navigation funnel do have a choice, even if it's only to get irritated and leave your site. So the purpose of your funnel usually isn't to force visitors anywhere. Rather, it's to see in a more sophisticated way how they're moving around on your site and how you can make them more comfortable and ease their travel—and in the process maybe steer them toward your goals. Think of college campus planners watching where students wear out the grass and then building sidewalks there.

Remember that as you're entering the funnel information you have the option to make the first page in the funnel navigation path a required one for the goal to be considered a conversion. Use this option sparingly; otherwise, you'll end up with goal conversions that don't appear to be conversions because users didn't hit the required page. However, if the user *must* go through a specific page to reach a goal conversion, you should include that as a required page.

Once you've defined the funnel navigation for one (or all) of your goals, within a few days you can begin to generate the report. It might look something like the Funnel Visualization report shown in Figure 12-5.

The report illustrates where users enter the navigation process and how they follow the funnel until they either leave it and eventually drop off the site, or reach the goal conversion. In some cases you'll see pages in the report that aren't part of your defined funnel navigation. This might mean you need to re-evaluate your funnel navigation. The same is true if you tend to lose users along a specific portion of the funnel navigation path, but that's covered more in the next chapter.

These two reports might not seem like much, but in truth they offer a wealth of information. And when you combine the information in these reports with the information that you can gather from other Google Analytics reports, you get a pretty good picture of what is driving your site visitors' behavior. Not bad for a free tool.

There's still a lot of information you can learn about your site visitors, however, so don't stop now. In the next chapter you'll learn how to integrate Google Analytics with your AdWords account. After all, we've spent a lot of time talking about AdWords in this chapter, so it's about time we connected the two, don't you think?

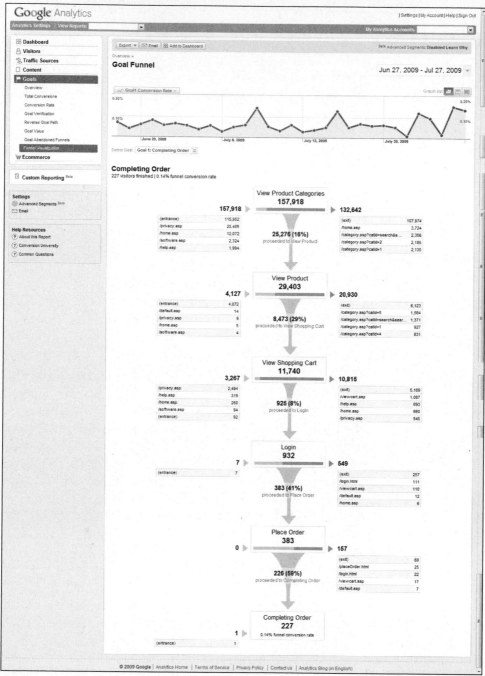

Figure 12-5: The Funnel Visualization report shows how visitors travel through a funnel.

CHAPTER 13

Google AdWords Integration

If there was ever a reason to sign up for your free Google Analytics account, then this is it. You can effortlessly sync your Google AdWords account to your Google Analytics account, enabling ROI measurement metrics for your AdWords marketing campaigns, a fourth Clicks tab, and a few jazzy reports that are available only if you sync your Google accounts.

In this chapter we're going to go that extra mile and not only show you how to do just that—we'll also show you how you can track your non-AdWords marketing campaigns, as well as stuff like banners and e-mail creatives/blasts.

Why Sync in the First Place?

Syncing your Google AdWords account with your Google Analytics account is the equivalent to adding rocket fuel to your 50cc moped. While AdWords already provides a great suite of reporting tools, your Analytics account gives you access to metrics, tabs, and reports that are not available anywhere else in the known world. Also, while your AdWords data is imported into your Google Analytics account, you'll be able to view or apply Goal Conversion, E-commerce (if applicable), Dimensioning, Filters, Custom Reports, and Advanced Segments at the Campaign, Ad Group, and Keyword level, which is tremendously beneficial.

For the most part, reporting at the AdWords level stops immediately after the click has occurred on your ad (unless you're using the Google AdWords

Conversion Tracking script). So while your campaigns may have high-quality scores, high click-through rates, and low cost-per-click averages, there's no way to really tell how effective your ads were at allowing your web site's visitors to perform the tasks they wanted to perform. Sure, you can analyze your conversion rates and your cost-per-conversion metrics, but without Google Analytics, how can you evaluate your landing pages and your conversion/shopping process, or know your true ROI?

Being able to sync your Google Analytics account to a cost-per-click advertising account is unique in the web analytics industry. Omniture SiteCatalyst, Coremetrics, WebTrends, Clicktracks, Unica NetInsight, and other great web analytics solutions on the market today do not have the direct pipeline to import AdWords data as Google Analytics does, which is one of the big reasons Google Analytics is as popular and widely used as it is.

Finally, syncing your AdWords account with your Analytics account saves you a boatload of reporting and analysis time, and it saves your right mouse button or your Alt + Tab keys a lot of wear and tear—you won't have to constantly switch back and forth between two tabs or windows.

NOTE Syncing your Google AdWords account with your Google Analytics account also helps you manage other Google products, such as Google Website Optimizer. If your e-mail address is an administrator of a Google Analytics account, syncing your AdWords account to it will enable you to create an Analytics profile just for your Google Website Optimizer experiment data, which can be a great add-on to your Google Website Optimizer experiments.

Syncing Your Google AdWords and Analytics Accounts

Now that I've convinced you, it's time to sync your accounts together. First, determine where you stand with your accounts—you will fall into one of the following four possible situations:

1. You have neither an AdWords nor an Analytics account (why not?).

2. You have an AdWords account, but not an Analytics account.

3. You have an Analytics account, but not an AdWords account.

4. You have both an AdWords and an Analytics account.

Even if your accounts are already synced, it's probably a good idea to review this part of this chapter, because there have been a few important changes recently with the AdWords/Analytics syncing process that may affect you.

You Have Neither an AdWords Nor an Analytics Account

Since you're reading this book, and since you've made it this far, you're at least considering creating an AdWords and/or an Analytics account, so there's no need to delay getting started. Here's what you need to do. First, open up your very own Google AdWords account by going to www.google.com/adwords. You don't need to start running your ads or bidding on your keywords quite yet—all you need is five dollars and the account is yours.

NOTE Remember, the e-mail address that you'd like to use for any Google product must be a Google account that includes Google AdWords. (Any e-mail address can become a Google account; it does not have to be a Gmail address.) Revisit Chapter 3 for instructions on how to create a Google account.

Next, click on the Reports tab, where a sub-menu that appears will give you the choice of Reports, Google Analytics, or Website Optimizer. Click on **Google Analytics** to be taken to the screen shown in Figure 13-1. From this screen, ensure that "Create my free Google Analytics account" is selected and hit **Continue**.

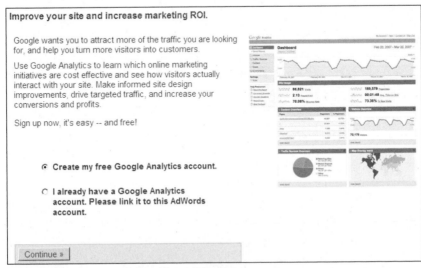

Figure 13-1: Syncing AdWords and Analytics

After that, enter your web site's URL and account name, as shown in Figure 13-2. Here you will also be exposed to two of the mechanics that make syncing possible, but that you won't see by opening up a stand-alone Google Analytics account: Destination URL Auto-tagging and AdWords Cost Data. Destination URL Auto-tagging enables campaign, ad group, and keyword information to be sent to Google Analytics, while AdWords Cost Data imports the metrics that you know and love: Impressions, Clicks, Cost-Per-Click, Click-Through Rate, and Total Cost.

In special cases you'll need to deselect Destination URL Auto-tagging and/ or AdWords Cost Data from each individual Google Analytics profile. We'll discuss that in a little while.

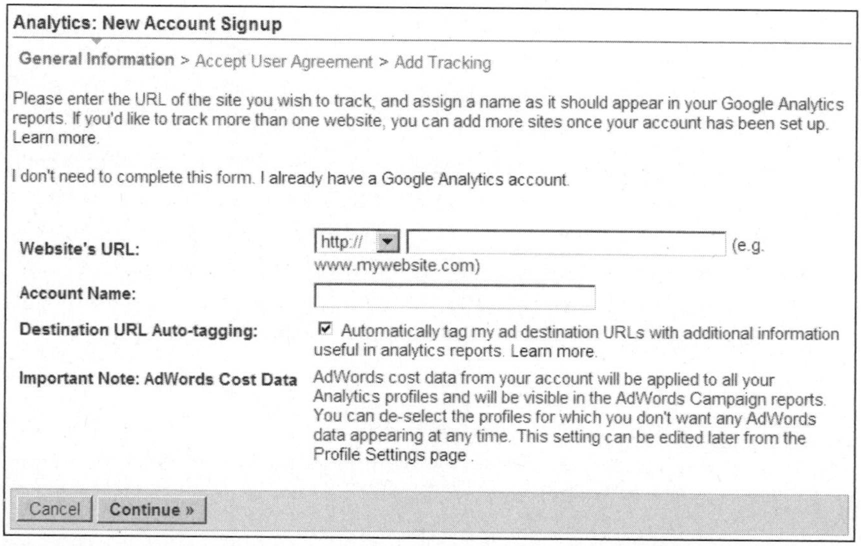

Analytics: New Account Signup

General Information > Accept User Agreement > Add Tracking

Please enter the URL of the site you wish to track, and assign a name as it should appear in your Google Analytics reports. If you'd like to track more than one website, you can add more sites once your account has been set up. Learn more.

I don't need to complete this form. I already have a Google Analytics account.

Website's URL:	http:// ▾ _____ (e.g. www.mywebsite.com)
Account Name:	_____
Destination URL Auto-tagging:	☑ Automatically tag my ad destination URLs with additional information useful in analytics reports. Learn more.
Important Note: AdWords Cost Data	AdWords cost data from your account will be applied to all your Analytics profiles and will be visible in the AdWords Campaign reports. You can de-select the profiles for which you don't want any AdWords data appearing at any time. This setting can be edited later from the Profile Settings page .

Cancel   Continue »

Figure 13-2: Destination URL Auto-tagging and AdWords Cost Data

After you click **Continue** and accept the AdWords terms and conditions, you will be able to grab the Google Analytics Tracking Code and finish creating your Google Analytics account, as I outlined in Chapter 3. Once you turn your campaigns on you'll begin to see AdWords data in the places that we'll discuss a bit later in this chapter.

You Have an AdWords Account, but Not an Analytics Account

Not everyone who has a Google AdWords account has a Google Analytics account (unfortunately), and if this is you, you can follow the same steps outlined in the previous section to open up your Google Analytics account. It's really that simple! Once you're done, refer to Chapter 3 to get your Google Analytics account up and running.

You Have an Analytics Account, but Not an AdWords Account

Haven't decided to advertise with Google AdWords until now? Not a problem—sign in to your Google account with the e-mail address that you want to use to log in to Google AdWords, and start the AdWords account-opening process as outlined in the section for those who have neither AdWords nor Analytics accounts. You must make sure that the e-mail address you use to log into your new AdWords account is an administrator on the Google Analytics account, or you won't be able to sync them.

You Have Both an AdWords and an Analytics Account

You have the best of both worlds, and if you want to connect them, no sweat. Simply assign administrative access to your Google Analytics account to the e-mail address that you use to log in to your AdWords account, and you'll be able to run through the syncing process. If that e-mail address doesn't yet have access to your Google Analytics account you'll need to create the new e-mail address in the User Access section of your Google Analytics account.

Special Cases and the GCLID

Depending on your individual situation, you may need to change the game plan a bit if you are missing AdWords data, or if you're receiving too much AdWords data.

AdWords is able to send click, keyword, ad group, and campaign data over to your Analytics account by appending a query string of parameters at the end of your destination URLs when a web-site visitor clicks on your ad. This query string of parameters is called the GCLID, and it's important that you be aware of its existence. As long as you have Destination URL Auto-tagging enabled you should expect to see something like this in your browser's address bar after someone clicks on your AdWords ad:

```
http://www.yoursite.com/page.php?gclid=CM3B_8rug5wCFQIxxgodAwNuRw
```

Without these encrypted characters Google AdWords can't do its magic of importing data into your Google Analytics profile(s). Every once in a blue moon a web server out there will not accept query parameters—this is normally to avoid a potential security risk. If you have Destination URL Auto-tagging enabled, and clicking on your ad results in an error page or security warning, work with your IT person or web developer to resolve this issue. Most of the time there won't be too many problems in allowing the GCLID to pass through.

Other times—more often than you'd like—the destination URL you're using in your ads is actually a redirect to another page, which may—and probably will—strip the GCLID off the URL in the address bar. If this is the case, either have the redirect removed or edit your ads and use the final destination URL where the visitor is ultimately taken to on your web site. Naturally, ensure that the Google Analytics Tracking Code is also present within the source code of your final destination URL page, especially if you are using uniquely created landing pages for your online marketing initiatives. You'd be surprised how many new landing pages go live without the Google Analytics Tracking Code that is on the rest of the web site.

Finally, in special situations you'll want to organize your AdWords campaign data in Google Analytics by using multiple profiles for different campaigns or ad groups. In some cases you don't want to expose the costs and monetary values associated with your AdWords campaigns for everyone to see. Cost Data is applied at the profile level, which means you can turn it on or off from any profile within the synced Google Analytics account. If you'd like to organize your AdWords campaign data with multiple profiles, you'll have to not only create those profiles but also use some custom include filters—Chapters 10 and 14 will show you exactly how to do that.

Tracking E-mail, Banner, and Other Non-AdWords Marketing

The most common question asked about Google Analytics when the topic of Google AdWords is discussed is usually something along the lines of, "Can Google Analytics track my Yahoo! Search marketing campaigns, too?" By default, no, it cannot. However, with a little bit of extra work, which we know you're good for, you not only can track your Yahoo! campaigns in Google Analytics, you can also track your Microsoft adCenter, Ask Sponsored Listings, Google Product Submit links, e-mail marketing campaigns, and about every other type of link under the sun.

You do this by manually appending a query parameter to the end of each of your destination URLs, or at the end of any link to your site in an e-mail campaign. This will allow Google Analytics to collect source, medium, campaign, ad content, and keyword data on your non-AdWords marketing campaigns. These five elements are normally referred to as the five dimensions of campaign tracking. They are also required for your search marketing campaigns if you'd like Google Analytics to differentiate between organic search result visits and pay-per-click advertisement clicks, because, by default, it can't.

Unlike the AdWords GCLID parameters that you just learned about, you cannot automatically apply this feature by selecting a checkbox—you're going to have to roll up your sleeves here and append parameters to your destination URLs one by one. With a bit of cunning you'll be able to make some simple formulas in Microsoft Excel that can partially automate this process for you, which we highly recommend doing after you learn the basics of URL tagging.

Let's take a look at the five dimensions of campaign tracking and how to construct your URL.

1. **Source:** This is pretty much what it sounds like—the source that was responsible for bringing the traffic to your web site. (Examples: Yahoo!, MSN, Ask, Shopzilla, newsletter, e-mail blast, etc.…).

2. **Medium:** This is the means by which a person accessed your web site. The standard that Google Analytics is expecting for pay-per-click campaigns is cpc, in lowercase lettering, but you can use cpm, e-mail, or banner, just to name a few. However, "cpc" in lowercase lettering is the only one that you should use for any non-AdWords cost-per-click marketing campaign.

3. **Campaign:** The campaign dimension can be used to group or *bucket* the visits from your non-AdWords marketing initiatives in a naming convention that makes sense to you. Most marketers use the same name for their campaign dimension that they use within the pay-per-click marketing program—it just makes life a lot easier. For e-mail or banner campaigns, it usually makes sense to use the name of the promotion, such as July Newsletter or B2B Banners.

4. **Term:** The term dimension is your keyword. Almost always this will be exactly what you're using in your marketing campaigns. The term dimension is normally not used for e-mail, banner, or referral links that don't need a keyword in order to be accessed.

5. **Content:** The last dimension that Google Analytics offers for manual URL tagging is the content dimension. For pay-per-click marketing campaigns this can be the title of your ad or a description of an ad, like 40% Off Sale Ad. The content dimension really is helpful with e-mail and banner/image marketing, as you can use it to identify a link's location (top link, bottom link, second link) or an image's size (150×600, 250×250, skyscraper).

Putting It All Together

Let's say that I'd like to tag my newest destination URL of http://www.yoursite.com/landing-page.html. I'm going to use the following for the dimensions:

- **Source:** yahoo
- **Medium:** cpc

- **Term:** green-shirt
- **Content:** discount ad
- **Campaign:** shirts and wearables

My final destination URL will look exactly like this:

```
http://www.yoursite.com/landing-page.html?utm_source=yahoo&utm_
medium=cpc&utm_term=green-shirt&utm_content=discount+ad&utm_
campaign=shirts+and+wearables
```

Notes and Tips about URL Tagging

Google Analytics will use exactly what you use for your dimensions in its reports under the Traffic Sources section, so it's strongly advised that you build your URL tagging carefully and with a bit of thought about how you want your data to look in the end.

There are also some miscellaneous items that you should be aware of when tagging your URLs. It's a bit tedious, but well worth the read:

- Source, medium, and campaign are required dimensions. You must use at least these three dimensions, or you risk your data's not being collected properly. The term and the content dimensions are both optional, but obviously you're going to want to at least use the term dimension for any URLs tagged at the keyword level.

- There is a reason that we used lowercase lettering throughout, especially in the medium dimension. If you don't use a lowercase cpc as your medium dimension, Google Analytics will not be able to recognize it as a paid keyword, and will lump the traffic under Other (visible on your dashboard and the Traffic Sources Overview report). Even CPC or Cpc will cause missing keywords and statistics throughout Google Analytics, so stick to lowercase and you'll be fine.

- We recommend using + symbols instead of spaces between words in the URL. Instead of green shoes, use green+shoes, and you'll not only make your report data come out nice and clean, but you'll also be insured against a broken link or error page being served up. (Some web servers do not allow spaces in the URL.)

- URLs on the Web can have only one question mark symbol. If your URL already has one before your URL tagging, make sure that it starts with an & symbol instead. (Use the Google Analytics URL Builder that we'll talk about next and it will take care of this for you automatically.)

■ At this time, report tables in Google Analytics are not expandable (as columns are expandable in Microsoft Excel). Therefore, try to keep your dimension names short and sweet—overly long names can make your report tables difficult to read.

The Google Analytics URL Builder

Fortunately, the fine folks at Google Analytics have a page in their help section that can build URLs for you, so you don't have to manually type them all up. Visit

```
http://www.google.com/support/googleanalytics/bin/answer
.py?hl=en&answer=55578
```

or simply search for "Tool URL Builder" or "Google Analytics URL Builder" on Google and click the first organic search result to get to the page displayed in Figure 13-3.

Simply enter your web-site URL, source, medium, term, content, and campaign names and click **Generate URL**. Voila!

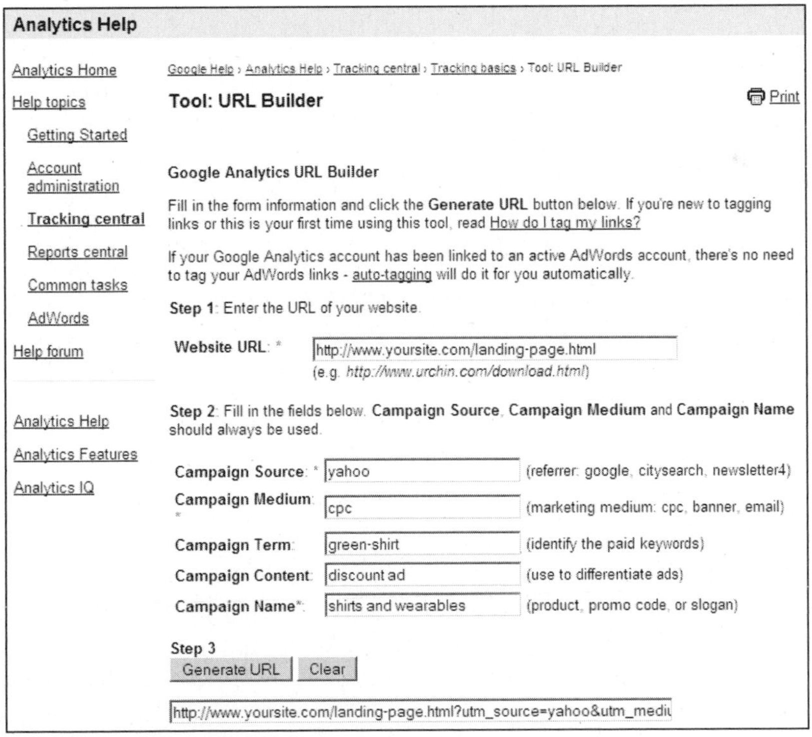

Figure 13-3: Google Analytics URL Builder

> **NOTE** If either you or your client is running multiple AdWords accounts at the same time, you can use manual URL tagging on the AdWords account that is not synced to the Google Analytics account, in lieu of using Destination URL Auto-tagging. Manual tagging should work just as well as auto-tagging with the GCLID parameters.

The AdWords Report Section

Now that I've bored you to death with technical implementation and URL tagging lingo, it's time for the big payoff—beautiful AdWords data in your Google Analytics account! At this time, Google Analytics offers three reports and a new tab for analyzing your AdWords marketing campaigns. You can find these by clicking on **AdWords** within the Traffic Sources section, where three report names will appear: AdWords Campaigns, Keyword Positions, and TV Campaigns. Start by clicking **AdWords Campaigns**.

The AdWords Campaigns Report

In the AdWords campaigns report you'll be able to view Google Analytics data, like average time on site and bounce rate, for each of your AdWords campaigns. You can use the data in the scorecard that runs horizontally across the report table to compare your AdWords campaigns' performance to site averages. Reach this report by clicking on Traffic Sources from the left-hand navigation, then click on AdWords, and click on AdWords Campaigns.

AdWords sent 7,810 visits via 35 campaigns

Site Usage	Goal Conversion	Ecommerce	Clicks			Views:
Visits	Pages/Visit	Avg. Time on Site	% New Visits	Bounce Rate		
7,810	**3.56**	**00:02:16**	**81.04%**	**52.33%**		
% of Site Total: 3.36%	Site Avg: 3.94 (-9.58%)	Site Avg: 00:02:40 (-15.19%)	Site Avg: 73.00% (11.01%)	Site Avg: 50.48% (3.67%)		

	Dimension: Campaign	Visits ↓	Pages/Visit	Avg. Time on Site	% New Visits	Bounce Rate
1.	National - Tennis Shoes	2,709	3.34	00:02:06	79.40%	42.12%
2.	National - T-Shirts	1,238	3.86	00:02:20	79.73%	48.30%
3.	National - Branding	658	8.98	00:06:34	52.58%	15.50%
4.	Florida - Tennis Shoes	561	3.53	00:02:33	85.38%	59.00%
5.	National - Content Network	455	1.13	00:00:15	96.70%	92.53%
6.	California - Surfing Wet Suits	406	1.83	00:00:55	95.81%	78.82%
7.	New York - Jogging Shoes	346	3.18	00:02:21	82.37%	58.38%
8.	Florida - Scuba Gear	247	2.53	00:01:31	85.02%	59.92%
9.	California - Rollerblades	225	2.19	00:01:17	87.56%	66.67%
10.	Arizona - T-Shirts	160	2.08	00:00:50	93.75%	71.88%

Figure 13-4: An AdWords Campaign report

As you can see in Figure 13-4, you can also view important goal conversion and e-commerce performance metrics by clicking those tabs at the top of the report table, just as you can anywhere else in Google Analytics. As I said at the beginning of this chapter, this is the type of critical performance data that's not available in Google AdWords and that can help you turn your average AdWords campaign into an awesome AdWords campaign. By the way—how much revenue are your AdWords campaigns generating? Are visitors from your AdWords campaigns completing tasks on your web site and converting? Do visitors from one campaign have a very high bounce rate? These are the critical questions that you can now have answered because you synced your AdWords and your Analytics accounts. Go you!

Now, look again at the top part of Figure 13-4. Do you notice a fourth tab, labeled Clicks, to the right of the Ecommerce tab? Clicking that tab will reveal your AdWords campaign statistics, such as clicks and cost-per-click, as well as three new metrics available only here. Figure 13-5 shows what it looks like when you click the Clicks tab.

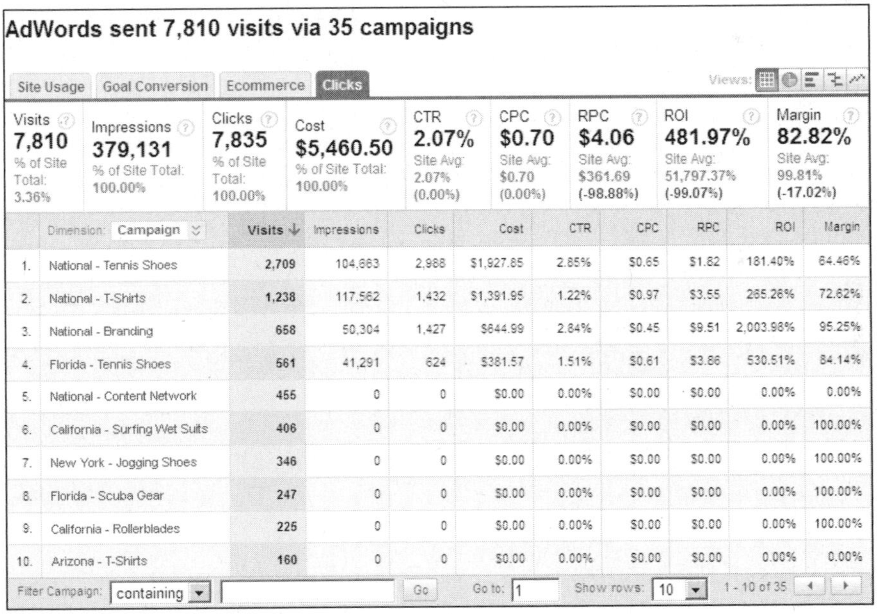
AdWords sent 7,810 visits via 35 campaigns

Site Usage | Goal Conversion | Ecommerce | Clicks

Visits	Impressions	Clicks	Cost	CTR	CPC	RPC	ROI	Margin
7,810	379,131	7,835	$5,460.50	2.07%	$0.70	$4.06	481.97%	82.82%
% of Site Total: 3.36%	% of Site Total: 100.00%	% of Site Total: 100.00%	% of Site Total: 100.00%	Site Avg: 2.07% (0.00%)	Site Avg: $0.70 (0.00%)	Site Avg: $361.69 (-98.88%)	Site Avg: 51,797.37% (-99.07%)	Site Avg: 99.81% (-17.02%)

	Dimension: Campaign	Visits	Impressions	Clicks	Cost	CTR	CPC	RPC	ROI	Margin
1.	National - Tennis Shoes	2,709	104,663	2,988	$1,927.85	2.85%	$0.65	$1.82	181.40%	64.46%
2.	National - T-Shirts	1,238	117,562	1,432	$1,391.95	1.22%	$0.97	$3.55	265.26%	72.62%
3.	National - Branding	658	50,304	1,427	$644.99	2.84%	$0.45	$9.51	2,003.98%	95.25%
4.	Florida - Tennis Shoes	561	41,291	624	$381.57	1.51%	$0.61	$3.86	530.51%	84.14%
5.	National - Content Network	455	0	0	$0.00	0.00%	$0.00	$0.00	0.00%	0.00%
6.	California - Surfing Wet Suits	406	0	0	$0.00	0.00%	$0.00	$0.00	0.00%	100.00%
7.	New York - Jogging Shoes	346	0	0	$0.00	0.00%	$0.00	$0.00	0.00%	100.00%
8.	Florida - Scuba Gear	247	0	0	$0.00	0.00%	$0.00	$0.00	0.00%	100.00%
9.	California - Rollerblades	225	0	0	$0.00	0.00%	$0.00	$0.00	0.00%	100.00%
10.	Arizona - T-Shirts	160	0	0	$0.00	0.00%	$0.00	$0.00	0.00%	0.00%

Filter Campaign: containing | Go | Go to: 1 | Show rows: 10 | 1 - 10 of 35

Figure 13-5: The Clicks tab in the AdWords campaign report

If you look toward the right-hand side of Figure 13-5, you'll see RPC, ROI, and Margin. These financially oriented metrics are available only here in this report within Google Analytics, and they can help you determine whether you're spending your advertising dollars wisely.

RPC is the acronym for *revenue per click,* which is the average revenue or average goal value for each click on your ads. The higher the RPC, the more revenue for you! If you're looking at your AdWords keywords in Google Analytics and you see a few keywords not performing very well, this could be a very good sign to stop financing those keywords, change the match type, or modify the ads within that ad group.

ROI (return on investment) doesn't really need a lengthy explanation, because it's a familiar term. In Google Analytics, ROI takes either the e-commerce revenue or the goal value, which means you don't have to operate an online shopping cart and sell products to have an ROI calculation, which is really nice! Refer to Chapter 11 to see how to set up goal values and what to use for your goal values.

Finally, Margin takes your e-commerce revenue (or goal value), subtracts the cost, and divides the result by revenue. This means that the margin will be represented as a percentage, and the closer the margin is to 100 percent, the more funds and budget you should feel comfortable allocating to that campaign. The lower the margin, the less likely that your campaign is a wise investment.

Clicking on the name of any campaign in this report will enable you to step one level deeper and view all the ad groups within that campaign. Clicking an ad group will bring up all the keywords within that ad group (Figure 13-6). Now you can view impression, click, RPC, and ROI data at the keyword level, all within the same report. Also, don't forget about the % of Site Total and Site Average metrics running across the scorecard on the top of the report table, giving you perspective on your set of ad groups or keywords.

Visits ⑦ **1,574** % of Site Total: 0.68%	Impressions ⑦ **69,466** % of Site Total: 18.32%	Clicks ⑦ **1,689** % of Site Total: 21.56%	Cost ⑦ **$1,037.88** % of Site Total: 19.01%	CTR ⑦ **2.43%** Site Avg: 2.07% (17.65%)	CPC **$0.6** Site Av $0.70 (-11.8

	Dimension: Keyword ⌄	Visits ↓	Impressions	Clicks	Cost
1.	green shirts	598	41,868	642	$366.62
2.	green t-shirts	158	4,954	145	$98.63
3.	green tee shirts	107	3,026	119	$78.82

Figure 13-6: AdWords keywords

About once a day, Google Analytics will go out to the Google AdWords account it is linked to and pull in data—keep this in mind when you're looking at your AdWords account statistics in AdWords when your date range is the default view of the last 30 days. Your data may be slightly different between the two interfaces, but don't worry—wait until tomorrow to see the complete data for today.

The Difference between a Visit and a Click

Flip back to Figure 13-5 and look at the campaigns in rows 5 through 10. Notice how none of those campaigns has any click data, but each campaign is showing visits? This isn't a mistake or a problem with Google Analytics; when your Analytics account is synced with your AdWords account, you will still receive visit data for campaigns that are no longer active, and if you do receive visit data it will appear in this report, alongside the actively running AdWords campaigns.

Old data may appear for a few different reasons. One reason is that when a user clicks on your AdWords ad, he or she bookmarks the URL, and then later on accesses your web site again via that same bookmark. Google Analytics uses the original referring information stored on a visitor's referral cookie to credit any visits that come from bookmarks, which means you will definitely see old or inactive campaign visits mixed in with your active campaigns.

Visits can also be accidentally labeled with older campaign names if you are using manual URL tagging for your AdWords destination URLs, but forget to update the utm_campaign dimension to the new campaign name. Old data can also get in if you're using utm_nooverride=1, which we'll cover in Chapter 14.

All this happens because a visit is completely different from a click, and those two metrics—visits and clicks—will most likely never match up identically in the same set of visitors. There are plenty of situations that help make these figures different: multiple clicks on your AdWords ads (by a comparison shopper or impatient web-site visitor), multiple visits from only one click on your ad (which we just talked about), or invalid clicks (fewer clicks than visits, because, while Google AdWords can remove invalid clicks from your AdWords account, Google Analytics will count a visit once it occurs on your web site.

The Keyword Positions Report

One of the real hidden gems, not only of the Traffic Sources reports, but of Google Analytics generally, is the Keyword Positions report. With it, you are able to view keyword performance across ad positions, which is sure to reveal some interesting information about your AdWords keywords and their performance per ad location.

Within the keywords report you can click on any keyword on the left-hand side of the report table to activate the results on the right-hand side. On the left you can sort your keywords by any site usage, goal conversion, or e-commerce metric with the small drop-down menu that defaults to displaying visits. On the right you can change the position breakdown of the selected keyword from the left-hand side with another small drop-down menu, which will also default to showing visits.

Figure 13-7 shows the keyword with the most visits selected, showing a position breakdown of e-commerce revenue. As you can see in Figure 13-7, most of the e-commerce revenue from this keyword is generated when its corresponding ad(s) are shown in either position Top 1 or position Side 1, with just a small bit of revenue coming from positions Top 2 and Top 3. In hindsight, it may seem obvious that this should be the case, but position Side 1 from the keywords report in Google AdWords is actually Position 4 in Google Analytics! (Translation: Google works hard to assure that buying a high position doesn't automatically guarantee clicks, revenue, or high-quality scores. So ad position 4 in Analytics may actually outperform positions 2 or 3 in AdWords.)

What this means is that if you use AdWords Position Preference, as many marketers do, or if you use a third-party ad bidding/management system, you'll probably want to make sure that your ads appear for your keyword more in Positions 1 and 4; these are the two highest positions on the results page, and generate more revenue for you than setting up your ads to show on Positions 1 through 3, which is a very common practice in both AdWords Position Preference and third-party bid-management platforms.

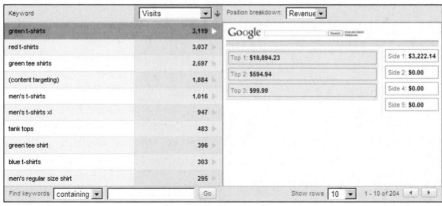

Figure 13-7: The Keyword Positions report

We highly recommend that if you use any report out of this section, it should be the one that you incorporate in your weekly analysis of your AdWords campaigns. Begin to analyze goal conversion and e-commerce performance metrics for your higher-spending keywords to see exactly where on Google's search results pages your ads are performing the best; then make position preference/bid management platform updates accordingly.

The TV Campaigns Report

One extension of the Google AdWords platform is the fairly new TV Ads program. With Google's TV Ads you are given a brand-new way to create, manage, and schedule your television commercials, right from within your Google AdWords interface. And, naturally, you can perform deeper analysis and obtain greater insights from your TV campaigns when your AdWords account is synced to your Google Analytics account. Even if you don't advertise on TV with Google TV Ads, read this section so that you can be exposed to even more of the possibilities of Google Analytics.

NOTE To learn all about the Google TV Ads program, including how TV Ads data is calculated, visit `http://www.google.com/adwords/tvads/`

Check out Figure 13-8 for what a breakdown of your TV campaigns may look like in your own Google Analytics account. From left to right on Figure 13-8, you can see each campaign listed in the first column, which is sorted by TV impressions in the second column. TV impressions are the total number of estimated viewers who saw your TV ad. Ad Plays displays the total number of times your ads were played; Viewed Entire Ad shows the estimated number of people, based on impressions, who watched your ad from beginning to end; % Initial Audience Retained is the proportion of your audience that watched your entire ad; and Cost and CPM represent the total dollars spent and the cost per thousand impressions for your TV ads, respectively.

Figure 13-8: The TV Campaigns report

One of the nice things that you can do with your TV ads data in Google Analytics is to compare it against your online traffic volume for your web site. Was there an uptick in traffic to your web site on the same day or hour that your TV ads ran?

Use the graphing tools above the report table to compare your TV ads impressions with your visits, page views, and bounce rate. A higher than normal bounce rate at the same hour or same day in which your TV ads ran could suggest a mixed message or visitor expectations not being met when they visited your site.

You can also use the graphing tools to compare your TV ad statistics against your goal conversion and e-commerce metrics, and as with anything else in Google Analytics, you'll be able to determine if your TV ads are worth it to your bottom line at the end of the day.

Other Reports Displaying AdWords and Non-AdWords Data

Earlier in the chapter, I talked a lot about URL tagging and tracking your non-AdWords data, and I don't want to leave you hanging with just implementation talk. I also want to show you some other places your AdWords data will appear, as well as where your properly tagged non-AdWords marketing data will show up.

For starters, check out your Search Engines report within the Traffic Source section, and click the blue **Paid** text link above the report table to view only paid (CPC) data. Everything tagged with a medium of cpc is going to appear here, including your Google AdWords CPC traffic. Use a combination of the graphing tools, report views, and goal conversion/e-commerce tabs to get an idea of how all your paid marketing efforts are doing across the board. A great thing to do afterward is to check out your keywords report. Here, you'll also want to click the blue **Paid** link and view the performance of all your paid keywords in all search engines. An intelligent strategy here is to dig into your top five or ten keywords, segment each one by source, and get an idea of which keywords you should probably invest more money with, and which ones you should pull back from. If your `brown t-shirt` keyword brings in more revenue from Yahoo! Search Marketing than it does from Microsoft AdCenter, guess where more of your money should go?

The campaign report is normally a favorite among paid marketers, since every campaign in their world is listed here.

> **TIP** When you're tagging your URLs for Google Analytics, be sure to place the search engine name at either the beginning or the end of the campaign name. This way, you'll be able to identify the source of each campaign without having to use the dimensioning drop-down, which frees you up to use it for something more interesting, like Visitor Type or Landing Page. Doing this will also separate the campaign data from each engine into its own line item in this report (This can either be really good or undesirable for you, depending on how you ultimately want to see and analyze your data. Think about how you want your data to appear before tagging your URLs.)

Now, what if you want to view more than just your CPC marketing efforts? In that case, it looks as if the All Traffic Sources report has your name on it. As the name suggests, and as you'll see when you reach Chapter 16, all your sources of traffic will be listed here, including all your banner, e-mail, and referral traffic together. Think of looking at this report as "zooming out" on Google Maps; you're getting a wider, broader view of all marketing efforts together.

NOTE Be very careful when comparing data from different types of traffic sources against one another. While all marketing efforts connect to and support one another, they also have very distinctive, unique properties, delivery methods, and audience types, which differentiate them from one another. For example, a visitor who heard your commercial on the radio may type in your web site's URL by hand (directly) and may be ready to buy your product, as your radio spot suggested. Another visitor may simply be interested in learning more about the product, and may click on your AdWords ad (CPC), along with some of your competitor ads to comparison-shop. Consequently, you may see a much higher conversion rate for direct traffic than you would for CPC traffic, in this particular example.

Therefore, use caution when comparing performance metrics between marketing channels. They aren't always comparable, and may ultimately leave you with a misleading choice of one channel versus the other channel. This may not be the best solution for you, since there are other ways of determining success and making a choice.

Chapter 1 introduced custom reporting and advanced segmentation. These are powerful tools that you won't be able to put down, once you're comfortable with them. Chances are that you have a lot of marketing questions to answer, and you need to be able to see and analyze your data with specific metrics and dimensions that aren't available in any standard Google Analytics report. Creating some custom reports and advanced segments for your AdWords and non-AdWords data may be the right solution for you. After all, it's your data; you should be able to do whatever you want with it, right? And yes, you can use advanced segments on top of custom reports—you won't crash Google Analytics.

You'll also want to consider creating a separate profile for either your cost-per-click data or your AdWords data (or both). When you create a duplicate profile for your AdWords data, you'll have a permanent record that does not need to be segmented or dimensioned. You'll also be able to take advantage of the ability to analyze your AdWords data with reports like Funnel Visualization and Site Overlay, which do not have advanced segment functionality at this time. Site overlay for your AdWords data can be particularly useful for you, because you'll be able to see exactly where your visitors are clicking on your landing pages. This can help improve the performance of your AdWords campaigns, and depending how far you take your optimization work, you may even sneak in a point or two on Quality Score—all because you were able to look at site overlay within your duplicate AdWords profile!

If this sounds like something that might interest you—and if you don't mind a few technical step-by-step instructions—then you should move on to Chapter 14, where I'll show you how to create a duplicate profile just for your Google AdWords data.

Hacking Google Analytics

What fun would Google Analytics be without a few tricks of the trade? Even though the default Google Analytics setup makes it a great tool to help web-site owners everywhere obtain highly insightful information, there are quite a number of helpful tips, tricks, and customizations that can make all the difference for you. We like to call these "hacks," and in this chapter you're going to find a whole lot of 'em. We've made it so that you don't have to be a computer science major or an MIT doctoral candidate in order to apply some of these hacks—or, at least, be able to tell a webmaster or IT techie how to do them.

Hopefully, you have free rein to make code modifications on your site, but please keep in mind that not every off-the-shelf or turnkey solution will allow you to edit source code and make customizations. Please work with your vendor to implement changes to the Google Analytics Tracking Code.

We have small hacks, big hacks, simple hacks, and a few complex hacks within the following pages. Which ones will be useful for you?

A Review of Subdomain/Cross-Domain Tracking

Some of you may be coming here because we recommended that you should from Chapter 6 ("E-commerce Concepts and Methods"). As we mentioned there, you don't necessarily need to have an e-commerce storefront for tracking your subdomain(s) or your multiple domain(s). Perhaps you have a blog on a subdomain from your primary domain (`blog.yoursite.com`), or maybe you have a sister web site as a part of your corporate umbrella (`www.secondsite.com`) that you'd like to track within the same Google Analytics profile.

Let's again review how to properly track your subdomain or a second domain.

Tracking Subdomains

On all pages of your main site and any subdomain site that you wish to track in one profile, use the following _setDomainName function in your Google Analytics Tracking Code as shown. Don't forget to keep the same UA number throughout:

```
var pageTracker = _gat._getTracker("UA-XXXXXX-X");
pageTracker._setDomainName(".yoursite.com");
pageTracker._trackPageview();
```

Naturally, replace `.yoursite.com` with your own domain name. Keep the leading period on the tracking code on both web sites to ensure cookie integrity.

Tracking Multiple Domains

Whenever multiple domains are involved you'll need to use both _setDomainName and _setAllowLinker on the Google Analytics Tracking Code on both web sites:

```
var pageTracker = _gat._getTracker("UA-XXXXXX-X");
pageTracker._setDomainName("none");
pageTracker._setAllowLinker(true);
pageTracker._trackPageview();
```

You'll also need to either use the _link function on all links that take users to and from each web site, or use the _linkByPost function on all forms that take a user to and from each web site

On hyperlinks (_link):

```
<a href="http://www.otherwebsite.com/"
onClick="pageTracker._link('http://
www.otherwebsite.com/');return false;">
Click here to go to our other web site!</a>
```

On forms (_linkByPost):

```
<form action="http://www.otherwebsite.com/processing.php"
name="form" method="post" onSubmit="pageTracker._linkByPost(this)">
```

Not using either _link or _linkByPost on both web sites will cause the second web site to drop its own set of cookies during a visitor's session, causing visitor and referral information to be lost. This is the number-one cause of self-referrals in reports (seeing your own web site as a top referring source).

> **NOTE** In Chapter 8, we recommended that you use calls to _setAllowLinker and _setAllowHash to track between multiple domains, instead of using a call to _setDomainName as we just did in the previous example. Both ways will most likely work, unless you have links between both sites that both use "www" and that don't use "www" (Example: links going to both http://www.site.com and http://site.com). If this is your situation, you'll want to use calls to _setAllowLinker(true) and _setAllowHash(false), instead of using calls to _setDomainName(none) and _setAllowLinker(true).

Tracking Multiple Subdomains and Multiple Domains

Here's something we didn't cover in Chapter 6. Let's say you have four properties that you'd like to track in a single profile:

1. Your main site (www.yoursite.com)
2. Your blog (blog.yoursite.com)
3. Your second site (www.secondsite.com)
4. Your second site's careers section (careers.secondsite.com)

In a situation where multiple domains and subdomains are involved, you'll need to use three functions on all pages on all sites: _setDomainName, _setAllowLinker, and _setAllowHash. Look closely at the next two coding examples of the proper way to use _setDomainName on each site. We'll use our four-site example to demonstrate:

On all pages of yoursite.com (www.yoursite.com and blog.yoursite.com):

```
var pageTracker = _gat._getTracker("UA-XXXXXX-X");
pageTracker._setDomainName(".yoursite.com");
pageTracker._setAllowLinker(true);
pageTracker._setAllowHash(false);
pageTracker._trackPageview();
```

On all pages of secondsite.com (www.secondsite.com and careers.secondsite.com):

```
var pageTracker = _gat._getTracker("UA-XXXXXX-X");
pageTracker._setDomainName(".secondsite.com");
pageTracker._setAllowLinker(true);
pageTracker._setAllowHash(false);
pageTracker._trackPageview();
```

You'll also need to use either _link or _linkByPost on any links to and from each site. However, _link or _linkByPost is not necessary on links between subdomains of each domain. (For example, don't use _link or _linkByPost on links from www .yoursite.com to blog.yoursite.com, or from www.secondsite.com to careers .secondsite.com).

Setting up Duplicate Profiles

Duplicate profiles have many different uses. You can create up to 50 separate profiles in one Google Analytics account, and the options are limitless as to what data you can track in each one of them. You can track 50 different web sites, all with different UA numbers, if you'd like to. However, with some nice filtering work you can do things like track all your Google AdWords data in its own profile from the same web site. Or track all e-mail marketing campaign data in its own profile. How about organizing your subdomain/multiple domain traffic with a few duplicate profiles?

Let's say you completed installing the Google Analytics Tracking Code, using the exact same tracking code on three separate subdomains that you wish to track in one profile:

1. Your main site (www.yoursite.com)

2. Your blog (blog.yoursite.com)

3. Your storefront (store.yoursite.com)

Here, what we would do is have four profiles for the same web site—one profile that collects all three sites' data (sometimes referred to as a "roll-up" profile), and an individual profile for each subdomain site.

The *main* or *master* profile that collects the data for all three sites does not need anything done to it. However, each one of the three *individual* profiles will need to have an *include filter* created for it. Remember, an include filter excludes everything but what you insert in its filter pattern.

Create a filter for each individual profile with the specifications shown in Figure 14-1, and apply it to the corresponding profile. You'll need to do this for each duplicate profile you create. Filters can be created within each individual profile's settings, or by clicking on the **Filter Manager** link, found toward the bottom of the Account Overview screen where all your profiles are listed.

> **NOTE** As you can see in Figure 14-1's Filter Pattern field, the name of the domain (the hostname) is written in Regular Expressions format. If you are not comfortable with Regular Expressions yet, please review Chapter 10 once more. Or simply copy our examples straight from the book—but be extremely careful when doing so, as one single mistake in a character (even an extra white space) can cause your filter to not function, or to do something completely unexpected and harm your data.

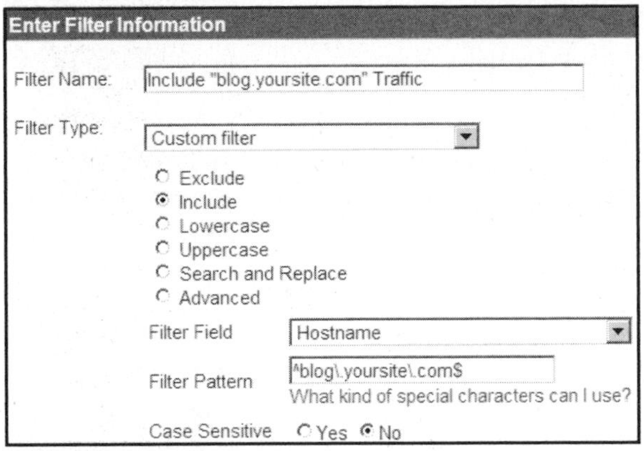

Figure 14-1: Include filter by hostname

Now let's say that you want to track all your Google AdWords data in a duplicate profile, so that you can have an entire suite of reports with nothing but your AdWords marketing data. In that situation you'll need not one but two include filters, as well as ensuring that you have Applied Cost Data checked.

After you've created your duplicate profile for an existing domain, create two include filters with the following specifications, and apply them to your newly created profile:

Filter #1

> **Filter Type:** Custom ⇨ Include
>
> **Filter Field:** Campaign Source
>
> **Filter Pattern:** google
>
> **Case Sensitive:** No

Filter #2

> **Filter Type:** Custom ⇨ Include
>
> **Filter Field:** Campaign Medium
>
> **Filter Pattern:** cpc
>
> **Case Sensitive:** No

If you plan ahead you can make other duplicate profiles using an include filter, such as to track all your e-mail Marketing efforts in one profile. If you plan on using the Google Analytics URL Builder that we talked about in the previous chapter, you'll want to use a consistent naming convention for your medium dimension for all your URLs. This makes creating these duplicate profiles much easier.

Let's say that you've used the word "email" for your medium dimension in all the URLs of your e-mail marketing efforts. Create the following include filter for your duplicate profile and you should be good to go:

Filter Type: Custom ⇨ Include

Filter Field: Campaign Medium

Filter Pattern: email

Case Sensitive: No

Another example of a duplicate profile that you could create would be one where you would exclude all your traffic from China, Japan, and South Korea. In this example you want any traffic from those countries to not be included in your report data. One exclude filter on a newly created duplicate profile can handle this request, with the exact specifications below:

Filter Type: Custom ⇨ Exclude

Filter Field: Visitor Country

Filter Pattern: china | japan | korea

Case Sensitive: No

NOTE A great way to check if your filter will work is to type in your filter pattern as you would when creating your filter in the filter tool at the bottom of most reports in Google Analytics. If the pattern works there as you want it to, it will also work as a filter.

Why Create Duplicate Profiles?

One question that you may be asking yourself is "Why should I create any duplicate profiles? Wouldn't it be easier to just use an advanced segment and possibly a custom report to get what I want?" There are a few important reasons why.

Creating a duplicate profile creates a permanent record of that traffic, based upon the filters that you apply to it. Advanced segments can be created and applied to reports, but they are not permanent. Duplicate profiles aren't subject to data sampling and can be assigned user access—advanced segments can be subject to data sampling and at this time can only be shared via a permalink.

The most important reason creating duplicate profiles can help is that certain reports in Google Analytics do not support advanced segments. These are the Keyword Position report, the Absolute Unique Visitors report, the Benchmarking report, the Site Overlay report, and the Funnel Visualization report. Creating a profile for all of your Google AdWords traffic, for example, enables you to view funnel visualization and site overlay data for that specific group of visitors, which can be invaluable in helping you to gain deeper insights into specific sets of visitors.

Filtering Out Internal Traffic

Along with subdomain/cross-domain tracking, excluding internal or corporate traffic is one of the things web-site owners ask about most frequently. You can do this in a number of different ways, depending on your situation.

Excluding a Single IP Address

If you—or everyone in your office—use a single IP address to access the Web, you will need to apply an exclude filter with the following specifications:

> **Filter Type:** Exclude all traffic from an IP address
>
> **IP Address:** ^192\.168\.254\.254$

You can also use the "Exclude all traffic from an IP address" filter type if your organization owns every IP address between `192.168.254.1` and `192.168.254.254` (where only the last octet of the IP address is different). You would use the following syntax in this situation:

> **Filter Type:** Exclude all traffic from an IP address
>
> **IP Address:** ^192\.168\.254\.*

This filter will still work in this filter type because it will match only one IP address at a time, be it `192.168.254.34`, `192.168.254.109`, or so on.

Excluding Two (or More) IP Addresses

Your IT director comes to you with two completely separate IP addresses to exclude from your Google Analytics reports. Let's say they are `192.168.1.5` and `201.34.1.72`. You can use a Custom ⇨ Exclude filter type, as shown in Figure 14-2. Notice the pipe symbol (|) between IP addresses—you can keep adding more IP addresses if the need arises. Keep in mind that the total length of the Filter Pattern field must not exceed 255 characters.

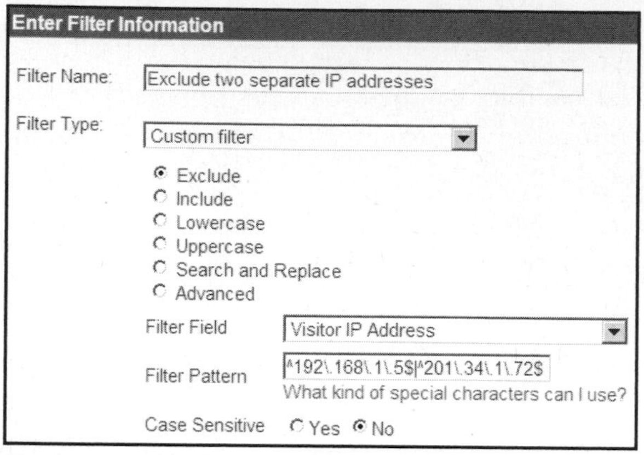

Figure 14-2: Excluding two IP addresses

Excluding a Range of IP Addresses

Imagine that you are the administrator of the Google Analytics account for a large organization that has a large range of IP addresses for all the computers on its network. That range of IP addresses just happens to be every IP address between `192.168.30.75` and `192.168.50.102`. If you are fantastic with Regular Expressions you will be able to write the filter in no time to exclude this range of IP addresses:

> **Filter Type:** Custom ➪ Exclude
>
> **Filter Field:** Visitor IP Address
>
> **Filter Pattern:** ^192\.168\.(30\.(7(5[-9] | [6-9][0-9]) | 2(5[5-9] | [6-9]
> [0-9]) | 3([0-9][0-9]) | 4([0-9][0-9]) | 5([0-9][0-9]) | 6([0-9][0-9]) | 7([0-9]
> [0-9]) | 800) | ((3[1-9] | 4[0-9])\.([0-9] | [1-9][0-9] | 1([0-9][0-9]) | 2([0-4]
> [0-9] | 5[0-5]))) | 50\.([0-9] | [1-9][0-9] | 1(0[0-2])))$

Yikes! That's a massive filter pattern, is it not? Even if you wrote the book on Regular Expressions, there's a far simpler way to come up with that same filter pattern without much hassle at all. Simply use the IP address range tool shown in Figure 14-3, from the Google Analytics Help Articles. This tool can create complex Regular Expressions like the previous one, or simple ones if you type in only one IP address, so it can be helpful if creating filters is something you're still getting used to.

This very helpful tool can be found at the following address:

```
http://www.google.com/support/analytics/bin/answer
.py?hl=en&answer=55572
```

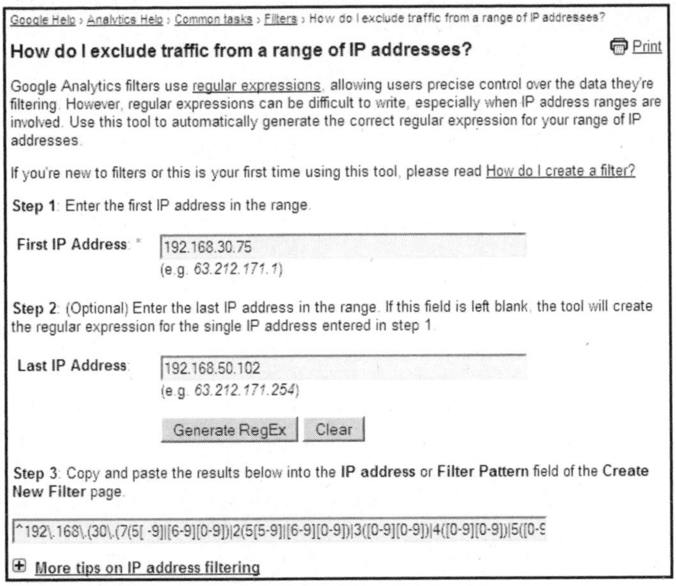

Figure 14-3: Creating a Regular Expression for a range of IP addresses

Excluding Internal Traffic That Uses Dynamic IP Addresses

If your organization uses dynamic IP addresses you won't be able to use the Visitor IP Address filter field to exclude your company's traffic (as your IP address is different with every visit). Most folks make the mistake of blocking the city (or cities) where their offices are located when dynamic IPs are involved, but of course that means that anyone else from those same locations will also not be reported.

What you can do instead is follow these steps. You will need the support of your colleagues on this one.

1. Create a simple web page, give it a unique name, and upload it live to your web server. Don't link this page from your navigation or integrate it with your site in any way—you don't want anyone in the world to have access to this page. On this page install the Google Analytics Tracking Code as you normally would on any other page on your web site. However, you will be adding a call to _setVar exactly as shown. (We talk more about _setVar a little later on in this chapter.)

```
<script type="text/javascript">
var gaJsHost = ((("https:" == document.location.protocol)
? "https://ssl." :
```

```
"http://www.");
document.write(unescape("%3Cscript src='" + gaJsHost +
"google-analytics.com/ga.js'
type='text/javascript'%3E%3C/script%3E"));
</script>
<script type="text/javascript">
try {
var pageTracker = _gat._getTracker("UA-XXXXXX-X");
pageTracker._trackPageview();
pageTracker._setVar("employees");
} catch(err) {}</script>
```

2. Create an exclude filter and apply it to each profile that you'd like to exclude internal traffic from, using the following setup:

   Filter Type: Custom ⇨ Exclude

   Filter Field: User-Defined

   Filter Pattern: employees

   Case Sensitive: No

3. Ask everyone in your office who might access your web site to visit this newly created page from every browser on his or her computer (Internet Explorer, Firefox, Safari, etc.…). Send your coworkers the URL or do it for them at their desks if you have to—it absolutely must happen in order for this to work.

Now—at least for the next two years—your internal traffic will no longer be reported on by Google Analytics! The _setVar function will drop a cookie with a shelf life of exactly two years on each person's computer. So two years from now you'll have to have everyone visit that same page again.

Other Neat (Advanced) Filters

Filters in Google Analytics aren't all about excluding your internal traffic or tracking subdomains. They have a variety of uses to make the data in your profile(s) more relevant for you and your business. There are so many different possibilities available with filters that Wiley Publishing could come out with a book entitled *1001 Google Analytics Filters* if they so chose. For *Google Analytics 3.0* we'll show you some examples of advanced filters that many folks have already used for their own profiles and that we think will be of use to you.

Writing the Hostname in Front of the Request URI

This type of advanced filter goes extremely well when you track subdomains and multiple domains within the same profile. Often subdomains and other domains will use the same page names, right down to the file extension. By default, when you're tracking multiple subdomains and domains, visits and page views on two identically named pages will be lumped together, which means you won't be able to tell which page of which site received what amount of visits. A filter like this one can help avoid this tracking issue, or it can simply satisfy your curiosity as to which page on which site gets more (or fewer) page views.

To set this filter up on your profile, create it exactly as shown in Figure 14-4. What we're doing here is taking the domain name (the hostname, be it www .yoursite.com or www.secondsite.com) and forcing Google Analytics to write it immediately in front of the page name (the request URI), so that we can tell which page is from which site when we look at any report in the Content section.

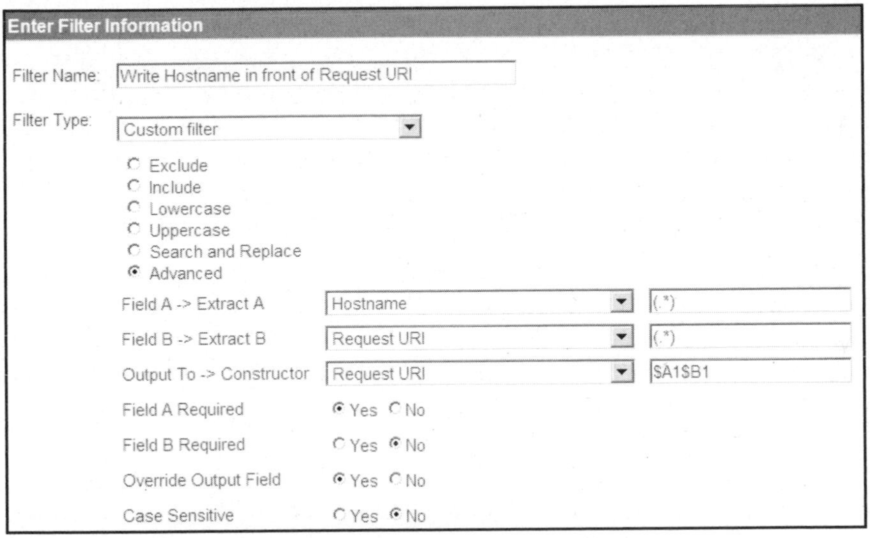

Figure 14-4: Writing the hostname in front of the request URI

Appending the Source after the Campaign

What the advanced filter does in Figure 14-4 is extract data from one dimension and append it onto another dimension. At present there are 37 different filter fields as well as two custom fields that can be used to build multi-step filters (see the very next example). One neat filter that marketers can take advantage of is created when you put the name of the source in front of the campaign. The output of this filter can be in the Traffic Sources ⇨ Campaigns report, and it, in essence, adds an automatic second dimension on that report, freeing up the dimensioning drop-downs for a third or a fourth dimension. If that sounds interesting to you, create a filter with the following attributes:

Filter Type: Custom Filter ⇨ Advanced

Field A ⇨ **Extract A:** Campaign Source ⇨ (.*)

Field B ⇨ **Extract B:** Campaign Name ⇨ (.*)

Output To ⇨ **Constructor:** Campaign Name ⇨ $B1 $A1

Field A Required: No

Field B Required: Yes

Override Output Field: Yes

Case Sensitive: No

Notice that in this filter our constructor is $B1 $A1, not $A1$B1. This will write the campaign name first, add a white space, and then write the campaign source after that. If you'd prefer to see those reversed, simply use $A1 $B1. We highly recommend the space between the two pieces of the constructor field to make report data look cleaner.

Three-Step Filter: Adding Campaign Source, Visitor Country, and Campaign Term to the Transaction ID

There are two filter fields—Custom Field 1 and Custom Field 2—that serve as temporary holding cells for data that was created by a filter and that is to be used in another filter. Since there are only two filter fields in an advanced filter, using these custom fields can be an excellent option if you need to combine more data than the default advanced filter allows for.

Here in our example we'll use three filters. The first filter will extract the campaign source and the visitor country, and dump this data into Custom Field 1. The second filter will then extract Custom Field 1 (which has campaign source and visitor country data), and also extract the campaign term and dump that data into Custom Field 2. Finally, the third and final filter will extract Custom Field 2 and combine and output it to the Ecommerce Transaction ID. The results of this three-step filter can be viewed within the Ecommerce ⇨ Transactions report.

Filter #1

Filter Type: Custom Filter ⇨ Advanced

Field A ⇨ **Extract A:** Campaign Source ⇨ (.*)

Field B ⇨ **Extract B:** Visitor Country ⇨ (.*)

Output To ⇨ **Constructor:** Custom Field 1 ⇨ $A1 $B1

Field A Required: Yes

Field B Required: Yes

Override Output Field: Yes

Case Sensitive: No

Filter #2

Filter Type: Custom Filter ➪ Advanced

Field A ➪ Extract A: Custom Field 1 ➪ (.*)

Field B ➪ Extract B: Campaign Term ➪ (.*)

Output To ➪ Constructor: Custom Field 2 ➪ $A1 $B1

Field A Required: Yes

Field B Required: No

Override Output Field: Yes

Case Sensitive: No

Filter #3

Filter Type: Custom Filter ➪ Advanced

Field A ➪ Extract A: Custom Field 2 ➪ (.*)

Field B ➪ Extract B: E-Commerce Transaction Id ➪ (.*)

Output To ➪ Constructor: Transaction Id ➪ $B1 $A1

Field A Required: Yes

Field B Required: No

Override Output Field: Yes

Case Sensitive: No

NOTE When working with multi-step filters such as the one in the preceding example, it is imperative that the assigned filter order is set, from top to bottom, as we show here. Filters will be processed in the order in which you arrange them, and it could get very nasty if a filter in a multi-step set of filters were out of order.

Tracking Google Search Engine Rankings

Another excellent use of Advanced Filters is to display the actual position of a keyword within Google's organic listings in your Traffic Sources ➪ Keywords report. In April of 2009 Google announced that it would be modifying the way queries are structured within its URLs, which opened the door for this type of filter to be created. (Thank you very much both to André Scholten from Traffic4U for creating the original 1.0 version of this filter, and to Corey Koberg from WebShare, who are both Google Analytics Authorized Consultants, for creating the 2.0 version.)

We will showcase the two-step filter, which assumes that you are running cost-per-click advertising (with AdWords). There is a single-filter version for non-cost-per-click advertisers, available on the WebShare blog via this link:

```
http://www.websharedesign.com/
display-search-engine-rankings-seo-in-google-analytics.html
```

Filter #1

Filter Type: Custom ➪ Advanced

Field A ➪ **Extract A:** Referral ➪ (\?|&)(cd)=([^&]*)

Field B ➪ **Extract B:** Campaign Medium ➪ organic

Output To ➪ **Constructor:** Custom Field 1 ➪ $A3

Field A Required: Yes

Field B Required: Yes

Override Output Field: Yes

Case Sensitive: No

Filter #2

Filter Type: Custom Filter ➪ Advanced

Field A ➪ **Extract A:** Custom Field 1 ➪ (.*)

Field B ➪ **Extract B:** Campaign Term ➪ (.*)

Output To ➪ **Constructor:** Campaign Term ➪ $B1 ($A1)

Field A Required: Yes

Field B Required: Yes

Override Output Field: Yes

Case Sensitive: No

After 24 hours check out your Traffic Sources ➪ Keywords report and click on the "non-paid" text link above the report table to display only organic keywords. You should start to see keywords with numbers next to them—the number represents the keyword's position in Google's search results at the time of the visit(s) to your web site.

Tracking PDF (and Other) File Downloads

Most web-site owners and Google Analytics account owners do not realize that with a simple JavaScript onClick event you can track any outbound link on your site, as well as any link to a PDF file, an MP3 file, or the link on your big rotating "E-mail Us" graphic on the bottom of your web site. (People don't still use those, do they?)

Even if you do still use a large rotating "E-mail Us" graphic on your "Sign My Guestbook" page hosted by GeoCities, that's OK, because it's trackable with Google Analytics.

Tracking PDF/Downloadable Files as Content

On any anchor tag (<a>) that opens up or downloads a file for one of your visitors when that visitor clicks the text link, you can use the _trackPageview function as a JavaScript onClick event, as shown in this example:

```
<a href="http://www.yoursite.com/white-paper.pdf"
onClick="pageTracker._trackPageview('/white-paper.pdf');">
Download a PDF</a>
```

After a few visitors have clicked your PDF link, check your Content ➪ Top Content report for white-paper.pdf, and you should see some visits listed for it. (In this case "visits" will actually be clicks on your downloadable file).

In some situations you may get thrown a scripting error after implementing this onClick event. If this happens you may need to move the standard Google Analytics Tracking Code above this onClick event in the source code, preferably immediately below the opening <body> tag.

Setting Up Goals for Your Downloadable Files

The advantage of using the _trackPageview function is that it registers the onClick event on your link as a page view in content reports. Because of this, you can set up this virtual URL as a goal in Google Analytics. Figure 14-5 shows the PDF file from our previous example being used as a goal in a Google Analytics profile:

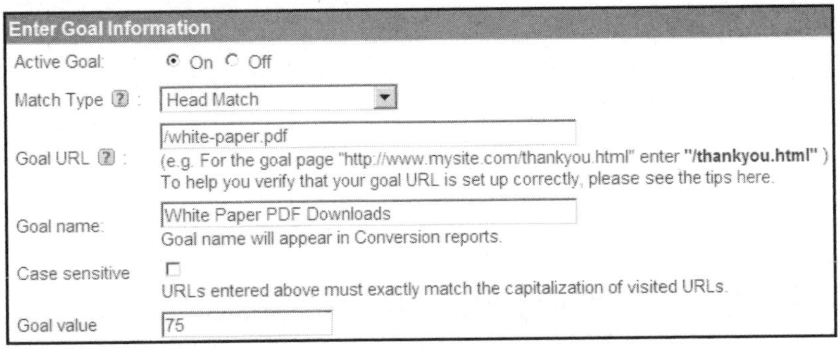

Figure 14-5: Goal Setup for your downloadable (PDF) file

The goal that we show in Figure 14-5 will match any instance of `/white-paper.pdf`. But what if you have multiple PDF files scattered throughout your site and you'd like to track any of the views or downloads of all those PDFs as a goal? Well, if you use a smart, consistent naming convention for all your _trackPageview values on all your PDF file anchor tags, you can write a simple Regular Expression to match any PDF download your site has to offer. Let's pretend for a second that all my PDF files have _trackPageview values of `/pdf/name-of-file.pdf`. I can set up my goal as follows:

Active Goal: On

Match Type: Regular Expression Match

Goal URL: ^/pdf/.*

Goal Name: Anything you want!

Goal Value: 75 (*ALWAYS* use a Goal Value for your Goals!)

After implementation (and after a few days or a week), visit your Goals ➪ Goal Verification report to see a breakdown of which PDF files were viewed or downloaded and counted as goals.

NOTE You can also track PDF (and other) file downloads as events, which will have their data populated within the Event Tracking subsection of reports. Please visit Chapter 19 ("Event Tracking") for examples of doing just that.

Customizations with the Google Analytics Tracking Code

You can make lots of different types of customizations with your regular Google Analytics Tracking Code. You can track virtual page views, you can track two (or more) Google Analytics accounts simultaneously, you can add your new favorite search engine as an organic source of traffic, and you can even turn on data sampling! We've tried our very best to compile the "greatest hits" in this section.

Tracking Virtual Page Views

We'll start right where we left off in the section on tracking downloadable files. Using the _trackPageview function within your Google Analytics Tracking Code is extremely useful for cleaning up long, bulky, SEO-unfriendly URLs. It's also great for a common situation on the Web in which different web pages share the exact same URL. This happens a lot on confirmation/receipt pages (thank-you pages), so using _trackPageview will allow Google Analytics to use another request URI (page name) instead of what it sees in the URL in the browser's address bar. Using _trackPageview is actually a requirement if your thank-you page shares the same URL as its previous form page.

Here's an example of _trackPageview being used within the Google Analytics Tracking Code:

```
<script type="text/javascript">
var gaJsHost = (("https:" == document.location.protocol)
? "https://ssl." :
"http://www.");
document.write(unescape("%3Cscript src='" + gaJsHost +
"google-analytics.com/ga.js'
type='text/javascript'%3E%3C/script%3E"));
</script>
<script type="text/javascript">
try {
var pageTracker = _gat._getTracker("UA-XXXXXX-X");
pageTracker._trackPageview();
} catch(err) {}</script>
```

Tracking Two Accounts Simultaneously

Who said Google Analytics can't track two separate profiles or accounts at the same time? Regardless of what you've heard or read before, the Google Analytics Tracking Code can most definitely support tracking two accounts simultaneously—as long as you are careful and set it up properly. In the following example we use a declaration of var secondTracker to define our other account's UA number and _trackPageview function. However, you can use any name you want—joeTracker, jerriTracker, myTracker—as long as it is consistent on all pages of your web site.

```
<script type="text/javascript">
var gaJsHost = (("https:" == document.location.protocol)
? "https://ssl." :
"http://www.");
document.write(unescape("%3Cscript src='" + gaJsHost +
"google-analytics.com/ga.js'
type='text/javascript'%3E%3C/script%3E"));
</script>
<script type="text/javascript">
try {
var pageTracker = _gat._getTracker("UA-XXXXXX-X");
pageTracker._trackPageview();
var secondTracker = _gat.getTracker("UA-YYYYYY-Y");
secondTracker._trackPageview();
} catch(err) {}</script>
```

In no time, both accounts should show the same number of page views for your web site.

Custom Segmentation (User-Defined)

Earlier in this chapter we showed an example that used the _setVar function to set a cookie on a visitor's computer so that we could block out our internal traffic that used dynamic IP addresses. When you use _setVar within the Google Analytics Tracking Code, the __utmv cookie gets set on the visitor's machine, which identifies the user with the label that you write into the _setVar function. This is helpful for tracking site registrants, shoppers, and other visitors who have performed specific actions on your web site.

```
var pageTracker = _gat._getTracker("UA-XXXXXX-X");
pageTracker._setVar("shoppers");
pageTracker._trackPageview();
```

The _setVar function can also be used as an onClick event on a hyperlink, just as with tracking file downloads:

```
<a href="http://www.yoursite.com/admin.php"
onClick="pageTracker._setVar('Administrator');">Administrator</a>
```

_setVar can also be used as an onSubmit function, as well as any other JavaScript function, such as for a user submitting a form:

```
<form action="http://www.otherwebsite.com/processing.php" name="form"
method="post"
onSubmit="pageTracker._setVar('interest');">
```

The data from your _setVar methods is all collected within the Visitors ⇨ User-Defined report, where you should see the labels that you assigned your _setVar functions across your site. Custom segmentation like this is key for obtaining a deeper understanding of your important visitors and their subsequent activity on your web site, so learning to embrace the User-Defined report and the _setVar function can only benefit you.

Modifying the Session Timeout

By default each visitor has 30 minutes to perform an interaction on your web site. If that visitor doesn't visit another page on your site after 30 minutes, the analytics session will time out and will start again when he or she returns to your site, returns to the computer, or comes back from lunch. This default session timeout may not work for your web site, as you may have videos and games that take longer than 30 minutes to watch or play—and you wouldn't want these highly-engaged visitor sessions to be timed out. Use the _setSessionTimeout function within your Google Analytics Tracking Code to increase (or decrease) the length of the session timeout. The _setSessionTimeout function uses seconds as its unit of time, and the default in Google Analytics is 1,800 seconds.

```
var pageTracker = _gat._getTracker("UA-XXXXXX-X");
pageTracker._setSessionTimeout("5000");
pageTracker._trackPageview();
```

Modifying the Campaign Conversion Timeout

Another editable default setting of Google Analytics is the campaign conversion timeout. Google Analytics will give credit for a conversion/transaction to the most recent campaign data stored in the visitor's __utmz cookie, if the transaction happens within six months (the default lifespan of the __utmz cookie). Your business may have a very long sales cycle, and six months may not be enough for you. Or six months may be far too long, in which case you'll want to shorten that time span. With the _setCookieTimeout function you can make this happen. Like _setSessionTimeout, _setCookieTimeout uses seconds as its unit of time. To give you a point of reference, 180 days (about six months) equals 15,552,000 seconds.

```
var pageTracker = _gat._getTracker("UA-XXXXXX-X");
pageTracker._setCookieTimeout("40000000");
pageTracker._trackPageview();
```

Modifying Conversion Attribution (Last to First)

It's high time that marketers everywhere received the proper credit for being responsible for generating conversions/transactions to their web sites. Google Analytics uses a last-visit attribution model for conversion data by default, but this can be changed to a first-visit attribution model by way of the utm_nooveride=1 query parameter in your marketing destination URLs. Let's say that someone visits your site via a Google AdWords ad, but doesn't make a purchase or doesn't visit that key page of your site. Then, two weeks later, the same user sees your e-mail newsletter with the same offer as your AdWords ad, and decides to click the link and convert. The conversion credit would go to the newsletter even though (arguably), some if not all of the actual credit for that conversion should go to the AdWords ad that originally introduced the visitor to your site. With utm_nooverride=1 you can give all the credit to the first referring source /medium/term/campaign.

Simply append the following bolded code to the end of a properly tagged destination URL. You must have the three required URL tagging dimensions in order for utm_nooverride=1 to function properly:

```
http://www.yoursite.com/landing-page.html?utm_source=google&utm_
medium=cpc&utm_campaign=T-Shirts+-+National&utm_term=green+
shirts&utm_nooverride=1
```

NOTE To learn all about URL tagging please revisit Chapter 13 ("Google AdWords Integration"), where we cover it in great detail.

Using the Anchor (#) Symbol in Destination URLs

Speaking of URL tagging, there will be rare cases where your web server won't accept the use of the ? symbol as the beginning of your URL parameter. If your URL-tagged destination pages lead users to an error page because of the query parameters, you can set the _setAllowAnchor method to true and use the # symbol instead:

```
var pageTracker = _gat._getTracker("UA-XXXXXX-X");
pageTracker._setAllowAnchor(true);
pageTracker._trackPageview();
```

Then use the # symbol instead of the ? symbol, as in this example:

```
http://www.yoursite.com/landing-page.html#utm_source=google&utm_
medium=cpc&utm_campaign=T-Shirts+-+National&utm_term=
green+shirts
```

Recognizing 'Nonstandard' URL Query Parameters

Sometimes URLs from other marketing efforts will already be loaded with their own query parameters, and you may not be able to add on additional URL parameters or edit the URL in any way. Not to worry—you can add up to seven different functions within your Google Analytics Tracking Code to detect (and accept) nonstandard dimensions (like utm_source, utm_medium, and so on).

Let's say that you have the following URL:

```
http://www.yoursite.com/email-landing-page.html?id=
12345&effort=Spring%20Sale&source=email&type=corporate&keyword=
green%20shoes&link=2&key=98769876
```

Here, you can see parameters like id, source, and keyword. These query parameters can basically be mapped into your Google Analytics Tracking Code and added to your profile data. The following functions would be added to your code on the landing page of the URL(s) you wish to track:

```
pageTracker._setCampNameKey("effort"); // Campaign Name
pageTracker._setCampMediumKey("type"); // Campaign Medium
pageTracker._setCampSourceKey("source"); // Campaign Source
pageTracker._setCampTermKey("keyword"); // Campaign Term
pageTracker._setCampContentKey("link"); // Campaign Content
pageTracker._setCampIdKey("id"); // Campaign ID Number
pageTracker._setCampNOKey("key"); // Campaign No-override
```

See the comment next to each function in the previous coding example—all of them except "Campaign ID Number" should look very familiar to you, if you've read Chapter 13 and everything in this chapter so far.

Counting Keywords and Referring Sites as 'Direct' Traffic

Some keywords, like your own domain name or mistyped brand names, and some referring sites, like an intranet help desk or partner web site, can be treated as "direct" traffic, instead of cluttering up your keywords and referring-sites reports. If there are certain keywords or referring sites that you'd like to do this for, use either the _addIgnoredOrganic or the _addIgnoredRef function in your Google Analytics Tracking Code, as our example shows:

```
pageTracker._addIgnoredOrganic("www.yoursite.com");
pageTracker._addIgnoredRef("second-site.com");
```

Keep in mind that neither _addIgnoredOrganic nor _addIgnoreRef will subtract or delete the page view counts that result from these keywords or referring sites that you are ignoring—such views just won't appear in your Keywords or Referring Sites reports, instead being lumped into the direct-traffic bucket.

Setting the Cookie Path to a Subdirectory

Do you have access to only one subfolder/subdirectory of a large site, and are you allowed to install the Google Analytics Tracking Code only there and nowhere else? No problem—use _setCookiePath in your code as in the following example, so that cookies get set to a specific subdirectory:

```
var pageTracker = _gat._getTracker("UA-XXXXXX-X");
pageTracker._setCookiePath("/folder/my-website/");
pageTracker._trackPageview();
```

Controlling Data Collection Settings

Let's face it—if you've made it this far, chances are that you're something of a control freak. Just kidding! Hey, even if you are, you're in good company here, because Google Analytics enables you to control whether or not you'd like to track the visitor's Flash version, browser information, and page titles, and even the sampling rate of all data that you collect!

Check out the following coding example for some more control functions:

```
pageTracker._setClientInfo(false); // Visitor Browser Data
pageTracker._setDetectFlash(false); // Visitor Flash Version
pageTracker._setDetectTitle(false); // Title in Content Reports
pageTracker._setSampleRate(75); // Controls the Sampling Rate (%)
```

_setClientInfo, _setDetectFlash, and _setDetectTitle can be set to either true or false, depending on whether or not you'd like to track each element. _setSampleRate is the percentage of traffic you'd like to track, represented as a whole number.

Data sampling can be very useful if you collect several million page views a month, or if you are tracking over 50,000 URLs. You wouldn't want to set this to either 0 or 100, because setting _setSampleRate to 0 would cause you to track no traffic, and setting _setSampleRate to 100 would not have any affect at all (in essence, setting it to 100 would be the same as not using the function at all).

Tracking a New Organic Search Engine

Finally, we saved one of the best code customizations for last. The _addOrganic function enables you to start tracking your newest favorite search engine as an organic source of traffic. By default, Google Analytics automatically detects over 40 different web sites as organic search engines, but new sites frequently pop up long before Google Analytics engineers can update the ga.js file. With _addOrganic there's no need to wait—simply add in the domain of the search engine along with the query parameter that the search engine uses, as our example shows:

```
var pageTracker = _gat._getTracker("UA-XXXXXX-X");
pageTracker._addOrganic("newengine.com", "q");
pageTracker._trackPageview();
```

By default all web sites that contain links to your site will be counted as referring sites. So technically you can use _addOrganic for any web site that has a search function on it. For example, did you know that CNN.com is automatically considered an organic search engine by the Google Analytics ga.js file?

Tracking Coupons and Discounts (E-commerce)

Here's a little-known fact about the Google Analytics Ecommerce Tracking Module, which we cover in great detail in Chapter 8: you can track your coupons or discount vouchers with Google Analytics! What you'll want to do is use a new _addItem line and a negative value for your unit price field. This will tabulate properly in your overall revenue and product revenue totals, which in a way enables you to balance your e-commerce revenue data to be more realistic. You'll also be able to see the number of vouchers redeemed or the number of coupons used in your Product Performance reports.

The only drawback to this method is that adding a new _addItem line will add to the total number of products sold, which, depending on your individual needs, could cause some confusion. Therefore, consider this method carefully before implementing it. Our recommendation: use this method anyway—the pros of tracking coupons far outweigh the cons of increasing the total number of products sold.

Here is an example of an additional _addItem line being used by the E-commerce module to track a coupon for $25 off:

```
pageTracker._addItem(
"135792468",
"ABC-123-XYZ0987",
"Coupon - 25 Dollars Off",
"Discounts",
"-25.00",
"1"
);
pageTracker._trackTrans();
```

Need a refresher in e-commerce tracking? Revisit Chapter 8 ("E-commerce Concepts and Methods").

Tracking Social Media

We couldn't close this chapter out without talking about social media. At this point you must have a social media presence as a part of your online strategy, or you will be left in the dust. Tracking social media efforts from Facebook, Twitter, LinkedIn, and YouTube is equally essential, because you can use the data collected by Google Analytics to refine and optimize your social media efforts.

It should be said that social media is so new that Google Analytics, as well as many other analytics packages, doesn't automatically detect referring traffic from Facebook, Twitter, etc., as "social media traffic." Such traffic is either counted as referring sites (which isn't too bad, though possibly confusing), or the traffic may be lumped in as "direct," which is not good. Once bucketed into "direct," there's no way to retrieve the original source of the traffic.

A staple of social media is the use of "short" or "tiny" URLs on status updates, tweets, and overall link sharing. When you use a URL-shortening site like `bit.ly` or `tiny.cc`, you can easily make the standard 140-character limit on your next Twitter update, which can now include a link to an article, a press release, or the latest "Will It Blend?" video.

However, when a user clicks a shortened URL he or she is redirected from `bit.ly` or `tiny.cc` to your web site. This means that the traffic you receive from shortened URLs will automatically be lumped in with the direct traffic segment, because of the redirect that allows the URL-shortening service to function properly. But what if you wanted to see how many clicks your latest office party video on YouTube received, or how many visits your latest blog post received from your LinkedIn status update?

What you'll need to do is actually quite simple—append the Google Analytics URL parameters to the end of your final destination URL before you run them through `bit.ly` (or your favorite URL-shortening service). This way the redirect happens first and your query parameters are saved for proper social media attribution. Most people using Google Analytics and a URL-shortening service do not realize that they can do this—until now.

> **NOTE** Some mobile device applications for social media sites automatically use URL shortening and do not provide end users with destination-URL-editing capabilities. Unfortunately, there may not be anything that you can do about that, apart from contacting your application vendor and requesting that it add the feature.

The Reports

Once you have Google Analytics set up to work for you, then it's time to start examining the reports that are available through the program. These reports can give you all kinds of insights into the minds of your site visitors.

Do you want to know where visitors come from, what pages they like best, or where you lose them? This is where you find out that information. In addition to telling you about how these reports work, we'll also give you insight into how to use the reports to improve your web-site traffic.

CHAPTER 15

Analyzing Visitors

One section of Google Analytics reports that many users seem to take for granted is the Visitors section. This group of reports contains lots of information about your visitors, including where in the world they are located, how many visits and unique visitors have been to your site, and how much time those visitors spend on your site. There's a lot more, too, but you'll find out all about the Visitors section as you read through this chapter.

One thing you should know going into this chapter is the difference between a visit and a unique visitor, as well as the difference between visits and page views. These metrics were covered back in Chapter 7, so if you don't remember the details you might want to flip back for a short refresher.

When you know the difference between the various measurements and how Google Analytics arrives at those measurements, then the reports in the Visitors section offer a lot of insight about your web-site visitors. These reports are your key to "getting inside their minds" to figure out what you are doing right with your web site (from the visitors' perspectives) and what you might be able to do better.

Visitors Overview

The Visitors report section is where you can find all the information you'll want to know about your visitors. This includes reports that show where your users are located, how they connect to the Internet, and how often they return to you.

The opening page for this report section is called Visitors Overview (though the actual report link on the left is just titled Overview). This page, shown in Figure 15-1, gives you a quick overview of the most important data in the Visitors section.

Figure 15-1: Visitors Overview highlights important numbers in the Visitors report section.

The information on this page includes visitor information such as the number of visits, the absolute unique visitors, and even the number of page views and bounces that your site experiences. You'll notice that each of these titles is a link to a report. Those are the same reports that are available from the navigation menu on the left side of the page.

Links to segmentation reports are also available on this page (as with all overview report pages). And at the bottom of the page is the technical profile for the visitors being tracked in the report. You can drill down into these reports by clicking the links in the Browser and Connection Speed tables. Or you can view the full Browser and Connection Speed reports by clicking the **view full report** link beneath the tables.

Visitors

Looking closer at the Visitors Overview, you'll notice that the top chart shows the number of visitors who have been to your site in the given time period. The next figure shows how you can change that chart to represent several different views of your visitor data:

- Visitors (the default view)
- Visits
- Page Views
- Pages/Visit
- Avg. Time on Site
- Bounce Rate
- % New Visits

Access these options by clicking the **Visitors** drop-down menu (displayed as the Visitors tab), as shown in Figure 15-2. Select the option that you would like to view to close the menu and view the selected data. There is one thing about changing this data that you should know: the change is temporary. If you navigate away from the Visitors Overview, when you return the report will again reflect the number of visitors to your site.

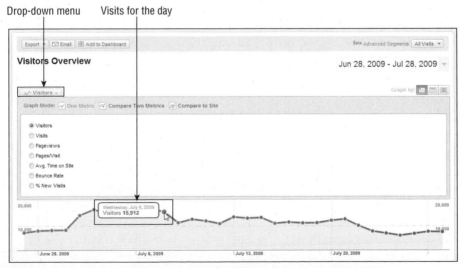

Figure 15-2: There is hidden functionality within the structure of a report.

Another nice feature in this section of the report is the ability to see how many visitors there were on a given day. Each dot on the chart represents a day. If you mouse over that report the number of visitors for that day are shown, along with the date (also shown in Figure 12-2).

Absolute Unique Visitors, Visitors, and New Visitors

Note that the actual Visitors graph shows the number for all visitors to your site, but beneath that graph is a metric for the number of absolute unique visitors and new visitors to the site. The numbers help you to see how many people come to your site in total, as well as how many of those people are really new visitors and how many are visitors who have been there before or who stayed on the site, went inactive, and then started navigating again (which makes them appear to be different visitors).

Suppose a visitor who's never been to your site before starts navigating through your site but gets a phone call while reading your pages. The visitor takes that call, which turns out to be from Mom, who wants to hear every detail of every aspect of her child's life. So, rather than be distracted, the visitor walks away from the computer for the hour that the conversation takes. Then this visitor returns and resumes surfing your site. That makes it look as if you've had two visitors, because one session expired and another was started later.

To further complicate things, your single visitor will show up as an absolute unique visitor (having never been to your site before), but also as a new visitor (because this is the first time in the specified time frame this visitor has been to your site). Then, when he or she picks up surfing through your site after the phone call, this is also going to show up as a return visitor (because the session expired before surfing began again, Google counted this person as another visitor who *had* been to the site before). Perfectly confusing, isn't it?

It all has to do with sessions versus visitors, which we covered back in Chapter 7. Your site visitor in this example is counted as a single visitor, but because of the length of time on the phone, he or she technically qualifies as two.

This kind of confusion can happen when you're using cookies to count visitors (which is what Google Analytics does). Fortunately, knowing that the overlap exists helps you understand what you're looking at when you're comparing absolute unique visitors with visitors and new visitors.

Deeper Insight with Graph Mode

One more feature of the Visitors graph that you might want to know about is the ability to change the graph mode that you're viewing. When you click the Visitors tab (as you did earlier to change the metric graphed) the dropdown gives you three Graph Mode options to choose from. By default the graph that's displayed is for One Metric. You can also choose to view Two Metrics or Compare to Site.

When you select the Two Metrics option your options change, as shown in Figure 15-3. From these options, choose the two metrics that you would like to compare, and the graph changes to show both metrics. This is an excellent way to compare your site visitors to the number of pages they viewed, or to view any other combination of the metrics available.

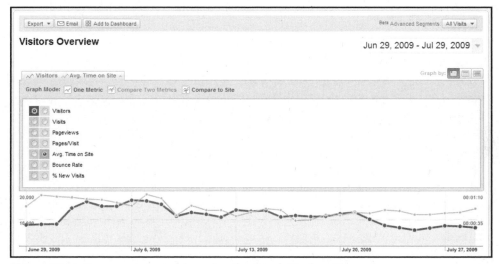

Figure 15-3: Compare two metrics using the Graph Mode options.

The other option that you have here is to Compare to Site. At the time of this writing, this option seems to still be in testing. It's linked to the benchmarking capabilities of Google Analytics, and in time should show you a comparison to other sites in your industry that are of a similar size to yours. Currently, however, the feature isn't showing a comparison, but rather is mirroring the visitors to your own site. It's a feature we hope to see more functional in future editions of this book.

Visitor Segmentation

The second section on the Visitors Overview is the overview of your visitor segmentation, as shown in Figure 15-4. As you've already seen, on the left side of the overview is a recap of the visitors to your site. Numbers and chart previews are provided for each of the categories listed at the beginning of the last section. The right side of the report provides links to other Visitor Segmentation reports.

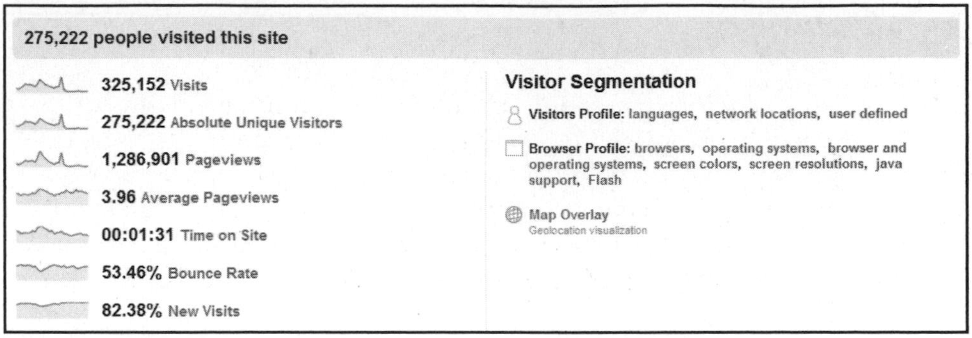

275,222 people visited this site		
325,152 Visits		
275,222 Absolute Unique Visitors		
1,286,901 Pageviews		
3.96 Average Pageviews		
00:01:31 Time on Site		
53.46% Bounce Rate		
82.38% New Visits		

Visitor Segmentation

Visitors Profile: languages, network locations, user defined

Browser Profile: browsers, operating systems, browser and operating systems, screen colors, screen resolutions, java support, Flash

Map Overlay
Geolocation visualization

Figure 15-4: Visitor Segmentation provides a quick glance at segmentation data.

All the blue links in this section lead you deeper into segmentation data. Those reports are covered later in this chapter. Just be aware that clicking any of those blue links takes you to the full report for that facet of visitor segmentation.

Technical Profile

The final section in the Visitors Overview is the Technical Profile. This section of the report briefly covers technical information about your visitors—what browsers and connection speeds they are using. Each listing on this report, shown in Figure 15-5, is linked to deeper information. Clicking the link enables you to drill down into the data to see more detail about how many of your visitors use a specific browser or connection speed.

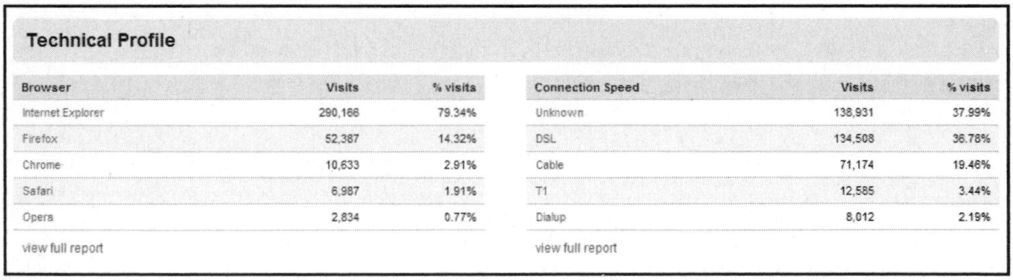

Technical Profile

Browser	Visits	% visits	Connection Speed	Visits	% visits
Internet Explorer	290,166	79.34%	Unknown	138,931	37.99%
Firefox	52,387	14.32%	DSL	134,508	36.78%
Chrome	10,633	2.91%	Cable	71,174	19.46%
Safari	6,987	1.91%	T1	12,585	3.44%
Opera	2,834	0.77%	Dialup	8,012	2.19%
view full report			view full report		

Figure 15-5: Technical Profile shows an overview of users' technical capabilities.

Like many of the other links on this page, these lead you farther into reports that cover the data in greater detail. We'll be covering those reports in order later in this chapter.

Benchmarking

By some definitions, a *benchmark* is a standard by which something can be measured or judged. In other words, something to compare against. As people, we unknowingly set benchmarks in our lives every day. For example, if your goal is to be a wealthy investor, your benchmark might be someone like Warren Buffett. By comparing your investment success and wealth to Buffett's, you have a clear picture of how far you are from the goal and some pretty good indications of what you might need to do to reach that goal.

Google Analytics offers the same capability in the Benchmarking report, shown in Figure 15-6. This report enables you to compare your site to other sites of similar type and size in your *industry vertical*.

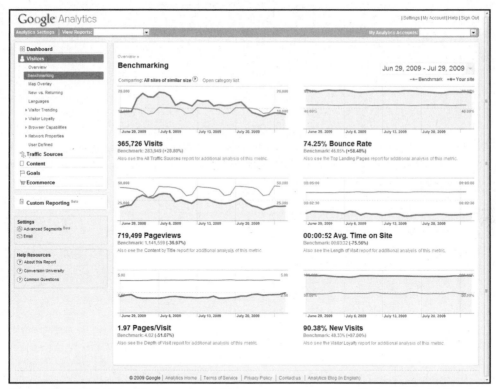

Figure 15-6: Benchmarking reports enable you to compare your site to other, similar sites in your industry vertical.

The benchmarking capabilities of Google Analytics became available in March 2009, so they're relatively new, which has a few implications that you should understand.

First, benchmarking reports are made possible by shared data from other Google Analytics users who choose to allow their web-site statistics to be anonymously monitored and entered into a pool of data against which similar sites can be compared. And by the very nature of that sharing relationship, the benchmarking ability of Google Analytics is still relatively small. Over time, as more and more users agree to share their information for benchmarking purposes, the comparisons should become more accurately representative of your industry vertical.

Wait. I can hear your objections already. Why do they need my information? What information do they need? What will others be able to see about me? And how accurate is this benchmarking, really? Let me see if I can answer some of those questions for you.

What's Collected and Why It's Needed

Benchmarking, by its very nature, involves comparison, and this means that to participate in Benchmarking you must be willing to share your analytics information so that it can be included in the aggregated data against which your web-site statistics are compared.

Sharing is anonymous. Google collects only what it needs to compare other sites against your own. It's not collecting anything that identifies you to others in your industry (that would likely be your competition). It just collects the numbers associated with certain measurements:

- Visits
- Page views
- Pages per visit
- Bounce rate
- Average time on site
- New visits

This information is then pooled and used to arrive at an average for each of those metrics. So when you want to know how your site compares to others in your industry, your actual data for each of these measurements can be compared to the average for your industry vertical.

At this time, Benchmarking is new enough that it's not all-inclusive. If you operate a web site that caters to work-at-home moms (WAHMs), it's not likely that you'll be able to get specific benchmarking statistics only for other web sites that target other WAHMs. However, you can find benchmarking statistics for other sites targeted to people with home offices, which is close enough to help you see how your web-site statistics compare to those sites'. And that comparison? Well, it's like comparing your wealth to Warren Buffett's. It won't tell you exactly how much he's worth, but it will tell you where you stack up against him, and by looking at some known (and measurable) facts, you can decide how best to reach for the goal of being Buffett Wealthy.

How Accurate Is Benchmarking?

You'll find that the Benchmarking report in Google Analytics isn't perfect. By the nature of analytics, anonymous data collection, and benchmarking in general, you're not going to get statistics that tell you exactly where your competition is in the market. Instead, you'll be looking at a general comparison to an average metric compiled from a lot of data.

That means that there is the possibility that some of the sites lumped together in the Home Office category will be very different from your web site that targets WAHMs. But as a general comparison, benchmarking is a good way to find out how you compare to others in your industry—not your niche.

Perhaps over time Google will collect enough information to tell you how you compare to web sites in your niche, but that time is not now. And it's dependent upon other web-site owners being willing to share their own information as well.

So the best thing that you can do, if you're interested in seeing how you stack up against others in your industry, is to share your data (again, it's anonymous, so you're not putting your web-site metrics in jeopardy) with the Benchmarking program. You're going to have to do it to see the Benchmarking reports, anyway.

Enabling Benchmarking on Your Site

Enabling Benchmarking on your Google Analytics profile will do two things for you. First, it will enable you to share your analytics data with Google. And it's also going to give you access to the Benchmarking reports. It's a bit like the share-and-share-alike concept that your parents tried to drill into your brain when you were a kid.

If you haven't already agreed to share your analytics data with Google, then when you click the Benchmarking link on the left-hand navigation bar you'll be prompted to change your sharing settings, as shown in Figure 15-7. Just click the link for **data sharing settings page** and then select the **Anonymously with Google and others** option and then the **Save Changes** button. This will enable both data sharing and the Benchmarking report.

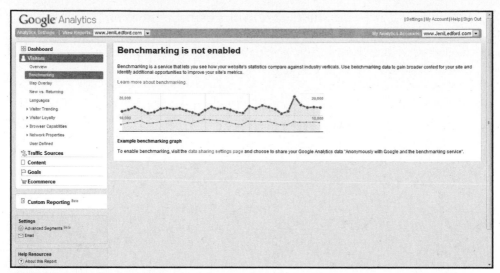

Figure 15-7: Before you can access the Benchmarking report, you must enable data sharing with Google and others.

Once you've enabled data sharing it could take up to two weeks for benchmarking data to be available on the Benchmarking report. Once it is, however, you'll be able to see how you compare to other businesses in your industry, as shown in Figure 15-8.

Highlight data point to reveal comparison data.

Click to change category.

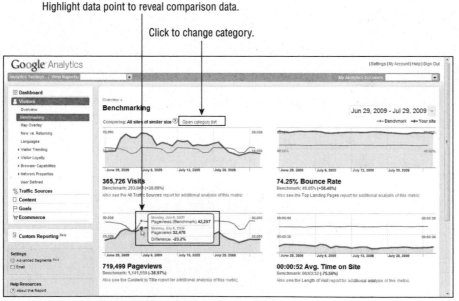

Figure 15-8: The Benchmarking report lets you compare your web site to the industry average.

When your benchmarking data does appear, you'll be compared to all the other industries that Google tracks by default. To specify one industry click the **Open category list** link (shown in Figure 15-8) and then select the industry and category that you want to compare your site to.

Also shown in Figure 15-8 is the comparison data revealed when you click any data point in any of the graphs available on the Benchmarking report. The top number given is the benchmark (or industry average) and the second number given is the actual statistics for your web site. Below that the difference is shown (in green if your statistics are higher, in red if they're lower).

Using this information you can get a good feel for where you stand in the industry. Are your numbers consistently higher than those of the industry you're comparing them to? Then you're probably doing something well. If your numbers are consistently lower, then you might want to kick up your marketing efforts to draw other visitors to your site or refine your approach to better target the right audience. Either way, with benchmarking statistics you'll know about where you stand in your industry.

Map Overlay

Wouldn't you be surprised if you looked at your site statistics and discovered that instead of the majority of visitors being from your country, they're from another country that you never thought to target? It happens. Many Japanese gaming sites find that US visitors make up a large portion of their traffic, especially right before the release of a new gaming console or device. And they aren't the only sites.

So how are you supposed to know what country the majority of your visitors are from? The Map Overlay, shown in Figure 15-9, is just the tool to give you that information.

This report shows you where your visitors are located geographically, but it also shows that information relative to site usage, the number of goal conversions, and the e-commerce value of each visit. That information can then be used to target specific segments of your web-site audience according to their locations.

There are several ways to dig deeper into the Map Overlay report. Of course, placing your pointer over any country will show you how many visits came from that country. But also, the actual map that you see is interactive, so if you click on any of the countries shown you'll be taken to a deeper view of that country.

Figure 15-9: Map Overlay shows the countries, regions, states, and cities visitors come from.

For example, if you place your pointer over the Americas and see that you have visits from that section of the world, you can click on them to be taken to the Country/Territory Detail view. Clicking the map that appears in the Country Detail takes you to the Region Detail (where available). Another click takes you to Country Detail, and another to State Detail. And if visitors within a state have been to your site, then you can click a city within a state to reach the City Detail report.

The Map Overlay page also gives you several options for drilling into your data. If you look below the map you'll see links that let you choose detail level. So, instead of clicking on the map repeatedly, you can click the link to go to City Details immediately.

One thing to keep in mind about the Map Overlay is that while it lets you see more clearly where visitors to your site are located, you've got to take this information with a little skepticism. When you get as deep as the City Details, there are dots that indicate visitor location. These dots could show the city where the visitor's ISP (Internet service provider) is located, rather than the location of the actual visitor. Generally the two are pretty close, but in some instances, if a visitor lives in a rural area, the location could be off just a little.

Still, the graphic is valuable in helping you to understand where the majority of your visitors are. For example, if your web site is very American-centric but the Map Overlay shows that a significant portion of your visitors are from Europe, you could be missing an untapped market. You'll also want to figure out what's drawing those European visitors to your site—but that's a topic for another chapter.

So you have the Map Overlay, and it shows you where in the world your visitors are located. How do you use it? Maybe you have a local computer repair business and your web site offers troubleshooting information designed to lead users to your physical location.

What happens if you look at your Map Overlay and find that the site is getting more visits from a nearby city than from the city where you're located? What you get is a clue that maybe there's an untapped market for your business in another location. So improve your targeting. Expand your marketing. Increase your business. Each task depends on the location of your visitors.

TIP When you're looking at the City Details of the Map Overlay, a few clusters of visitors are probably hard to distinguish. When several visitors from one location are counted, the spots that represent those visits may be piled on top of one another. There's good news, however. You can zoom in on the graphic by selecting the city from the list below the map. This takes you yet another level deeper in the information.

New vs. Returning

The New vs. Returning report, shown in Figure 15-10, quickly tells you what portion of your visitors is new to your site and what portion is returning.

Of course, this information is set according to the cookies placed on a user's hard drive, so if a user doesn't allow cookies, or has cleaned them out, that could affect the way the user is counted in each category of visitors.

Figure 15-10: Use this report to separate new visitors from ones who visited earlier.

This report shows you the number of new and returning visitors to your site in the context of site usage, goal conversions, and e-commerce, just as the Map Overlay did. To see this information, click the appropriate tab in the table below the Visits graphic.

So why do you need this information? Simply put, you need it to see how often your new and returning visitors reach your goal pages. If you offer a free report from your web site and have the download of that report as one of your goals, you can track how often that happens. And if you find that only first-time visitors download it, what does that tell you? Maybe that the report is drawing traffic to the site, but also that something else is pulling returning visitors back. It could be another of the goals that you have established for the site, but it could be something entirely different. This report is the first stop along the way to finding those answers.

Languages

The Language report, shown in Figure 15-11, is a quick glance at the set language for your site visitors.

Figure 15-11: The Language report shows you the set language of visitors.

As with the Map Overlay report and the New vs. Returning report, you can view this information in the context of site usage, goal conversions, and e-commerce by clicking the tabs in the report table. You can also view the statistics about a specific language by clicking the link for that language in the Language column of the report.

It's a pretty good bet that the majority of your web site's visitors will have their language preferences set to your native tongue, but if your figures show that you have a high number of visitors with different language preferences *and* there are a lot of goal conversions for those visitors, something on your site is drawing them. You need to find a way to capitalize on that.

The visitors to your site can tell you a lot about the effectiveness of your site design, your marketing efforts, and even organic factors over which you have little or no control. These first three reports in the Visitors section of Google Analytics should help you begin to get to know your visitors a little better.

Visitor Trending

Visitor trending is a fancy way to talk about what your site visitors did while they were on your site. The Visitor Trending report section in Google Analytics takes some of the most commonly used trending reports and places them all in one section. With these reports you can quickly see how many visitors you had, how many were first-time visitors, how many pages those visitors looked at, how long they spent on your site, and how many visitors came to a single page and then left immediately.

The information provided in these reports is a first step toward seeing how effective your web site is at keeping people engaged. The longer a visitor is engaged on your site, the more likely that visitor is to reach one of your conversion goals. For example, if one of the goals for your site is to have first-time visitors sign up for your newsletter, the trending information in these reports will tell you how your first-time visitors might reach that goal.

Visits

The first report in the Visitor Trending report section is the Visits report, shown in Figure 15-12. This report includes the number of visits you've had to your site. That means not only new visitors, but returning visitors as well.

The Visits report shows you bar graphs that represent the total number of visitors to your site on a given day. By default you're shown a month's worth of visits, and this includes all the visitors to your site, whether they're absolute unique or returning visitors.

This is a plain-vanilla report. There isn't any hidden functionality. It's designed to give you a quick overview of the traffic on your site for the defined time period. There isn't even an option to change the way the data is displayed. But that doesn't make this report less valuable.

In truth, this report lets you see very quickly how effective your marketing efforts are. You won't find any additional information, but at a glance you can see how many people came to your site. If you need a site-usage figure on the fly, this is the report that provides it.

Absolute Unique Visitors

Before we get too deep into the Absolute Unique Visitors report, it's necessary to understand how visitors are classified for trending purposes. By Google's standards there are two types of visitors to your site: absolute unique visitors and returning visitors.

Absolute unique visitors are people who have never been to the site before, right? Not exactly. There are certain qualifications that make visitors absolutely unique. For example, did you know that a person can visit your site this month as an absolute unique visitor and then return to the site next month and also be an absolute unique visitor? It can happen.

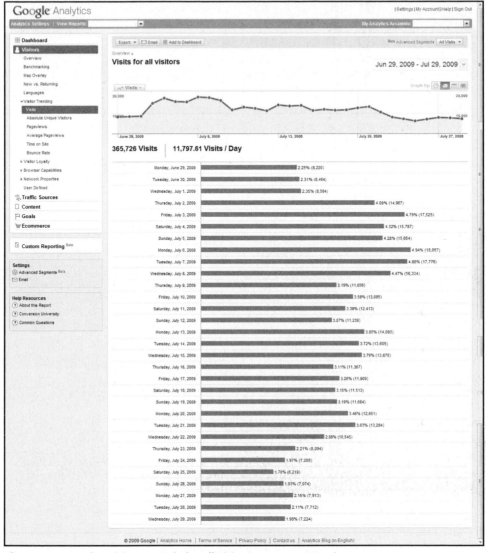

Figure 15-12: The Visits report is for all visitors, new or returning.

It's one of those situations in which things may not always be as they seem—like stepping on the scale first thing in the morning. It seems that you weigh about two pounds less than you do by lunchtime. Surely you're not putting on two pounds in four hours, right? Don't worry, you're not. But first thing in the morning your body may be slightly dehydrated. So, naturally, you're going to weigh less when you first get out of bed than you will at lunchtime, after you've had several drinks and probably even some food.

That's the problem with measurements of any kind. You can be absolutely certain that a comparison is accurate only if the circumstances of both measurements are completely identical. Fortunately, Google Analytics makes it possible for you to recreate those circumstances easily.

An absolute unique visitor is a person who visits your web site for the first time during a stipulated period. This means that people can visit your site once this month and be counted as absolute unique visitors, but be counted as returning visitors, not absolute unique visitors, if they return later in the month.

However—and here's where it gets hinky—when these same visitors return to your site for the first time the next month, they are counted as absolute unique visitors again, but only one time for that month.

The one-month time frame isn't anchored in concrete. In fact, the period may be a week or an hour, depending on how you set the date ranges for your reports. But a month is pretty much the industry standard. The time frame you determine will designate how often your returning visitors are counted as absolute unique visitors. (If you were to set a weekly time period, you could end up counting the same person as an absolute unique visitor four times in a month.)

Then there are return visitors, who form a pretty self-explanatory category. They've been here before in the time period and decided it was worth coming back.

You may be wondering how Google Analytics knows the frequency with which a visitor comes to your site. It's possible to use two small pieces of technology to determine this. The first is a user's IP address. Every computer has an IP address; it's like your street address on the Web. Just as a street address designates your house, your IP address designates your computer—the physical *where* of your location.

Of course, just as your street address can represent the physical location of several people, the IP address can also represent the location of several people. That's most common when a household has a central computer that multiple people use. This is another of those areas where Google Analytics can't be 100 percent accurate. But then, neither can any analytics program that tracks people by IP address. It represents a very small number of the visitors to your site, and so isn't really something that you need to stress about.

Another tool, and the one that Google (and every other company on the Web) uses to keep up with visitor comings and goings, is called a cookie. A cookie is a small piece of information placed on a visitor's computer; it contains information about the visitor relevant to the site that places the cookie.

Think about the last time you logged on to Amazon.com. If you've ever used Amazon, you were probably prompted to create an account that included a username and password. The next time you returned to Amazon, did you happen to notice that near the top of the page, as shown in Figure 15-13, you were greeted by name and even directed to a store designed specifically to recommend items similar to those you've purchased in the past? That's what cookies do for you. They make it possible for companies to know that you've visited before and even to know some information about those past visits to help them serve you with better, more targeted content.

NOTE One thing you should know about cookies is that it's not necessary for you to log into a web site for a cookie to be placed on your site. That's just one of the ways that cookies are used. But a web site can place a cookie even when you just surf through that site.

Content personalization
enabled by cookies.

Figure 15-13: Amazon uses cookies to personalize the content it serves to visitors.

All this is to say that a cookie makes it possible for Google Analytics to know whether a visitor is an absolute unique visitor or a returning visitor. And that information helps you understand how many visitors return to your site and how often. This information in turn can be used to optimize your site content for those categories (or to achieve those categories of visitors, i.e., turn a new visitor into a returning visitor).

When a new visitor comes to your site, Google Analytics places a cookie on that visitor's browser profile. Every time that user returns, Google Analytics reads the cookie it set the first time and knows whether the user is an absolute unique visitor or a return visitor.

NOTE If one person has more than one account on more than one computer (rather than the same account on more than one computer), then GA counts as many unique visitors as there are computers. In other words, three computers are equal to three absolute unique visitors, which just means that, really, people aren't counted as visitors, computers are. Also, if a user turns off all cookies settings (and many do for privacy reasons), Google Analytics cannot track them at all. These users look like new, absolute unique visitors every time they visit the site.

It does get a little strange, but these are pretty good guidelines for understanding how Google counts visitors as absolute unique visitors or as returning visitors. And now that we understand the difference between absolute unique visitors and returning visitors, it's time to look a little more closely at the concept. The Absolute Unique Visitors report, shown in Figure 15-14, shows additional information about these site visitors.

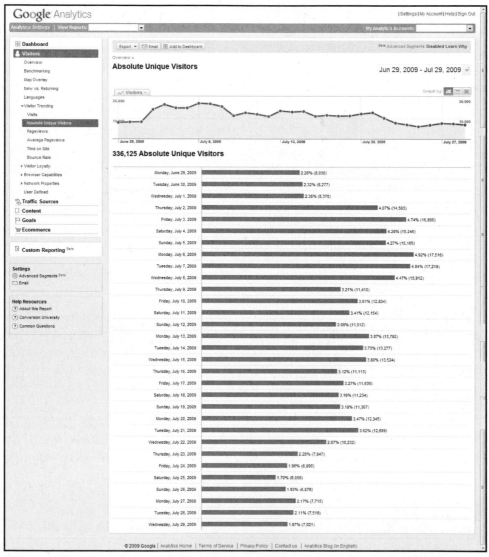

Figure 15-14: This report shows how many site visitors are absolute unique visitors.

The Absolute Unique Visitors report, much like the Visits report, is quite simple. It shows you exactly how many of your visitors are absolute unique visitors, but no additional drill-down information is available in this report.

Still, you can use this information to see how effective your marketing efforts are at driving absolute unique visitors to your web site. If you were tweaking an existing marketing campaign to drive more of these visitors to your site, this information would help you decide how future iterations of that marketing campaign could be changed or enhanced to bring in more absolute unique visitors, as well as more returning ones.

Page Views

There may be a distinct difference between the number of visitors to your site and the number of page views on your site. A visit is counted when a person first navigates onto your site, whether it's by clicking a link that leads there or by typing your URL directly into the address bar of a web browser.

The number of page views on your site is how many pages visitors actually clicked. For example, if one person visits your web site, that counts as one visit. However, while visiting, that person might look at five different pages. Those are page views.

The Pageviews report, shown in Figure 15-15, shows you how many pages your visitors viewed while they were on your site.

What the Pageviews report doesn't show, however, is how many pages were viewed by each visitor. It's a subtle distinction, but an important one. The next report, Average Pageviews, gives you that information.

In this report all you see is the number of pages that were viewed by all visitors each day. So, for example, if you're looking at page views over a month (as shown in Figure 15-15), then each day is represented by a bar in the graph. However, if you're looking at a single day or a week, then you still see the number of page views per day.

This general look at page views isn't really useful as a marketing tool. Although the numbers for page views can seem impressive, the truth is that this number is a collection of all the visitors to your site and all the pages those visitors looked at. So, while it gives you an accurate indicator of how much traffic your site receives (which helps you to plan for and manage the resources needed to support those visits), it doesn't tell you anything about how accurate your marketing efforts are.

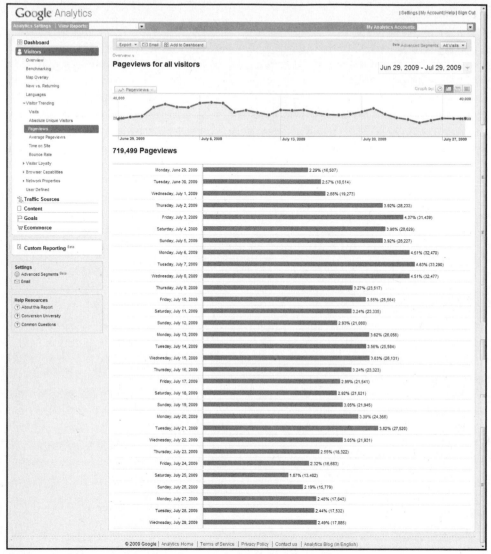

Figure 15-15: The Pageviews report shows how many pages were viewed in a specified period.

Average Page Views

The Average Pageviews report is a little different from the Pageviews report. This report, shown in Figure 15-16, shows you an average of how many pages were viewed per visit.

This is the total number of pages viewed in a given day divided by the number of visitors on that day. What that means is that this report doesn't show you how many actual pages each visitor went to. Instead it shows the average number of pages each visitor viewed on a given day.

Figure 15-16: Average Pageviews shows the average number of pages per visitor.

Now, even though this information isn't exact, per visitor it's still useful. One of the benefits of having this information is that it tells you how your users are interacting with your site. If, for example, you have a high average number of page views on your site immediately after a content update, then you know that users are paying attention to that site.

So, more accurately, this is a measure of web-site quality. A higher number of page views is a direct reflection of the quality of the content on your site. Users tend to view more pages when the content on those pages is relevant to the reason they visited your site.

Time on Site

The Time on Site report, shown in Figure 15-17, is a slightly different measurement of visit quality from the Average Pageviews report. Instead of showing you how many pages your visitors looked at, this report shows you how long, on average, they spent on your site.

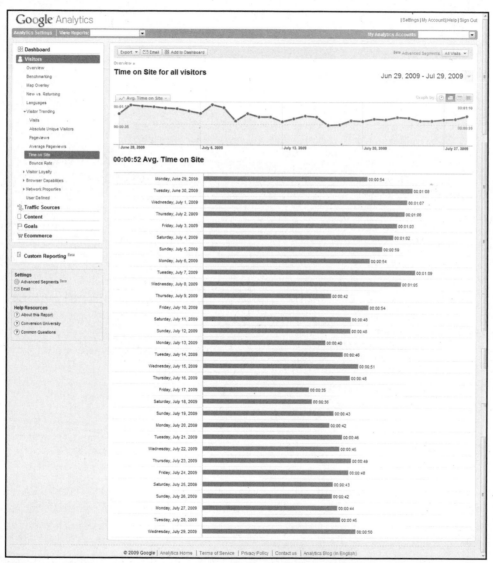

Figure 15-17: The Time on Site report is another indicator of site-content quality.

I hear you already: Why does it matter how long a visitor spends on my site? It matters because if they aren't on your site, they're probably spending their time on a different one. Because you want them to spend as much of their available Internet time as possible on your site, you need to have content that draws them in and keeps them busy for a while.

How long is a while? That's a question for which there is no right answer. The time a person spends on each of your web-site pages depends on numerous things: what the user is looking for, what your page has to offer, how quickly users read/scan pages and find additional information to navigate to, and how often the phone rings while they're on the page. Really.

Here's a situation for you. On Monday a visitor comes to your site, spends about 10 minutes surfing through the various pages, and then leaves. On Tuesday that same user returns but spends only eight minutes because on Monday he or she saw all the pages and the return visit today is to hit some of the dynamic content on your site (think blog, podcast, or new articles).

Then on Wednesday this user returns again. This time the user is in the middle of surfing through the same dynamic content, but the phone rings. Rather than close out of the page, this user takes the call and 20 minutes later, when the call is over, goes back to your site to finish reading a blog post.

Now you have this strange blip on your length-of-visit graph. It shows that one day, your average time on site is considerably higher than other days. Woohoo!

Just don't get too excited, because unless it happens consistently, chances are that it's just a fluke. On the other hand, if something is consistently drawing multiple users who spend an unusually long time surfing your pages, you may have a factor upon which you can capitalize.

If the number shows the opposite, you know that you need to add something to your pages to keep users there longer. What you add should be determined by what your users need. And that's a topic best left for a web-design book.

Bounce Rate

One more report that you'll find useful in this section of the Visits category is the Bounce Rate report, shown in Figure 15-18.

A bounce happens when a visitor arrives on a page and immediately leaves. In essence, a bounce means: *Did not visit another page. Did not collect $200.* For the purposes of this report (and only this report), a visit, a visitor, and a page view are pretty much all the same thing.

Bounce rates can show how effective pages on your site are. Visitors come into a site, and some of them leave immediately. When you consider additional information, such as sales info or goal conversion, you can deduce the effectiveness of your site or the ad bringing in those visitors. Both those observations require action from a business standpoint.

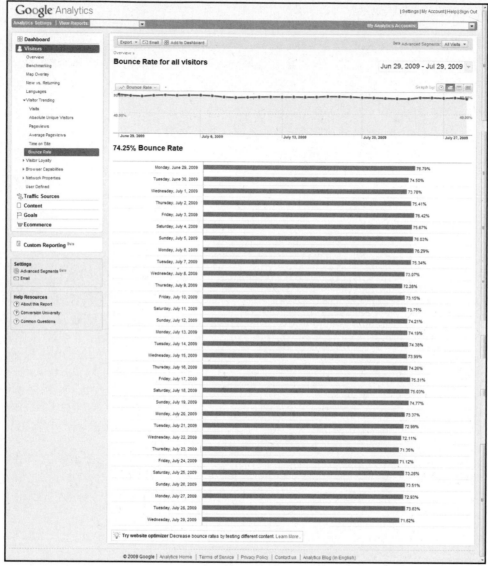

Figure 15-18: Bounce Rate data shows the percentage of visitors who saw only one page.

It's important to remember that you can't look at Google Analytics' metrics in isolation from other information about your business. As capable as Google Analytics is, it's still a medium-tier product. It won't function like a high-end (read: expensive) analytics package. You're going to have to use your head when applying outside data—such as actual sales—to Analytics' metrics. Analytics won't do everything for you.

Visitor Loyalty

Visitor loyalty—it is one of the most sought-after aspects of drawing visitors to your web site. And it's not easy to achieve. The Internet makes it really easy for users to pop into your site and then take off to find another if what they are looking for isn't immediately apparent.

It's not at all like the real world, where you might go into a store looking for something only to find that what you're looking for is a little more expensive, or that the store doesn't carry the exact brand you want. Because you had to drive to the store, get out of your car, and find whatever it was you were looking for, you're less likely to take off and go to another store if the exact product you're looking for isn't available. It's just a pain to repeat that process.

On the Internet, however, moving on is as simple as clicking a button. And users will move on for all kinds of reasons. If your web site is slow to load, visitors go to the next web site on their list. If users find your site through a product or information search and what they were looking for isn't right there as soon as they click into your site, they'll move on. Any number of things can prompt a user to find another site.

It is also hugely expensive to continue drawing new customers. If, however, you can build a core of loyal users—users you know will return and will regularly be the source of a goal conversion for you—then you don't have to put quite as much time, effort, or money into drawing new visitors.

Yes, enticing new visitors to come to your site is a constant effort for every web site. However, if you are always searching for new visitors and not serving return visitors, then you'll invest far more in your efforts than the site that had a sizable group of regular users.

The reports in the Visitor Loyalty section help you to see how effective your efforts at creating loyal visitors really are. Each of these four reports is a quick, easy-to-read graphic that shows you exactly what you're looking for and nothing more. There is no hidden functionality or deeper data to view in any of these reports. What you see is all there is. But that doesn't make these reports less valuable. They are just more efficient.

Loyalty

How often do visitors return to your site? Is it once? Two hundred times? You can't know without some kind of indicator, and that's what you get with the Visitor Loyalty report, shown in Figure 15-19.

What's it all mean?

The histogram—bar graph—shows you exactly how many times your site visitors return to your site. In the case of Figure 15-19, the maximum number of times a visitor has returned to the example site is more than 201.

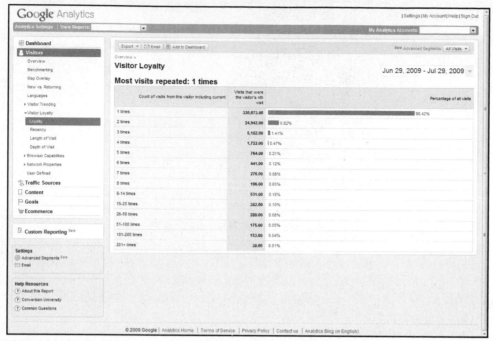

Figure 15-19: The Visitor Loyalty report shows you how often visitors return to your site.

The information contained here is used to gauge how loyal your site visitors are. If you find that you have a low number of returning visitors, it could indicate that you need to add something more to your web site to draw visitors back regularly. Using time-shifted content, such as newsletters, blogs, and podcasts, is a great way to increase visitor loyalty.

Recency

A number that goes hand in hand with visitors' return visits to your site is how often they return—the recency of their visits. Do visitors come back every two days? Once a year? Knowing when visitors return to your site helps you understand what's driving them to return.

The Recency report is shown in Figure 15-20. The graph shows the visitor from zero days through more than 366—over a year. So at a glance you can tell if visitors come once each year for your annual sale or if they return for your daily podcast review.

Visitor behavior reveals a lot about the efficacy of your web site. Metrics such as visitor loyalty and visit recency show you when (or if) your site visitors return, and give you cues as to what works to drive traffic or returning traffic to your site. What you do with that information will determine how successful your site is in the long term.

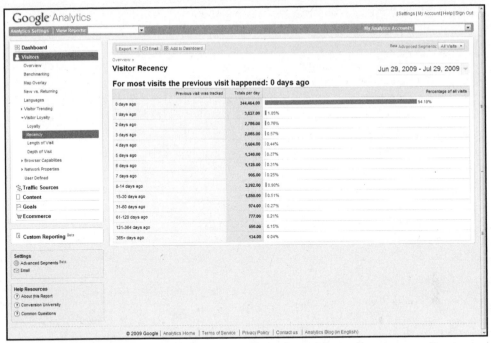

Figure 15-20: The Recency report shows you how often visitors return to your site.

Length of Visit

Knowing how long a visitor spends on your site is one way that you can determine how effective your site content is. The Length of Visit report, shown in Figure 15-21, shows you how long visitors spent on your site, broken down by seconds.

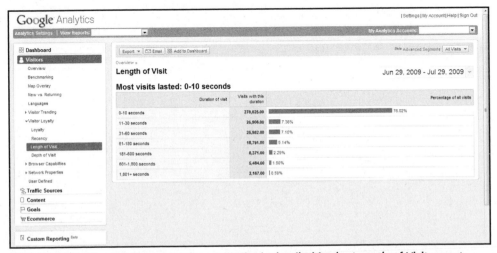

Figure 15-21: Time visitors spend on your site is detailed in the Length of Visit report.

Looking at the length of a visit gives you valuable clues to your users' habits. For example, if most of your visits fall in the zero- to 10-second range (as the report in Figure 15-21 shows), then you know that there is a problem with your site. Maybe the site is classified wrong, maybe your content is not enticing enough, or maybe there is some other reason entirely. Or maybe your visitors are just finding the site for the wrong reason. Whatever the case, your site is not effective at holding visitors.

In fact, if visitors are leaving within the first 10 seconds of a visit, then you know that those users are bouncing off your site just as quickly as they get there. It might take some investigative skills, but if you pay attention to the length of visit in combination with the most frequent landing pages, you should be able to tell what pages are turning visitors away. From there, it's a matter of design and content to turn those short visits into longer visits. And ultimately, a longer visit is what you're striving for. The longer visitors stay on your site, the more likely they are to reach goal conversions.

Depth of Visit

Depth of Visit is a quick little report designed to show you one thing—how many pages users visited during their brief stops on your web site. It's like travelers who stop at a roadside store during a journey. One traveler might make a pit stop in the restroom, then swing by the soda cooler, stop at the chip display, and finally end up at the register to make a purchase. A different traveler might dash into the restroom and then leave without making a purchase. A third could come in only to purchase a soda and never even approach the restroom.

There's a lot to be learned about people's habits by studying their stops along a journey, even if their journey is a virtual one through your web site.

The Depth of Visit report, shown in Figure 15-22, shows you just how many stops your visitors make as they pass through your site.

Functionally, this information might seem a little obscure. Why in the world would you want to know how many pages your visitors viewed? Well, in short, the more pages viewed the better. But if you look at this information and you find that your visitors are more the get-in-and-get-out types, you know that there's nothing compelling those readers to dig deeper into your content. So how can you change that?

It will take some experimentation. What drives your visitors? What would catch their attention and make them spend longer on the site? As an example, let's consider the (completely fictional) site BusyMommy.com. A visitor coming to this site is obviously very busy. The visitor is likely female, and has children—probably young children—vying for her attention. So when she stops by your site, she's looking for something specific. And she doesn't want to spend too much time looking for it.

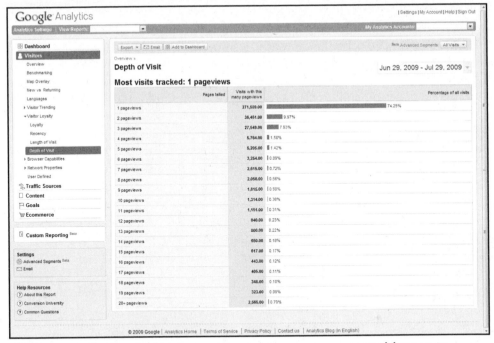

Figure 15-22: The Depth of Visit report shows how many pages your visitors go to.

But if Busy Mommy finds what she wants and it leads her to something else that she didn't know she needed, she might spend a few extra seconds on your site or visit an additional page or two. Your content, of course, has to be very compelling and has to entice her to dig deeper into your site.

Now, this report won't tell you how to create that content, but it will tell you if you're reaching your audience in the way you want. If visitors are hitting one page and leaving, and your site consists of hundreds of pages, there's some problem you should be worrying over. If your site is only a few dozen pages long, and visitors are hitting most of them, you know that you're appealing to those users. All you need to do is figure out how to capitalize on that.

Browser Capabilities

Web design parameters are the different factors that affect the way users see your web site. And those parameters can have a huge impact on the number of visitors who come onto your site and bounce right back off, and on the number of visitors who stick around, browsing and reading the content that you've provided.

One goal of your site should be to make visitors stick around for a little while—at least until they reach one of the goals that you've set for your site.

But if your site is hard to use, doesn't render well, or frustrates users for any reason, they will leave. The reports in the Browser Capabilities section of Google Analytics help you to see how different aspects of your site design and structure could affect how your visitors see, and use, your web site.

Browser

Web-site design affects how the site renders in different browsers. For example, some web sites are best viewed with an Internet Explorer browser. If you try to view those sites using a non–Internet Explorer browser, such as Firefox, Opera, or Safari, very often the page won't display properly. Sometimes graphics won't show up. Other times the graphics show up but the text behaves badly.

To help you avoid having a site that's not designed well for all the users who visit, the Browsers report, shown in Figure 15-23, shows what browsers most frequently accessed your web site in a given time frame. This enables you to see at a glance how your visitors viewed your site.

Figure 15-23: The Browsers report shows browsers used to access your site.

NOTE It's worth mentioning that sometimes designing your site with the intention of catering to every browser out there (or even just more than one of them) can be a very bad idea. When you look at the Browsers report in Google Analytics, you might find that 99 percent of your visitors access your site with Internet Explorer. The other 1 percent might use Firefox. If that's the case, you have to ask whether it's worth it to expend time and money to ensure the site is visible to that 1 percent of visitors who are not using Internet Explorer. In many cases the answer is no. If that's the case, then leaving your site alone is the best plan of action.

The usual tools are also there to help. You'll find tabs for Site Usage, Goal Conversions, and Ecommerce. The really interesting part of this report, however, is that you can see the version of the browser your site visitors are using. Click the name of any browser and you'll be taken to its specific browser analytics page, where there are links to the browser versions that accessed your site. Clicking those links takes you to the detail page for the browser version, as shown in Figure 15-24.

Figure 15-24: The Browser Version detail shows the final level of browser data.

Browser, Browser Type, and Browser Version detail pages show the same type of information. The Site Usage, Goal Conversions, and Ecommerce tabs enable you to see the number of visitors in the context of those elements. And the graph at the top of the page shows you the number of visitors per day for that browser, browser type, and browser version. The only place you really get any variation is the Browser Version detail page. That's as far into the data as you can go, so you won't find links to any additional information and there is no pie graph showing you comparisons among browsers or versions.

Operating System

More often than not, web sites are designed to work well with only the dominant browser. But not having the capability to work with older browsers may not be good business. For example, if you support Windows Internet Explorer 8.0 only, then users who are working from Windows Internet Explorer 6.0 might be left out in the cold, especially if there are downloadable media files in the mix.

The Operating Systems report shown in Figure 15-25 shows which operating systems are being used by visitors to your site, and how many visitors used each type of operating system listed.

Figure 15-25: The Operating Systems report tells you the operating systems visitors use.

As with the Browser Version report, you can click any listed platform to drill down deeper into what version of that operating system visitors use.

Browser and Operating System

Visitors don't come to your site using a browser that is independent of an operating system. Nor do they come using an operating system that's independent of a browser. And very often the operating system that a browser is running on affects the way the browser behaves. So Google Analytics makes it easy for you to figure out what combinations of platforms and browsers are used most often to access your web site.

The Browsers and OS report, shown in Figure 15-26, shows you the combinations of web browser and operating system used most frequently.

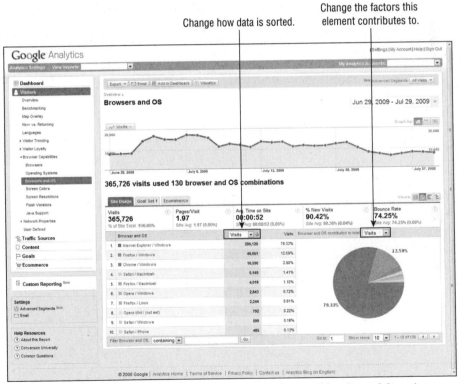

Figure 15-26: The Browsers and OS report shows the combinations visitors use.

All the drill-down capabilities that you've seen in the other reports in this section are available in this report. But there's one more capability you haven't really looked at yet—the ability to sort the data by categories other than the number of visitors to the site. Additionally, you can change your data view to see how the browser-and-operating-system combinations affected other aspects of your data. Both of these capabilities are labeled in Figure 15-26.

When you change the data you're viewing, you see differences. These subtle differences, however, can mean huge differences in what you do with that information. For example, if you're looking at these browser/OS combinations sorted by visits, but then you change the Contribution view to reflect the amount of time each user spent on your site, you might learn that while three different combinations of operating systems and browsers could access your site, one alone accounted for 100 percent of the time spent on your site.

This information can be interpreted in a couple of ways, but the most likely interpretation is that visitors using the combinations that accounted for no time on your site bounced right back off when they landed on your page. The site might not have rendered properly for them, or it could be something else. Watching these numbers over time should help you come to some conclusions. And once you know there is a problem, it takes only a little time and effort to fix it.

Screen Colors

Anyone who has ever printed a color picture or ordered a colored garment over the Internet knows that colors on a screen can be vastly different from colors in real life. What you might not realize, though, is how different colors look on different types of monitors.

Because some web sites have a very specific color scheme, it's essential to ensure that all the colors on the site are distinguishable. To help with that, the Screen Colors report, shown in Figure 15-27, shows what color-rendering standard most of the site's visitors are using.

This report breaks down the graphic viewing capabilities of your site visitors so that you can be certain they're actually seeing what you intend them to. It also gives you access to the additional capabilities—tabs and different views of the data—that you've become familiar with in other reports.

If you're not targeting the right graphics capabilities with your web site, users could be seeing red when you want them to see fuchsia.

Screen Resolution

How Jerri views a web site from her Windows-based laptop might be different from the way she views it on the 19-inch monitor of her desktop computer, and that's certain to be different from what someone else sees on an iBook. The screens and screen resolutions that visitors use to view your site will make all the difference in the world in what they see.

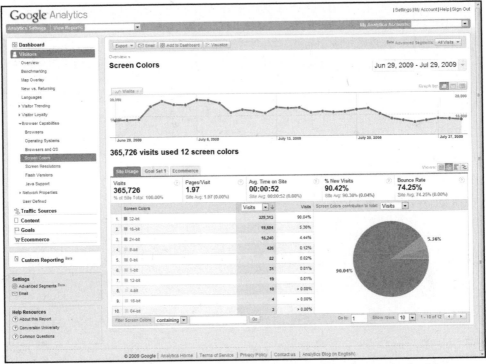

Figure 15-27: The Screen Colors report shows what color-rendering standards visitors use.

To help you determine whether your site is displaying as well as it can for the majority of users, the Screen Resolutions report, shown in Figure 15-28, ranks visits according to screen resolution.

Users are ranked according to the resolutions of the screens they are using, and you can click any resolution or use the calendar functions to dig deeper into the information or to view a different time frame. You can also switch between tabs to see how screen resolution affects your goal conversions or your e-commerce transactions.

Flash Version

Here's a news flash: most web-site visitors hate Flash (not because it's a bad technology but because it's very often used in advertising). This means that when visitors see Flash graphics coming up on their pages, they're a little reluctant to download a new version of Flash just to be hit with an advertisement that renders better.

On the other hand, Flash openers are more acceptable (to Jerri at least), and can be very cool. But it's still a technology that must be used with care.

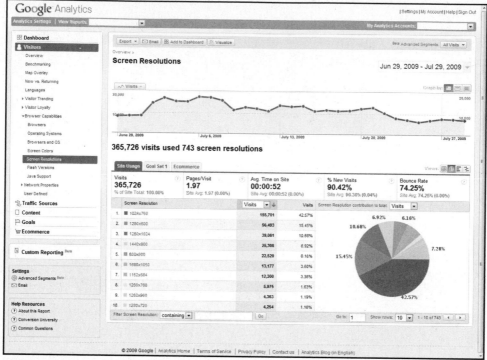

Figure 15-28: Use the Screen Resolutions report to find out how visitors see your site.

If you absolutely must have one of those exceptionally cool Flash splashes on your site (I know you would never use Flash advertisements), the Flash Versions report, shown in Figure 15-29, will show you what version of Flash the majority of your users have installed.

Once you know what Flash version the majority of your users have, you can use that version to create your Flash opener. That way the fewest possible number of visitors will have to install a new version of Flash support. And you still get the super-cool opening page that will make your visitors go "Oohhh … ahhhh!"

Java Support

To Java or not to Java? That is the question. Okay, so maybe it's corny, but if you're considering putting a Java-enabled application on your web site, it's a question you could be asking yourself.

Figure 15-29: The Flash Versions report suggests what Flash version to use for openers.

Web-site visitors are a fickle bunch. Scores of studies have been done to show what users want and don't want from a web site. Among those reports are some that focus solely on Java, and the findings generally suggest that users who don't have a capability installed usually don't want to install it. So if you're putting Java on your site, you should probably make sure the majority of your users have Java-enabled browsers, unless you have a very good reason for doing otherwise.

The Java Enabled report is your way to tell. The report, shown in Figure 15-30, tells exactly how many visitors have Java capabilities and how many do not. With that knowledge in mind, you can make an informed decision about how valuable adding a Java application to your web site might be.

The remaining controls on this report are the same as those on previous reports, and you can drill into the information to see how the data breaks down for each category of visitors.

When you're building your web site, it often seems that the design and structure of the site is far less important than things like keyword placement and meta-tagging. But the truth is that your design and structure are just as important. And if your site is not user-friendly, visitors are going to leave—quickly. Use the reports in this section to ensure that your site is as user-friendly as you can make it.

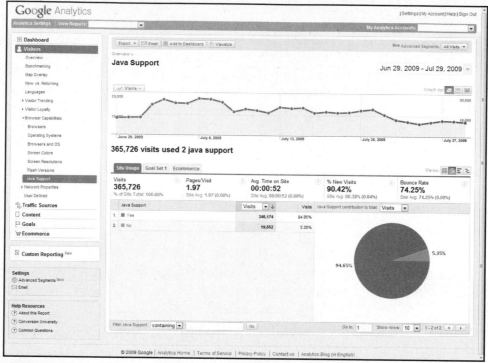

Figure 15-30: Learn how many of your visitors have Java support.

Network Properties

Pick up any book about building web sites and it's pretty much guaranteed to have at least a few pages on usability. Usability is simply how usable your web site is to visitors. And as you saw in Chapter 12, there are a lot of usability factors that affect your web-site traffic. But those are all factors directly related to the web site.

Usability doesn't end there, however. There are some elements of usability over which you have absolutely no control. Most notably, the network properties available to your site visitors can have a huge impact on the usability of your site. Factors such as network location, hostnames, and even connection speeds can change the usability quotient of your site. And that's exactly why it's important to monitor these factors.

The Network Properties section of Google Analytics shows you some of the important measurements that you might otherwise take for granted. The data collected for these reports isn't earth-shattering; however, the data will help you design your site so that it's accessible by as many visitors as possible.

Network Location

When you see the term *network location*, you might think it refers solely to the geographic location of a network. In this instance you'd be wrong. The Network Location report, shown in Figure 15-31, is misleading because it actually tells you to what ISP (Internet service provider) or corporate network visitors to your site are connected.

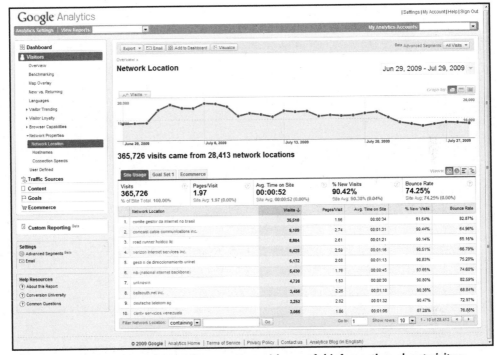

Figure 15-31: The Network Location report provides useful information about visitors.

What can you possibly gain by knowing the ISP or corporate network to which your users are connected? Watch for anomalies in the network location (like maybe universities or other unusual ISPs) and then consider what those locations might mean about your site. If it's a university network, what about your site is drawing university students or professors? Look at your own statistics over time and think creatively about how you can use them to improve your business or solve a business problem.

It also helps to look deeper at the available data. On the Network Location report you can click the name of any ISP to be taken to the specifics for that report. Once there, you can use the Segment drop-down menu to view further segmentation of your visitors.

Hostnames

Some web-site owners have multiple domains pointing to the same physical web space. If you park an old domain on your current site, separating old traffic from new can be difficult. But with Google Analytics it's not. Analytics provides the Hostnames report, shown in Figure 15-32, to help you see which site got what traffic.

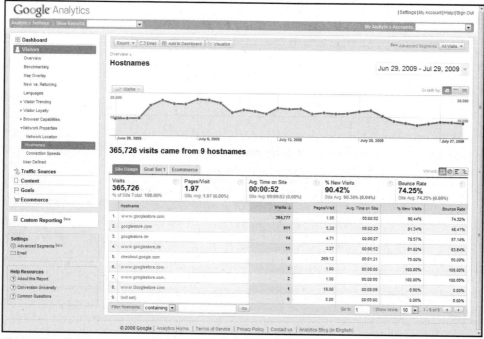

Figure 15-32: The Hostnames report shows which URLs users accessed to reach your site.

> **NOTE** This report is one means of seeing if someone else is copying your web site's source code to build his or her own site or to create a spoofed copy of your site. If a web site appears in this list that doesn't belong to you, it's possible that the site owner has copied your source code (and even your content) to use as his or her own.
>
> Before you get all up in arms, make sure that it's not the proxy or cache of an ISP, which, by law, is allowed to maintain copies of your pages. This is a place where it's worthwhile to note that because the proxy copies the whole page, including the Google Analytics code, page views that might escape a log-based analyzer like AWStats don't get lost in the shuffle. To Google Analytics they look no different from page views served directly from your site.

With the Hostnames report you can monitor the URL that users visit to access your site. Say, for example, that my actual web site is www.JerriLedford.com. But maybe my first web site was www.technologywriter.com. Users who have been visiting my site since it was www.technologywriter.com might still use that web address to access it. My Hostnames report, then, would break down my site visitors into those who typed www.JerriLedford.com into their browser bars and those who typed www.technologywriter.com.

That fact can help you to know how long you should hold on to a web site that is simply a referring site. If you find that your Hostnames report lists only one site, the other might no longer be necessary.

Connection Speeds

Back in the late 1990s and early 2000s, scores of reports were put together about web-site usability. The concept behind such usability studies was to provide web sites that were easy for visitors to navigate. At the time, the studies looked at a variety of factors, including how long it took for a web page to load.

What was discovered was that Internet users are an impatient lot. We like to have our pages served up to us in less time than it takes to nuke a cup of coffee. Remember the days of going out for Chinese while a page loaded? These days, if a page takes more than a few seconds to appear, we're ready, willing, and able to move on.

Today, more and more users are connecting to the web via high-speed broadband connections, but there are still some users who have dialup connections, including the vast majority of non-American users (except in Korea). And those users don't want to deal with pages that take forever (in Internet time) to load. The Connection Speeds report, shown in Figure 15-33, illustrates the speed at which your users connect to your site. With this information you know how complicated (or how simple) your web site can be and still draw users without testing their patience.

Understand that there are various levels of Internet service, from the slowest (which is dialup Internet access) to the fastest (which would currently be cable). If your site visitors are all either dialup users or broadband users, you may see only two categories. However, you can also have other categories, such as T1 and DSL. Both of these types of Internet service are faster than dialup, yet slower than cable.

Simple things such as network location, hostnames, and connection speeds might not seem to be big factors for visitors to your web site. But in truth, they can have a major impact on the number of visits to your site. Knowing these details helps you to make your web site accessible to even more people.

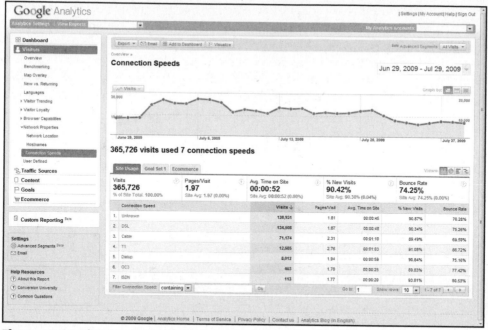

Figure 15-33: The Connection Speeds report shows what level of Internet service visitors use.

User Defined

Dump a box of multicolored, differently shaped blocks on a table, and at some point someone will come along and separate them by color, shape, or both. It's human nature. We want to make sense of things, so we place everything in its own compartment.

This tendency to compartmentalize things serves other purposes, too. Think about working in your yard. If you reach down to pull a weed and spot something long and rounded, it's a pretty good bet you'll yank your hand back before you're even certain what you see.

That's the result of compartmentalization—also called segmentation. We give objects general classifications, like *long, rounded, hairy, green,* or *fat,* because that helps us know quickly where those objects belong. And it's not just objects. Basically everything can be classified as one thing or another.

Visitor segmentation works the same way, except that it applies to your website visitors. By segmenting visitors, first generally and then more specifically, you can determine how effective portions of your site are, what groups of visitors are the most valuable (or spend the most money), and which group of visitors provides the best return on investment.

Google Analytics gives you a good standard selection for visitor segmentation. There are even plenty of options for customized segmentation, but as useful as the existing segmentation reports are, you'll probably want (or need) to segment site visitors in a way that's very specific to your business. The User Defined report, shown in Figure 15-34, enables you to segment your visitors according to differentiators that you define, and it shows you how those users measure up in conversions and e-commerce values.

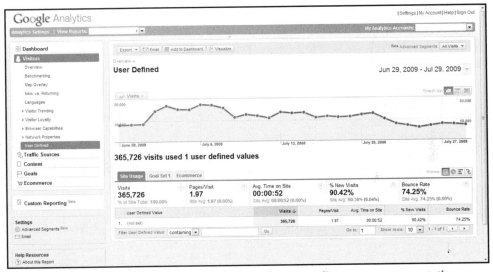

Figure 15-34: The User Defined report displays data according to your segmentation requirements.

When looking at Figure 15-34, you'll notice the only data there is labeled "not set." In that report, a user-defined segmentation measurement hasn't been added, so Google Analytics is keeping up with all the data, instead of just the type of data you tell it to. But adding a differentiator isn't all that difficult. It requires a snippet of JavaScript code placed on your web page, below the tracking code that you've inserted so Google Analytics can collect visitor data from your site.

Adding a Variable

One measurement that you can use to segment your visitors is information from a form that visitors complete on your site. For example, if you push site visitors through a registration form when they enter a specific point on your site, you could include a drop-down menu in that form that allows users to select their specific job titles. The job title can then be used to track how registrants from each job category navigate through your site.

The User Defined segmentation in Google Analytics works by setting a cookie on a user's computer that points to a specific piece of data being monitored by a JavaScript function. So the first thing you need to do to set a user-defined variable is to add the Java Script code to your web site. The code should include the utmSetVar() function. It looks like this:

```
<script type="text/java_script">__utmSetVar('Marketing/PR');</script>
```

Replace the script language with the script that you're using. There's also a piece that reads ('Marketing/PR'). This is a variable and you should replace this portion of the code with the name of the variable that you want to track. So for our example of segmenting visitors by job title, your code might look like this:

```
<form onSubmit="__utmSetVar(this.mymenu.options
[this.mymenu.selectedIndex].value);">
<select name=mymenu>
<option value="Technical/Engineering">
Technical/Engineering</option>
<option value="Marketing/PR">Marketing/PR</option>
<option value="Manufacturing">Manufacturing</option>
<option value="General Management">General Management</option>
As you can see, each of the job titles that you've listed in your
online form should be given a line in the code. That way, Analytics
knows to track each of the separate job functions.
You can also track separately users who click certain links. The code
for that segmentation might look like this:
<a href="link.html" onClick="__utmSetVar('Marketing /PR');"
   >Click here </a>
```

One other option you have is to track users according to a specific page that they visit. For example, if you have a visitor who stops by your Marketing/PR page, you can set a segmentation variable that will then track that visitor's movements through your site as a part of the Marketing/PR segment. Your code for this type of tracking might look something like this:

```
<body onLoad="javascript:__utmSetVar('Marketing/PR')">
```

What to Segment

One of the most difficult parts of using User Defined segmentation is knowing what to segment. The general segmentation settings included in Google Analytics seem (at first glance) to cover just about everything that you would need to know about your site visitors. And if you are looking at those segmentation categories in very broad terms, they might. But when you get into the normal daily workflow associated with your web site and the goals you have set for the site, then you begin to understand that there could well be other aspects of user demographics or behavior that might be important for you to understand.

For example, if your web site is a content site, then it might be important to you to learn how many of your users sign up for your newsletter every day. You can set up a user-defined report to show you this answer, and then you can further segment that data by using the provided segmentation reports.

Determining the right metric to monitor in user segmentation isn't always easy. A good rule, however, is that any User Defined segmentation that you create should apply to your specific business goals for your web site. Using a truly important measurement enables you to drill down into your data to see what emerges to drive meaningful action on your site. So when you're creating User Defined segmentation, the question you should be asking is, "Of what value to my business is this measurement?"

Visitor segmentation is all about figuring out how certain groups of your visitors behave in the context of that grouping. There's a lot to be gained from segmenting your users. If you're segmenting by information included in a form, such as job titles, you can quickly learn how engineers use your site versus how IT managers use it. This is an easy way to learn quickly which are the most profitable segments among your site visitors.

Traffic Sources

Understanding where your site visitors are coming from—not geographically, but from where on the Web—can help you target users to bring even more traffic to your site. But to do that you have to know basics such as how many of your visitors came directly to your site and how many were referred by outside sources, search engines, or advertisements.

The reports included in the Traffic section give you all that information. Then you can use that data to draw (or drive) additional traffic to your site. And that's hugely important because the more people who see your site, the more likely you are to achieve the goal conversions you're trying to reach. (Remember that goal conversions mean that transactions are completed, whatever those transactions might be for you.)

What Traffic Analysis Can Tell You

Where does your web-site traffic come from? Do you know? Do you know why you should know?

Where your web-site traffic comes from is one of the most basic analytics measurements, but that doesn't make it less valuable. It's important to know where your site traffic originates because this helps you to know where to target advertising dollars and marketing efforts.

Here's an example. Say you have a web site that's been around for a while. Every week you have an overview of your traffic sources sent to you from Google Analytics and after a while you begin to notice a pattern: nearly 25 percent of your traffic is coming from one web site that you haven't done business with in years. So you follow the links in the report and learn that what's driving that traffic is an old advertisement that you placed on a related web site about five years earlier.

Wait just a minute! A five-year-old advertisement that's not costing you a dime is pushing 25 percent of your site traffic? Now that's something you can work with. Maybe you decide to update the advertisement on the referring site. Maybe you choose to write an article and offer it to the site. Or maybe you purchase additional advertising on the site. Whatever action you take because of that information, you can rest assured that it will likely increase your site traffic. And the reason you can be so sure about that is that you have some very compelling evidence in the analytics of the value of a single ad.

This isn't really a "what if" situation. It's a situation that Jerri faced with her web site. When she began using Google Analytics, she learned that a link from a web site she hadn't even visited in years was driving a sizable portion of her traffic. And that is what analyzing your traffic sources can show you—patterns of visitors' behavior that you would never have guessed otherwise.

Traffic Sources Overview

When you click into the Traffic Sources reports (from the navigation menu on the left), the first thing you see is the Traffic Sources Overview report, shown in Figure 16-1.

The graph still shows the number of visits to your site, but if you look immediately below it you'll see percentages for the source of your traffic. In the case of the example shown in Figure 16-1, 8.83 percent of the traffic was direct traffic, meaning the visitor typed the URL for the web site that's being monitored directly into the browser's address bar.

The majority of traffic (83.62 percent) came from referring sites, or other web sites that included a link back to the web site that's being monitored, and 7.56 percent of the traffic came from search engine results.

You can click through any of these links to see a detailed report, but we'll be covering those reports later in this chapter, so I won't go into them here. The analytics contained in this report are all just quick overviews of the other reports in this section. However, you can click any of the links to be taken to a full view of that report.

Figure 16-1: The Traffic Sources Overview is a quick snapshot of your site traffic.

For example, at the bottom of the overview screen is a section labeled **Top Traffic Sources**. In this section is a list of the top sources and the top keywords. Click any one of the links in the source list and you'll be taken to a corresponding report for that link, whether it's a search engine, direct traffic, or referral traffic. Click any of the links in the keyword section and you'll be taken to the keyword report for that specific keyword (which is one level below the Keyword report).

The one frustration with these overview pages is that you cannot change them to reflect the metrics that are most important to you in a section. You can, however, export the Overview in PDF, XML, CSV, CSV for Excel, or TSV formats. To access this function, click the **Export** button right above the report title, as shown in Figure 16-2.

When you click the **Export** button, the file options to which you can export the report appear. Select the file type and the report is automatically opened in that application. So if you select PDF, the file opens in Adobe Reader. If you select CSV for Excel, the file opens in Excel.

The purpose behind exporting reports is to share your analytics with others without giving them access to your Google Analytics account. Export and save or print files to distribute to management and project or team leaders, or even to include as visual aids in a presentation.

Click to open Export options.

Figure 16-2: Export reports in various formats to share with management and colleagues.

> **NOTE** The Export capability is available in all the reports in Google Analytics, except the Site Overlay. You can export any report to share with others in the same way.

One other reminder about your reports. You can schedule automatic e-mail delivery of any report in Google Analytics (except the Site Overlay) by clicking the **Email** button above the report name. Or if you're not really into sharing but you want to have this information available from your main Analytics dashboard, you can click the **Add to Dashboard** tab to place the report on your dashboard.

Direct Traffic

Direct traffic is those visitors who come directly to your site by selecting your site address from a favorites list or typing your URL directly into the address bar of their browsers. The **Direct Traffic** report, shown in Figure 16-3, is a measure of how many of your site visitors qualify as coming directly to your site and not through some outside source.

Direct traffic can be an indicator for a couple of factors about your web site. First, direct traffic can point to the popularity (or lack of popularity) of your brand. A brand is the image that users have of your company, which is associated with a general topic. For example, when you think of software, you probably automatically think Microsoft. And when you think of search capabilities, you probably think Google. That's because Microsoft and Google are more than just company names. They are also brands.

Figure 16-3: Direct Traffic shows how well the public knows your site or brand.

If your brand is well established, then when people think of a topic related to you, your name should come immediately to mind. And at that point, users who want to access your web site will first try typing www.*yourname*.com into the address bar of their web browsers. That's direct traffic.

Direct traffic can also indicate the effectiveness of your marketing or advertising efforts. If these efforts are reaching the right audience, then you're likely to see a boost in the number of direct-traffic visitors to your site.

Glancing at a Direct Traffic metric just once isn't going to give you a clear picture of the trending for direct traffic, however. This is a measurement that is best used over time. Ideally you want your direct-traffic visitors to rise over time, because you want to create a community of loyal users who come to your site directly because they are comfortable with your brand. However, you'll find there will be bumps—times when the direct traffic jumps considerably only to fall back to a more normal level. These bumps will tell you how you're doing in your efforts to increase direct-traffic numbers.

Referring Sites

Among the big questions about web sites are, "Where do users come from?" and "Who refers them?" Knowing where your traffic comes from makes it easier to target marketing efforts. It also lets you know if your current marketing efforts are working.

So where does traffic come from? There's always the direct route. But then there are links that you've paid to have placed on other sites and links from banners, as well as newsletters and other marketing efforts. And then you also have the web searches by which people stumble onto your site. These are all lumped together as referring sites.

People come to your site from all manner of sources. To see what those sources are, there's the Referring Sites report, shown in Figure 16-4.

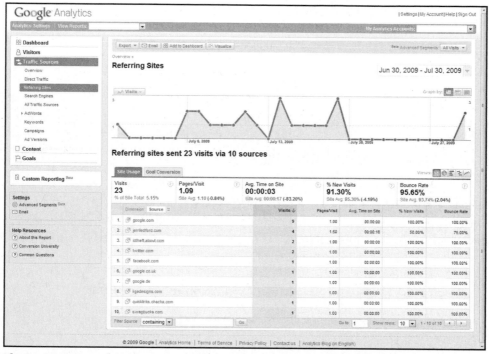

Figure 16-4: See where your site traffic originates in the Referring Sites report.

This report lays out the referral sites for your visitors and then illustrates how those visits translate into goal conversions and e-commerce data. Do the visitors who come from your newsletter buy more than the visitors who come from your AdWords campaigns? Or do the visitors who come from a high-end referral link spend more than visitors from a less costly referral link? The only way you'll ever know is to look at this report.

Of course, the report comes with all the standard tools. Each link in the report takes you further into the details of that referring site. And you can see how your data applies to goal conversions and e-commerce considerations by using the tabs. You can also further segment your data using the Dimension or Advanced Segments drop-down menus.

As previously mentioned, you can use this report to help build on the potential that you might be missing, but even more important, the report also makes it obvious where something is not right. If you expect that products featured on your front page should generate more traffic or revenue than they actually do, you can easily see there's a problem that needs to be addressed.

Using this report you can also see clearly how well your marketing and advertising efforts are generating revenue. You do need to tag the marketing links to persuade the report to track them, but by now you should be pretty comfortable with the process of tagging these links.

Search Engines

The topic of search engines—or more accurately search engine optimization—is highly important when it comes to creating traffic for your site. Some people spend virtually all their time learning which search engines bring the most traffic and how to target those search engines in order to rank higher in search results.

It's no wonder there is a report that shows specific analytics for the search engines that refer visitors to your site. The Search Engines report, shown in Figure 16-5, lists the search engines that referred visitors to your site and how many visitors came from each.

Figure 16-5: The Search Engines report shows how search engines affect site traffic.

The default view for this report is all traffic. In other words, when you click on this report you see all the traffic that was pushed to your site by search engines, no matter whether the occurrences of that traffic were the result of organic search engine rankings or paid search engine rankings. However, you can change that view using the "paid" and "non-paid" links to look at only the specified segment of search engine traffic.

This is an excellent way to tell how well your *organic ranking efforts* are working, and how effective your paid listings are. Organic ranking efforts are design elements that you include in your site to ensure that it appears as far up in search rankings as possible. For example, many people use keywords in the HTML of their site design to ensure that search engine crawlers will list the site correctly in search engine rankings. Even the links that you have on your site can have a bearing on the ranking you get.

So if you're looking at this report and your non-paid referrals are high, you know that your organic ranking efforts are paying off (because, of course, organic means you're not paying for the ranking). If, on the other hand, your paid rankings are higher, then you can tell how effective those paid rankings are. If they're low, you might consider changing the rankings or even not using them at all. But if they're higher, then you know your targeting is right on.

Some people (sometimes called SEOs, or search engine optimization specialists) spend all their time manipulating sites to take advantage of both paid and unpaid search rankings. You may not want to put that much time into it, but having a report that shows you how many site visitors were referred by search engines and whether those were organic or paid referrals can go a long way in helping to determine if your efforts to draw visitors to your site through search engines are working.

All Traffic Sources

A way to tell how one type of traffic to your site compares to another type is to use the All Traffic Sources report, shown in Figure 16-6.

This report shows you both the source of your traffic and the medium that pushed the measured traffic to your site. A source is the web site or search engine that leads users to your site. The medium is the type of marketing campaign that leads users to your site.

When you're looking at the All Traffic Sources report, you're viewing traffic by both source and medium. However, you can separate that traffic into those two categories by using the drop-down **Show** menu that's directly below the bold statement about the number of visitors from the number of sources and mediums.

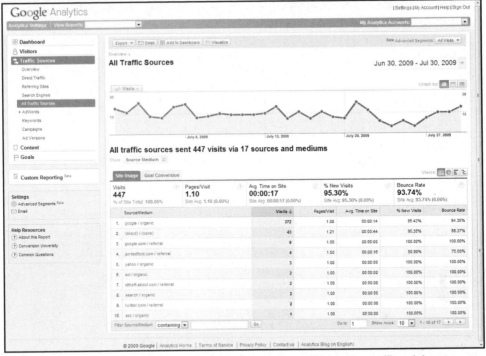

Figure 16-6: The All Traffic Sources report shows where all your site traffic originates.

When you choose the **Source** option in that menu you're taken to a report that shows only the sources for your traffic, as shown in Figure 16-7. Using the tabs on this report you can also look at those sources in the context of Goal Conversion (how many goal conversions each source contributed) and Ecommerce (how valuable the visits from each source were).

You can drill even deeper into the data to learn just what media were responsible for which sources, as shown in Figure 16-8. All you have to do is click the link for one of the sources. The information included in the detail page will help you understand how that particular source affected areas such as the average time users spent on your site and the number of pages per visit for that source.

This information can be very valuable when you're trying to draw new customers to your site, and even for keeping track of what returning visitors are doing while they're visiting you. If the source or medium that draws users to your site is highly effective, you'll see that in these reports.

Switch among Source, Medium,
or Source/Medium (both).

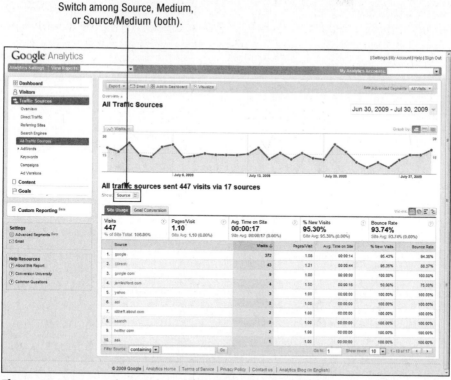

Figure 16-7: Learn what sources drive traffic to your web site in this report.

Figure 16-8: The Source/Medium detail report shows how these are connected.

Of course, that doesn't really explain the medium. The medium is the type of marketing campaign that leads users to your site. If you're running a marketing campaign and you have your web pages tagged accordingly, then by using these reports you'll be able to tell quickly which campaigns are responsible for what percentage of site traffic and what percentage of goal conversions, as well as the e-commerce value of the visitors the campaign is pushing to the web site.

A medium can also be organic, as is the case with the report shown in Figure 16-8. The source (Google, in this case) organically pushed 372 visits to the web site being monitored. *Organic traffic*, as you probably already know, is traffic that comes to your site naturally, through your marketing efforts and not through page sources.

All of this is valuable information. If you're looking to improve your site traffic and begin building a base of loyal users, this report will point you in the right direction. It also helps you to quickly discern which marketing efforts are effective for what types of sources.

> **NOTE** Source and medium are two of the five dimensions of tracking marketing/advertising campaigns. The other three elements are term, content, and campaign. The term is the keyword or phrase users type into a search engine. Content is the version of an advertisement that users clicked through. And the campaign differentiates product-specific promotions, such as Free Day with 5-Day Rental or Buy One Get One Shoes. These campaign labels are tagged in your site/advertising code, as explained in Chapters 3 and 6.

AdWords

If you have a web site, you know it's not all that difficult to get your site listed in search engines such as Google or Yahoo! For the most part, especially if your web-site URL and title are the same, all you have to do is put the site up and wait. In many cases, within a few days a potential visitor can type the name of your web site into a search engine and it will appear in the search listings, albeit probably deep in the rankings. Give it a little more time and you might even make it to the first page of the results, if your site is well-designed and properly targeted.

That's the only easy part of search engine marketing. If you have a service or product that you want to market by search engine, landing good placement in search engine results is like catching electric eels by hand. Not only is it slippery and unpredictable, but if you do manage to do it, there's a very good possibility that you're going to get a serious shock.

To help combat the difficulties of creating web pages that actually land on a relevant search-term result, an entire discipline of marketing is targeted at optimizing search engine results. It's called *search engine optimization*. At the heart of this marketing strategy are keywords and keyword marketing.

Lumped together, this all adds up to *search engine marketing*—the art of gaining prominent placement in search engine results. And if you're trying to improve your search engine results, you're probably using some kind of *keyword marketing*.

Keeping up with the results of that marketing can be a difficult task that leaves you wishing you had a clone or maybe six of them. It's a difficult, time-consuming process. Or at least it was. Now that Google Analytics offers metrics for search engine marketing, all you really have to do is tag your keyword campaigns properly and Analytics will provide your tracking reports.

AdWords Campaigns

Google AdWords is a keyword marketing service offered by Google. The basics of AdWords are that you can bid on keywords to use in your advertising. The keywords are bid on by others as well, and the person with the highest bid and the best-quality rating is the one who gets the best ad placement for that keyword. So, for example, if you're bidding on the keyword "cell phone," then you're competing with every other person or company that also wants to use that keyword in search engine advertising.

The more people bidding on a keyword, the more expensive it is likely to be. Therefore, many web-site owners try to use keywords that are completely relevant, but that might not be the same terms every other person in that industry is interested in. Once you've won the right to use a keyword, then advertisements for your business (you create these short bits of text) are displayed on related web sites and when someone searches for related content. How often your keyword advertisement is displayed determines how much traffic the keyword leads to your site.

The AdWords Campaigns report shows how your AdWords campaigns perform. You probably remember from Chapter 13 how and why AdWords integrates with Google Analytics. This report is the proof of that integration, so to speak. When you click into the AdWords Campaigns report you're taken to the Site Usage tab, as shown in Figure 16-9. From this tab you can learn how your AdWords campaigns performed in terms of site visits—how many pages were visited, how long the visitor spent on each page on average, and how many visitors were new visitors or bounces.

The truly useful information in this report, however, comes from the Clicks tab. If you select that tab, the report shown in Figure 16-10 is displayed.

Figure 16-9: The AdWords Campaigns report tells you how campaigns perform.

Figure 16-10: The most telling data about AdWords campaigns is on the Clicks tab.

This information includes:

- **Visits:** The number of visits to your site as the result of clicks through an AdWords advertisement
- **Impressions:** The number of times your ad was shown to search engine users
- **Clicks:** The number of times visitors clicked through an AdWords ad to get to your site
- **Cost:** The cost of the AdWords clicks received
- **CTR (click-through rate):** The percentage of impressions that resulted in visitors clicking your AdWords ad
- **CPC (cost per click):** The average cost of each click earned through an AdWords ad
- **RPC (revenue per click):** The average revenue per click on AdWords ads. Revenue can be either the value of e-commerce sales or goal value as defined by you.
- **ROI (return on investment)**: What are you making from your AdWords campaigns versus what you are spending on them? This measurement tells you.
- **Margin:** What percentage is your margin? In other words, how much are you making on your products when you consider how much you're spending on them?

Each AdWords campaign listed on this report is a link to a more detailed report about that specific campaign. For example if you click the **Newbie Campaign** link in the report you're taken to the AdWords Ad Groups report, shown in Figure 16-11. This report shows you the same information that was shown in the AdWords Campaigns report; however, it is specific to a single AdWords campaign, rather than to all the campaigns you're running.

Within each AdWords campaign it's possible to run more than one keyword. When you click into the AdWords Ad Groups report you'll see a list of the keywords being used in that campaign. If you click one of the keywords in the Ad Groups report, you're taken a level deeper into the report to learn more about that specific keyword, as shown in Figure 16-12.

Finally, you can click one level deeper into this report to see how each individual keyword performed. This report, shown in Figure 16-13, gives you another way to look at the data for that specific keyword.

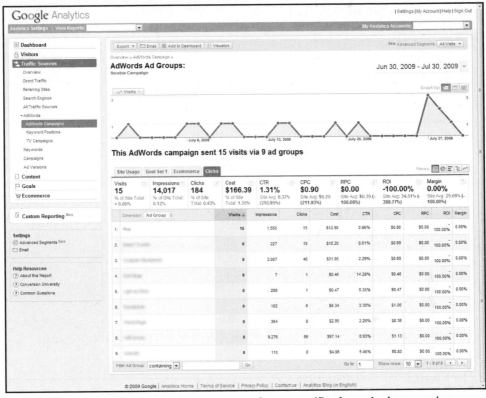

Figure 16-11: The AdWords Ad Groups report shows specifics for a single campaign.

Figure 16-12: Click a keyword in the Ad Groups report to go deeper into the data.

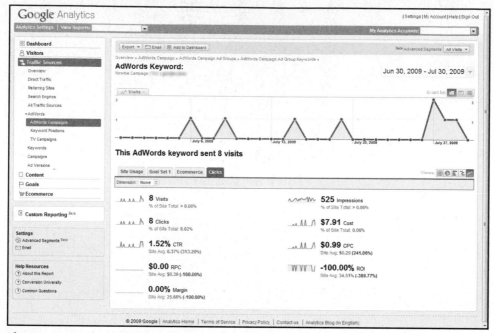

Figure 16-13: The AdWords Keyword report lets you look at data in yet another way.

So what does all of this mean? What can you do with it? If you've used AdWords, then you already know how valuable this information is. If you haven't, this is a great time to try it. The information shown in these reports helps you to see quickly which of your AdWords campaigns are performing well and which are not. You can then use the information to determine what campaigns need to be changed or discontinued and which ones might be worth investing more in.

Keyword Positions

How often have you wondered where your AdWords ads appear? Obviously you can't see every single time an ad is shown on the Google search results page, so you're left to wonder how often and where that ad is shown.

Ads can appear in two places on the Google search results page—either the top of the page, above the search results, or on the side of the page, to the right of the advertisements. The Keyword Positions report shows you where, and how often, your keyword ads appear on the Google search results page, as shown in Figure 16-14.

Figure 16-14: In the Keyword Positions report you can see where your keyword ads appear.

The most useful part of this report is the actual graphical representation of where your keyword ads appear on the Google search results page. On the lower right side of the report each ad position is shown, along with the position number and the number of times that your ad was placed in that position. Of course, if you don't have ad placements in one of the two positions, nothing is shown there.

Once you can graphically see where your keyword advertisements appear on the Google search results page, then you can begin to correlate your keyword performance with the keyword placement. Do you want to know why your keyword doesn't draw more than 94 visits even though there were more than 600,000 impressions for that keyword?

It could have something to do with the fact that your keyword ad appears only on the side of the page, and most of the time it's in a lower position because you're not investing enough in that keyword to warrant better positioning. Of course, that may not be the only reason your keywords aren't performing as well as expected, but it's certainly an indication that you might need to reconsider your keyword advertisements.

Again, none of the data collected in these reports is meant to be used alone. Sure, you can look at a single report and learn from it, but the truly useful information is in the combination of the analytics from several different reports.

TV Campaigns

Never one to be outdone, Google is always improving and adding new features to all its products, including Google Analytics. The linking of your Google Analytics account to your Google AdWords and AdSense accounts is just another step in the process of making all of Google's products more useful (and in helping them all work together).

If you are an AdWords user you probably already know that in the recent past Google has been adding some offline-to-online capabilities. For example, it's now possible to tap into television advertisements through Google AdWords, if you have the desire and the budget to do so. So it goes without saying that Google would be remiss if it didn't add the ability to track metrics for the different ad types in Google Analytics.

Never one to be remiss, Google Analytics has just such capabilities. Tracking abilities for AdWords TV campaigns are available in Analytics, even if they are limited at this time. Over time, and as use of this service increases, Google Analytics capabilities for the report will likely grow. For now, however, you can find the basic metrics that show how your television ads are performing.

The TV Campaigns report, shown in Figure 16-15, gives you an overview of how the TV campaigns you're running through AdWords are performing.

Figure 16-15: The TV Campaigns report lets you see how your AdWords TV campaigns are faring.

Included in the metrics that you can see in this report are the total TV impressions, the number of times the ad was aired (Ad Plays), how many people viewed the entire ad, what percentage of your original audience was retained, the cost of the campaign, and the CPM (cost per thousand impressions).

There are some important details about how these numbers are arrived at that you probably should know. First, Google measures these ads through set-top cable boxes. In other words, people who have a cable converter box through their cable company are counted. This means that those people who are not using set-top boxes (i.e., those who use a direct cable line) are not counted.

Furthermore, Google counts as an impression anyone who stayed on a channel for at least five seconds of the ad in question. This can be the first five seconds of the ad, the last five seconds of the ad, or any five seconds in between.

That's where the metrics for the Viewed Entire Ad and % Initial Audience Retained numbers come in. The difference between the number of visitors who viewed the whole ad and those who viewed less than the whole ad (including those who viewed only five seconds) can be pulled out of these stats. Also, the percent of the initial audience (those watching when the ad started) lets you know who stayed through the whole thing from beginning to end.

As with all of Google's reports, you can click a specific campaign to drill down into results for specific campaigns.

Keywords

The Keywords report is similar in structure to the All Traffic Sources report. The report, shown in Figure 16-16, shows you the metrics for all keywords, both organic (or unpaid) and paid. And as with the other reports, you have the option of viewing this information in the context of goal conversions and e-commerce value.

If you use the **Show** links you can also change your view to analyze just paid or just unpaid keyword results. And, of course, you also have the segment drop-down menu to further segment the keyword data by campaign details, geographical location, or technological capabilities.

But how do you use the information? To start with, use it to see what keywords are most effective at drawing visitors to your site. You may find, as you analyze the data, that an unpaid keyword is outperforming your paid keywords. Or you could find that a paid keyword is not performing at all. You can then use this information to tweak the keywords that you invest in.

You can also use it to find out where the highest number of goal conversions is coming from and the visit value for each keyword. A high number of conversions that results in low sales tells you that the visitors drawn by that particular keyword may not be as valuable as conversions that come from a different keyword that might have a higher sale value.

Figure 16-16: The Keywords report shows what keywords are drawing visitors to a site.

Don't look just at the most valuable keywords; look at the least valuable ones, too. These are keywords that indicate you either need to make changes to the advertisement driven by them or eliminate them altogether.

Keywords used in pay-per-click advertising are usually purchased through either a flat fee or a fee per click. But in the case of very popular keywords, you have the opportunity to bid within the confines of the daily budget that you've set. If you find that a keyword is performing poorly, you can remove that word from your list and return its cost to your budget. In turn, that additional budget can be used to purchase higher-priced, more frequently converting keywords.

Another hint you may get from this report is what keywords (that you're not already using) you should consider including. If you find that a specific keyword or set of keywords seems to be performing well, you can test similar keywords to see how well they perform.

Finally, if you find that a keyword or set of keywords has activity but that this activity is lacking either conversions or visit value, you know that something within your site probably needs to change. Maybe you need to modify the pages that users land on when they click a keyword.

For example, if you find that the keyword "pomegranate" has a lot of hits but a low conversion rate, you should consider changing the page that this keyword leads to. Maybe you have only one product on that page, or maybe that page just happens to have a strange navigational structure that makes it hard for the user to find other items on your site.

Try changing aspects of your site—improve navigation, feature additional products, or entice visitors to click deeper into the site—and continue to monitor the keyword performance. Sometimes something as simple as putting a recommendations bar on one side of the page will improve the length of time visitors spend on your site and the amount of money they spend while they're there.

The Keywords report is a useful tool for helping you fine-tune your keyword marketing efforts. Use the various aspects of the report to improve high-performing keywords and weed out the ones that are as worthless as two left shoes.

How can you use information about organic keywords that are generating conversions and high visit values on your site? Do you even know what those keywords are?

It's not enough to know that some keywords organically funnel visitors to your web site. You also have to know what they are. Then you need to find a way to use them.

The most obvious way to use these words is to convert them to paid keywords using a CPC (cost-per-click) program such as AdWords. But you don't necessarily have to spend money to get mileage from these keywords.

One of the ways to use this report is called *search engine optimization (SEO)*. SEO is the concept and strategies used to optimize your web site for search engines. Remember how bots, spiders, and crawlers probe your site? Those programs are looking for keywords and metadata tags (which are like keywords on steroids) that can be used to classify your web site when users search for specific keywords.

If your Keywords report shows that certain organic keywords are frequently used to find your site and that these seem to result in a high number of goal conversions or a high-value visit, you should consider using those keywords in prominent places on your web site.

For example, you might find that three organic keywords are especially effective for a selected time period. These keywords can be planted in a web site to help draw users to the site. However, this is a bit of a tricky situation.

One of these keyword combinations could be several words long and it might be hard to work into the body of a web site. You can include the individual words in the text and the metadata tags, but the exact combination might not always work. If you can't put them into the web-site text, you can't take advantage of the traffic they are naturally generating. If, on the other hand, you can logically work them into the site, the chances are good that you'll be able to build on the traffic that your site is already generating.

The thing to remember when working these keywords into your site, however, is that you don't want to overdo it. Including the keyword or keywords on a page too many times could cause a search engine to view your page as keyword spam. When that happens you can be delisted from the search engine; instead of gaining ranking, you could lose it altogether. It's a science that can be very hard to master.

But keyword optimization, when done right, can be a low-cost means of generating traffic—traffic that leads to goal conversions and increased visit values.

LEARN MORE ABOUT KEYWORD MARKETING

Keyword marketing is a very precise science. There are more nuances than can possibly be covered in a single book. But if you'd like to learn more about keyword marketing and how to use it to enhance your Internet business, here are a few titles that will get you started:

BEGINNER

- *Pay Per Click Search Engine Marketing For Dummies* by Peter Kent. Wiley. ISBN: 0471754943.

- *Pay-Per-Click Search Engine Marketing Handbook: Low Cost Strategies to Attracting New Customers Using Google, Yahoo & Other Search Engines* by Boris Mordkovich and Eugene Mordkovich. Lulu Press. ISBN: 1411628179.

INTERMEDIATE

- *Search Engine Marketing, Inc.: Driving Search Traffic to Your Company's Web Site* by Mike Moran and Bill Hunt. IBM Press. ISBN: 0131852922.

Campaigns

Tracking the effectiveness of your marketing campaigns is just half the battle. The other half is understanding how the campaign affects the number of people who reach a defined goal on your web site. This is called goal conversion. And marketing is all about conversions.

The goal could be for a visitor to make a purchase, sign up for a newsletter, or even just link to the page. Whatever your desired marketing campaign results, the number of conversions can be looked at in a variety of ways, and each conversion view tells you something about the effectiveness of your marketing campaign.

If you're running only one marketing campaign, keeping up with the results of that campaign won't be too difficult. But it's more likely that you're running multiple paid (and free) campaigns. And keeping up with multiple campaigns might leave you feeling as if you've been chasing your tail—lots of work for very little return.

The Campaigns report, shown in Figure 16-17, is a quick glance at how all your marketing campaigns are performing in terms of visits, pages per visit, average time on site, bounce percentage, and percentage of new visitors.

Figure 16-17: The Campaigns report quickly shows you how all your campaigns are performing.

The Campaigns report shows you your top-performing marketing campaigns, as long as they have been tagged for tracking by Google Analytics. Each of the lines in the table beneath the graph is dedicated to one marketing campaign that is either auto-tagged or tagged for a specific campaign.

NOTE The Campaigns report looks very similar to the AdWords Campaigns report, but it is *not* the same report. The AdWords Campaigns report is specifically for AdWords campaigns, while the Campaigns report is for all your marketing and advertising campaigns.

You may remember that Google tracks all instances of marketing campaigns—organic, referral, and direct. An organic campaign represents visits from an unpaid search engine; referral is the indicator used for visitors who clicked through an untagged marketing link; and direct indicates visitors who typed the URL for your site into the address bar of their web browsers.

The tag [not set] may also appear in your list of campaigns. This indicates visitors who came to your site through all methods that are not specifically tagged. For example, organic and direct visitors are qualified as [not set] because there is no campaign tag associated with these visitors. Referral visitors, on the other hand, will usually come from an advertising campaign, and can be tracked by campaign if you tag your campaigns properly.

You can quickly look at all these reports and see how many visits are related to each category and how those visits translate into goal conversions for each of the goals set for the site. With this information you can then adjust marketing campaigns to improve performance in an area where some campaigns aren't performing as well as you think they should.

If you are tracking more than one campaign, the information can also tell you which campaigns result in the highest visit value. This information can then be used to expand or shape future marketing campaigns.

The term *source* refers to the web site or search engine that led users to your site. If you're using cost-per-click advertising from Yahoo! or Google's AdWords, then when a user clicks through one of your AdWords advertisements, the page (Yahoo! or Google) that referred the user becomes a source of traffic for your site.

Each of the campaigns listed on the Campaigns report is a link to further information. If you click through one of those links you're taken to the Campaign detail page, shown in Figure 16-18. This report shows the same information that is collected in the Campaigns report, but here that information is specific to the campaign to which the report is assigned. So instead of seeing the number of visits for all campaigns, you're seeing that information for a single campaign.

Figure 16-18: The Campaign detail report shows a specific campaign.

Stepping back one page to the Campaigns report, you should pay particular attention to the dimension and segmentation capabilities. There are similar capabilities on almost all reports (they do change slightly on some). However, they are extremely useful on this report because they give you even more detailed information about your advertising campaigns. The following sections describe some of the most important segments that you should consider examining.

Source

The Source segmentation shows you the top sources driving traffic to your site and how valuable those sources are in terms of conversion and visit value. The report, shown in Figure 16-19, is similar to others that you've seen. The source tracking is what sets this one apart.

Figure 16-19: The Source dimension enables you to see what sources drive traffic.

Once you have segmented the campaign data by source, you can further segment it by clicking the Goal Set or Ecommerce tabs to see how each source translates to goal conversions or visit value.

Medium

You may remember that we have defined a *medium* as the type of marketing campaign being tracked—e-mail campaigns, banner advertisements, and organic searches are just a few examples of what's considered a medium. The Medium dimension shows you which of these types of marketing efforts is performing best in terms of visits or, if you switch between the tabs, in terms of goal conversions or e-commerce.

The Medium dimension is shown in Figure 16-20, and is another of those reports that are similar in appearance to others but different in content.

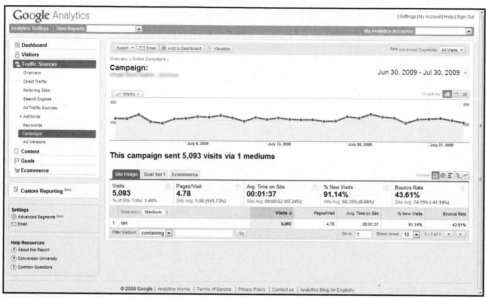

Figure 16-20: The Medium dimension enables you to see which ad medium performs best.

The key to using the Medium dimension report effectively is to evaluate each marketing medium according to the number of goal conversions, and the visit value if you have e-commerce capabilities. It's not enough to have goal conversions if you don't have the sales to support them.

By switching among the tabs in this report you can determine where you should increase your marketing investments to capitalize on the user's purchasing trends in relation to goal conversions. If you don't see any success (or you see only small success) in your goal conversions and visit values, you can tell which marketing media are not working, and your investment can be redirected to more successful efforts.

Ad Versions

Ad versions are different aspects of, or slants on, the same advertising campaign. For example, many companies create one advertisement that differs slightly from region to region. Those are considered ad versions. Keeping up with your ad versions is essential in determining which works best and how to capitalize on that fact. The Ad Versions report, shown in Figure 16-21, ranks your site visitors according to how each version of a campaign has been tagged.

Figure 16-21: The Ad Versions report tracks different versions of an ad campaign.

A/B Testing

The first step in testing any marketing campaign, or group of marketing campaigns, is to compare one against another. (The A/B in the preceding title simply refers to comparing one thing with another.) This type of comparison has been going on for as long as there have been advertisements. Heck, you may have even started studying advertising way back in grade school when you were scrawling "Roses are red/Violets are blue/If I looked like Susie/I'd join the zoo" in a note, passing it around, and waiting for results.

It wasn't nice, but it does illustrate the point. If it was a note not too many people saw, you were safe. If everybody saw it, Susie would be checking out handwriting and heading your way, fire in eye, brick in hand. Different ads perform at different levels in different places. And your online ads work in very much the same way. If one ad is performing better than another, you want to know it, and it's all right there in the Ad Versions report, in clearly defined detail.

On the other hand, you may be running only one ad. Or maybe you don't have any ads running. In that case, when you pull up your report it will have little or no information included in it. To change this either you need to begin running ads (such as keyword ads from AdWords or other types of ads that are properly tagged), or you need to tag your own ads properly.

In Chapter 13 we discussed tagging and gave you a little preview of how to go about doing it. You can flip back now if you need to. It's okay. Really. We'll wait.

Finished? Good. If you need more information on tagging your campaigns, you can find it in the Help section of Google Analytics by searching for tagging.

So exactly how do you use this Ad Versions report? Well, you start with tagging your advertising campaigns (which is why you just flipped back for a refresher). For the comparison to work you have to tag two different ad campaigns in different ways to distinguish them.

Specifically, what will change for each advertising campaign are the tag elements: `utm_source`, `utm_medium`, `utm_term`, `utm_campaign`, and `utm_content`. (Some but not all of these were mentioned in Chapter 13.) And you don't have to use all of them—use only what applies to your specific needs. If you were tagging, say, to track your newsletter name, you might change `utm source` to `utm source=MyNewsletter`. If you wanted to tag keywords for a specific ad, you might make it `utm term=running+shoes`.

You might also need to use the `utm_campaign` tag to compare different marketing campaigns. For example, if you're using a 15-percent-off coupon in e-mail to drive traffic to your site and you also have a link in an industry newsletter, you can use the `utm_campaign` tag to compare the effectiveness of the two campaigns. You can then use that information to determine which campaign should have more capital investment, based on the return on that investment.

URL Builder

Before you start muttering to yourself about the complexities of tagging, we have good news. Google Analytics provides a URL Builder tool, shown in Figure 16-22, that makes it easy to create the tagging URLs. To find the URL Builder tool, search Help once you've logged in to your Analytics account.

Once you have the tag, all you have to do is insert it in your campaign. For example, if you're using two different types of links you'll generate a URL for each link and replace the direct URL (in a form such as `http://www.example.com`) with the tagged URL, like this:

```
http://www.JerriLedford.com/?utm_source=Newsletter&utm_medium=link&utm_
content=textlink&utm_campaign=exampe_ad
```

Figure 16-22: The URL Builder tool helps create tags for different campaigns.

NOTE Remember that AdWords automatically tags the source and medium of your keyword campaigns. However, you may want to add an utm_term addition to your keywords to track specific, paid keywords. This also can be done in the URL Builder tool.

One more note about tagging your ads. Remember that these tags are very sensitive. They translate exactly what you tell them to translate, so if you are inconsistent in naming your campaigns (Spring-Sale versus Spring_Sale), Analytics will assume the tags refer to different campaigns.

With the information that you garner from comparing one ad campaign to another (or from comparing different ads within the same campaign), you can analyze the performance of those campaigns (or ads). That information in turn lets you know where to invest more or less of your advertising dollars, based on the results those campaigns generate.

Tracking ad versions isn't difficult, but it does require a little more effort than simply tracking your web site. Use the URL Builder tool, however, and you'll be tracking different advertising campaigns in no time at all.

CHAPTER 17

Content Overview

One of the most important elements of any web site is the content on that site. And content optimization is no easy task. It requires an understanding of what content draws users and how they interact with that content.

To truly understand how content optimization affects your site, you need some metrics to tell you how each aspect of the content performs. How does the content on your web site affect your traffic patterns? Does it lead users to the site? Does it drive users to make a purchase, sign up for a newsletter, or fill out a form that you have on the site? Is there content on your site that performs better than you expect it to?

These are all questions the reports in this section can answer. The content on your site—the content users land on when they arrive—plays a big role in how long users stay and how much deeper into the site they go.

If you have an e-commerce site, there might be a natural driver that pushes users deeper. Maybe users come to your site because you have a great price on laptop computers. But how is your content going to direct users once they land there? If you do the content well, you might be able to drive additional sales or create return users.

The only way you're going to know if your content is done well is to analyze the metrics associated with how users *use* your site. The reports in this section will show you exactly that. What you do with that information determines just how useful it is for you.

Determining the Value of Web-Site Content

People who own content-only web sites but don't sell actual products often assume that their content has no value. Even people who have e-commerce sites may assume that the content on their site is of little value. What's important, they may feel, are the products that sell and create a stream of revenue. That assumption would be wrong, however.

Content is one of the most important drivers for your web site. It's one of the reasons so many different types of content—articles, blogs, newsletters, podcasts, training videos—have become so popular on the Web. People want information, and they want it in a variety of ways, depending on what they're looking for.

That's what makes determining the value of your web-site content so very important. You can even go so far as to assign a monetary value to the content, which is something you learned about in Chapter 11. Now, however, we're just going to focus on what content interests your site visitor. *That* content is of value to you, because it results in visits and *stickiness*, or the quality of visitors staying on your site longer. The longer visitors stay, the more likely they are to make a purchase or to return to the site in the future.

But how do you determine which pieces of your content are most valuable? The answer is in the metrics, which Google Analytics provides through both the Content Overview report and the other reports in the content section. Each report tells you something a little different about each piece of content you're tracking. And when you take those different facts as a whole, you can see a pattern that points to what users want, and to what doesn't interest them.

Content Overview

The Content Overview report, like all the overviews you've seen to this point, is a bigger-picture look at your different content metrics. The report, shown in Figure 17-1, gives you a quick glance at the number of page views and unique views, and the bounce rate. But there is also a report module for Top Content, which we'll look at a little more closely later in this chapter, and links to additional information including Navigation Analysis, Landing Page Optimization, and Click Patterns.

Most of the report links in the Content Overview report actually lead deeper into some aspects of the Content reports. For example, when you click **Navigational Summary** you're taken to a sub-report for the Top Content report section. However, this is the only way you can get to that particular report. If you were to click **Top Content** the report you'd see would differ greatly from the Navigational Summary.

Figure 17-1: The Content Overview shows the most important data on your content.

Here's a closer look at the subsections for the Content Overview report.

Navigation Analysis

Understanding how your site visitors navigate your site can give you insight into what catches and holds their attention and what doesn't. The links in the Navigational Analysis section of this report take you to Top Content sub-reports, which are designed to show you a little more about how your visitors navigate your site.

Where your visitors come into your site, where they leave it, and what they do while there are all clues to what they want from your site. When you know the path a user is taking, it's easier to determine that user's final destination.

Navigational Summary

The Navigation Summary report, shown in Figure 17-2, shows you how often the given web page was an entrance page, what pages were viewed *before* this page, how many visitors left your site from this page, how often visitors exited your site from this page, and what pages were viewed *after* this page.

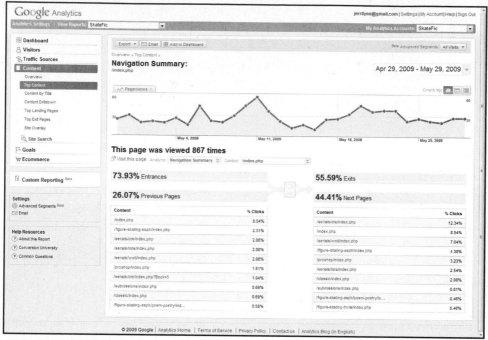

Figure 17-2: The Navigation Summary shows how the page fits into the path users took through your site.

By default the page shown is your main web page (your index page or the page that ends with /). You can, however, change this setting to reflect the navigation summary of any page on your web site. Use the Content drop-down menu, shown in Figure 17-3, to select a different page on your site or to search for a page if it is not included in the drop-down menu.

You are also not limited to just navigation data. You can choose to view the data through other standard filters as well:

- Content Detail
- Entrance Paths
- Entrance Sources
- Entrance Keywords

These filters are available through the Analyze menu, shown in Figure 17-4, and they enable you to see different details for the pages of your web site.

Once you have these reports, they can give you a picture of how your users come into, navigate through, and then leave your web site. They also provide additional detail about the way users *use* your site. This all gives you a clearer picture of what works for your visitors. It will also point out, in no uncertain terms, which pages *don't* work.

Use the content drop-down menu to view the
Navigation Summary for a different web page.

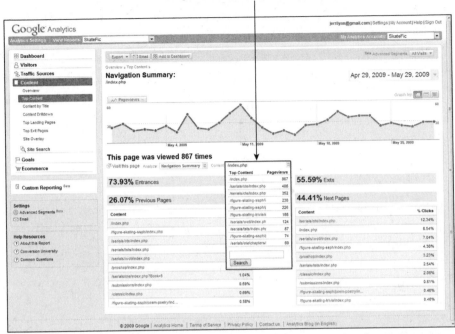

Figure 17-3: Examine navigation data for any page on the site using the Content menu.

Analyze additional content data.

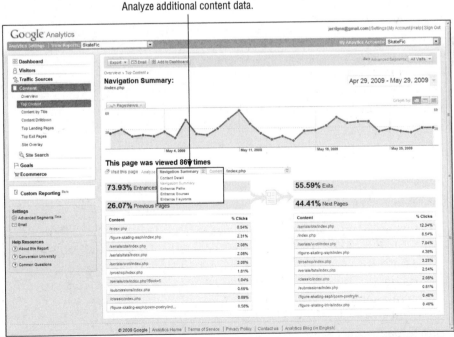

Figure 17-4: Use the Analyze menu to see navigation data that's filtered differently.

You can then use this information to further hone your page styles and content until you have successful pages throughout your site. Combining what you learn from analyzing this data with what you learn from analyzing other data (such as the e-commerce data or goals data) should give you a clear picture of how users use your web site.

Entrance Paths

An *entrance path* is quite literally the page on which a user enters your site. For example, most web sites have a high entrance path that starts at the page whose name ends with a slash (/), as in www.JerriLedford.com/. Another frequent entrance page is labeled /index.html (as in www.JerriLedford.com/index .html). In both cases, this is where users jump onto the site, and in both cases that's usually because they type the web site's address directly into the address bar of their web browser (in some cases, the number of visits to these main pages can be attributed to search engine referrals).

The Entrance Paths report, shown in Figure 17-5, illustrates where visitors came onto your site and where they went from there. In the Content drop-down menu you can choose any page that you're tracking as a starting point. In Figure 17-5 the start page is the main index page. From that page, users visited the pages in the list (labeled "Then viewed these pages"). You can then select each page in that column to find out where visitors went from there (in the "And ended up here" column).

Figure 17-5: Use the Entrance Paths report to learn where visitors started and ended.

This information helps you figure out where your visitors enter and exit your site, but it also does more. For example, if the majority of your visitors come into your site via your main page (the page denoted by a slash) and also leave from that page, what does that tell you?

To me, it would say there are a high number of bounces on that main page, and that it needs to be made more reflective of the topic you want users to see. So if your site is showing as a search result for ice skates when you actually sell skating fiction, you need to make it much clearer that your site is about content related to skating, not about ice skates as products. Then when users find your content through a search engine, they'll actually find what they're looking for.

Landing Page Optimization

Landing pages are the pages that site visitors land on when they come to your site. This is important, because you may have a different landing page for each campaign you're running. It's essential that you track all the pages and see which perform the best in terms of stickiness and keeping your visitors on your site.

Landing-page optimization is an industry all its own. You can find hundreds (or thousands) of articles about the best way to optimize your landing pages to ensure that the right visitors find your site and stay there once they find it. A first impression is important and you want it to be the best possible.

That's where the reports in the Landing Page Optimization section come in handy. The Entrance Sources and Entrance Keywords reports give you some insight into what's drawing visitors to your site. And knowing what gets them there might make it easier for you to decide how to satisfy the need that leads those visitors to you.

Entrance Sources

Entrance sources differ from entrance paths in that sources are where the traffic comes to your site from and paths are where the traffic on your site starts. Of course, the Entrance Path is just the first page in the navigational path that a user might take through your site. But that traffic has to come from somewhere, and that's what the Entrance Source is. The Entrance Sources report, shown in Figure 17-6, shows what sources sent traffic to each page of your site. By default the data for the main site page is displayed, but you can change that setting using the Content drop-down menu.

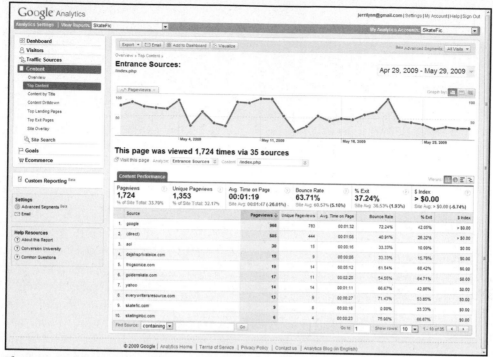

Figure 17-6: The Entrance Sources report shows where users came to each page from.

Entrance Keywords

The Entrance Keywords report, shown in Figure 17-7, is similar to the Entrance Sources report, except that here you see which keywords led visitors to your site. This information is helpful when you're looking at the keywords that seem to work for your site. For example, if you find that the keywords included in the top positions on this report are organic keywords, then you know that you're spending money unnecessarily on paid keywords that aren't as effective as you need them to be.

As with the other reports that you've seen in this chapter, you can use the Content drop-down menu to see what keywords draw visitors to other pages on your web site as well.

Click Patterns

The Click Patterns heading contains a link to only one report: the Site Overlay report. The Site Overlay report shows you navigational information directly on your web page. For now, it's enough for you to know that this report can give you detailed information about how users click through your content. For more detailed information about this report, including screenshots that show you what it looks like, keep reading. It's covered near the end of this chapter.

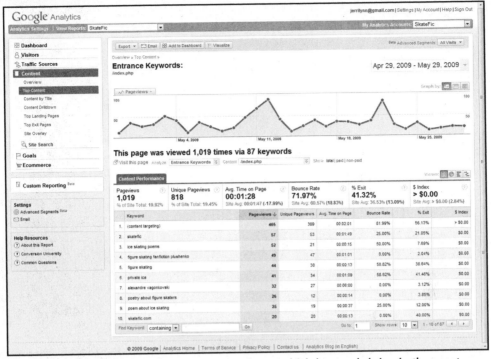

Figure 17-7: The Entrance Keywords report shows which keywords bring in the most traffic.

Additional Content Reports

As useful as the Content Overview is, especially with all the sub-reports that it leads you to, there's still much more you can learn about the content on your web site. Google Analytics supplies additional reports in the navigation links on the left side of the page. Each of those links leads to a different report that you can use to learn even more about the content on your web site.

Top Content

In many cases the top content on your site (the page your users came to directly most often) will be your front page—also called your index page. This is usually the first page that users see when they type your URL directly into the address bar on their web browsers. But that's not so in every case. If you're running a marketing campaign that pushes users to a page that's deeper in the site, *that* could be your top content. The only way to know for sure is to look at the Top Content report, shown in Figure 17-8.

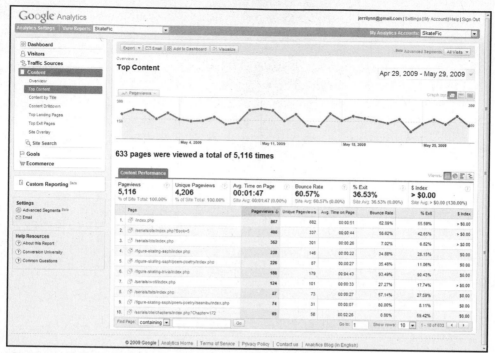

Figure 17-8: The Top Content report shows the pages users came to directly most often.

In this report, content pages are listed according to how frequently they were visited. You'll also find measurements for the number of page views for each page, the average time users spent on that page, the percentage of exits, and the value index. This last measurement (the value index) helps you see what content is leading visitors to goal conversions, and this will come in handy later when you're tracking your funnel-navigation process.

Another measurement on this report to which you want to pay special attention is the percentage of exits for each page. If you have a page that seems to have an unusually high number of exits, the content on that page could be the reason visitors are leaving. If you can use this report to locate the pages where you're losing visitors, you can change or update those pages in an effort to improve stickiness.

You may also want to make note of the average time users spend on each page. There's no guideline that says users should spend x amount of time on each page, but obviously some (such as content pages) will require more time to view than others. You have to figure a baseline for your site using the measurements available to you. Then if you decide that, on average, users should spend a minute and a half to two minutes on each page, and you find you have a page (or pages) on which users spend less than a minute, you know you should analyze it to find out why users are clicking through (or worse, exiting at) that page.

Of course, each of these measurements alone is valuable only for that measurement. When you look at them as a whole, however, you begin to see a larger picture—such as how many users are exiting a page after only 15 seconds or how many users are clicking through a page after two minutes to make a large purchase or complete some other goal you've established.

These traffic patterns give you insight into the minds of your users. Use them to improve goal conversions and sales through your site, and to funnel visitors to the pages that you consider most important in reaching those conversions or sales.

Content by Title

Another way to view the traffic to your site is with the Content by Title report. This report, shown in Figure 17-9, shows the value of your web pages by page title, using the same measurements as before: page views, unique views, average time spent on the page, bounce rate, percentage of exits that occur on the page, and value of goal conversions that result from the page.

Figure 17-9: The Content by Title report shows content metrics by title, not URL.

It's not at all unusual to see a page that has not only the highest number of page visits but also the highest number of exits. It's just naturally the way visitors tend to come and go from a site. However, if you happen to notice that a page with a low number of visits has the highest percentage of exits, you know that there's likely some kind of problem with that page and it needs to be changed or updated in some way.

The most important factor for you to know about this report is that page titles are determined by HTML titles. In the design of your page there was probably some titling algorithm that set the HTML tagging and titling for the page. It's also possible that you set the titling manually. Either way, that's what is used to classify the page for this report. Here's the catch: if you happen to have multiple pages with the same HTML title, those pages are going to be counted as a single page for measurement purposes. (It's possible to tinker with the HTML to separate them, but your skills have to be pretty sharp.)

So while these measurements are useful, they can be a little deceiving in their presentation. However, as long as you remember that each of these measurements could feature more than one page, you should be able to use the information to determine where you need to change or improve your content.

Content Drilldown

How is your web site designed? Do you have pages that have subpages? Maybe you have a page on your site that includes articles about issues related to the products on your site. And on that page maybe there are links to past articles. Those past articles are probably located on subpages. So how do you know if those pages are of any value to your site at all?

Another consideration to keep in mind when looking at this report is the pages of *dynamic content* that might exist on your web site. When you think of dynamic content you probably think of things such as articles or blogs—content that changes frequently. But that has nothing to do with dynamic content here. Most blogs are actually *static pages*—pages pre-built and stored in their final form on the web server—which were created on submission of individual entries.

Dynamic content refers to pages for which one file may be associated with multiple pages of content. *Dynamic pages* are built on the fly with a technology such as PHP, ASP, or JavaServer Pages (JSP). These technologies use variables in the URL, called *page-query terms*, to dictate what content goes together to form the finished page. Site-search and catalogue functions are generally dynamic pages. Other sites implement dynamic pages for various other reasons.

Dynamic pages present unique tracking challenges because what differentiates one dynamic page from another is not the file name, but the query term or combination of terms.

The Content Drilldown report, shown in Figure 17-10, shows how each of your pages performs, and whether that page is considered dynamic content or *static content* (which is content that rarely, if ever, changes).

Figure 17-10: The Content Drilldown report shows how valuable subpages are.

For every page that you're shown in this report, there is a set of measurements that includes the unique views and pages, the average time spent on the page, the percent of visitors who exited from that page, and the value of pages that are commonly visited before a high-value conversion during that visit. The conversion could be a sale or another type of goal conversion, depending on how you have your conversion goals set up. You can also click each page title to see more detailed information about the visits to that page.

The purpose of this information is much the same as the purpose of the Top Content report. Use it to determine which pages need to be changed or updated and which pages work well, as indicated by visits, goal conversions, and the value of those conversions.

Top Landing Pages

As we've discussed before, a bounce occurs when a visitor arrives on a page and immediately leaves. It differs from an exit, which refers just to the page from which the visitor left the site, possibly after visiting other pages. A bounce means "Did not visit another page. Did not collect $200." For the purposes of this report (and only this report) a visit, a visitor, and a page view are pretty much all the same thing (subject to the caveats about counting unique visitors and the length-of-visit limitation discussed in Chapter 7).

The Top Landing Pages report, shown in Figure 17-11, illustrates how often visitors entered your page through a specific page and how often they bounced right back off your site from that page.

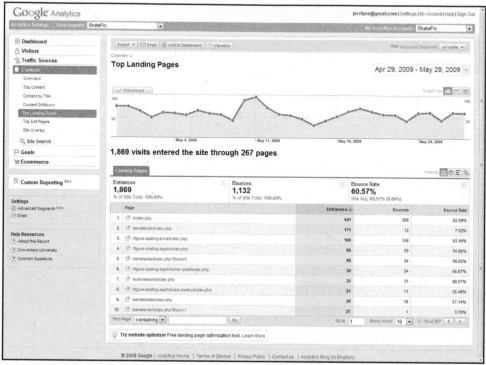

Figure 17-11: The Top Landing Pages report shows where visitors landed—and bounced.

Bounce rates can show how effective a particular page is. For example, in Figure 17-11, the top landing page on the site (which also happens to be the main page) has the most bounces.

The bad news is that about 62 percent of the visitors who arrive on this page also leave immediately. The good news is that at least some of those people were looking for the information on the front page of the web site. Having found what they wanted, they left. That's not a bad thing. Giving visitors what they're looking for is what a content site is supposed to do.

However, the main page also has another specific goal—to lure visitors deeper into the site. And the bounce rate reflected in this report shows that's not happening in about 62 percent of the cases. This could indicate that your site is classified wrong in search results, which could mean you need to retag the site, or it could mean that you need to reconsider how you see your site versus how visitors see it.

If I haven't made this point enough, I'll say it again: it's important to remember that you can't look at Google Analytics' metrics in isolation from other information about your business. As capable as Google Analytics is, it's still a medium-tier product. It won't function like a high-end (read: expensive) analytics package. You're going to have to use your head when applying data—such as bounce rates—to an analysis of your site. Analytics won't do everything for you, and sometimes understanding what the metrics mean requires a little experimentation on your part.

Top Exit Pages

While knowing where visitors arrive is important, so is knowing where they're leaving from. You'll note that it's fairly common for your busiest pages overall to also be the busiest from the entrance and exit standpoints. In Figure 17-12 you can see this effect.

Unlike with the entrance pages, you can't assume that each page view on the Exits report represents a visitor. A visitor could load the page, then wander off deeper into the site and eventually wander back. However, because you can assume each page view here represents a visitor in the Entrance Pages report, you can do interesting things with the Exits report. You can isolate how many visits ended on a particular page when it's not the first and last page visited.

Figure 17-12: The Top Exit Pages report shows the pages from which visitors leave most often.

For example, let's say SkateFic's index page is ranked number two in exits and in bounces. Each entrance is a page view, so subtract entrances from page views for that line. So, if SkateFic has 3,575 page views and 2,086 entrances, the equation would look like this:

```
3,575 - 2,086 = 1,489
```

What this tells you is how many page views came from visitors who had come in from other parts of the site. Now, assume that SkateFic has 1,243 bounces and 1,824 exits.

Technically speaking, bounces are exits, so subtract Bounces from Exits to remove duplicate exit counts.

```
1,824 - 1,243 = 581
```

This indicates how many of the visits entering from other parts of the site left once they hit this page. That in itself is an interesting metric, but it means more if you translate the two new figures to a percentage.

```
581/1489 = .39 or 39%
```

So overall, while 51 percent of page views mark the end of a visit and 60 percent of new visitors leave from there immediately, only 39 percent of visits that include other pages leave from here.

To put it another way:

Once visitors get into the site they are much less likely to leave from this page. For the homepage (which SkateFic.com is), it may not mean much, but this kind of additional analysis can be helpful for other pages, such as those involved in the sales process.

Site Overlay

Sometimes it's easier to understand a complex set of metrics if you draw a picture. That's exactly what the Site Overlay is. Each page of your web site has an overlay, and on the overlay are small boxes, one for each link on the page. If you click a box you get an overview of information for that link. But the point is that you can see at a glance how the various links on a single page are performing compared to one another.

Figure 17-13 shows the Site Overlay for one of Jerri's web pages. As you can see, most of the small boxes show little or no activity.

However, one of the boxes, shown in Figure 17-14, seems to be responsible for all the traffic. And when you hover your pointer over that box you get a quick view of some of the most important metrics for that link. That view includes the number of clicks for that link and the goal value for the link (that is, the revenue it generates).

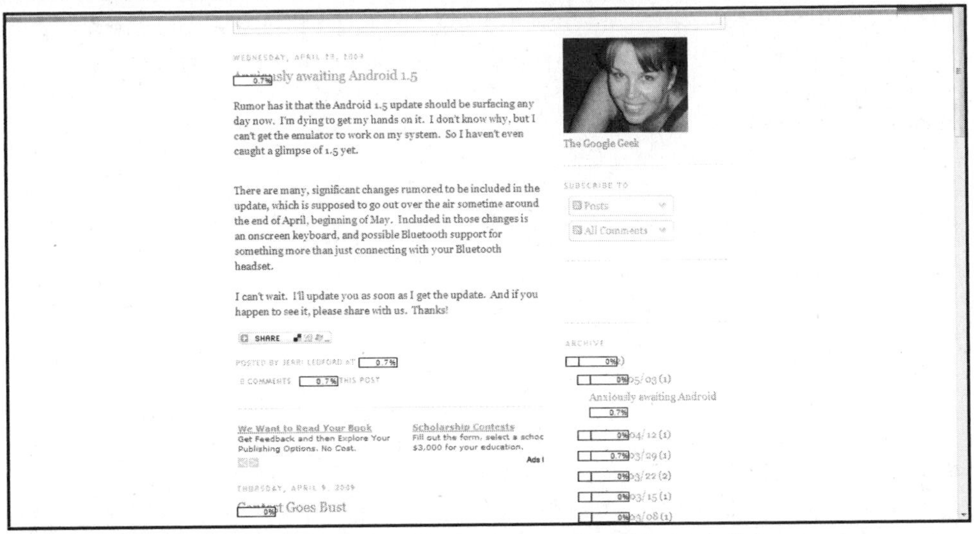

Figure 17-13: The Site Overlay report shows how many clicks each link gets.

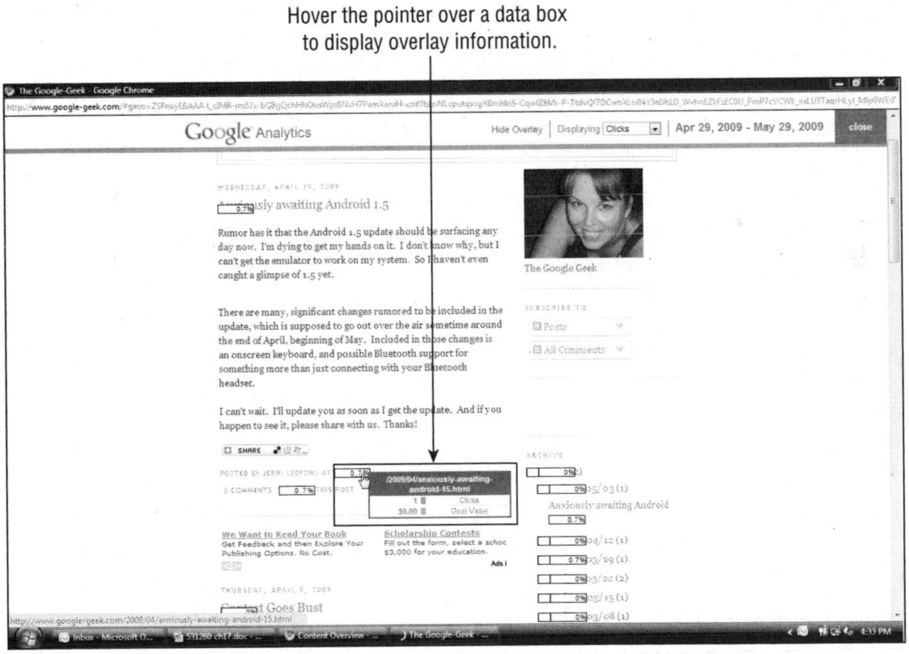

Hover the pointer over a data box
to display overlay information.

Figure 17-14: The quality of your links is displayed in the pop-up box.

So essentially the Site Overlay illustrates very clearly what links on your page are performing, and how well. It's a graphic representation of where users are taking action on your pages.

And One More...

There's one additional report in the content section that you're probably going to be interested in. It's the Site Search report. But we're not going to get into it in this chapter, because it's pretty involved. Instead we'll cover it in the next chapter, so flip on over whenever you're ready. We're all done here.

CHAPTER 18

Site Search

One of Google Analytics' "hidden treasures" that can help uncover some amazing insights into the pulse of your web site's traffic is the Site Search section of reports, which is located within the Content section of your "Favorite" profile. Site Search can collect the actual search queries performed on your own web site's search function, including the number of refinements your visitors need to make, the page that they perform their searches on, and the category that the search query falls under, just to name a few.

This section of reports is a direct pipeline of data between you the web-site owner and your web site's visitors. One of the very few ways in which your site's visitors can communicate with your web site is by what they type into your search tool.

Configuring Your Profile(s)

In order to begin tracking your web site's search function with Google Analytics, you need to perform a few administrative tasks first. In most situations, this should be a piece of cake for your administrator (and if that means you, then you'll definitely be able to appreciate how easy this is going to be!).

> **NOTE** Depending on your search function's vendor, there may be additional steps that need to be performed, such as ensuring that your web site is configured for subdomain or cross-domain tracking, or using the Google Analytics Tracking Code to dynamically populate the search query if it does not appear in the URL. Check with your site search vendor to ensure that it can accommodate Google Analytics tracking.

1. Log in to your Google Analytics Account and click the **Edit** link underneath the Actions column on the far right of your Account Overview screen.

2. Next, click the white **Edit** link on the top right of the Main Website Profile Information page. Scroll down to the bottom to find the Site Search section, and click **Do Track Site Search**, which will make these form fields appear (Figure 18-1):

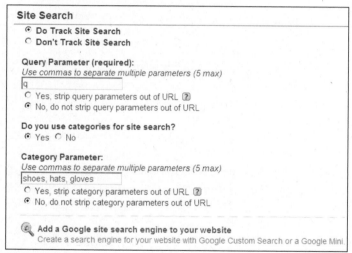

Figure 18-1: Site Search configuration options

3. Next, you must perform a search on your web site and find your search query parameter. There are **thousands of different** types of search features, but if you're using Google Site Search the query parameter will be the letter q, as shown in Figure 18-1. In case you're curious about where that letter q originates, the URL in your browser's address bar may look like this after you perform a site search (look for the "q" in the last line):

```
http://www.yoursite.com/google-results.php?cx=000054
728233934906451%3A92y8tmfvku8&cof=FORID%3A11&ie=UTF-
8&q=analytics&sa=Search#12345
```

TIP   A common mistake in setting up Site Search is to include the = symbol after the query parameter. Inserting the = symbol will cause Site Search to not track any data. Simply insert the query parameter without the = symbol, and you should be good to go.

4. If your search function makes use of categories, then you insert up to five comma-separated categories, which get their own individual reports in the Site Search section. Again, there are thousands of different possibilities here, but the URL in your address bar could look something like the following, if you're using categories in your search function:

```
http://www.yoursite.com/
search.php?q=nike+mens+running+shoes&shoes=mens+shoes
```

5. Once you hit **Save Changes** you will have access to the Site Search section of reports, found within the Content section. You won't see any data yet, but don't worry—wait a few hours and you may start to see some!

NOTE   Remember, changes to one profile in your Google Analytics account will need to be duplicated in every other profile that you wish to track Site Search for.

What If I'm Not Using Google Site Search?

There are so many different available solutions for a web-site search function that we could devote about 10 full chapters of this book to them alone. So we'll leave it up to your vendor of choice, and whether or not your software program enables you to install the Google Analytics Tracking Code on it.

If the answer is "No," then I'm very sorry to be the bearer of bad news— you won't be able to track your web site's search function activity in Google Analytics. You should consider upgrading to a solution that enables you to install JavaScript tags, if that's feasible.

However, if the answer is "Yes," then the site search world is your oyster! Here are two common situations that you'll most likely run into with a non-Google site search solution:

The first, and most common, situation is that there is no query parameter present in the URL at all. Unfortunately, this is the case with some non-Google site search solutions. If, after a search on your site, the URL in the address bar looks like this:

```
http://www.yoursite.com/search.cfm?page=results
```

then you will need to get with your webmaster to have the query parameter appear within the trackPageview function of the Google Analytics Tracking Code. This should be something that your webmaster can easily accomplish—assuming your site search solution is a flexible one.

Figure 18-2 shows how the trackPageview function can be used within the Google Analytics Tracking Code to collect the search query. Notice the /?q= part inside the parentheses on line 145 of Figure 18-2—the letter q here is the search query letter that would be used in the Main Website Profile Information that we showed in Figure 18-1.

```
131        </tr>
132        <tr>
133          <td height="5" align="left" class="bottom"><img src=
"images/dot_clear.gif" width="1" height="5" /></td>
134        </tr>
135      </table></td>
136    </tr>
137 </table>
138 <script type="text/javascript">
139 var gaJsHost = (("https:" == document.location.protocol) ?
"https://ssl." : "http://www.");
140 document.write(unescape("%3Cscript src='" + gaJsHost +
"google-analytics.com/ga.js' type='text/javascript'%3E%3C/script%3E"));
141 </script>
142 <script type="text/javascript">
143 try {
144 var pageTracker = _gat._getTracker("UA-XXXXXX-X");
145 pageTracker._trackPageview('/?q=google+analytics+book');
146 } catch(err) {}</script>
147 </body>
148 </html>
```

Figure 18-2: Using trackPageview to collect the search query

The second situation: If your site search solution resides on another domain—that is, on another web site—you'll need to update the Google Analytics Tracking Code on both your site and the search vendor's site for cross-domain tracking. Refer back to Chapter 14, where we show some examples of how to do this.

What If I'm Not Using Any Search Tool?

After you've finished reading this book, go to google.com and search for "site search." Clicking on the first organic result will take you to Google's Site Search web site, at which point you should pick up the phone or fire off an e-mail to your webmaster or IT director and ask—no, demand—that the Google Site Search engine be installed on your web site!

As mentioned at the beginning of this chapter, Site Search is a direct pipeline of communication between you and your web site's visitors. It's through a web site's search function that your visitors can ascertain whether or not your site has what they are looking for, where they should go, and what they should do after obtaining this information. If you are an e-commerce retailer of any size it's almost a requirement that you have a properly working, cutting-edge search function like Google Site Search installed on your site. Even if your web site is not an e-commerce store, you should still install a search function. As you're about to find out, you may be very surprised to learn what your web site's visitors are searching for while they are on your site!

Site Search Overview (Metrics)

Enough already about setting up Site Search! Now let's get down to what's important, which means obtaining insights from the reports! With the Site Search section of reports, you'll be introduced to some brand-new metrics exclusive to this section of Google Analytics. Figure 18-3 shows a part of the Site Search Overview report, which lists all the new metrics that you'll begin to fall in love with. This report overview will list all these flashy new metrics for you, equipped with links to each individual metric's histogram within the Trending report. Click on any metric to view a daily breakdown.

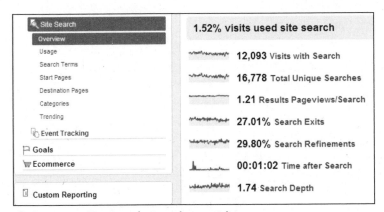

Figure 18-3: Site Search Overview metrics

Here are a few points about these metrics:

1. **The percentage of visits that used Site Search** is displayed right away in the gray bar. Depending on a number of factors this percentage can range anywhere from an infinitesimal amount to as high as 15 percent, and in some rare cases even higher than that.

2. **Visits with Search** shows the total number of visits (not visitors) for which your Site Search function was used.

3. **Total Unique Searches** displays the total number of unique searches performed. This is not to be confused with the total number of *original* searches performed, which can be obtained within the Search Terms report.

4. Now it starts to get interesting. The **Results Pageviews/Search** metric shows the average number of times a visitor viewed a search results page after performing a search. A high average number here can suggest that your search function isn't displaying relevant results that match up with what users are searching for, which could be bad news for you. We'll talk a bit more later on about what action(s) you should take, and where to take them.

5. The percentage of **Search Exits** is the percentage of visitors who leave your web site immediately after performing a search. In other words, it's the bounce rate of your search function. This is an overall performance metric that you'll need to keep an eye on. If this percentage is very high, ask yourself ,"What is my search function displaying to users after they perform a search?" Sometimes a very high percentage can indicate a technical problem with your search function, such as an error page being displayed to your users (in which case you'll want to sound the general alarm and get it fixed pronto).

6. **Search Refinements** occur when visitors perform additional searches (within the same session) after they've already performed a search. It's tough to predict what a user's intentions are in refining a search—perhaps the user searched for something that doesn't exist on your web site? Maybe he or she misspelled the search term and is trying again? Or loved your search function enough to take it out for another spin? The old rule of thumb states that users should find exactly what they're looking for on their very first attempt, and shouldn't have to refine a search. But that's why it's the "old" rule of thumb—maybe these refining visitors don't exactly know what they are looking for in the first place, and need to search first before knowing what it is they really want.

7. **Time after Search** is another one of those metrics that you shouldn't read too much into. Naturally you'd like for all your users to spend as much time as possible on your site, but if they only spend a minute or two after searching for something, it doesn't necessarily mean that they were unhappy, or that they didn't find what they were looking for.

8. Finally, **Search Depth** shows the average number of page views users make after interacting with your search function. Bear in mind that this metric is not the same as Results Pageviews/Search—that metric measures strictly the average number of results pages after a search, while Search

Depth measures the average number of any page views performed after a search. For example, after performing a search, a visitor views three total web-site pages. One of those three pages is the second search-results page. Google Analytics will count this visitor's search depth as 3 (pages), and this visitor's Results Pageviews/Search as 2. It will then tally up all the Search Depth and Results Pageviews/Search counts for all visitors with Site Search to provide average numbers.

Now that you're familiar with these new metrics, let's dive into the reports in this section and find out what all the fuss is about.

Site Search Reports

The Site Search Reports within the Content section in your Google Analytics profile feature six insightful reports (excluding the Overview Report): Usage, Search Terms, Start Pages, Destination Pages, Categories, and Trending. In this section, we'll review each report and provide key insights for each.

The Usage Report

Figure 18-4 shows the Usage report, splitting your visitors into two groups: those who used Site Search and those who didn't. While anyone can do the math and figure out how many site users did not use the search function, don't discard the potential that this report can bring to the table. Use the Goal Conversion and E-commerce tabs—along with the other metrics within the scorecard and the two drop-down menus within the report table—to determine different behavioral patterns between users and non-users. Do users of Site Search convert at a higher rate than non-users? Are the non-users spending more time on your site than the Site Search Users? Do folks who interact with your search function account for a higher revenue per transaction than folks who don't? These are all valid questions that you can ask yourself here.

Insights: If you see that very few visitors are using your site search function, consider implementing the search function on every page of your web site, including the homepage and any other high-volume pages. (Check your Top Content report to find out which pages are the high-volume ones.) If you already have the search function on all your site's pages, consider drawing more attention to it, or moving it to a more prominent place on your site, such as the top left-hand side of your pages. If you find that users are indeed using your search function, but they are simply not converting or making purchases like non-site search users, evaluate the search results that your search function is displaying to users, and see if there are any ways to optimize the search results.

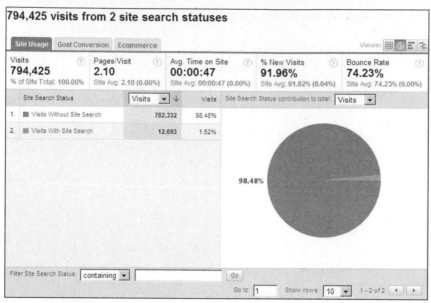

Figure 18-4: Site Usage report

The Search Terms Report

What makes the entire Site Search section awesome is the Search Terms report, which lists every search term that your site's visitors entered into your search function. In this report you can also get the number of original searches, which is not available in the Site Search Overview report.

Figure 18-5 shows an example of the Search Terms report. As you can see, you'll be able to drill one level deeper and see metrics like %Search Exits, Time after Search, and Search Depth for each individual search term, thus getting a more precise overview of how users are using your search tool. You can also use the Goal Conversion and E-commerce tabs to see which search terms have directly led to outcomes for your web site, and as with any other report in Google Analytics, you can use the filter tools at the bottom to dig for specific search terms.

NOTE Site Search terms are case-sensitive. Therefore, the search term "google" is not the same as the search term "Google" or the search term "GOOGLE." These will be counted as three separate, unique search terms, and won't be combined into one line item.

There were 16,778 unique searches via 12,658 search terms

	Site Search Usage	Goal Conversion	Ecommerce					Views:

Total Unique Searches	Results Pageviews/Search	% Search Exits	% Search Refinements	Time after Search	Search Depth
16,778	**1.21**	**27.01%**	**29.80%**	**00:01:02**	**1.74**
% of Site Total. 100.00%	Site Avg: 1.21 (0.00%)	Site Avg: 27.01% (0.00%)	Site Avg: 29.80% (0.00%)	Site Avg: 00:01:02 (0.00%)	Site Avg: 1.74 (0.00%)

	Dimension: Search Term	Total Unique ↓ Searches	Results Pageviews/Search	% Search Exits	% Search Refinements	Time after Search	Search Depth
1.	shoes	84	1.33	51.19%	4.46%	00:00:33	0.94
2.	hats	78	1.42	35.90%	9.91%	00:43:29	3.03
3.	ties	74	1.16	17.57%	16.28%	00:01:35	4.49
4.	sneaker	58	1.03	37.93%	10.00%	00:01:18	3.02
5.	t-shirt	57	1.09	17.54%	19.35%	00:01:18	3.23
6.	bag	55	1.35	18.18%	18.92%	00:02:31	3.51
7.	shoe	50	1.30	40.00%	26.15%	00:00:30	0.98
8.	tie	50	1.10	24.00%	30.91%	00:01:10	2.04
9.	sex	50	1.50	30.00%	16.00%	00:01:00	2.48
10.	free shoes	47	1.06	27.66%	12.00%	00:01:16	3.53

Filter Search Term: containing ▾ [   ] Go

Go to: 1   Show rows: 10 ▾   1 - 10 of 12,658 ◄ ►

Figure 18-5: The Search Terms report

Insights: Are there search terms appearing in this list that have nothing to do with your web site, products, or services? It's a great time to ensure that you are sending irrelevant searches to a creative "Sorry, no results" page that will let users re-enter the search process and refine their searches. On that note, are there search terms appearing here for products you don't carry, or services you don't offer? Now would be a fantastic time to consider adding these products or services to your business. Finally, is one search term suffering from a very high % Search Exit figure? Do a test search on your own web site with this term to ensure that a technical issue isn't throwing a monkey wrench into your program, or that your search function isn't serving up an inordinate number of irrelevant search results. Nothing can frustrate a user more than an irrelevant search result. Just ask Google about that—it has the science of search pretty much down.

P.S. Don't worry about a search term like #9 in Figure 18-5. You're guaranteed to have some search queries like that popping up here and there. Simply ignore them.

Start Pages and Destination Pages Reports

Where did your users start their searches? What pages were they taken to after their searches? These two reports can answer those questions for you, and enable you both to perform analysis one level up from the Search Terms report and to view the start and end points of your visitor's Site Search experience. Depending on the structure of your site, and where your search function is located, your web site's pages can experience radically different results, even though you're using the same search function everywhere.

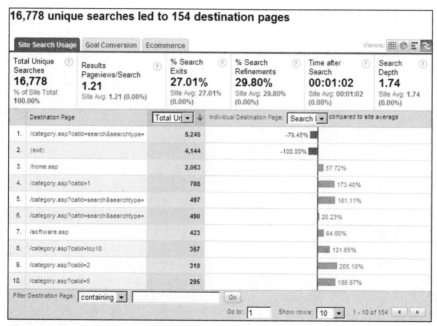

Figure 18-6: Destination Pages report

Insights: For your Start Pages report, it's imperative to identify the "winners" and the "losers" among your highest starting Site Search volume pages. As with most reports in Google Analytics, you can ascertain the "what," the "who," and the "how many," but the "why" part of the analysis equation is something you'll need to take charge of. It needs to be your responsibility to step out of the site marketer/owner role and step into the everyday visitor role, by performing searches on your own site. There may be a technical issue or a search result relevance issue with some of your start pages that will need to be hashed out to improve start page performance.

For your destination pages, it's all about identifying the quality of your tool's search results. Are folks going to irrelevant pages after performing a search? Are they going back and refining their searches? Or are they exiting the site immediately en masse after performing a search? Use this critical line of questioning in your own head when looking at these kinds of reports in Google Analytics, and let regular, old-fashioned common sense guide you.

The Categories Report

If your site search function makes use of categories (and if you've configured your category names properly in your Main Website Profile Information, shown in Figure 18-1), then this report will break down the volume of searches per category for your convenience. Most search functions don't use categories, so if you're one of the lucky ones, take advantage of a report like this to identify which types of products are being searched for the most. For example, if your hats category is racking up most of the search volume, chances are that there may be enough interest in hats to run a special sale or promotion.

You can also use the Categories report to evaluate your marketing efforts. Did you run a big direct mail campaign about your special on shoes this week? Or did you send an e-mail blast to your loyal subscribers about this month's special on home and garden? If you're not seeing much in terms of a boost in sales from those departments, AND if you're not seeing much search volume in those categories, it can serve as a big sign to you that your next marketing efforts may need some tweaking.

The Trending Report

Rounding out the Site Search section of reports is the Trending report, which is a standard type of report that you'll find for most main sections of Google Analytics. With the trending report, you'll be able to get a monthly, weekly, daily, or hourly breakdown of all the searches performed on your site. By default you'll see a daily breakdown, but simply modify your view in the trending graph to update the report accordingly.

As Figure 18-7 shows, you can click on the **Trending** drop-down menu, underneath the total daily number of visits with search, to view the Trending report by any one of the site search metrics available in this section. This type of report is mainly for informational purposes—there aren't too many actionable items that you can extract from this high-level type of report. So you shouldn't read a lot into it when people perform searches on your site. Be happy that they're using it in the first place!

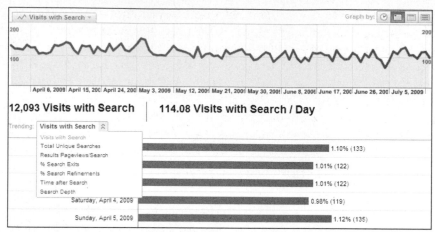

Figure 18-7: Site Search Trending report

The Philosophy of Site Search

As I mentioned at the beginning of this chapter, site search is a direct line of communication between your web site and its visitors. It's very important to keep that line of communication free of static (broken pages, irrelevant results, difficult user experience, and so on). And, as also mentioned in this chapter, nothing is more frustrating to a user than a broken, irrelevant, or out-of-date search function. You may have the best site in the world, but if your site search frustrates, irritates, and confuses your users, all your efforts will be in vain.

With things like Twitter and Facebook updates available to everyone, you also run the risk of frustrated users telling all their followers how much they hated searching for something on your site. Yes, you should take it that seriously.

So, what can you do about all of this? Here are some tips that may help you make your Site Search function a good one:

1. **Test, test, test!** That sounds like something a Google Website Optimizer engineer may say, but the only way to know how your site search is really working is to perform some test searches on it. Are the results relevant to your query? Are the listings updated? Do the listings even work when you click them?

2. **Get smart about your "Sorry" page:** We touched on this earlier in the chapter and it bears repeating here. On the Web, you're bound to get your fair share of irrelevant searches that have nothing to do with your web site

or your business. However, that doesn't mean you should discard these searches and send them off to a cold, lifeless, unwelcoming "Sorry" page that looks like an error page, with one line of text across the top reading "Sorry, no results found.".A great way to decrease the number of % Search Exits is to get creative with your "Sorry" page and try to get that user to refine his or her search. Work with your webmaster or IT person and come up with some creative content, links, and possibly a nice image to keep that visitor engaged with your web site. Did someone search for chrysanthemums on your red roses storefront? No problem— show searchers a nice image of a dozen bright red roses, and they may even go for it!

3. **Make your search results pages look like part of your web site**: There's no better way to scare the pants off your visitors than by sending them to a search results page that looks like someone else's web site. Imagine the feeling you would get if you walked into JCPenney, went down the perfume aisle, and all of a sudden found yourself ordering a milkshake at Burger King! This is what you want to avoid at all costs. Again, commission your favorite web developer and work with that person to customize your search function so that it looks like a part of your web site. Work with your site search vendor to accomplish this if you use a search function hosted on a separate domain. Send the vendor a template or a shell of your web site within which the vendor can place the search results. Make clear it's of the utmost importance and has to be done.

4. **Search Relevance:** If you use Google Site Search, you probably don't have to worry about this too much. If you use anything else, you will definitely want to stay on top of it, though. If you search for "light bulb" on your search function, the very first result that comes up should be something about "light bulb," not about "tile floors" or "carpeting." (These examples sound ridiculous, but unfortunately they wouldn't be out of place today). Once again, make your IT person or your site search vendor your best friend—then push your friend to update the search algorithm or optimize the search results for increased relevance.

5. **Accept imperfection**: Along with irrelevant searches, you can also expect your fair share of misspelled searches, searches with apostrophes, exclamation points, and currency symbols, searches with non-ASCII characters, and searches in all caps. Ideally your search function can accept searches like this without too much of a problem. Do what Google does and ask searchers if they meant something else when they made an honest mistake.

Why Are People Searching on My Web Site in the First Place?

If there were ever a $64 million question, this would be it. While it's impossible to ascertain the exact reason someone searches on your site, downloads that PDF file, or watches your message from the CEO video, it's very important to be aware of the way in which your search function is being used.

Take a look at Figure 18-8. It shows the top 10 search queries performed on a web site (from the Search Terms report on Figure 18-5) against the top 10 organic search engine keywords used to find a web site (From the Traffic Sources > Keywords report). Do you notice the big difference between these sets of search terms? The top site search terms are very broad, general, and short. Searches from Google, Yahoo, and Bing.com are more refined, specific, and longer-tail queries (longer-tail being search queries with multiple words, usually more than three words per search query).

A lot of people aren't aware that there is a difference between pre-site searches on search engines and on-site searches on your site's search function. A lot of folks probably feel that these types of searches should be very similar, while others haven't even thought about it until reading this paragraph. Thanks to Google Analytics, we can clearly see that visitor search behavior changes drastically when users are on a site as opposed to using a search engine. Pretty interesting, isn't it?

From our experience in analyzing hundreds of Site Search reports, and in speaking with hundreds of web-site visitors and colleagues directly, people generally don't feel that they should need to phrase their queries as formally or have as precise an idea of what they're searching for on a web site as on Google or Yahoo. They feel that the web site they are searching should know exactly what the visitor is typing into the web site's search function, AND that the search function should be able to provide them relevant results that will make sense. They don't feel like typing in three- or four-word queries.

So what does this mean for you, the hard-working web-site owner with many other things to deal with day in and day out? It means that your search function must be running at optimal levels at all times. By testing your search function out every once in a while, and by analyzing the Site Search section of reports that we covered in this chapter, you'll be able to determine if your search function is doing its job in helping people find what they are looking for quickly and effectively. Is it fair to you that your search function must be able to read visitor intent, and bring up relevant search results to a user based upon single-word search queries like "hats" or "cameras"? No, it isn't fair, but that's the online world that we live in.

The bottom line is this: if your search function isn't up to par, your web site's visitors will find another one on another web site, and you stand a great chance of losing those customers. Use the reports outlined in this chapter to help you achieve Site Search success, and you'll be one happy web-site owner in no time!

Dimension: Keyword ⌄		Dimension: Search Term ⌄	
1.	womens running shoes	1.	shoes
2.	womens sneakers	2.	hats
3.	xj990 womens running	3.	ties
4.	running shoes xj990	4.	sneaker
5.	1770 running shoes	5.	t-shirt
6.	fedora hats	6.	bag
7.	white running shoes	7.	shoe
8.	xj90 for women only	8.	tie
9.	womens running shoe	9.	sex
10.	1770 shoes white	10.	free shoes

Figure 18-8: Comparing the top 10 keywords and the top 10 search terms

Event Tracking

Earlier this year Google Analytics finally released Event Tracking to all Google Analytics accounts across the globe. Event Tracking opens the door for web-site owners to track the activity of their rich media content, such as movies, games, widgets, loading times, and Flash and AJAX applications. As web sites incorporate more "Web 2.0" elements with each passing day, it has become essential to be able to properly track visitors' interactions with dynamic elements. Event Tracking for Google Analytics was designed with the ability not only to track rich media and Flash, but also to provide insightful and useful information about their activity.

In this chapter we'll cover your options for tracking implementation, as well as for understanding the report data in order to extract value out of it.

Why Bother with Event Tracking?

Web-site visitors have evolved since the early 1990s, when the Internet first exploded. They are becoming more demanding in terms of site usability, content, aesthetics, and, if you are a merchant, pricing. Their demand has exponentially increased the supply of bigger, better, faster web sites over the years, sites that provide more, and more…and even more to the user. What used to be a one-page listing of hyperlinks in 1994 on Yahoo.com is now a multifaceted, interactive global community, chock-full of videos, games, Flash content and social media applications.

The same can be said for the web analytics industry. In the late 1990's, tracking "hits" from search engine spiders and signups on "guestbook" pages, and downloading raw server log files to plug data into your favorite Microsoft Access database, was the way to go. As web sites and web visitors have evolved over the years, so have web analysts, and their need to track and obtain valuable data.

Enter Event Tracking in Google Analytics. As we explained in the beginning of this chapter, the event tracking module enables you to track special interactions with the many Web 2.0 elements that web sites all over the Internet now feature in abundance. As you'll learn very shortly, because of the advanced technology now available, event tracking is not bound by rigid restrictions and exacting syntax, like the standard Google Analytics Tracking Code or the Ecommerce tracking module. It can be taken in many different directions, which means you can mold it to fit your tracking needs.

NOTE Event tracking with Google Analytics requires that you use the `ga.js` tracking code. You will not be able to take advantage of event tracking if the pages on your web site are coded with the legacy (`urchin.js`) coding module. If event tracking sounds like something you want to use, this may be a great time to migrate to the `ga.js` tracking module.

Implementing Event Tracking

If you are familiar with Google Website Optimizer, you know that the very first step in a successful experiment is the planning phase. So before you start any coding, get together with your IT team or your Flash expert and iron out the following important questions:

1. What elements do you wish to track?

2. What do you wish to learn from event tracking?

3. What insights do you want to obtain from event tracking data?

Having a meeting to answer these questions will set a good foundation for your event tracking success. Do you want to track each time a user clicks the huge Play button on your homepage video? Do you want to track the live chat usage that's on the left navigation bar of all of your site pages? Do you want to learn how to improve your live chat applet by studying its interaction? Do you plan on taking action and optimizing your interactive "Design Your T-Shirt" system if your users don't seem to be interacting with key elements? If these types of questions begin racing through your head, you're already in the right mindset for event tracking success.

The Event Tracking Module

OK, let's get down to business here. Event Tracking uses the _trackEvent function, which can be used with the regular Google Analytics Tracking Code, as a JavaScript onClick or onSubmit event, and, naturally, in any Flash or AJAX applet.

The format for the _trackEvent function is made up of four parameters: categories, actions, labels, and values. The following code snippet shows the schematic of the _trackEvent function:

```
_trackEvent(category, action, optional_label, optional_value)
```

Out of the four event tracking parameters, you are required to use both a category and an action. The label and the value parameters are optional ones. Let's take a look at each of the four parameters:

1. **Category (required):** The category parameter in the _trackEvent function should be used for the name of the object, or the type of object that you wish to track. Think of the category as the highest-level name that you plan on using. For example, if you're tracking elements from a video, the word "Videos" may work fine. The category parameter name should be used consistently across all desired trackable events, so you have a nice organizational structure when looking at reports later.

2. **Action (required):** The action parameter is pretty much what it sounds like—the action that a visitor will perform on the event that you wish to track. Continuing with our video example, if you want to track when visitors click the Play button on your video, the word "Play" could be used as the name for this action. Other possible ideas for actions that you could track with a video include clicks on the Fast-Forward or Rewind buttons; volume adjustments (raising or lowering of the volume); or enlarging/ zooming in on the video. Also, you can't forget about a very important element to track—clicks on the Pause or Stop button(s).

3. **Label (Optional):** The label parameter is completely optional for you to use with event tracking, but we recommend that you make use of it. Labels do get their own report in the Event Tracking section, so you might as well. The label parameter can be used for a specific movie name ("Transformers Movie Trailer"), or, if you're tracking file downloads, the Request URI (file path) of the downloaded file (/downloads/file.pdf). The name for your label should probably be the deepest-level name you would assign

something, in contrast to the name of a category, which should have the highest-level name.

4. **Value (Optional):** Lastly, the value parameter is a field that supports only integers and not text. This is where you can assign numerical values to any event you wish to track, which in a way is very similar to assigning numerical values to your goals, which we discussed in Chapter 11. This is where you can insert special elements such as the time it takes for your video to load, or the number of baseball cap logos selected in your "Create a Cap" interface. However, you can't use negative integers for "bad" or "unwanted" events—they are not supported in the value parameter.

Putting it all together, here's an example of a code snippet that uses values from our previous examples:

```
pageTracker._trackEvent("Videos", "Play Button",
"Transformers Trailer", "37");
```

The following code example shows what this could look like in your Flash source file using ActionScript 3. Keep in mind that this is just a sample—with Flash, there are far too many different possibilities to be able to cover them all in this book. Our best advice is to become best friends with an expert Flash developer and work with this person closely to track the elements that you want to track.

```
myMovie.addEventListener( MouseEvent.CLICK,
onButtonClick );
function onButtonClick( event:Event ):void
{
  tracker.trackEvent ( "Videos", "Play Button",
"Transformers Trailer", "37");
}
```

NOTE If you had access to earlier versions of event tracking as part of a limited beta, please note that the previous specification for the _trackEvent function has been deprecated. If you are using the (action, label, value) specification, you will need to update to the newer (category, action, label, value) setup in order for event tracking to function.

Implicit Count: What It Is and What You Need to Know

When you think about a page view and unique page view with standard Google Analytics tracking, you should know that they may not necessarily be equal to each other. If a user views the same page three times in the same session (visit), Google Analytics will consider this as only one unique page view, because there was only one unique view of that page within that user session. However, three page views will be associated with this session for the same page.

Event tracking uses a similar implicit count methodology for tabulating events. As you'll see when we start introducing event tracking reports, the Total Events metric will count the total number of events performed by a user in a session, but the Visits with Event metric will only count one time per user session, whether that visitor performs one or one hundred event actions.

Keep this in the back of your mind whenever you're looking at event tracking reports and wondering why the sum of a few metrics may not equal the total(s) represented.

Does Event Tracking Affect Bounce Rate?

In short, it does.

Events in Google Analytics are considered *interaction hits*. As you've learned, a bounce is a single-page visit on your web site, and the bounce rate is the percentage of visits to your site that are single-page visits. When a user lands on a page of your site and performs an action that is coded with _trackEvent, the visit will not be considered a bounce, even though the visitor may still leave the site without visiting any other pages. Because of this, event tracking will affect Time on Site metric calculations as well, since bounces in Google Analytics have an Average Time on Site of zero seconds.

At this time there is no way to toggle or manipulate this setting, unless you can do some fancy scripting on your end. So if event tracking is in the cards for your web site, keep in mind on what pages you implement it, and what may happen with your Bounce Rate and Average Time on Site metrics.

Are There Any Limitations on What I Can Track?

You can track anything you'd like with event tracking—PDF file downloads (see the very next section of this chapter for an example), videos, games, widgets, Flash interactions, and anything else that you can think of tracking.

The limitations of event tracking are not on what you can track; they are on how much you can track. Google Analytics limits each user session to 500 requests, be they event tracking requests or those accumulated by the standard Google Analytics Tracking Code (page views). It would be almost impossible to reach this limit by actually attempting to view 500 pages in one session (legitimately), but the limit can be easily reached and exceeded with event tracking.

Therefore you must be very careful how you're using event tracking, because you don't want to have to sacrifice tracking regular user activity on your site.

We recommend that you avoid tracking elements or actions on your site that could easily be repeated several dozens or several hundreds of times in a single visit. These include:

1. Every second a user is on your site. If you do this, then in a little over eight minutes (480 seconds = 480 events) the session will reach its request limit.

2. onMouseOver and onMouseOut events, which can add up extremely fast with dynamic navigations and other Flash elements

3. Clicks during games, animated banners, and applications in which visitors may click their mice hundreds of times in a matter of minutes, like shoot-'em-up games

4. Every second listening to your audio player or every second watching your video

5. Any other type of mouse action or keyboard shortcut action that can potentially add up fast, causing tracking limits to be reached

If you have a game on your site in which users shoot grenades at enemy targets for points, consider tracking an event for every 5,000 points reached, or the number of lives used. If it's a video, track the clicks on elements pertaining to the video player, not every second viewed. Or, if you want to track something more "static" like a web form, don't track each instance of a user typing data into a text field—especially if you have a large form.

Tracking File Downloads as Events

We mentioned in Chapter 14 ("Hacking Google Analytics") that you could track file downloads, like downloads of PDF and MP3 files, as events, if you did not wish to track these as page views with the _trackPageview function. Luckily for all of us, _trackEvent is a very flexible function, as it enables you to track static JavaScript onClick functions as well.

Here is the PDF example that we used in Chapter 14, only this time we're using _trackEvent and not _trackPageview with our JavaScript onClick event:

```
<a href="http://www.yoursite.com/white-paper.pdf"
onClick="pageTracker._trackEvent("PDF", "Downloads", "white-paper.pdf",
"125");">Download a PDF</a>
```

Notice how we used the name of the file (`white-paper.pdf`) for our optional label parameter, and a value parameter of 125, which is also optional. Remember that both category (PDF) and action (Downloads) are required in order for event tracking to function.

Can Events Be Tracked as Goals?

When you use the _trackPageview function on any file or outbound link, a page view will be associated with that user's action. Because of this you can create a goal, because goal tabulation in Google Analytics looks for the total number of unique page views that match your goal URL within the specified date range. (You can see your unique page view count in the Top Content report.)

The _trackEvent function, on the other hand, is not as fortunate. At this time, goal tracking with events is not supported. This can throw a monkey wrench into your program, but if it's any consolation, you are not alone—goal tracking with events is a very hot topic of discussion on the Google Help forums, which are read by Google employees. Lots of folks would like this feature to be added, so perhaps someday you'll be able to track events as goals.

Event Tracking Reports

You've worked with your IT team and your favorite Flash developer, and you have event tracking configured on all your neat Web 2.0 site elements. Now it's time to visualize what all the fuss is about! Within the Content section of reports within Google Analytics you will see a subsection titled Event Tracking, right underneath Site Search. Click **Event Tracking** to be taken to the Event Tracking Overview report.

The Event Tracking Overview Report

The Event Tracking Overview report is the highest-level reporting about your overall event tracking activity. All events triggered throughout your site in the specified date range will appear here, along with an overview of the top categories, as shown in Figure 19-1. Notice that to the right of the tracking statistics are three questions: "What event categories are most common?", "What actions are people using in each category?", and "What labels are being recorded the most?" This is a change of pace from the standard sectional overview reports, which simply provide links to the different report sections. Here Google Analytics wants you to think about questions that you may ask about your event tracking data, which are a foundation for mining insights. You can expect to see Google Analytics adopt this style more and more within its interface.

Going back to the bottom left-hand side of Figure 19-1, we can see the top three actions on the "Transformers Video" that we're tracking. We haven't even left the report overview, and we can already see something very interesting: the second-most popular event action is Volume Down. This should immediately scream out to you (no pun intended) that the video's volume is far too loud for most people's speakers. The actionable item to take away from this is that you should work with your video person and decrease the volume so that visitors do not have to replace their computer speakers after your video has blown them out ☺.

Right away the work that you've put into implementing event tracking is paying off with valuable information that you couldn't have received anywhere else.

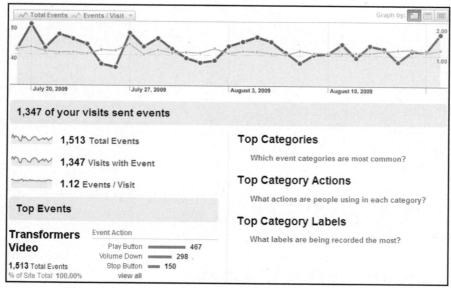

Figure 19-1: The Event Tracking Overview report

The Event Tracking Categories Report

Once in one of the event tracking reports you will see the standard Google Analytics report table that you know and love. The Categories report enables you to see which event categories were responsible for recording actions, with a breakdown of total events, unique events, event value, and the average value of each category. As shown in Figure 19-2, the event tracking report tables give you the standard Site Usage tab and, if it is enabled within your profile, the Ecommerce tab. Remember that events cannot be counted as goals in Google Analytics at this time; therefore it does not make sense to have the Goal Conversion tab in this section. However, you can easily see if any event categories led to any e-commerce transactions, which (we hope) can justify the costs of creating videos and other rich media. Your awesome product demo video may very well be your top online salesperson, and thanks to event tracking you will now be aware of it.

Don't forget about using the date-range slider to compare your event tracking data to that of a previous period. This enables you to easily evaluate the progress of your event categories as you optimize and refine them over the course of weeks or months. Use the Ecommerce tab in addition to a date comparison to attach the almighty dollar figure and substantiate your efforts.

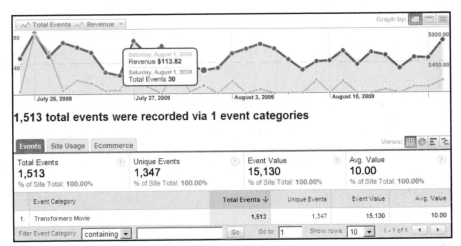

Figure 19-2: The Event Tracking Categories report

The Event Tracking Actions Report

Every one of your actions that has been recorded at least once will appear in this report. Here, all the actions from all your categories will appear together; if you'd prefer to have a breakdown of actions by category, simply edit your event tracking coding to include the name of the category in the action parameter.

In Figure 19-3 we have a couple of things going on at the same time. First, we are looking at our top event action—Play Button—over the span of two weeks, which is a result of using the date-range slider's Compare to Past checkbox. Second, we're using the Ecommerce tab to determine whether our event actions are responsible for increasing profitability. In this situation, our Play Button action resulted in a transaction in the most recent week. How exciting!

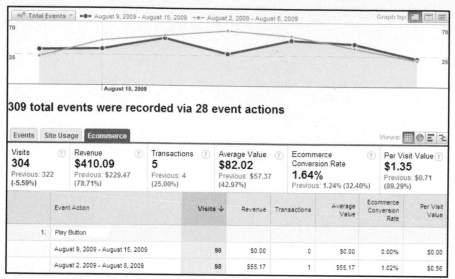

Figure 19-3: The Event Tracking Actions report

The Event Tracking Labels Report

If you use the optional labels parameter in your event tracking coding, you will see the collection of all of your labels in the report displayed in Figure 19-4. Remember from earlier in the chapter that labels can either be the file path (if you're tracking file downloads or outbound links) or the specific name of a movie or a game (e.g. "Transformers Movie," "G.I. Joe Trailer," "Race Car Wars," etc.).

In Figure 19-4 we're analyzing the average order value of the top 10 event labels, where clearly our top breadwinner is our "Transformers Movie," earning an average of $859.50 per event! In this same figure we are also comparing the percentage of unique events to the site average, by having our comparison table view enabled. We can use the combination of the comparison view and the average order value of each event label to get a good feel not only for which events are popular on your web site, but also for which ones are profitable. Even with something as "not profit-generating" as event tracking, it's important to use the value parameter and tie in either a numerical value or a currency value to each event. Doing this helps quantify your events into more meaningful units of measurement.

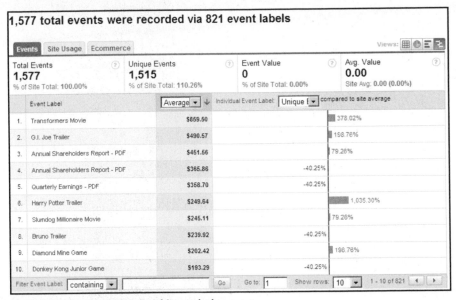

Figure 19-4: The Event Tracking Labels report

The Event Tracking Trending Report

The Trending report in the Event Tracking section shows you a very simple break-down of the total number of events accumulated per day. In Figure 19-5 we've changed the graphing option to "hour," which not only changed the trending graph to show each hour's events vertically, but also updated the histogram below the trending graph to display the same breakdown as a horizontal bar graph.

You can also modify the trending view to show Visits with Event or Events per Visit by clicking on the drop-down menu toward the upper left-hand side of Figure 19-5.

The Event Tracking Hostnames Report

Finally, you can view a complete breakdown of all your events by hostname with this last nifty report. This could prove very useful for you if you have the Google Analytics Tracking Code and event tracking coding on multiple domains. You can then use this report to get a sense of which web sites are sending more event interactions your way. However, chances are fairly high that your hostnames report will look something like the Hostnames report shown in Figure 19-6. You should see your domain name receive the bulk of the events, if not almost all of them, followed by the canonical version of your domain (the "non-www" version), as well as internal IP addresses or staging/development servers.

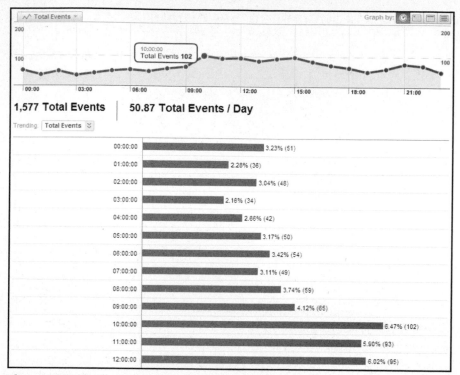

Figure 19-5: The Event Tracking Trending report

Figure 19-6: The Event Tracking Hostnames report

Using Events in Advanced Segments

As we mentioned in the very first chapter of this book, advanced segments are powerful, deeply insightful tools that enable you to gain a richer understanding of your visitors from customized segments that you can create and manage at will. With advanced segments you can define the dimensions, metrics, conditions, and values that are important for you and your business, or specific data that you're just curious about.

Very recently the Google Analytics team enabled event tracking dimensions and metrics within the Advanced Segments creation interface. Figure 19-7 shows an example of a rather simple custom advanced segment being created. We want to see any event that came from a source containing the word "google," be it a paid visit from AdWords, an organic visit from a Google search engine result, or a visit from Google Images or another Google property.

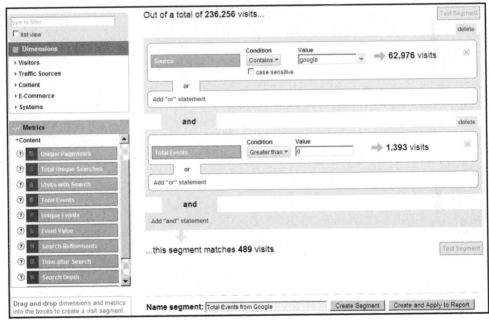

Figure 19-7: Setting up an advanced segment with events

Figure 19-8 shows our newly created custom advanced segment on our All Traffic Sources report:

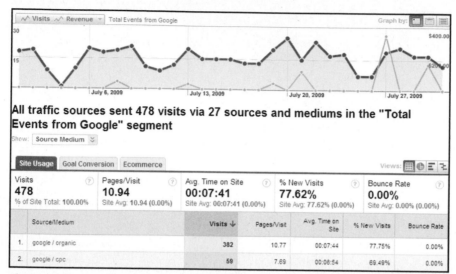

Figure 19-8: An advanced segment applied to Google Analytics

Notice in Figure 19-8 how the Goal Conversion tab is now present. Even though events cannot be tied into goals at this time, you can still see whether or not visitors who had interactions with events eventually converted for you. Also notice how the bounce rate in the scorecard is 0.00%—this is because Google Analytics considers an event an interaction hit. (Flip back to earlier in this very chapter where we talk about this.)

Keep in mind that advanced segments in Google Analytics are applied throughout your entire profile when enabled. So for our example from Figures 19-7 and 19-8, every report that we bring up will show us visits from Google that have at least one event interaction in the session. This excludes the Funnel Visualization, Benchmarking, Keyword Position, and Absolute Unique Visitor reports, as they do not have advanced segment capabilities at this time.

CHAPTER 20

E-Commerce Tracking

Transactions, revenue, product performance—all these are elements or factors in an e-commerce business. They're also measurements of how successful your e-commerce business is at driving sales.

These measurements are important in helping you track and monitor what works and what doesn't in your e-commerce infrastructure. How many days does it take before a user makes a purchase? How much time do visitors spend on your site? And most important, how does this information fit with all the other data that you've examined in Google Analytics?

Your e-commerce measurements can tell you. Commerce is defined as the buying and selling of goods. On a macroeconomic level, commerce could represent all of the sales within a city, state, or region, but we're not concerned with macroeconomics. Rather, we're concerned with microeconomics—the buying and selling of goods on a specific web site: *your* web site.

Even more specifically, you're probably concerned with how much you're selling from your web site. It's not enough just to know what you're selling, though. You also need to know how those sales happen because when you know, you can duplicate the process.

Google Analytics provides reports that help you understand the circumstances under which your products are sold. For example, do you sell more products on Monday than on any other day of the week? You can know for sure using the reports in this section.

> **NOTE** There's more to enabling e-commerce tracking than just turning the reports on in Google Analytics. That's the easy part. Depending on what type of shopping cart you use, you may have to do some fancy code work to get it all working properly. In Chapter 8 we covered some of the basic shopping carts that you might use and provided information about how to start tracking e-commerce, so in this chapter we're just covering reports. Important information, that.

Ecommerce Overview

As with the other report categories that you'll find in the left-hand navigation menu, the first report in the E-commerce section is the Ecommerce Overview. You know the drill about overview reports—they're just a quick glance at the top metrics in the section. In the case of the Ecommerce Overview, shown in Figure 20-1, the metrics you're viewing are Ecommerce Conversion Rate, Sales, and Top Revenue sources.

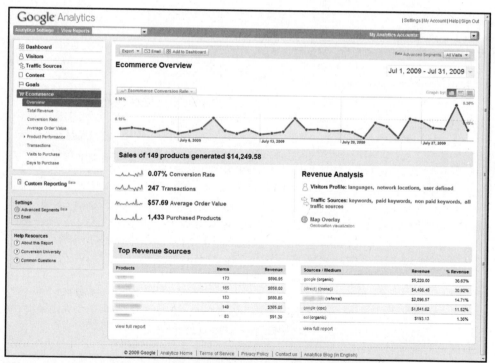

Figure 20-1: View basic e-commerce metrics on the Ecommerce Overview report.

Each report section contains links that lead to other reports, where you can find more (and better segmented) data about that specific topic. For example, if you click the **Conversion Rate** link, you're taken to the **Conversion Rate** report (which is covered later in this chapter). And if you click the **Purchased Products** link, it takes you to the **Product Overview** report—as does the **Products** report at the bottom of the page.

The data in this report is your first step in understanding how income is generated on your site. Using this report, you can quickly see what your average order value is and what your top products are. This information can then be leveraged to tweak advertising campaigns, or even to change the direction of an advertising campaign that's not showcasing a product well. Or it can be the catalyst to create an advertising campaign for a product that's doing better than expected. Of course, before you make all those decisions based on this overview report, you might want to look a little closer at the more detailed reports that each section of it leads you to.

Total Revenue

Revenue and transactions are the basis of any commerce reporting. What are your sales, and how many transactions did it take to reach that sales level? The Total Revenue report, shown in Figure 20-2, illustrates the revenue part of that equation.

The top chart (Revenue) in this report shows your total day-by-day revenue in a very graphic way. The chart lets you quickly see the highs and lows for the cycle that you're tracking. You can also compare date ranges in this report, which gives you the ability to see revenue increases or decreases over time. For example, one of the busiest months of the year for retailers is December. If you want to know how your December this year compares to that of last year, you can use the date ranges feature to quickly see the difference.

A little further down the page is a histogram that shows your transaction values by day, and the average value of those transactions. It, too, is very graphical, enabling you to quickly see where your highs and lows fall. Is one time of month better for sales than another? Or maybe a particular time of week or year is better, or whatever the case may be.

So how do you use this information? Aside from the obvious quick-glance format, which you can use to tell quickly where your revenue and transactions stand for the given time period, you can also use it to determine which day of the week the most revenue and transactions are generated.

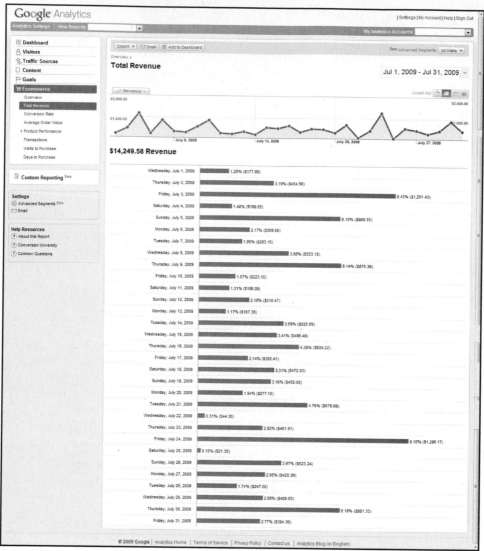

Figure 20-2: View revenues by day in the Total Revenue report.

Use this information over time to find patterns in user purchases and spending, or combine this information with other reports (such as the marketing reports) to learn what's driving customers to your site on a given day.

For example, if you send out a weekly newsletter, compare your revenue report to the Campaigns report for that particular time frame to find out if the newsletter is driving revenue and transactions on your site.

Conversion Rate

By now, you should be pretty familiar with conversions and the difference between a conversion and a goal. A conversion is the measure of how well you do at driving users to complete a transaction on your site. And transactions per visit is the name of this game. The Conversion Rate report, shown in Figure 20-3, illustrates the percentage of visitors who reach a conversion goal in a given day.

Figure 20-3: The Conversion Rate report tells how many visitors reach conversion goals.

Conversions can be defined in a number of ways. There is, of course, the exchange of money for goods. This is what most people commonly think about when setting conversion goals. You want visitors to buy your products.

However, not all web sites are about selling products, and even some that are have conversion goals that aren't specific to selling products. You can also consider a visitor's signing up for a newsletter, downloading a file, or completing a form as a transaction. It requires that you set that specific action as a transaction and give it a monetary value.

One last aspect of these reports: You also have the same capabilities that you had in the previous reports to change date ranges and compare by date ranges.

Average Order Value

Companies, such as McDonald's, understand the importance of average order value. That's why the person behind the counter always asks if you want to upsize your Extra Value Meal. Higher average order values translate into higher revenue. And even e-commerce sites need to keep track of this metric, especially if that site happens to be the type that changes products or layout on a regular basis.

The Average Order Value report, shown in Figure 20-4, shows you what the average value of transactions is on your site. Whether you have 50 sales or 500, the high-value transactions are interesting, the low-value transactions are depressing, but the average value tells the tale.

With this information, you can watch, over time, as changes in your site affect your revenue. The information is also useful for learning when you need to boost sales programs or increase resources and capabilities (if your average order values are consistently rising). What's more, if you implement a new marketing campaign, the Average Order Value is where you can see just how effective that campaign has been at increasing your order value.

This report really isn't any more detailed than the other reports in this section, but that doesn't mean the information isn't valuable to you. It simply means that you use this information, combined with the other facts that you can learn, about your web site, marketing campaigns, navigational structures, and even product information, to increase the sales efficiency of an e-commerce site or simply the exposure of a content site.

Ultimately, it's all about improvement. Right?

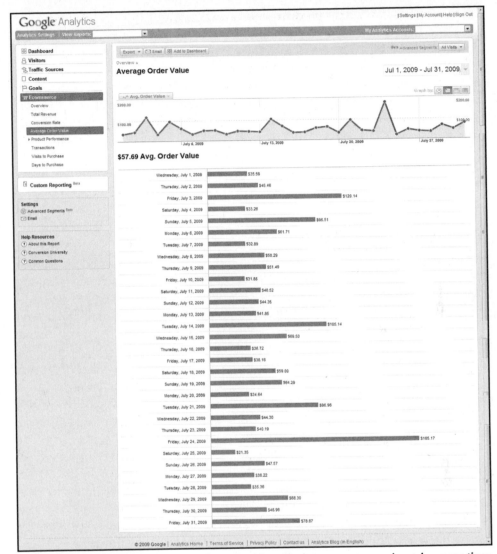

Figure 20-4: The Average Order Value report breaks down average order value over time.

Product Performance

Every item in every store you've ever been in has been strategically placed right where it is so that you'll see the item in a certain light or at a certain time in your visit. It's called product merchandising, and companies spend millions of dollars each year ensuring that product placement is just perfect because it really does matter when it comes to sales and revenue.

Several years ago there was a large craft company with several dozen sizable stores scattered around the southern United States. The company generated several billion dollars in revenue each year and spent millions on ensuring that products were placed within the stores in a way that was intuitive for customers. A large part of every employee's job was to make sure each department conformed to company standards for product placement.

Then a new CEO took over. One of his first orders of business was to change the layout of every store. The problem was that the CEO didn't understand how customers shopped in the stores, and customers were not happy with the new layout. They began shopping elsewhere, and within three years the company went belly-up. It probably wasn't only because the merchandising in the store was off, but that played a part in the overall demise of the stores.

If that CEO had looked at some of the measurements indicating how product merchandising affects revenue, he might have corrected his mistake before it was too late (or never made it in the first place). Measurements like the ones in this chapter are essential to tracking the health of your product merchandising and how it affects revenue.

Google Analytics understands that it's all about the placement, and it supplies the tools you need to monitor the important merchandising metrics for your e-commerce business.

Product performance measurements give you insight into how well the product is being placed, priced, and displayed. In bricks-and-mortar stores, these are the all-important measurements. In e-commerce stores, it's a little trickier. You may need to play with your page placement to find the best place to display your products.

The Product Performance reports are designed to help you see how well (or poorly) your products sell. The report shows the number of items sold, the total revenue, the average price, and the average order quantity for each product you sell online.

Additionally, you can click any product category to drill down to specific SKUs (Stock-Keeping Units) for more detailed information about sales.

These numbers are important because poorly performing products could indicate poor placement. If you find that an item that should perform well does not, consider moving the item to a different page on your web site or featuring the product more prominently on the front page of the site.

These measurements are also a good indicator of product-specific marketing that you may be conducting. If the marketing is driving sales, you should see an increase in sales for that specific product. If you do not, the marketing may not be performing effectively.

Product Overview

In previous chapters, we've defined source as the link or advertisement that leads visitors to your site. Now it's time to look at the purchases those visitors make once they come to your site. The Product Overview report, shown in Figure 20-5, illustrates sales for general categories of products and how much revenue those sales generated.

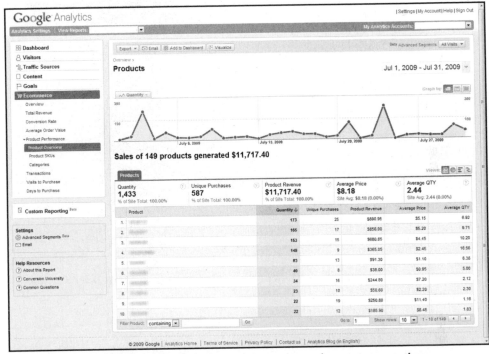

Figure 20-5: The Product Overview report shows sales and revenues over time.

The report shows the number of items sold in what number of transactions—important information because the more items sold per transaction the higher sales tend to be. It also shows product revenue, which is the amount generated by all sales, as well as average price and average quantity. Using these numbers, you can gauge how effective your product selections are, how effective your marketing efforts are (especially if they are geared toward one specific product or category of products), and what kind of return you're making on your product investment.

Additional information about a category of products can be gained by clicking the name of a product category in the product list. This takes you to a product category detail, which includes SKUs that might fall under that product category, as shown in Figure 20-6.

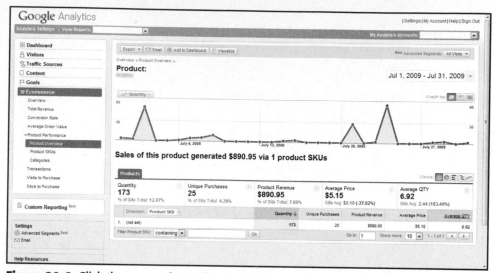

Figure 20-6: Click the name of a product to drill down into additional data about it.

This information can be used to target your sales to your site visitors much more effectively. One way to do that would be to offer a discount coupon, available only to readers of your organization's newsletter. Another way might be to develop an article that features organization tips and recommends the product that's available on your web site. You could then offer the article, free of charge, to other newsletters sent to Internet users. The result should be increased sales from that specific audience.

With this information, as with much of the information supplied by Google Analytics, you can improve your marketing techniques and increase your sales. And just as with the other capabilities in Analytics, you don't necessarily have to have an e-commerce site to take advantage of these measurements. You just need to assign a value to the various goals you have in place. Then, when it all comes together, you still have access to all of the capabilities that Google Analytics has to offer.

Product SKUs

A *Product SKU* is the number by which most retailers (and e-commerce dealers) track the products ordered versus the products sold. In the Product SKUs report, shown in Figure 20-7, the product SKUs that generate revenues for your site are shown along with information about the number of items, transactions, product revenues, average price, and average quantity.

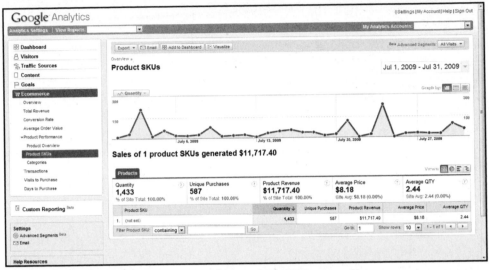

Figure 20-7: The Product SKUs report shows which SKUs generate revenue.

The Product SKUs report enables you to quickly see which of your specific products are producing the most sales. But clicking an SKU number in the Product SKU list leads you to a drill-down report. This SKU detail report provides additional information specific to that SKU. For example, in the SKU report shown in Figure 20-8, you can quickly see how many items were sold in how many transactions, and what the average price of those items are.

Figure 20-8: The Product SKUs detail report shows additional drill-down data for that SKU.

Now, why would you want to know the average price? Maybe there has been a sale on that item. Or perhaps some customers have store-wide discount coupons. This report lets you see the average value of each item sold of that SKU. This helps you to keep track of how much you're earning on a product versus how much you've spent acquiring that product.

The data collected about product SKUs allows you to see, without doubt, which of your products sells best and which sells worst. With that kind of information, you can make adjustments to the amount and type of stock that you make available to site visitors, to capitalize on your return on investment (ROI).

If you're running a content site and don't have products to track, you can track content using the SKU report. However, it has to be downloadable content. The tracking won't work if you try to track the content pages. That's what Content reports are for. If you do have downloads on your site, however, you can label each one with a different SKU, and then track those SKUs just as you would track them for an e-commerce site.

Categories

Product categories are another helpful indicator of web-site performance and product merchandising. For example, if you have two categories of products on your site—racing memorabilia and sports memorabilia—knowing which of the categories performs the best is essential to understanding how you should display those products.

If the racing memorabilia are selling better, you may decide to feature those products more prominently and increase articles about race car drivers or racing teams. If you really wanted to increase visitor interaction with the site, you could add a quiz or game related to racing.

The Products Categories report (shown simply as Categories in the left-hand navigation bar), shown in Figure 20-9, gives you the measurements that show which category of products on your site is generating the most revenue.

The report shows the number of items sold, the total revenue, the average price, and the average order quantity for each product you sell online. You can also click the name of each category of products. This returns you to the Product Overview report you just saw.

NOTE You may notice in Figure 20-9 that there's only one category listed, and it's listed as (not set). This is because the categories for this web site have not yet been set up. Remember, back in Chapters 12 and 13 when we showed you how to set the utm variables? Those are the variables you need to set to determine categories for your products as well. If you need a refresher, flip back to those chapters to access that information.

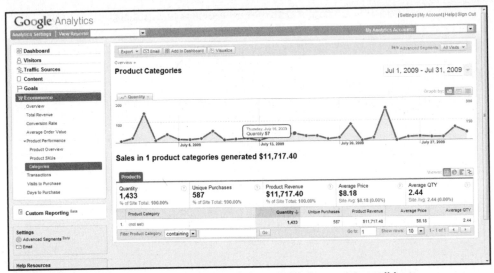

Figure 20-9: The Product Categories report shows which categories sell best.

The purpose of all of the Product Performance reports in this section is to help you better manage the products that you offer on your site. Remember that you don't necessarily have to sell products to use these tracking tools. A little ingenuity will have you learning more about your non-product transactions before you know it.

Transactions

There are so many elements that go into e-commerce. Not only do you need to watch the number of transactions that are completed on your site, but you also need to keep track of how those transactions take place, and also what's included in the transactions. Using these metrics, you can monitor thoroughly the effectiveness of your web site—everything from content to placement to product selection. You can also use these metrics to make educated guesses about products (or content, or services) that might be effective for your site in the future.

All the reports in this section seem minor when taken by themselves. When you combine these reports with additional information, however, you begin to put together a clear picture of how your site is performing and how that performance leads to conversions, transactions, and revenue. Then, if you need to follow up, having a complete list of transactions makes auditing easier and provides additional information on the transactions.

The Transactions report is exactly what it says, a transaction list. As shown in Figure 20-10, the report lists all of the transactions for your site within a given time frame.

Figure 20-10: The Transactions report shows each transaction in a given timeframe.

This information is most commonly used for auditing purposes, to ensure that actual transactions are represented properly in records and reports. It's a useful report if you want to see more details about the transactions that generate revenue.

This report has columns for tax, shipping, and the number of items in a transaction. This additional information gives you a method for monitoring changes in these categories. So if you find that the number of items in the average transaction is only two, you know you might need to recommend additional products using recommendation software or incentives to customers.

As with other reports in Google Analytics, clicking through a link, such as the link represented by each transaction number, takes you to a page on which you can view additional detail. In this case, clicking a transaction number takes you to the Transaction detail report, shown in Figure 20-11. This report shows exactly what products were purchased in the same transaction. The price and quantity of each item are also included. This information can be used in a variety of ways.

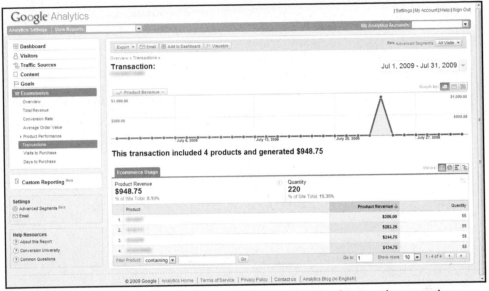

Figure 20-11: The Transaction detail report adds information about each transaction.

For example, if you're selling multiples of a single product during a majority of transactions, and this is unexpected, then you know this product has a special draw to your site visitors. Maybe it's just placed well on the site, maybe the content leading consumers to that product is especially well written, or perhaps you are the only e-commerce vendor on the Web who has that item in stock (don't laugh, it happens). Whatever the case, you know that particular item is driving revenues, and that's a fact you can capitalize on, even if only for a short while.

Visits to Purchase

The Visits to Purchase report, shown in Figure 20-12, shows you the number of visits that it took before a site visitor made a purchase.

In the Visits report, the measurement is the number of visits a user made to the site before making a purchase. So you're monitoring how many times they came to the site before being persuaded to buy.

This report might seem a little unnecessary, but it's not. How many of your visitors make a purchase the first time they visit your site? How many visitors come to your site five or more times before they make a purchase?

These measurements help you learn whether the content on your site is doing its job—making it easy for the visitor to make a decision. If your users have to return to your site numerous times before making a purchase, that probably means they were out comparing prices, reading reviews, or learning more about the product.

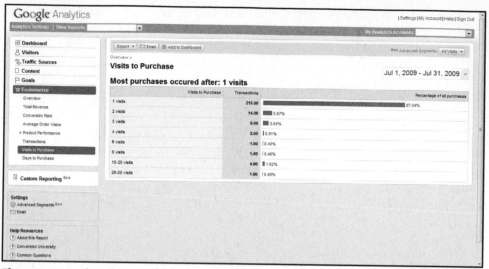

Figure 20-12: The Visits to Purchase report shows how many visits before a purchase.

Can you provide any of the same information so that the user doesn't have to leave your site to find it? If you can provide it, you have a greater chance that the visitor will make a purchase with you. It's all about convenience. And he who provides the most convenience wins.

Use this report to build more convenience into your site. It tells you how often visitors leave and come back; now all you have to do is change that. Web-site designers should take into consideration all the information that consumers need to make a decision. Put that information at the customer's fingertips, and you're likely to decrease the number of times a visitor leaves your site before making a purchase, which in turn increases revenue. It's timeless economics. What's new now is the medium.

Days to Purchase

I know a person who spends a lot of time thinking about a shopping decision. He compares prices at all of the web sites that carry the product he seeks, he visits a page multiple times before making the decision to purchase, and he may even start the purchase several times and never complete it because he's indecisive about spending money, especially if he's looking for a high-ticket item.

This describes a large number of people in today's world. Money is tight for almost everyone, so we agonize over making purchases of all sizes. That's why you've designed your site to help your users make those purchasing decisions. If you have a good site, there might be reviews of the product included on the product page, or maybe there are articles about how the product could improve the user's life or workflow. It's even possible that you've included video testimonials from other users who have purchased the product and were happy with it.

The point here is that very often, users don't make a decision about buying a product on the first day. It's more likely they'll take several days to make the decision, but once it's made, the purchase is usually completed fairly quickly. Are your customers the instant-gratification types who want it right now, or are they more like the Thinking Man, stuck for a time in indecision?

The Days to Purchase report, shown in Figure 20-13, should answer that question for you. If you find that the majority of your users make purchases on their first visit, you know that whatever is drawing them to your site (it could be newsletter coupons, advertisements, or word of mouth) is working to complete the sale.

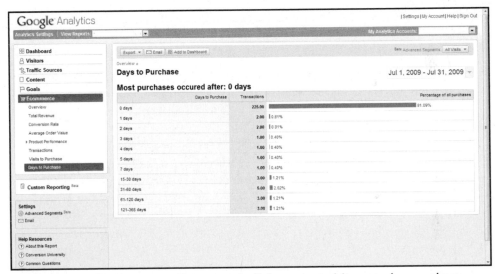

Figure 20-13: The Time to Purchase report tells how many visits precede a purchase.

On the other hand, if your users seem to take several visits to make a purchase, how could you improve that? What information could you provide to the user to close the sale? This graph shows you which area you should concentrate on: driving more traffic or decreasing the time-to-purchase ratio.

All of the reports in the E-commerce reports section are designed with one goal in mind: to help you improve your e-commerce capabilities. Whether that improvement is through better targeting, better product placement, better marketing, or through some other means altogether is up to you. Using the information that you gather from these reports should help you decide what it is that you need to do differently. And even for the best sites, there's always something.

Where To Go from Here

If you've gotten this far, then you've learned quite a bit about Google Analytics. But the truth is that there are people who are still learning Google Analytics after several years of using it. There is always some new scenario for what you need, a feature change, or some question that comes to mind. And there's just no way that we can address everything there is to address in a single book about Google Analytics.

Fortunately there are plenty of resources available to help you out. Of course you'll want to keep this book handy for a reference, but for the things that aren't in this book (especially as you go from being a beginning or intermediate user to being an advanced user) the resources out there on the Web will be invaluable.

Google Resources

Google never does anything halfway. That's true with Google Analytics too. There are a ton of different Google-operated resources where you can find answers and even more training for Google Analytics and all of Google's other applications.

The problem is that sometimes those Google resources are a little hard to find. Sure, there's the help link in the upper right corner of the screen, but where do you go from there? And what if what you're looking for isn't immediately available when you click Help?

Don't worry! Google's got you covered.

Navigating Google Help Files

When the first and second editions of this book were written, Google's help files were very hard to use. They were circular and it was easy to get stuck in a loop where you never found the answer you sought or even a way to search for that answer.

Fortunately, Google has listened to the complaints that the help files could be better (what do you expect when a bunch of geniuses are trying to write help files?) and they've begun to put some work into how those files—which are more accurately called help articles—are written and arranged.

Still, it's possible to get into the help center and find yourself not only not finding the answers that you need, but also hopelessly lost. So it helps to know a few tricks about how to use those help files.

The first thing to understand is that no matter where you are when you click the help button, you're taken straight to the main Google Analytics help page. There you'll find a list of links to other (general) help topics.

If you click the link for one of the help topics, you'll be taken to an overview page for that specific topic. There you'll find a basic article about the help topic, and links to related topics. Those links may be embedded in the text of the article, or they may be in a list of links or in a set of tabs to the left of the article.

Right now the help topics are still being redesigned, so they're not always consistent. Once the redesign is complete, the topics will be linked through text and tabs only, with lists of links appearing only rarely, and only when essential.

Each level deeper you click into the help topics, the more specific the information gets. For example, if you click the **Getting Started Guide** and then click **Getting to know Analytics** ➪ **Profile Settings** you'll be taken to a page that tells you how to edit and manage your profile settings.

You may also notice that there's a link on the left side of the page for **Analytics Help**. This just takes you back to the main help page.

Below that is a link for **Analytics Features**. This takes you through an explanation of the features of Google Analytics. And the **Analytics IQ** link will take you to a page that lists the available Analytics IQ lessons that you can work through to learn more about Google Analytics.

These lessons are video lessons, but there's also a text overview to let you know what to expect in each lesson. And when you're done there's a Google Analytics Individual Qualifications test that you can take to help you quantify your knowledge of Google Analytics.

Conversion University

The Analytics IQ lessons are part of another feature of Google Analytics called Conversion University. Conversion University is a learning center where you can take courses that are specifically geared to helping you learn how to use Google Analytics.

Two levels of courses exist in Conversion University. There are the Analytics IQ lessons and Professional Services. Professional Services are the courses that are offered to those who wish to become Google Analytics Authorized Consultants. For most people, only the Analytics IQ lessons are necessary.

There is one other level of course in Conversion University. It's more a resource than it is specifically a set of training courses, however. The **Code Site** link leads you to the Google Analytics developer site, where you can learn more about the Google Analytics code and how to use it. The information that's covered on the code site, however, is geared more toward the programmer or developer level, and less toward the level of the ordinary Analytics user.

Searching Help Files

You can also search through the Analytics Help files if you're not in the mood to browse around until you find the answers that you seek, or if you're not ready to commit to learning as much about Google Analytics as you can learn through Conversion University.

The search results for the help site can also be a little confusing. Search results are drawn from the help files, from Google Analytics forums, and from Google Analytics blogs where appropriate. When you're using the help search, it's a good idea to look at where the result was pulled from before you click the result link.

Beneath each help listing, a pathway is shown. For example, it might be Analytics Help ⇨ Glossary, which just means the article in question is located in the Glossary section of the Analytics Help pages. You could also see something that says Analytics Blog or `http://groups.google.com/`. The Analytics Blog listing means the search result leads to a Google Analytics blog, and the groups.google listing means the search result leads to a forum in a Google Groups community list.

Using the search option isn't my favorite way to find articles about a specific topic in Google's help files, but if you're in a hurry and you're paying attention to what you're reading, you can find great answers this way. It just takes some getting used to.

Google Analytics Forums

One more resource that you'll find through Google's help pages is the Google Analytics forums. This is nothing more than a group of message boards where you can converse with other people who also use Google Analytics. The message boards are monitored semi-regularly, and users of all levels participate in the forums.

I would urge, however, that you use good forum etiquette in the Google Analytics forums. Not only do you not want to incite some flame war over a posting, but you also don't want to be banned from the forums. And it does happen.

Posting respectful and informative messages is the best way to participate in the forums. Ask the questions that you have and offer your own answers or opinions in the threads that you know enough to join. People appreciate it when there's give and take within a forum, as long as that give and take is friendly.

Google Analytics Blogs

Among your most useful tools for learning more about Google Analytics are the Google Analytics blogs. Of course, Google sponsors blogs about all its applications, but in addition to the Google-provided blogs are dozens of others that you might find useful. Here's a short list to get you started.

Advanced Web Metrics

www.advanced-web-metrics.com/

Analytics Market

www.analyticsmarket.com/blog

Analytics Talk

www.epikone.com/blog/

Conversion Room

http://conversionroom.blogspot.com/

Google Analytics Blog

www.analytics.blogspot.com

Google Analytics Results

www.googleanalyticsresults.com/

Kaizen Analytics

www.kaizen-analytics.com/

Lies, Damned Lies

www.liesdamnedlies.com/

Measuring Success

www.advanced-web-metrics.com/blog/

Mine That Data

http://minethatdata.com/blog/index.html

Occam's Razor

www.kaushik.net/avinash/

OX2 Web Analytics Blog

http://webanalytics.ox2.eu/

ROI Revolution Blog

www.roirevolution.com/blog/

Visual Revenue

http://visualrevenue.com/blog/

VKI Studios

http://blog.vkistudios.com/index.cfm

Web Analytics Demystified

http://webanalyticsdemystified.com/

Web Analytics Management

http://wam.typepad.com/

Web Analytics Zen

www.webanalyticszen.com

Index

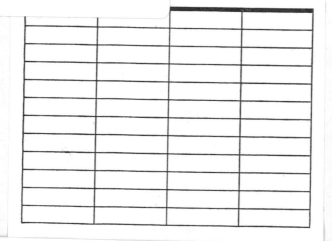